SECTS, 'CULTS'
AND
ALTERNATIVE RELIGIONS

'There is a principle which is a buffer against any information, which is proof against all argument and which does not fail to keep every human being in constant ignorance. This principle is to condemn before researching.'

Herbert Spencer (1820–1903)

'Pilate saith unto him, "What is truth?"'

John 18:38

SECTS, 'CULTS' AND ALTERNATIVE RELIGIONS

A World Survey and Sourcebook

DAVID V. BARRETT

BLANDFORD

First published in the UK 1996 by Blandford
A Cassell Imprint
CASSELL PLC
Wellington House
125 Strand
London WC2R 0BB

Reprinted 1997, 1998
First paperback edition 1998

Distributed in the United States by Sterling
Publishing Co. Inc., 387 Park Avenue South,
New York, NY 10016–8810

**A Cataloguing-in-Publication Data entry for this
title is available from the British Library**

ISBN 0-7137-2567-2 (hbk)
        0-7137-2756-X (pbk)

Typeset by Business Color Print, Welshpool, Powys
Printed and bound in Great Britain by
Biddles Ltd, Guildford and King's Lynn

To the memory of my father,
the Rev. Theodore L. Barrett (1910–93),
for whose parish magazine I first wrote
about alternative religions many years ago

And for my mother,
Emily Barrett,
who believes that unquestioning simple
faith is the best

With love

CONTENTS

PART ONE
BACKGROUND

PART TWO
CHRISTIAN ORIGINS

PART THREE
EASTERN ORIGINS

PART FOUR   ESOTERIC AND
NEO-PAGAN MOVEMENTS

PART FIVE
PSYCHOLOGY AND SELF-HELP

ACKNOWLEDGEMENTS

With many thanks to all the religious movements, and individuals within them, who have been so helpful in the preparation of this book. It would be unfair to single out any specific organization or person, but some deserve especial thanks for their cooperation and generosity.

Particular thanks to all those who provided books, booklets, photographs and other items. All quotations are copyright their original authors and publishers, and all photographs are supplied courtesy of the relevant organizations unless otherwise credited, they are used with thanks.

Thanks also to Diana Atkins and Chris Bell for reading the manuscript and correcting some of my infelicities. Any that remain, and all unattributed opinions, are my own responsibility.

◆

Every effort has been made to ensure the accuracy of the entries in this book. If I am made aware of any factual errors, they will be corrected in future editions of the book. Any religious movements that are not featured and wish to have an entry in future editions should contact me via the publisher.

DVB, 1996

INTRODUCTION

In 1978 some 900 members of the People's Temple, a Christian sect, committed suicide in Guyana. In 1993 the world watched the headquarters of the Branch Davidians, another Christian sect, explode into flame at Waco, Texas with the death of some 80 people. In 1994 another very little-known cult sprang on to our television screens with the deaths in Canada and Switzerland of a couple of dozen members of the Order of the Solar Temple. In March 1995 the Japanese authorities blamed a small Buddhist revivalist sect, Aum Shinrikyo, for killing 12 people by releasing poison gas in the Tokyo underground system. Its leader, Shoko Asahara, was arrested by Japanese police two months later (see p.272).

These are the headline-catchers, but they make us aware that many hundreds of thousands of ordinary, intelligent people all over the world belong to movements, usually called sects or cults, which to most non-members appear strange, often disturbing, sometimes even frightening. Some are Christian-based; others have their roots in Eastern religions.

What are these strange movements? What do their members believe? Why do people want to join them? Do the families and friends of members have anything to worry about?

In addition to these organizations, the mainstream Christian Church is becoming increasingly worried by the numbers of people using Tarot cards, runes or I Ching, wearing talismans and amulets, practising healing and professing belief in ancient gods. Is the New Age movement just another type of cult? What do modern-day Neo-Pagans believe? What do the Druids do at Stonehenge? Do witches really perform magic? Is there any difference between Neo-Paganism, witchcraft, Druidry, high ritual magic and Satanism?

Not according to Christian Fundamentalists, who themselves are causing increasing concern as they become more involved in 'the moral majority' and right-wing politics.

And then there are all the self-improvement philosophies, many of them apparently unconnected to any religion. Occasionally they too attract headlines, and they certainly attract members. Are they beneficial, in that they help people to improve themselves, or should they also give cause for concern?

APPROACH

This book examines the beliefs and practices of many of today's 'alternative' religious movements: groups and organizations other than the mainstream denominations of the major world religions. It explains where they come from and what they believe, and it gives them the opportunity to answer the questions many people want to ask. It is aimed at the ordinary non-specialist reader who genuinely wants to know more about these movements.

Many of the movements included in this book might object to being among the others here, either because they don't claim exclusivity ('We are simply one path among many') or because they do ('We have the only truth; all the others in your book are deluded').

If any organization believes it has the only truth, then by definition everyone else must be wrong, including all mainstream religions and all the other alternative religions. This book does not attempt to judge the 'truth' of any of the movements, but presents their beliefs and practices, often in their own words. It aims to be as unbiased as possible.

Many books on sects and cults have an agenda, whether declared or undeclared. Those written by Evangelical Christians, as well as levelling the usual charges of brainwashing, often set out to 'prove' that sects and cults are wrong because their theology is out of line with the author's own beliefs. The vast majority of Christian books about Neo-Paganism are unfortunately so full of factual errors, illogical arguments and unexamined assumptions that they are worthless. Other more anecdotal books are sometimes deliberately sensational, filled with case histories, horror stories of brainwashing, sleep deprivation, teenagers stolen away from their families and so on. These approaches are valid – anyone promoting their own beliefs, whether religious, moral, political, economic or whatever, has every right to do so, and rubbishing the opposition is a fairly standard technique – but only within their own parameters.

Another type of book warns of very real social and psychological problems. But again the approach is limited. In both cases, because of their starting points, the axes they have to grind, they tend to be very selective, both about the sects they examine and about the information they choose to give us. An outsider with preformed views is looking in, picking out the bits that offend and highlighting them.

Evangelical Christians who criticize another religion or religious movement for not being completely in line with Evangelical Christianity are missing the point. To make an analogy: an English-language purist might say, quite correctly, that American English and Australian English are not 'pure' English, or Queen's English, or received pronunciation, but to go on to attack them for being 'wrong' is not valid; they are self-evidently variants of English, which the purist might dislike but has no legitimate grounds for attacking. It would be even less valid (and rather more stupid) to criticize Spanish or Swahili for not being English. They never claimed to be; they are different languages. Yet books abound which attack Jehovah's Witnesses, Christian Science and Christadelphians for straying from 'the Truth' while calling themselves Christian, and attack Krishna Consciousness, Neo-Paganism and Scientology on the grounds that their beliefs are quite different from Christian beliefs. Of course they are; that's the point.

The approach of tabloid newspapers is no better. 'Thousands of people dedicate their lives to God' is hardly a lively front-page headline. 'Evil cult stole my daughter', on the other hand, grabs the attention and sells papers.

Very rarely are these religions given an opportunity to speak for themselves, to say what they believe in and what they do, to defend themselves against the charges levelled against them. In medieval times, Christians were told that Jews stole and ate babies. In Renaissance times, countless thousands of ordinary men and women were tortured and killed because unfriendly neighbours hinted at witchcraft or heresy. Their guilt was assumed – and it is next to impossible to prove innocence.

Little has changed. Modern sects and cults have replaced baby-eating Jews in the popular imagination. And the lives of hundreds of decent people have been wrecked because over-zealous social workers accused them of 'Satanic ritual abuse' of their children; again, their guilt was assumed.

This book gives a large number of movements the opportunity to speak for themselves, to set out their own stall, and to respond to criticism. I have no personal axe to grind. I simply wish to portray a wide diversity of religious beliefs and to attempt to correct some popular misconceptions. My task, made easier by the helpfulness and openness of most of the movements, has been more editorial than authorial. I have tried to keep my personal views out of the picture and not to judge.

This method is based in part on the phenomenological approach to religious studies promoted by Professor Ninian Smart of Lancaster University in the mid-1970s, when I took my own degree in the subject. The aim is not to say whether, for example, what the Mormons believe is true; rather it is to say, 'It is true that the Mormons believe x, y and z.' By telling what the religious organizations believe, rather than filtering their beliefs through my own beliefs and preconceptions, I hope I have made this book as unbiased as possible. To a large extent I believe I have succeeded, though of course anyone who is looking for bias will find it.

In allowing the movements to speak for themselves, I obviously run the risk of leaning over too far in the opposite direction: no organization is willingly going to dwell on the shadier sides of its character and operation. That is why many of the entries include criticisms. Where there are genuine doubts about historical accuracy, or substantiated acccusations of, for example, sleep deprivation, indoctrination, financial irregularities, sexual impropriety or outright lies, these are pointed out. The movements are then given the opportunity to defend themselves if they can, to explain, excuse, refute – or accept – the accusations.

Nearly a quarter of the questions in the questionnaire I initially sent to each organization focused on criticisms. This book is not intended to be a whitewash job for sects and cults.

There are two things in particular which might cause the strictly unbiased approach to slip a little. I will not tolerate intolerance and I will not accept deception. Intolerance usually brings with it both self-righteousness and a 'nanny-knows-best' imposition of (usually ultra-right-wing) moral strictures, as well as denying people freedom of will, of thought and of choice. Evidence of deception causes me to doubt the integrity of a movement's leaders; if they're prepared to lie about their history or about their founder, how can they be trusted on anything else? It is bad enough to deceive an outsider, but even worse to deceive your own members deliberately.

There is plenty of factual information about religions in this book which ordinary members of those religions might not know. But it should not be forgotten that they have something which outsiders do not: the genuine personal experience of being a member of that religion.

♦

This book, then, is based very largely on firsthand information from the movements themselves, though of course a number of books have been invaluable for providing background information which then enabled me to ask more pertinent questions of the religions. These particularly included Benjamin Beit-

Hallahmi's *The Illustrated Encyclopedia of Active New Religions, Sects and Cults*, and several excellent reference books by the American authority on the subject, J. Gordon Melton (see Bibliography), though three of these became available to me only a few weeks before completing the book. When it has not been possible to check the factual details gleaned from such sources with the movements themselves, I have tried to obtain corroboration from other sources to minimize any perpetuation of error.

TERMINOLOGY

The usual terminology in this subject is loaded. The words 'sect' and 'cult' are applied by outsiders rather than members and generally have pejorative overtones. Few if any of the movements in this book would call themselves sects or cults. To avoid this problem, some authorities now use the term 'new religious movements' or NRMs, coined by the British authority on the subject, Professor Eileen Barker of the London School of Economics. I prefer the term 'alternative religions', in which I include Christian offshoots, Eastern-inspired movements, the New Age, Esoteric and Neo-Pagan groups, and Personal Development organizations. What all these movements have in common is that they are alternatives to the established religions. Some of the movements in this book aren't new; some say they are not religions; and some, in the technical sense of the words, actually are sects or cults. Throughout the book, the words 'movement', 'organization' and 'Church' are used almost interchangeably, except when a different usage of the words is clearly meant. Sometimes a movement will be referred to as a religion. And sometimes the terms sect and cult will be used, though without any pejorative intent.

Let's look at some of these terms. What is a sect? What is a cult? How are they different from a denomination or a religion? What do we mean by the word 'heresy'?

A sect is a subdivision or splintering off from an already established religion, so Jehovah's Witnesses and Mormons may correctly be described as Christian sects (Evangelicals would call them heresies, but more liberal Christians would regard their beliefs as aberrant rather than heretical).

A cult is usually a focusing on one person, on their teachings and their personality. In Roman Catholicism, 'the cult of Mary' means, quite simply and legitimately, the veneration of Mary (not the worship of Mary, a common non-Catholic misperception). In general usage, though, the word 'cult' usually implies a criticism of the practices rather than just the beliefs; cult members are thought to do something unsavoury or strange, from brainwashing converts to wearing peculiar clothing.

Heresy covers any beliefs which are substantially at variance with those generally accepted and which are condemned or disapproved of by the powers-that-be – that is, the establishment at that particular time. Mainstream Christian theology today contains several elements which, at different times in the first few centuries of Christianity, were condemned as heresy. Three obvious examples are the Trinity; the question of whether the Holy Spirit is a separate person of the godhead or just 'God-in-action'; and the balance of humanity and divinity in Jesus.

Over the early centuries, Christianity was riven by such disputes. Anyone who has ever been on the committee of a local political party will remember long and tedious debates (usually instigated by one nit-picking person) on the exact meaning of and desirability of the rewording of Clause 5, Section III, Subsection B, Paragraph vi of the Constitution. The well-loved creeds recited by millions of Christians every Sunday, particularly the Nicene Creed, are the results of very similar wranglings. The original reason for such creeds (from the Latin *credo*, 'I believe') was not so much to provide a succinct statement of beliefs as to set out the correct *established* beliefs, and so make it easier to label any alternative interpretation as heretical.

To a mainstream Christian, a Unitarian, a Christadelphian or a Seventh-day Adventist is a heretic, though many of their beliefs overlap with 'standard' Christian beliefs. A strict Roman Catholic and a member of the Exclusive Brethren would each claim that the other was not a true Christian.

Within this book, the word 'Evangelical' is used to mean a Bible-believing Christian who has been saved – or born again – through individual acceptance of Christ's atoning sacrifice. The words 'evangelism', 'evangelist' and 'evangelistic', on the other hand, simply refer to preaching the gospel.

Fundamentalists are those who have absolute conviction of belief in the fundamental principles of their faith, to the extent that they will not accept the validity of any other beliefs.

It is perhaps necessary to distinguish between conviction of belief and fact. I shall discuss later how sincere believers of any religion might say, 'I *know* this is true', rather than 'I *believe* this is true.' This inner knowledge, or conviction, is indisputable to the believer; he or she *knows* it. But that does not make it a *fact*. It is a fact that the earth orbits the sun. It is a fact that the majority of people on earth have a head, a torso, two arms and two legs. It is a fact that many of those people believe in God, or gods. It is a fact that some people believe there is an afterlife, a heaven or a hell, while other people believe in reincarnation. It is *not* a fact that God, gods, heaven, hell or reincarnation actually exist, provable to everyone.

It is very disturbing to find in the *Webster's New Reference Library*, a one-volume compendium of different dictionaries and reference sections aimed at 'Home, School and Office', the statement: 'Always remember that the Bible is God's infallible, inerrantly inspired word. There are no mistakes in the Bible. God has included everything in the Bible that He wants you to know and that is necessary for you to know concerning salvation and your Christian life.'[1] That statement would be fine in a devotional book written specifically for believing Christians. It is absolutely out of place in an encyclopedic reference book. The editors have not distinguished between fact and conviction of belief.

One further word needs explaining. In popular usage, the word 'myth' means a story which is untrue. The actual meaning of the word is a story *which may or may not* be factually true, but whose importance does not rest on its factual basis. For example, the wealth of stories about King Arthur and his knights is a body of myth. The fact that those stories still fire the imagination today has nothing to do with what, if anything, actually happened at Camelot. The influence is more important than the actuality. If the word 'myth' is used about Joseph Smith finding the *Book of Mormon* inscribed on golden plates, this is not to cast doubt on the historical veracity of the event (though neither does it assert that the story is factually correct). Similarly, when religious scholars speak of belief in the myth of the virgin birth of Jesus, they are not saying it is untrue; they are saying, as with the golden plates, that it *is* true that millions of people believe the story.

It should also be pointed out that the negative propaganda against sects and cults has also become a myth – again, in the true sense of the word. In some cases, with some religious movements, on some occasions, some of the common accusations of brainwashing, low-protein diet, sleep deprivation, 'heavenly deception' and so on almost certainly have some basis in factual truth. But because of the activities and pronouncements of some of the cult-watching organizations, and because of sensationalist tabloid journalism, and because people tend to believe there's no smoke without fire, the general perception is that these quite probably fairly rare occurrences in a handful of movements some years ago apply across the board to all movements now. Thus every alternative religious movement is a cult, and every cult is dangerous. The reality is usually not given a chance to speak for itself. In this book, it will be. However, because such stories are now indivisibly a part of the mythology of many of the movements, they will be mentioned where relevant – usually prefaced by 'Critics have said that . . .'

SCOPE AND STRUCTURE

Many of the religious or semi-religious movements covered in this book are fairly new in origin, often having an unswerving dedication to their founder, with a set of beliefs and practices distinct to themselves. In many cases, for whatever reasons, outsiders may be uneasy about them. These are the movements usually called sects or cults. But the book includes others as well. Inclusion of a movement in this book does not imply authorial approval or disapproval, or any other value judgement of it.

Established non-Christian religions – Hinduism, Buddhism, Judaism, Islam, etc. – and established denominations of Christianity – Roman Catholicism, Anglicanism, Methodism, Presbyterianism, etc. – are not covered in the main body of the book. However, Chapter 1 provides a very brief overview of the main historical world religions, to give a context for the movements covered in the remainder of the book, most of which have sprung, in one way or another, from Christianity, Hinduism or early polytheistic religion. The outlines of their origins and beliefs are not intended to be in any way comprehensive, but rather to show where they fit in with the other world religions and how they might provide a springboard for new religious movements.

All the movements which are covered – Christian, Eastern, Esoteric and Neo-Pagan, and Personal Development – can be regarded, in one way or another, as alternatives to the mainstream religions.

The largest section of the book, Part Two, covers movements with Christian origins. Some of these are more than a century old and are now well established. By no means all of them are labelled as 'sects' or 'cults'. Several are quite well respected (though often misunderstood) by non-members. Yet they are still not part of the religious establishment, hence their inclusion here as 'alternative religions'.

At the beginning of this section we examine briefly the early days of the Christian religion and the development of its beliefs, and discuss why there have always been so many different variants of Christianity. For anyone brought up with 'standard' Christian beliefs, and even more so for Evangelical Christians, this discussion might be disturbing or even offensive. There are two reasons for its presence. First, it forms a necessary background to the entries on new Christian-based religious movements, many of which have revived old 'heresies'. Second, the majority of readers of this book will live in 'Christian countries'; the religious buildings in their towns and the assumptions behind what they were taught in school will be largely influenced by Christianity. If one is going to examine unfamiliar religious beliefs and practices, it is a good idea to step to one side for a moment and examine the religion which is a fundamental part of one's own culture from a different perspective. No disrespect is intended.

The main body of the book, divided into four parts, covers over 50 'alternative religions', divided into categories. In most cases they are easy to place: for example, Mormonism is clearly a Christian offshoot and ISKCON (the Hare Krishna movement) has an Eastern background. Others are a little more problematical. Theosophy, Anthroposophy and related movements, for example, are included in the Esoteric section, though they contain some Eastern and some Christian elements. Transcendental Meditation is included among the Personal Development movements, despite its Eastern origins, because of what it teaches. The Emin see themselves as 'Human Potential/Philosophical', and so are also in the Personal Development section, despite the Esoteric nature of some of their beliefs.

The Bahá'í Faith does not fit into any of these four later parts. As a new world religion in the same mould as Judaism, Christianity and Islam, it is covered in Chapter 1, but because of its more recent origin, it is given a full-length entry.

The Conclusion looks at why people join alternative religious movements and what they get out of them. It considers some of the reasons why these movements might be criticized and the efforts of 'cult-watchers' to help people to leave them. This section includes personal observations.

Most of the entries on individual religious movements are divided into two sections, 'History' and 'Beliefs and Practices' – usually, but not always, in that order. Some of the shorter entries combine the two for convenience.

◆

No book of this type can ever claim to be complete. Some of the entries are less detailed than we would like them to be; a few are missing entirely. The 50 or so which are included are representative of the many alternative religions and semi-religious movements currently available in Britain. They are inevitably less representative of the many, many more in the USA (although a lot of these are simply slightly different variants of each other).

In line with our basic principle that each movement should have the opportunity to speak for itself about its beliefs and practices, and be able to answer criticisms about itself, we have reluctantly not included entries on a few organizations which did not reply to our repeated inquiries, or on the very few which did reply but refused absolutely to have anything to do with this book.

We are aware that one group of recent religious movements is entirely absent from this book: offshoots of Islam and Judaism such as the various black Muslim groups, the Nation of Islam, the Holy Tabernacle Ministries, the Nubian Hebrews and others. Attempts to gain information from these movements (as opposed to information about them) have so far been unsuccessful. We would be very happy to include them in future editions of this book.

◆

All Bible quotations are taken from the King James Authorized Version.

PART ONE

✠

BACKGROUND

ONE

A BRIEF HISTORY OF WORLD RELIGIONS

EARLY RELIGIONS

Religion has been with mankind ever since we were able to consider such things as the mysteries of birth and death, and where people go to, if anywhere, in their dreams and after death. Animals had to be hunted, crops had to be grown, and physical strength and the weather were all-important. At one time every tribe had its own gods and goddesses, who protected the people, helped them in war and helped their crops to grow. It was accepted that other tribes had their own gods. If another tribe defeated your own, their gods were probably stronger than yours. As tribes defeated each other, traded with each other, migrated, intermingled and intermarried, gods and the worship of gods also intermingled, and religious beliefs and practices developed.

As human society developed, so did the specialist task of dealing with the gods. The priesthood, in one form or another, ranks with prostitution and spying as one of the oldest professions. (A case can be made for the fairly early development of a more sophisticated belief system, one in which the true belief was actually in one supreme being, the Source of all life, the Oneness of the otherworld, the world of nature and man himself; the spirit of a tree, a river or thunder was not God, or even a god, but an aspect of the Source. Although the spiritual leaders, the shamans and priests, might have thought of them in this way, the common man was perhaps more likely to have believed that these were individual gods.)

So, in early religion there was often a multiplicity of gods or powerful spirits (the distinction is now not always clear) who all had their own responsibilities and, as religious ideas developed, their own personalities, and each of whom had to be persuaded or appeased in an individual, appropriate way.

Sometimes there was one or more deity who was so big, so powerful and so distant that he or she could not be approached directly. The lesser gods were more approachable, more immediate. They could understand the need for rain, or sun, or healing from an injury, and might be persuaded to do something about it.

Sometimes gods would work together; at other times they would seem to be working against each other. As the gods developed personalities, they developed relationships and family hierarchies; they became humans writ large, with all the virtues and faults of humans magnified. Greek, Roman and Norse mythologies are full of stories of such gods. At times it is difficult to distinguish between the exaggerated stories of human heroes and the exploits of the gods. The latter were often based on the former, but also, to add to the prestige of a hero, he would often assume attributes of one of the gods, or be declared a god after his death.

Man-like gods and god-like men are common in mythology and early history. In some societies the king was the living embodiment of the god. In early crop fertility religions, the king was literally or symbolically sacrificed to represent the death of crops and of the sun in winter, and would be brought back to life to symbolize the rebirth of green shoots in the new year. The echoes in Christianity are obvious. (So are the differences. In nature, a plant dies in winter, then comes back again the following spring; it is possible that this simple observation is the origin of belief in reincarnation.)

The local pantheons of gods, neglected for centuries, are resurfacing in the Celtic revival in Britain, in the interest in Native American shamanism in America and in the Northern Tradition in central and northern Europe.

HINDUISM

Hinduism is the oldest of the major established religions, though it might more fairly be called a group of interrelated religions. The word 'Hindu' actually refers to the people and culture of the Indus Valley region, now on the border between Pakistan and India, so effectively it means 'the religion(s) of the Indian peoples'. The earliest of the beliefs now incorporated in Hinduism date back to maybe 3000 BC, though the sacred book of 1,028 hymns, the Rig-Veda, was composed around 1400–1200 BC.

For the Westerner, Hinduism has a bewildering variety of gods and goddesses, and an equally wide range of ways of worshipping and serving them. For this reason, Hinduism has been called the ultimate pagan religion. As Hinduism spread geographically, its inherent flexibility enabled it both to absorb and to adapt to local religious ideas. Of the literally millions of gods and demi-gods (some say 33 million), most of them unique to individual villages, the best known are the 'trinity' of Brahma the Creator, Vishnu the Sustainer and Shiva the Destroyer, and also, these days, Krishna, an avatar of Vishnu.

Given the number of gods and the age of the religion, it is hardly surprising that there are many quite different varieties of Hinduism, and that new movements with Hindu origins can be quite different from each other.

Hindus believe in reincarnation, the idea that after death the soul is reborn into another body. The quality of the next life you live depends on what you do and what you learn in your current life. This is the basic idea of *karma*, which is central to the present-day, Eastern-inspired, Esoteric and Neo-Pagan religious movements.

BUDDHISM

Buddhism is sometimes very loosely described as Hinduism without the gods. The word 'Buddha' means 'Enlightened One', and there have been a number of Buddhas over the centuries, the best known (and founder of Buddhism) being Siddhartha Gautama (*c.* 560–480 BC).

By practising morality and meditation and gaining wisdom, Buddhists aim to escape from the cycle of reincarnation and attain nirvana (literally 'no-being'), the ultimate, peaceful, transformed consciousness.

The two main strands of traditional Buddhism are Theravada and Mahayana, which split from each other very early on. Theravada (sometimes called Hinayana) Buddhism lays great stress on an individual's own self-improvement and salvation, though this can be attained only by living a strict monastic life. The Mahayana lifestyle is less strictly ascetic, depending more on faith and devotion. Mahayana Buddhism lays more emphasis on the possibility of anyone becoming a *bodhisattva*, or someone destined for enlightenment, who then delays his passage or nirvana until he has helped others along the same path. Celestial *bodhisattvas*, or *mahasattvas* are effectively equivalent to gods, and this helped Buddhism take hold in Indian villages, with their individual Hindu beliefs. Tibetan, Chinese and Japanese Buddhism all stem from Mahayana Buddhism. A third strand, Tantric Buddhism, is more text-based and ritualistic, with much recital of mantras.

Zen Buddhism, very fashionable in the Western world since the 1960s, and therefore often misunderstood and misrepresented, is a fusion of Mahayana and Chinese Taoist beliefs. Its aim is the direct experience of enlightenment (*satori*). Teaching, texts and worship can be useful, unless they become important in themselves and so get in the way of *satori*. All ordinary aspects of life, from cooking a meal to driving a car, are seen as a form of meditation. Zen particularly lends itself to blending with other religious traditions.

ZOROASTRIANISM

Zoroaster, or Zarathustra, was probably the son of a pagan priest, living in Persia from *c.* 660 to 583 BC, or perhaps earlier, *c.* 1400 BC. At the age of 30 he had a religious experience in which the one god, Ahura Mazda (the Wise Lord), told him to reform the polytheistic beliefs and sacrificial practices of his land. In a practical move, the earlier gods were absorbed into the new religion as assistants to the one god. Although monotheistic, Zoroastrianism is responsible for the idea of a good spirit of god and an evil spirit of god, light and darkness, two equal but opposite demi-urges. This dualist belief has informed much of later religion, whether overtly, in some of the Gnostic religions, or covertly, in the Christian counterparts of God and the Devil. Zoroastrianism has also had profound effects on Jewish, Christian and Islamic beliefs in the afterlife, including resurrection, heaven and hell. Fire is central to Zoroastrian worship, symbolizing God's power and purity. Zoroastrianism has high moral ideals and (unlike later monotheistic religions) treats women well.

When Islam took hold in Persia in the seventh century, many Zoroastrians moved to India, where three-quarters of the roughly 150,000 total live today, known as Parsees. There are about 3,000 Parsees in Britain, and perhaps as many in North America.

JUDAISM

Judaism is a landmark in the history of world religions. It is the last of the important religions to be associated almost entirely with one people: the Jewish race and the Jewish religion are inseparable. When an African tribe was found to have a religion almost indistinguishable from Judaism, it caused tremendous debate: was it possible to be a Jew by religion if you were not a Jew by blood? It is, of course, possible for the opposite to occur, for a Jew by birth to join another religion. This century there has been a very strong missionary campaign by the Christian Church to convert Jews to Christ. One remarkable statistic put out by some of the cult-watching organizations is that a quarter of recruits to the more recent new religious movements are Jewish by birth.

Judaism is unusual in that it does not actively seek to recruit new members from other religions.

Judaism became the first of the great monotheistic religions. Although initially Yahweh was seen as a tribal god – 'I am the God of thy father, the God of Abraham, the God of Isaac, and the God of Jacob' (Exodus 3:6) – and greater than any other gods – 'Thou shalt have no other gods before me' (Genesis 20:3) – as the religion developed he became the only true god, all others being false rather than lesser.

Both the exoteric and the esoteric influence of Judaism on Christianity and Islam – particularly the idea of the Creator God having a personal relationship with his people – cannot be overestimated. The Christian God the Father and the Muslim Allah are the same as the Jewish Yahweh. The great prophets and leaders of Judaism are also recognized in the two later religions, as are many of the Jewish scriptures.

The Cabbala is a mystical philosophical system based on the esoteric interpretation of the Jewish Scriptures, especially the Torah, the first five books of the Bible. Its deepest roots are unknown, but it developed into a formulated system in eighth-century Spain, and was further developed in the Zohar, a mystical work written in the late thirteenth century. The Cabbala's diagrammatic Tree of Life is used symbolically to represent the relationship between God and man. The Cabbala has been called 'the foundation of the Western Mystery Tradition', and its study lies at the heart of many Esoteric religious movements, including Esoteric Christianity.

CHRISTIANITY

The essence of Christianity is that God came down to earth as a man, to pay once and for all the necessary sacrifice for the sins of mankind, so that God and man might be reconciled.

Christianity originated as just one of many Jewish sects of the time. The Pharisees, Sadducees, Zealots and Essenes are all well known. There were prophets everywhere. For example, John the Baptist was already a well-established teacher, preacher or prophet when Jesus started his ministry. Part of his message was 'He that cometh after me is preferred before me' (John 1:15), paving the way for the new teacher, Jesus.

Christianity might have died with the death of Jesus if not for the one thing which distinguished it from most other Jewish sects: the instruction to believers, 'Go thou and preach the kingdom of God' (Luke 9:60). But if it hadn't been for Paul, Christianity would probably have remained a fairly minor Jewish sect; Peter, the natural leader after Jesus' death, initially saw no need to spread the faith to non-Jews, until God gave him a vision (Acts 10:9–29).

Christianity spread, developing as it went. Paul, and others, took the message to Rome, the hub of the empire. Again, it could easily have died out in those first few years. But the early Christians, who seemed to thrive on persecution, kept preaching and the movement grew. In the year AD 312, the Roman emperor Constantine invoked the Christian God for help in a war. He won, and the rest is history. Over the next few centuries, Christianity was taken to most of Europe, including the British Isles. By around the year AD 1000, even the Norse were letting the new 'nailed god' supplant Odin, Thor, Balder and the rest.

(Some things the Christian Church was too late to change. The days of the week in English are named after the Sun, the Moon, the Roman god Saturn, and four Norse gods, Tyr/Tîw, Woden/Odin, Thor and Frigga or Freya.)

By around the fifteenth century, the great seafaring nations were the British, the Spanish, the Portuguese and the Dutch, and all were Christian. Everywhere they went, from the New World (north and south) to Africa, to the East, to little scattered islands all around the world, they took their religion – and, for better or for worse, imposed it on the native peoples of those lands. The fledgeling United States, colonized by Christian Europeans, imported slaves from Africa and made them Christian too.

Christianity had long left behind its origins as a minor sect of one of many Middle Eastern tribal religions. Now it was the 'establishment' religion of the 'civilized' world.

ISLAM

Muslims rightly object to being called Muhammadans; Muhammad (AD 570–632) was the Prophet, not God. In AD 611 Muhammad began to have meetings with the angel Gabriel. The teachings he received were written down in the Koran (or Qur'ān), which for all Muslims is a far more sacred work than the Bible is to most Christians. Although the Koran may be 'interpreted' in other languages, it can never properly be translated because its expression in Arabic is an integral part of its holiness. It was written in Arabic and is still read in Arabic by all Muslims, thus simultaneously maintaining the purity of that language and identifying Islam largely with Arabic-speaking peoples.

'Islam' means 'submission' or 'surrender' to the will of God. The essence of the Muslim 'creed' is 'There is no God but God (Allah), and Muhammad is His Prophet.' There is only one God, but there have been several prophets, including Adam, Abraham and Jesus; Muhammad was the last of the prophets, with the final revelation.

Because of the Middle Eastern origins, Allah is the same God as the Jewish Yahweh and the Christian God the Father. The three great monotheistic religions are known as the Religions of the Book.

In AD 622 Muhammad, encountering religious opposition to his teachings of the unity of God and his denunciation of idolatry, moved north from his birthplace Mecca to Medina, both in Saudi Arabia. This *hejira* marks the start of the Muslim calendar. All Muslims must attempt to make a pilgrimage to Mecca and Medina at least once in their lives. This is one of the five Pillars of Islam, the others being belief, prayer, fasting and alms-giving.

Like most religions, Islam has suffered schisms over the centuries. The main one occurred within a few years of the founding of Islam, when followers of the fourth caliph, Muhammad's son-in-law Ali, decreed that all future caliphs must come from the line of Ali. They also denounced the first three caliphs, who had all been close associates of Muhammad. The Party of Ali *(Shi'at al Ali)*, known as Shi'a or Shi'ite Muslims, became more hardline than the majority Sunni Muslims (*sunna* means 'the rule or custom'), and today are found in their original Iraq, Iran and Pakistan. Shi'ites were led by 12 imams, descended from Ali; the twelfth disappeared and is expected to return one day as the Mahdi ('guided one') to restore pure Islam to the world. Other Muslim sects include the Ismaelis, who split from the Shi'ites around AD 765.

Historically, most Muslims were actually more tolerant of other religions than were Christians. Like Christian countries, Muslim nations and tribes took their religion into the countries they conquered, but generally they allowed Christians and Jews to retain their faith and practices, though as second-class citizens. The Crusades, being both territorial and religious military campaigns, created a tension and distrust between Muslims and Christians the repercussions of which are still with us today. The other main cause of tension is that Islam has always been both religious and political in nature. An Islamic nation is ruled by an Islamic government with Islamic laws, which do not sit happily with the more relaxed laws and customs of Western liberal democracies which, in turn, Muslims see as degenerate.

Islam initially spread in the West as Indians and Pakistanis emigrated to Britain and the USA. In the last few decades there has been a growth in two areas: a more militant expression of Islam among Asian, Middle Eastern and North African Muslims in the West; and the rapid development of Black Muslims. The latter began among African–Americans in the USA in the 1930s as the Nation of Islam, and has since split into various factions, some returning to Sunni Muslim orthodoxy and others being more politically motivated, upholding black rights against both whites and Jews.

SUFISM

Sufism is the mystical side of Islam, dating as far back, probably, as the first century of Islam. The word 'sufi' is Arabic for 'wool-clad', referring to the traditional coarse robe of the ascetic believer. It might also have links with the Arabic word *safa*, meaning 'purity', the Hebrew term *en sof*, a term for the Divine in Jewish mysticism, and maybe with the Greek word *sophia*, meaning 'wisdom'. Sufism is rich with beautiful poetic literature, music and ecstatic dance – the famous whirling dervishes of one of the Sufi orders (or *tariqas*, meaning 'ways'), the Mawlawiya or Mevlevis. One way of getting close to God by contemplation is to repeat his name continuously.

Perhaps partly because it puts the believer's personal relationship with God before the strict outward observance of religious practices, Sufism has been regarded with suspicion by Islam itself since the very beginning, while at the same time being highly respected for its spiritual and intellectual worth. A further reason for suspicion is that Sufis have always had a close relationship with mystics and philosophers of other religious traditions, including Neo-Platonism, Greek

Orthodoxy and Hinduism. A deep, loving communion with and experience of God is valued, whatever the religion. In the Middle Ages Sufis and Cabbalists exchanged knowledge freely. The Knights Templar had links with Sufis, and it can be argued that Sufi symbolism influenced early Freemasonry. For influence in the other direction, there are elements of both Christian mysticism and Gnosticism in Sufism.

In the first few centuries of Islam Sufis were persecuted and some were executed. In the twelfth and thirteenth centuries a *rapprochement* took place, particularly with Sunni Islam, but there is still sometimes an uneasy tension between Sufis and orthodox Muslims. In Pakistan the Ahmadi order of Sufis is currently facing tremendous persecution from Fundamentalist Muslims. Shi'ite Muslims are particularly antagonistic towards Sufis.

Among the twentieth-century Sufi writers who are influential in Britain and America are Hazrat Inayat Khan, who brought Sufism to the West, and Idries Shah. Sufism has influenced several of the more esoteric and mystical New Age movements in the West, where it is less strongly linked with its Muslim origins, claiming rather to be a universal religion. The emphasis is on dance, chanting the names of God and healing; the aim is a loving union with God. Gurdjieff (see p. 176) was also influenced by Sufism.

SIKHISM

Although the Sikh religion (*sikh* means 'disciple') is sometimes seen as a fusion between Hinduism and Islam, its founder, Guru Nanak (1469–1539), wrote, 'There is neither Hindu nor Muslim, so whose path shall I follow? I shall follow God's path. God is neither Hindu nor Muslim and the path which I follow is God's.' In this Nanak followed the teachings of the mystic Kabir (1440–1518), some of whose words are contained, along with Nanak's and several other Sikh gurus, and some Hindu and Muslim writings, in their scriptures, the *Granth* ('the Book'). Because of its geographical origins and the beliefs of both Nanak and Kabir, however, Sikhism inevitably contains elements of both religions, specifically Bhakti Hinduism (devotion to God rather than religious ceremonial and idol worship), Advaita (founded by Samkara or Shankara – see p. 149) and elements of (Muslim) Sufism.

The Sikhs, largely originating from the Punjab, on the borders of India and Pakistan, have often been caught between Hindus and Muslims. The Moguls in particular were hostile towards them and the Sikhs developed into a warrior people. Their common male surname Singh means 'lion' (the female surname Kaur means 'princess'), and a devout Sikh wears not just a turban but a sword at all times. (This is part of the five Ks: *kesh*, unshorn hair; *kangha*, comb; *kirpan*, sword; *kara*, steel bracelet; and *kachch*, short trousers for ease in fighting.) During this century they have fought more through politics than the sword; their political party is the Akali Dal. But in recent years there has been armed conflict between Sikhs and Hindus, intensified by the Indian troops' storming of the Golden Temple at Amritsar, and the Sikhs' retaliatory assassination of Prime Minister Indira Gandhi. There is also traditional hostility between Sikhs and Muslims.

Although for historical reasons Sikhism is often seen as a militant religion, at its heart it is deeply democratic and egalitarian, with keen social awareness and a spirit of reconciliation. Sikhism is monotheistic, with God seen as the supreme guru. The ten gurus from Nanak to Gobind Singh (1666–1708) are deeply revered. The *Granth*, containing their teachings, is the immortal guru.

Of the 6 million Sikhs worldwide, over a quarter of a million live in Britain. Sikh revivalist movements have taken hold in America throughout this century. One in particular, Sikh Dharma, is better known by its educational wing 3HO (the Healthy, Happy, Holy Organization). Kundalini yoga, which through breathing regulation and being 'centred' helps one to meditate on God's name, is also widely taught by Western Sikhs.

BAHÁ'Í FAITH

In the last 30 years membership of the Bahá'aí Faith has grown at an astonishing rate. By their own figures, in 1963 worldwide membership was 400,000 living in 11,000 localities and organized into 56 national and regional communities. By 1994 membership had risen to 5 million, living in over 120,000 localities and organized into 165 national communities. There are approximately 6,000 registered Bahá'ís (adults and children) in the UK.

Although this is a relatively new religion, and although it had its origins in Islam, the Bahá'í Faith claims to be no more a Muslim sect than Christianity today is a Jewish sect. It is a new worldwide religion, the next in order after Judaism, Christianity and Islam, worshipping the same one God as they do.

From time to time God sends his prophets or messengers to earth; these have included Abraham, Krishna, Moses, Zoroaster, Buddha, Jesus, Muhammad – and now two others, the Báb and Bahá'u'lláh. Each has revealed God to the people of a particular time and place.

HISTORY

The Bahá'í Faith began in Persia, now Iran, when in 1844 a young Muslim merchant called Mirza Ali Muhammad (1819–50) started to preach that the Day of God was at hand. He proclaimed himself to be the Báb or Gate, and said, like John the Baptist, that he was the forerunner of one greater than himself who would initiate a new age of peace and justice. Although initially within Islam, the Báb's teachings grew further away from that religion and in 1848 he formally announced that Bábism was a new religion. He was executed by firing squad in 1850.

There are several versions of the Báb's martyrdom, but most Bahá'ís believe that when the smoke cleared, the Báb was found to be back in his cell, unharmed, teaching one of his disciples. Only when he had finished did he say to his guards, 'Now you may proceed to fulfil your intention.' This time the bullets found their mark.

After the death of the Báb, one of his closest followers, Mirza Husayn-Ali Nuri, the son of a wealthy government minister, was arrested and flung into gaol. On his release he was banished, first to Baghdad and then to Kurdistan, where he spent two years in solitary contemplation. Returning to Baghdad, he took over the leadership of the Báb community, and in 1863 he announced that he was the Bahá'u'lláh, the Glory of God, the one whom the Báb had foretold.

Bahá'u'lláh spent much of the rest of his life as a prisoner or in exile in various cities in the Ottoman Empire. From 1868 until his death in 1892, he lived in Acre, in present-day Israel. He was succeeded by his son, Abdu'l-Bahá (1844–1921) and great-grandson Shoghi Effendi (1897–1957), each of whom played a key role in the development of the Bahá'í Faith.

The Báb wrote a sacred book, the *al-Bayan*, and Bahá'u'lláh wrote vast numbers of books and letters, including *The Hidden Words*, 'a distillation of the spiritual guidance contained in the successive revelations of God', the *Kitáb-i-Íqán* or *Book of Certitude*, the principle exposition of his doctrinal message, *The Seven Valleys*, a small mystical work in poetic language, and the *Kitáb-i-Aqdas*, or *The Most Holy Book*, which contains the laws and institutions for the new world order. Unlike the Gospels, Bahá'ís say, these books are first-hand writings by God's messenger, rather than second-hand accounts about God's messenger; Bahá'u'lláh's writings are counted as equal to the Bible and the Koran. The original handwritten texts, in Bahá'u'lláh's handwriting, still exist.

◆

It is interesting that Bahá'ís claim 1844, the year when the Báb began to preach, as the beginning of their religion. Many Millenarian Christians, including the forerunners of the Seventh-day Adventists, foretold the Second Coming for 1844, their calendraic calculations based on a particular interpretation of biblical prophecies. The Bahá'ís, then, can point to their faith as being in line with Christian prophecy for the return of Christ.

Critics have suggested that the choice of this rather convenient date is somewhat arbitrary; it would be the same as beginning the Christian calendar from when John the Baptist began to preach, rather than from the supposed date of the birth of Christ. The Bahá'ís could have chosen 1817, when Bahá'u'lláh was born, or 1863, when he announced that he was the Promised One, or 1892, when he died; or 1819 or 1850, the years of the birth and death of the Báb.

Although Bahá'ís today tend not to mention this, there was dispute at the very start of their religion. After the death of the Báb, Bahá'u'lláh and his brother Mirza Yahya originally took over leadership of the new faith together; Mirza Yahya was actually the Báb's appointed successor. Two factions developed, the majority eventually accepting Bahá'u'lláh's claim to be the messenger of a new religion, the minority (Azali Bábism) following his brother, who saw Bábism as a movement within Shi'ite Islam. There are currently only a few thousand members of Azali Bábism, living mainly in Iran.

There was also factionalism after Bahá'u'lláh's death, with Abdu'l-Bahá's half-brother Mirza Muhammad Ali claiming to be the legitimate successor.

Similarly, Bahá'ís often claim that unlike every other religion the Bahá'í Faith has never splintered into sects. In fact, there have been several: the New History Society was founded in New York in 1929 by an excommunicated Bahá'í, Mirza Ahmad Sohrab; the Bahá'í World Union, or the World Union of Universal Religion and Universal Peace, was founded in Germany in 1930, banned by the Nazis and relaunched in 1948; the Bahá'í World Federation, founded in 1950 by Amin Effendi, the last surviving grandson of Bahá'u'lláh, united several dissident groups opposed to the leadership of Bahá'u'lláh's great-grandson Shoghi Effendi; Bahá'ís Under the Hereditary Guardianship, or the Orthodox

Bahá'ís, were founded in 1960, in a leadership dispute after Shoghi Effendi's death; and a further small splinter group from this, Bahá'ís Under the Provisions of the Covenant, was founded in 1971. Most of these movements, however, have had few members. 'Sectarianism has sporadically surfaced though no single group has become a significant threat to the larger community,' says Dr Stephen Lambden, a leading Bahá'í scholar.[1] The position of the main Bahá'í organization seems to be that these groups, simply by being dissident, have gone against the World Order of Bahá'u'lláh and have violated the Covenant. They can no longer be considered as having anything to do with the Bahá'í Faith and are not, therefore, Bahá'í sects.

BELIEFS AND PRACTICES

Although Lambden points out that this is 'highly generalized', it has been said that Judaism brought knowledge of God's law; Christianity brought grace, salvation and a relationship with God; Islam brought submission to God's will; while the Bahá'í Faith brings unity of all peoples under God.

> Bahá'ís believe that in every age God sends a Messenger to mankind . . . Each Messenger builds upon the Messages of Those gone before, leading us to new spiritual heights and bringing social teachings designed for that particular age . . . Bahá'ís believe that, although the Messengers are all different individuals, it is the same spirit, the spirit of God, which animates them all . . . We believe that the same spirit which was in all the Messengers is in Bahá'u'lláh.[2]

Bahá'í beliefs about the afterlife are fairly similar to those of Christianity:

> When the human body dies, the soul is freed from ties with the physical body and the surrounding physical world and begins its progress through the spiritual world . . . Entry into the next life has the potential to bring great joy. Bahá'u'lláh likened death to the process of birth . . . The physical world provides the matrix for the development of the individual soul. Accordingly, Bahá'ís view life as a sort of workshop, where one can develop and perfect those qualities which will be needed in the next life . . . In the final analysis, heaven can be seen partly as a state of nearness to God; hell is a state of remoteness from God. Each state follows as a natural consequence of individual efforts, or the lack thereof, to develop spiritually.[3]

For a major world religion the Bahá'í faith is unusual in having no priesthood and no set liturgy for services. The religion operates a grass-roots-up democracy by which representatives are elected at every level from local community to senior worldwide administration, in a process which not only forbids canvassing for votes but also has no candidates. The electors, at whatever level, vote for anyone they wish 'who can best combine the necessary qualities of unquestioned loyalty, of selfless devotion, of a well-trained mind, of recognized ability and mature experience'.[4] After Shoghi Effendi's death, a new senior governing body, the Universal House of Justice, was set up, elected by national and local spiritual assemblies.

The Bahá'í Faith has grown from nothing in 1863, when Bahá'u'lláh announced that he was the Expected One, to more than 5 million followers in over 200 countries today; it is the second most globally widespread religion after Christianity. Several factors have contributed to this phenomenal growth.

Much of its appeal to members of the other Religions of the Book – Judaism, Christianity and Islam – is that the Bahá'í faith is a continuation of the same theme: one God, the Creator, who cares enough for his people that he sends them a messenger. The familiar prophets of each of the religions are accepted and respected by Bahá'ís. For Jews, Bahá'u'lláh is seen as a descendant of Abraham and a fulfilment of Old Testament prophecy: 'And there shall come forth a rod out of the stem of Jesse, and a Branch shall grow out of his roots' (Isaiah 11:1). For Christians, Jesus' uniqueness as *the* Son of God, and the uniqueness of his sacrifice – 'after he had offered one sacrifice for sins for ever' (Hebrews 10:12) – are necessarily lost, but because the Bahá'ís see Jesus as a prophet rather than as God himself, they can point to Bahá'u'lláh as the promised return of Christ. For Muslims, Bahá'u'lláh could be seen as fulfilling the promise in the Koran for the 'Day of God' and the 'Great Announcement', when God will come down to earth; in addition, the Báb began his teaching within Islam, saying that he himself was the one promised in the Koran.

Because Bahá'ís accept a number of previous messengers of God, they can say to Hindus that Bahá'u'lláh is the new incarnation of Krishna, the 'Tenth Avatar', while for Buddhists, he is the foretold Maitreya, the Buddha of universal fellowship.

There is, then, both a continuity and a familiarity in the Bahá'í Faith for members of many other religions who might feel that their own religion is not as relevant as it could be in today's world.

The Bahá'í Faith also has an appeal to those interested in New Age ideas. Bahá'ís speak of the new Age of Aquarius, and adopt the terminology of New Age proponents: 'The former age was dominated by male characteristics, leading to aggression and obsession with power, but the new age concept is based on a balance of male and female qualities, leading to a more complex and rounded human character and civilization.'[5]

The New Age, from the 1960s onwards, has been characterized by syncretism, seeking after truth, and peace. The Bahá'í faith is tailor-made: 'Truth is one in all religions, and by means of it the unity of the world can be realized . . . If only men would search out truth, they would find themselves united.'[6]

The democratic nature of the Bahá'í faith is also appealing. There are no priests or bishops, gurus, imams, ayatollahs or popes. All members are equal, all have a say in every decision at local level, and all can take part in electing their representative at national and international levels. Consultation and group decision-making is paramount in Bahá'í thought.

Bahá'ís are also very strong on the equality of all races and the equality of the sexes. Women can hold any position in the religion, except membership of the nine-strong Universal House of Justice, the international governing council of the Bahá'í faith. This one exception was apparently laid down by Bahá'u'lláh himself, with no explanation; Bahá'ís themselves cannot explain it.

Although the Bahá'í Faith has a strong spiritual aspect, it is perhaps at its strongest in the community. Education is very important to Bahá'ís, particularly at local level in Third World countries. Education should be 'compulsory for all; be based on spiritual principles; be equally available to all children, but if any preference has to be given it is to the female child; and be based on the realization of the absolute oneness of all mankind, to be implemented by the teaching of world citizenship,' says Hugh Adamson, Secretary-General of the National Spiritual Assembly of the Bahá'ís of the United Kingdom.[7]

Healthy living is important to Bahá'ís; alcohol and drugs are forbidden, smoking is discouraged and vegetarianism is recommended as being healthier than eating meat, though 'most Bahá'ís today are not vegetarians and are not pressurized to become so,' says Stephen Lambden.[8] Traditional sexual mores are also firmly taught.

PART TWO

✠

CHRISTIAN ORIGINS

TWO

VARIETIES OF CHRISTIANITY

Christians generally *know* that they have the truth, mainly because of Jesus' words, 'No man cometh unto the Father, but by me' (John 14:6), and possibly, to a certain degree, because of historical imperialism.

Sometimes committed members of individual Christian denominations know that *they* have the truth. Talk to a dedicated Roman Catholic. He is right; he has history and the pope behind him. Talk to an Anglican or an Episcopalian. He is right; he has history but he's rejected the spurious authority of the Bishop of Rome. Talk to a Baptist. He is right; he has thrown aside the man-made accretions of history and gone back to the one legitimate source, the Bible. But then, so have the Exclusive Brethren. And the Pentecostals. And the Seventh-day Adventists. And the Christadelphians.

They all share the same sacred text, the Bible, they all believe in the same God and they all preach the words of the same young Jewish man who was executed nearly 20 centuries ago. Yet each of these Churches knows that it is right. Many of them will say that the others are wrong.

There are exceptions, of course. The ecumenical movement draws Christian denominations together to share the 99 per cent they have in common, rather than argue about the 1 per cent that separates them. In Britain most of the Presbyterians and the Congregationalists merged to become the United Reformed Church. In Canada and in India, the major Protestant denominations merged to form national Churches. The Church of England claims as both its greatest strength and its greatest weakness the fact that it is a broad church, ranging from 'high church' Anglo-Catholics to 'low church' Fundamentalist Evangelicals, with a troublesome left wing of outspoken liberals, including a Bishop of Woolwich who declared in the 1960s that God was dead, and a Bishop of Durham who in the 1990s said that it wasn't necessary to believe in the virgin birth and the literal resurrection of Jesus.

But still there are many denominations, many different Churches, each one believing that it is right.

THE 'EXPLOSION' OF CULTS

The newspapers and the cult-watching organizations often give the impression that the profusion of sects, cults and other new religious movements in recent years is something new. It could be, they say, a reaction against materialist philosophy, which was in turn a reaction against dogmatic Christianity; or it could be a repeat of the Millenarianism witnessed shortly before AD 1000; or it could be a sign of the Last Days before the return of Christ – 'For there shall arise false Christs, and false prophets, and shall shew great signs and wonders; insomuch that, if it were possible, they shall deceive the very elect' (Matthew 24:24).

It could be any or all of these things, and a host of others. But the proliferation of Christian sects is no new phenomenon. There has been no sudden 'explosion of cults' in the last few decades. True, many of the organizations covered in this book sprang up in the twentieth century, but several of them are nineteenth century in origin, and some are much older and are simply reappearing in a slightly different guise.

Religious sects are nothing new. In 1827, the fifteenth edition of *A Sketch of the Denominations of the Christian World* was published, shortly after the death of its author, John Evans. After running through 'Christian sects, According to the Person of Christ' (eight), 'According to the Means and Measure of God's Favour' (five) and 'According to the Mode of Church Government' (19), Evans lists a further 'Twenty-four Miscellaneous Sects, not reducible to the above three-fold Division'.

This last list is fascinating. A few have continued to the present day, in the main as respected denominations, but for most we can only ask, 'Where are they now?' and smile at some of the names.

These are Evans's 'Twenty-Four Miscellaneous Sects': Quakers; Methodists (plus *Lady Anne Erskine, Character of*); New Methodists; Primitive Methodists, or Ranters; Bryanites; Jumpers; Universalists; Destructionists; Sabbatarians; Moravians; Sandemanians; Hutchinsonians; Shakers; Dunkers; New American Sect; Mystics; Swedenborgians; Haldanites; Freethinking Christians; Joanna Southcott, Muggletonians, and Fifth-Monarchy Men; Seceders from the Church of England; Sauds, or Saadhs; Jerkers and Barkers; and Millenarians.

These were all Christian sects, each worshipping in its own way and recruiting new members early in the nineteenth century. There were no doubt others as well.

It has often been pointed out that in America one can find a different Church on every corner: a store-front church, a converted cinema or car showroom. A lot of these originate when one member of a 'Free Church' congregation disagrees with his pastor over a perhaps minor doctrinal or organizational detail; or sometimes there is a battle of succession after the death of the founder, or sometimes just a clash of personalities. Whatever, the member walks out, taking a few supporters with him, and a new Church is born. Few of these last much beyond the lifetime of their last founder member, but some do, and spawn daughter congregations. A very few grow into national or international denominations or Churches.

PROBLEMS IN INTERPRETATION

The majority of alternative religions encountered in Britain, Europe and the USA are offshoots, in one way or another, of Christianity: the word 'sect' is accurate, not insulting. Christianity has always been a many-hued creature. From its very beginnings it sprouted in different directions, as different groups emphasized different aspects of it, or formulated its developing theology in different ways. If the 12 apostles could have travelled forward in time just 200 years, they would have found some difficulty in identifying the religion with the Jesus they had known; 1,000, 1,500 and 1,900 years on and they would have been astonished – and at times horrified – at what professed to be Christianity, at its beliefs, its rituals and the way it treated other people.

Many of the variants of Christianity today began as honest attempts to return to the simplicity of the original message. Why, then, are there so many of them, with so many major differences? If they are all trying to get back to the original, why can't they agree on what the original is?

Part of the problem is that the New Testament (let alone the whole Bible) is not a manual of doctrine. It contains four overlapping but different accounts of the life and teachings of Jesus, each angled in a different way for a different audience; an account of the lives of some of the disciples after Jesus' death; 21 letters; and a vision. The Old Testament contains, among other things, history, law, poetry and prophecy. The whole assemblage was written by several dozen people over several hundred years, and the package which we now call the canonical Scriptures was listed as we now have it only in AD 367, by which time the people who made the choice of which books to include and which to leave out had their own doctrinal agenda. There isn't such a thing as a statement of belief, a creed, in the Bible. If you want one, you have to study, search, analyse and interpret the Bible, and write your own.

A further problem is that everyone is convinced that their own interpretation is the only correct one. Ask a dozen well-educated people to state the main points of Marxism in a few hundred words, or to say what Plato's *Republic* or Shakespeare's *Tempest* or Dickens's *Hard Times* or Wordsworth's *Prelude* is about, and in each case there will be a dozen different replies. This is even more the case when spiritual matters are involved. The Evangelical Christian says, 'My beliefs come solely from the Bible', and will point out exactly where every Christian sect strays from the Biblical truth. But most Christian sects also say, 'My beliefs come solely from the Bible.' Talk to the Evangelical or talk to the sect member, and each will say, 'This is the true interpretation; anyone else's interpretation is man-made and Devil-inspired; God's word speaks clearly.' It doesn't, of course, or we wouldn't have all this diversity of interpretation in the first place.

A third problem is that the events of the New Testament took place in a particular geographical, historical, social and religious setting. There is no reason why the truths at the heart of Christianity should not be relevant for everyone, everywhere, at all points in history; but individual sectarian interpretations sometimes focus in on specific points which were relevant to a Jew living in a Mediterranean country occupied by Rome 2,000 years ago, but which might have been stated somewhat differently if Jesus had been talking or Paul had been writing in fifteenth-century Venice or twentieth-century Chicago. This can easily be forgotten by present-day Christian sects.

A fourth problem is deciding which parts of the Bible are to be taken at their literal face value and which are metaphorical. Most Evangelicals will say that the whole Bible should be taken literally, but even they will accept that 'the mountains skipped like rams' (Psalm 114:4) is not a factual description of a major earthquake; it's a poetic metaphor. But where do you draw the line? Were the 5,000 actually fed by five loaves and two small fishes? What about the 4,000, who had a slightly better deal with seven loaves and 'a few small fishes' between them (Matthew 15:32–9, 16:6–10), and who had only seven baskets of leftovers, whereas the 5,000 had 12? If we accept the miracle, are we to take each of these numbers as literal fact? Or do they simply mean 'a little food and a lot of people'? If so, what other small details in the Bible are not really significant? Or are the two stories different versions of one event? Or are they both metaphors (Matthew 16:11–12), and not factual at all?

Where do you draw the line? When Jesus said, 'Be ye therefore perfect, even as your Father which is in heaven is perfect' (Matthew 5:48), did he mean that it is possible for people to achieve perfection in this life? The Holiness Churches would say so, but most other Christians would say that this is blasphemy, because only God can be perfect; what it really means, they say, is that we should strive to be perfect, we should aim for it, even though we can never achieve it. But that's not what Jesus said; he said 'be'. So who is right? Who is interpreting the Bible correctly?

If there are such differences of opinion on such familiar texts, it is not surprising that questions about the nature of heaven and hell, and the exact timetable for 'the last things', should divide Christian sects as they do. Does the word 'perish' mean to become non-existent or to suffer in hell for ever? When believers die, do they go to be with God immediately or are they put on hold until the last judgement? Will there be a literal battle at Armageddon, and a literal thousand-year direct rule of God on earth?

These are the very questions which separate most Christian sects from mainstream Christianity (which contains enough doctrinal differences of its own). There are no straightforward answers in the Bible to any of these questions. There are plenty of clues, but piecing them together in different ways leads to quite different solutions – which is why there are so many varieties of Christianity, and why so many of them contradict each other on fundamental points of doctrine, and why mainstream Christianity regards most of the Christian sects as heretical.

A HANDFUL OF DOCTRINAL DIFFERENCES

Before we look at heresies, let us consider briefly just a few of the differences in points of doctrine (including both belief and practice) within mainstream Christianity itself. In some cases, these are more fundamental than those separating some of the small offshoots of the Christian religion from the mainstream.

SATURDAY OR SUNDAY

Today, Seventh-day Adventists are accepted by many as a denomination rather than a sect. Their main difference from mainstream doctrine (as with their offshoots the Worldwide Church of God and the Branch Davidians) is that the Christian holy day should be Saturday, not Sunday. They point to Exodus 31:15–16, which says, 'Six days may work be done; but in the seventh is the sabbath of rest, holy to the Lord . . . Wherefore the children of Israel shall keep the sabbath, to observe the sabbath throughout their generations, for a perpetual covenant.' Present-day Jews still stick to this; it's one of the Ten Commandments, but mainstream Christianity changed it.

The reason given for the change is that Jesus rose from the dead on the first day of the week. (One or two of the new Churches have argued, albeit rather tortuously, that from the Gospel accounts even this standard belief isn't absolutely clear; he first *appeared* to someone on the first day of the week, they say, but he might have *risen* on the Sabbath, the day before.) Also, the disciples met on a Sunday. In Acts 20:7 we read that 'upon the first day of the week, when the disciples came together to break bread, Paul preached unto them'. However, this doesn't say that the Sabbath should be shifted from Saturday to Sunday, any more than the common habit of a Wednesday night prayer meeting or Bible study makes Wednesday the new day of rest and worship.

Within the first two centuries, though, Sunday became accepted as the Christian day of worship. To take just one of several examples from the Church Fathers, Justin Martyr (AD 100–165) wrote, 'Sunday is the day on which we all hold our common assembly because . . . Jesus Christ our Saviour on the same day rose from the dead.' But if one looks solely for biblical evidence, the theological argument is probably stronger for maintaining Saturday as the day of rest. Throughout mainstream Christianity, then, a major change rests more on tradition than on Scripture.

TRANSUBSTANTIATION OR REMEMBRANCE

The Roman Catholic Church believes that the bread or wafer at the Eucharist actually becomes, in its true nature, the body of Christ. The Protestant Churches say it represents the body of Christ – 'This do in remembrance of me' (Luke 22:19) – and that the Catholics are sacrificing Christ anew at every mass, which is biblically unsound – 'after he had offered one sacrifice for sins for ever' (Hebrews 10:12). The Roman Catholics, in return, simply point to the description of the Last Supper: 'And he took bread, and gave thanks, and brake it, and gave it unto them, saying, This is my body which is given for you' (Luke 22:19). 'This *is*', not 'This *represents*'.

Millions of words must have been written on this one point of doctrine alone; two paragraphs here cannot possibly approach the complexity of the problem, or the brilliant exegesis of attempts to reconcile the issue. The fact remains that it is a major point of doctrine at the very heart of Christian worship and that there are fundamental and essentially irreconcilable differences of belief about it within the main strands of established Christianity.

PRIESTS OR THE PRIESTHOOD OF ALL BELIEVERS

The Roman Catholic Church has the pope, cardinals, archbishops, bishops, priests and deacons. The Orthodox Churches have patriarchs, bishops and priests. The Anglican Church has archbishops, bishops, priests and deacons. The Methodist Church has ordained ministers and a wide network of lay preachers. The Baptist Church has pastors. The Presbyterian and Congregationalist Churches, now largely joined as the United Reformed Church, appoint leaders from the Church members. Other Free Churches have no equivalent to ordained ministers at all.

Two main theological points divide all of these. Evangelicals believe in the universal priesthood of all believers; if you are a Christian, you don't need any other intermediary between yourself and Christ. Although some people clearly have a teaching or preaching vocation, they are not separate from other church members.

At the other extreme is the authority of continuous apostolic succession. The Roman Catholic Church believes in an unbroken line of laying-on-of-hands from Christ, through Peter, through all the bishops of the last 20 centuries, to every bishop today. A new bishop is consecrated by several other bishops. A priest at ordination, or a child at confirmation, is touched on the head by the hands of a bishop, and this touch goes right back to, and represents, Christ himself.

The Anglican Churches claim apostolic succession in that their first bishops were originally consecrated as Roman Catholic bishops, so the line is unbroken. Methodist ministers don't have apostolic succession, because John Wesley was a Church of England priest, not a bishop, so his ordination of ministers was technically invalid.

To non-Christians and to some members of Free Churches, apostolic succession might seem a somewhat esoteric if not trivial point of difference; but those Churches which have it value its authority, and it has been a major sticking point in ecumenical negotiations. For the Roman Catholic Church, for example, any ordinations in secessionist Churches, though valid, are illegal, even if they claim apostolic succession, because the first Anglican bishops had turned their backs on the Church of Rome, wherein lies the only authority.

PREDESTINATION OR FREE WILL

This is another extremely complex issue, which can only be touched on very briefly here. If transubstantiation and apostolic succession are among the issues dividing Roman Catholicism from Protestantism, predestination splits Protestantism, including the Free Churches, into two distinct groups, Lutheran and Calvinist.

To put it at its simplest, Lutheran theology states that Christ died for the sins of everyone; we can all be saved, but it is up to each individual to accept or reject salvation. Calvinist theology, summarized equally simply, states that God, knowing everything, already knows who is going to be saved and who isn't; as the future is foreknown, it is therefore foreordained, or predestined. It's a small step from knowing to choosing. God has chosen some to be saved and some to be damned. We cannot therefore know that we are saved, as Lutheran Evangelicals believe.

The Calvinist or Reformed Churches include the Presbyterian and Congregationalist Churches, hence their new name of the United Reformed Church.

DEVOTIONAL ART OR IDOLATRY

Roman Catholic churches are full of paintings and sculptures; Eastern Orthodox churches have icons; Anglican churches have a cross on the altar; many Nonconformist 'low' churches don't even have that. In the older established denominations the priests wear richly patterned vestments; a Baptist minister will usually wear a suit. At a sung Eucharist the choir will sing anthems, perhaps in Latin; in a house fellowship someone might strum a guitar. Evangelicals claim that they are returning to the simplicity of worship of the early Church, and accuse the Catholics in particular (and any priest who even bobs his head at the cross) of idolatry – 'Thou shalt not make unto thee any graven image' (Exodus 20:4). Anglicans, Orthodox and Catholics point out the difference between worship and veneration, and stress the important teaching and meditational value of stained-glass windows, paintings and carvings of the Stations of the Cross. As the eighth-century John of Damascus said, they are 'books for the illiterate'.

On one level these are simply two different viewpoints: Evangelicals prefer to have a lack of clutter around them when worshipping God, while traditionalists find that beautiful visual aids help them to get closer to God. If that were all, there should be room for both viewpoints, and each should be able to accept the other. But Evangelicals, in inveighing against Catholic idolatry, can very easily swing too far the other way. The presence or absence of paintings in a church can become symbolic of indulgence in the pleasures of the flesh on the one hand, and of a hard, moral Puritanism on the other.

Evangelicalism has created little great art. Not just churches and cathedrals, but art galleries, public buildings and concert halls throughout the Western world are full of beautiful paintings, statues and music. Much of the artistic culture of the Western world stems from traditional Christianity. A few guitars and tambourines, and a couple of Day-glo posters on the walls of a Free Church somehow don't have quite the same resonance. This is a sadness for many Free Church Christians, who, while wanting to keep their theology, would actually like to have some of the grandeur of a Bach oratorio or the beauty of a Michelangelo painting as part of their worship.

As one ten-year-old girl chorister said, 'Latin is lovely to sing in once you know it well. I would hate to sing *Ave Verum* in English.'[1]

It has been argued that by stripping the Gospel message of all its later accretions, Evangelicalism has removed both mystery and mysticism from worship. Raising your arms in the air and shouting 'Hallelujah' with 500 other people is one way of feeling God's presence; but so is silent, individual contemplation of a statue of Mary holding her baby.

There has been at least one attempt to bring Evangelical beliefs and traditionalist practice together. The Catholic Apostolic Church, also known as the Irvingites, was founded by Edward Irving in 1831. Its doctrine was Evangelical; its liturgy and ceremonial were as complex and artistically fulfilling as anything in the Orthodox, Catholic or Anglican Churches, from which they were largely borrowed. The Church also believed in speaking in tongues and prophecy, and in the imminent return of Christ, thus simultaneously taking on aspects of the New Testament Church and of many present-day new Christian movements. Detractors would see it as one of the first modern Christian sects.

It should be said that, particularly with the growing influence of African and West Indian Christianity, some Evangelical Churches are now integrating costume, dance and drama into their worship.

NON-CHRISTIAN ELEMENTS IN CHRISTIANITY

To step back to the early days again, American car-showroom churches have had their equivalents since the first Christians picked themselves up after their teacher was killed and asked, 'What do we do now?' Even in the New Testament we see individual churches being put right when they strayed from what the early leaders had decided was the party line. The problem was that no one had yet set down a statement of beliefs and practices. The message of the first Christians was simply, 'We preach Christ crucified' (I Corinthians 1:23), but what exactly did this mean?

This problem was compounded by the various elements which went into Christianity. There was its background in Judaism, of course. The Christian God the Father was the same as the Jewish Yahweh or Adonai; Jesus said that he came 'not to destroy, but to fulfil [the Law]' (Matthew 5:17); the main Jewish Scriptures became the Christian Old Testament. But how much of Judaism should be carried forward into Christianity? There was a group of specifically Hebraic Christians up to the fifth century; and today there is a small but highly active movement of Jews who have converted to Christianity without giving up their Jewish religion.

But Christianity also absorbed other elements, from Neo-Platonism, from the various Mystery religions around at the time, from the Roman Mithraism and elsewhere. Paul quotes from Pagan writers in his letters, and makes no apology for it. The idea of a god dying for his people and coming back to life again is by no means unique to Christianity; it is one of the oldest religious ideas of all, and was at the very centre of the earliest solar religions and crop-fertility religions. The concept of the Eucharist or communion service, central to the beliefs of traditionalist Christians, was borrowed from Mithraism, which at the time of Jesus was the religion followed by many Roman soldiers. The idea of the virgin birth was widespread long before the Blessed Virgin Mary was visited by an angel. Indeed, if you wanted to be taken seriously as a prophet – or even as a military leader – it was almost compulsory for you to have had a non-human father; the Norse god Odin, the All-Father, was renowned for fathering children of mortal women.

For small, individual Christian Churches in the very early days, the difficulty lay in knowing which bits of other religions it was all right to borrow and which bits were unacceptable. One clever solution, proposed by the second-century Justin Martyr, was that God had allowed some of the truths of Christianity to be made known to earlier thinkers, and so 'whatever things were rightly said by any man, belong to us Christians'.

Even the writers of the Gospels and Epistles had their differences in emphasis, if not in doctrine. Peter, Paul and the writer of John's Gospel held widely differing views of the substance of their belief; it's partly because of this lack of cohesiveness in the New Testament that so many 'heretical' movements over the centuries have been able to claim that the Bible supports their beliefs.

HERESIES

It is useful to look at Christian 'heresies' through the centuries, since many of their beliefs resurface again and again, particularly in today's new religious movements. From the books listed in the Bibliography, four will show the point.

Sects and cults, as we have said, are nothing new. David Christie-Murray's excellent *A History of Heresy* (1976) spends 243 pages covering 'heresies' from New Testament times to the mid-twentieth century. *A Handbook of Heresies* by M. L. Cozens was first published in 1928. The 16 brief chapters of its 1974 edition include Protestantism among the 25 heresies covered; for traditional Roman Catholics, any other variant of Christianity is a heresy. From the opposite end of the theological spectrum, *Heresies and Cults* is by the Evangelical preacher J. Oswald Sanders; its 1962 edition describes 21 heresies, including Roman Catholicism. The bias in both Cozens and Sanders is very evident. Finally, the *Lion Concise Book of Christian Thought* by Tony Lane is a very sound work from an Evangelical publisher which covers the development of Christian teaching over the centuries; its index lists 24 'heresies and schisms', only nine of which overlap with Cozens' list.

Christianity has been riven with disagreements from its very beginning. Part of the problem is the basic simplicity of the Christian message, perhaps most perfectly set out in John 3:16: 'For God so loved the world, that he gave his only-begotten Son, that whosoever believeth in him should not perish, but have everlasting life.'

The message of the New Testament Christians, 'We preach Christ crucified', is only rendered slightly more complicated by today's Evangelicals: 'You are a sinner bound for hell; God loved you and sent his son Jesus to take your punishment on himself; believe and be saved.' A simple message.

Unfortunately, it's not that simple. What do we mean by sinner, hell, God, son, Jesus, take, punishment, believe, saved? To give just one example, why are we sinners? Is it actually possible for a human being *not* to be a sinner? No, because 'All have sinned, and come short of the glory of God' (Romans 3:23). So is this our fault, because of free will, or God's, for creating us that way? If God knows everything, he already knows (in fact, he knew before he created Adam) who will be saved and who will be damned. But is this foreknowledge or predestination? Are we condemned because of Adam's sin or our own? Does 'original sin' mean that because birth results from sexual intercourse, the parents' sinfulness passes into the baby, and does that mean that sex is sinful?

Similar questions can be asked – and discussed endlessly – about every single term in Christian theology. The basic message may be simple . . . until you start defining what the words actually mean.

Most of the 'heresies' which the mainstream Christian Churches condemn in today's sects were hotly debated 17 or 18 centuries ago, and very often it was the precise usage and definition of words which were in dispute. One of the fundamental questions concerns the nature of Jesus: how much was he God and how much man? This makes an enormous difference to every other point of Christian theology. It's like a complex series of mathematical equations; if you change one value early on, it affects everything else.

If, for example, the virgin birth didn't occur, then Joseph was Jesus' father and Jesus was born a normal man. Did he remain 'just a man' or did he take on the nature of God at some point, perhaps at birth, or perhaps when the dove came down upon him when John the Baptist baptized him? But this is man-become-God, rather than the God-become-man of what is now standard Christian belief; it takes away Christianity's uniqueness and makes it more possible to view it alongside Islam and the Bahá'í Faith.

The dove represents the Spirit of God, the Holy Spirit – another bone of contention since the earliest days. Is the Holy Spirit, as standard Trinitarian Christians believe, an equal third person of the Trinity? Or is the Holy Spirit God-in-action? A person or a process? He or it? Or is the Holy Spirit the missing female portion of the Judaeo-Christian deity, Sophia, the Wisdom of God?

Brilliant theologians have spent hundreds of years and millions of words discussing these problems. Whatever varied conclusions they arrived at, the very amount of work proves, if proof were needed, that these are real, complex issues; there are no simple solutions. Those who claim that there is one straightforward outline of Christian beliefs ignore the centuries of dispute and discussion which formulated the particular set of beliefs which they now hold to be true, and refuse to allow the validity of the hundreds of variant sets of belief held true by others.

There is no such single thing as 'the Christian belief-statement'.

THE EARLY CHURCH AND EARLY HERESIES

Even at the time the books of the New Testament were written, there were different versions of the story of Jesus circulating. Paul writes of 'another Jesus, whom we have not preached' (II Corinthians 11:4), and rebukes those who preach 'a different gospel' (Galatians 1:6–9). During this first century or so, there were some who believed in Jesus the man, who may or may not have attained some measure of godhood, and others who believed in the Christ, either as a Jewish Messianic (revolutionary) figure or as God. And there were some who believed that Jesus the man was also Christ the God, which became the prevailing view of what we now know as Christianity.

Fundamentalist Christians believe as an article of faith that every word of the New Testament is divinely inspired; Bible scholars tend to hold the more liberal view that, for example, the Gospels of Matthew and Luke were based on Mark, with large sections of a 'Sayings of Jesus' known as Q, plus material from other sources; and that both the Gospels and the Epistles were much edited, rewritten and added to over the years, by people other than their original writers, to highlight particular points. They also look at the large number of Gospels and Epistles which didn't make it into the New Testament, for a deeper understanding of the varieties of belief that existed at that time.

Even if the Fundamentalists are correct, and the books of the New Testament are divinely inspired and true and accurate in every word, the evidence of the non-canonical works shows that there never was one original gospel message which was accepted by all of the Christians of the first 200 years. Christianity, right from the start, came in many varieties. Different churches and their leaders had different beliefs – beliefs which would soon be judged heretical.

The difficulty was, as already mentioned, that Christianity did not exist in a spiritual vacuum. In the earliest days a Jewish Christian, or one preaching to Jews, would describe Christ and the new faith in terms relevant to Judaism. Similarly someone educated in the Greek philosophers would naturally find points of comparison between their teachings and Christian beliefs. Neo-Platonist and Gnostic beliefs found their way into different versions of Christian theology.

Many of the great Church Fathers, who have for over 1,500 years been revered for formulating the finer points of Christian doctrine, were at one time or another judged to be heretics.

Justin Martyr (c. AD 100–165) for example, wrote, 'Next to God we love and worship the Word', implying that the Word, Logos, or Christ was not actually God.

Tertullian (c. AD 160–220), probably the first Christian theologian to write in Latin, and one of the first to make the Holy Spirit equal to the Father and the Son in the godhead, fought against Gnosticism, but embraced one of the very earliest Christian offshoots, Montanism.

Founded in AD 156, Montanism was remarkable for many things, and was the forerunner of many more recent Christian movements. It must have been the earliest sect to demand a return to the beliefs and practices of the original Christian Church, only a century and a quarter after the death of Jesus. It practised speaking in tongues and prophecy (it had two main women prophets), both features of the nineteenth- and twentieth-century Pentecostal Churches and the Charismatic movement in both Protestant and Catholic Churches today. It preached the imminent return of Christ and end of the world, a common feature of many later movements; as with them, many of its adherents sold all their property in anticipation; and as with them, the failure of the world to come to an end on schedule apparently didn't affect membership too much. Montanists longed for martyrdom to prove their faith and were highly critical of anyone who fled from it. They were also extremely ascetic, with long periods of fasting and with complete celibacy. Amazingly, the movement lasted until the fifth century.

Clement of Alexandria (late second century AD) believed that although Jesus ate and drank like a man, he didn't actually need to for bodily sustenance.

Origen (c. AD 185–250) was the first major Christian theologian, who systematically set out the principles of Christian faith. Several of his beliefs were heretical. He treated parts of the Old Testament as allegorical rather than literal. He accepted the Trinity, but he taught that the Father was greater than the Son, and the Son greater than the Holy Spirit; they were all eternal, but so were the next level of the hierarchy, 'rational beings', including angels and men. He also believed in a sort of two-stream Christianity: the basic message of salvation through faith was fine for the uneducated, but for the more intellectual and spiritual, salvation came through contemplation. He was officially branded a heretic in the sixth century.

Cyprian (d. AD 258), Bishop of Carthage, insisted on the authority and indivisibility of the Church, condemning all schismatics; it was not possible to have divergent views of any kind and remain in the Church. Conversion and baptism by a schismatic church was not only worthless but evil – 'it makes sons not for God but for the Devil'. Ironically, even the Bishop of Rome was more lenient to schismatics. It was Cyprian who created the authoritarian and unforgiving stance of the Catholic Church throughout the centuries towards anyone with differing beliefs.

Eusebius (c. AD 260–340), Bishop of Caesarea, was the great historian of the early Church. He was a strong supporter of the emperor Constantine, who first called on the Christian God in the middle of a war in AD 312 – an event with enormous consequences for the Church, both for good (the spread of Christianity throughout the Roman Empire) and for bad (the combination of Church and state). Eusebius, among many other bishops, accepted the beliefs of Arius, the most influential heretic of the early centuries.

Arius (d. AD 342) taught that only the Father is God. Although through the Son he had created the universe, he had first created the Son out of nothing, and there had been a time, however far back, when the Son had not existed.

Arianism has resurfaced many times through the centuries, including in the present-day Jehovah's Witnesses. In the early fourth century it was splitting the Church, with many bishops and their churches accepting it. Roman Christians and Arian Christians might sometimes live side by side or fight in the same army, but neither regarded the other as true Christians; although they preached from the same Scriptures, they were further apart theologically than Catholics and Calvinists centuries later.

Emperor Constantine was unhappy about the divisions in the Church and called the Council of Nicea in AD 325 to resolve them. Unfortunately (like the later Synod of Whitby in AD 664, when Celtic Christianity was thrown out of Britain in favour of Roman Christianity), the Council of Nicea was an example of what happens when politics gets involved in religious debate. Several of the bishops signed up to its outcome more to please (or not to displease) the Emperor than because they actually accepted it.

The Council of Nicea finally agreed a creed (*not* the Nicene Creed, which came out of the Council of Constantinople in AD 381), which condemned Arianism:

> But the holy catholic and apostolic church anathematises those who say: 'There was once when he [Christ] was not' and 'He was not, before he was begotten' and 'He was made out of nothing' and those who assert that he is from some being or substance other than the Father or that he is mutable or liable to change.

One of the main opponents of Arius was Athanasius (late third century AD − 373), the Bishop of Alexandria, who, incidentally, was the first to set out the canon of the New Testament as we know it today, as late as AD 367. He devoted much of his life to fighting Arianism and defining the correct balance of manhood and godhood in Christ. For Athanasius, if Christ was not fully God as well as fully man, the whole of Christianity fell apart. He also argued for the full equality of the Holy Spirit within the Trinity. The Athanasian Creed, though dating from around AD 500, was ascribed to him because of his detailed work on the Trinity.

> Such as the Father is, such is the Son, and such is the Holy Ghost.
> The Father uncreate, the Son uncreate, and the Holy Ghost uncreate.
> The Father incomprehensible, the Son incomprehensible, and the Holy Ghost incomprehensible.
> The Father eternal, the Son eternal, and the Holy Ghost eternal.
> And yet they are not three eternals, but one eternal.
> And also there are not three incomprehensibles, nor three uncreated, but one uncreated, and one incomprehensible . . .
> The Father is made of none, neither created, nor begotten.
> The Son is of the Father alone; not made, nor created, but begotten.
> The Holy Ghost is of the Father and of the Son: neither made, nor created, nor begotten, but proceeding . . .

And in this Trinity none is afore, or after other; none is greater, or less than another;

But the whole three Persons are co-eternal together, and co-equal . . .

Well over half of this Creed concerns itself with the Trinity; a further quarter with the nature of Christ; with the remaining few verses rushing through a brief synopsis of the passion and purpose of Christ. This degree of definition, which might seem astonishing today, was necessary to pinpoint the 'errors' of the 'heretics'.

Arianism was not the only heresy to cause dissension in the early centuries. Monarchianism (sometimes known as Sabellianism), which began before AD 200, held that there is only one God, not three-in-one; it saw Trinitarian belief as Tritheism. The Father, the Son and the Holy Spirit are all one being, simply performing three different roles, like an actor playing several parts. This version of the heresy was sometimes called Patripassian, because it implied that the Father suffered on the cross. A variant belief, Dynamic Monarchianism, stated that Jesus was a normal man with divine power in him, a belief held by many alternative religions today. At least one Bishop of Rome and a Bishop at Antioch, among many others, believed in a version of Monarchianism.

Even the great theologian Augustine, Bishop of Hippo, Saint Augustine (AD 354–430), is said to have been inclined to Monarchianism. Also, for 12 years earlier in his life, before he turned to more-or-less conventional Christianity, Augustine was a follower of Manichaeism, a semi-Christian, semi-Gnostic religion much influenced by Zoroastrianism. Two deities, of light and darkness, are in perpetual conflict; the god of light is the creator of the soul, but we live in an evil world of matter created by the god of darkness. Manichaeism later resurfaced as the background to the Albigensians or Cathars of thirteenth-century France.

Perhaps because of his earlier beliefs, Augustine devoted much of his time to fighting heresy. His major battle was against Pelagianism, which held that it was possible for a man, albeit with a great deal of effort, to live a sinless life. 'Not so!' thundered Augustine, and went on to clarify the Church's teaching on original sin. Everyone was a sinner, including newborn babies, because of Adam and because of the sin of the parents (not least of which was the sexual intercourse which had created the baby).

The debate between Augustine and Pelagius, who was a Scots or Irish monk, occupied educated Christians throughout Europe for decades; eventually, and inevitably because of his power base, Augustine won, defining a central plank of mainstream Christianity which many schismatic Churches are still rebelling against.

The doctrine of original sin resulted in two other doctrinal innovations: infant baptism, so that babies who died need not go to hell; and (much later) the belief in the immaculate conception of Mary, on the grounds that Jesus was by definition sinless, so he could not have been born of a sinful woman, so if Mary had been without sin, she herself must have been conceived without sin. (This, which became official doctrine only in 1854, is a rare example of a Roman Catholic belief which is judged heretical by the entire Protestant world, on the grounds that it puts Mary on a fairly equal footing with Jesus; in the words of a Catholic archbishop of the time, it made her 'above all our co-redemptress'. There was actually a minor pressure group in the nineteenth-century Roman Catholic Church wanting to make Mary 'the fourth member of the Trinity'.)

Augustine was responsible for various other teachings which were to affect the Church for centuries to come. He taught that the sacraments are valid even if administered by an unholy priest, which allowed for many of the clerical excesses of later years. He taught that it was permissible to coerce people into belief – or out of heresy – by force if necessary; this provided theological justification for the Church's treatment of heretics in medieval and Renaissance times. He also taught that many people nominally within the Church were not really Christians; only God knows who the true believers are. This led him into a belief remarkably similar to Calvinism 1,000 years later: God not only knows who will be saved but chooses to whom he will give the grace to accept him.

Taking these last two teachings of Augustine together explains (though it cannot condone) the reputed words of the papal legate Arnaud, Abbot of Cîteaux, at the French city of Béziers in 1209, when a soldier asked him how they should distinguish between true believers and heretics, Roman Catholics and Cathars: 'Kill them all; God will know his own.' More than 15,000 men, women and children were massacred at Béziers; some of them while claiming sanctuary in the church.

Three other heresies to split the Church during the third to fifth centuries were Apollinarianism, which stated that Jesus was the Word in a human body, but did not have a human mind or soul; Nestorianism, which painted a clear distinction between God the Word and Jesus the man – Nestorius was Bishop of Constantinople in *c.* AD 429; and Macedonianism, which said, once again, that the Holy Spirit was not an equal member of the godhead.

Brief mention must be made of Gnosticism, which resurfaces in many of the present-day Esoteric movements. Gnosticism, like Christianity, existed in many varieties – some were extremely ascetic, others extremely libertarian – but in all of them the emphasis was on direct knowledge (in Greek, *gnosis*) of God. In general, Gnosticism follows Zoroastrianism in its concentration on the opposing forces of good and evil, light and dark, spirit and matter. The Gnostics of the first few centuries were rooted in Christianity, and concentrated on the secret teachings of Jesus; this made them even more dangerous to the established Church, which systematically destroyed both them and their writings – many of which were lost until 1945, when a large number of texts were found at Nag Hammadi in northern Egypt.

Gnostic Christianity bears much the same uneasy relationship to mainstream Christianity as scholars of the Cabbala do to Judaism, or as Sufism does to Islam. Indeed, these three often get on better with each other than they do with their own 'parent' religions; mysticism, personal devotion and individual scholarship cannot readily be brought under the control of Church authority.

Of the many heresies which occurred in medieval times – including the Paulicians, the Bogomils, the Waldenses and others – I shall outline only one: the Cathars, or Albigensians. Their beliefs came from Manichaean Gnosticism, and sprang up in southern France – the Languedoc – in the late eleventh century. They believed that spirit is good and matter is evil; the material world was created by the evil demi-urge. For the extreme *parfaits* or *perfecti*, this meant abstaining from food and from sex, because the one sustains the flesh and the other sustains the race.

The Cathars (meaning 'pure ones'), with their own distinctive theology and their lack of respect for priestly authority, were a threat to the Church. Pope Innocent III launched the Albigensian Crusade under Simon de Montfort, which culminated in the massacres at Béziers in 1209 and at the Cathar's last stronghold, the fortress of Montségur, in 1244.[2]

SIXTEENTH – SEVENTEENTH CENTURIES

The sixteenth and seventeenth centuries rival the nineteenth and twentieth for new Christian ideas; they saw many revolutionary movements within Christianity, with Germany and Switzerland as the main breeding grounds. Martin Luther nailed his famous Ninety-five Theses to the church door at Wittenberg in 1517. Ulrich Zwingli began to proclaim his Protestant ideas in the 1520s, and John Calvin started off what became known as Reformed theology in the 1530s. From this John Knox founded Presbyterianism as a Scottish church system around 1560. The idea of small, independent, self-governing Congregationalist churches began to spread in England during the reign of Elizabeth I.

The Anabaptists, who believed in adult baptism for believers, grew up in the early sixteenth century. The beginnings of formal Unitarianism can be traced to Laelius Socinus (1525–62) and his nephew Faustus (1539–1604), though its ideas had been around in central Europe for some years previously.

There were many other varieties of belief, stemming from individual scholars who had formerly been members of other Churches – some of them Catholic priests; many of these independents were considerably more tolerant than the Churches they had left.

It shouldn't be thought that each separate type of belief was self-contained; there was some overlap between them, and great divisions within them. The different groups of Anabaptists, for example, kept trying to work out a common creed, but had so many differences of belief that this proved impossible.

Neither should it be thought, because of the profusion of beliefs, that this was an age of religious toleration. Everybody condemned everybody else as a heretic. The Anabaptists in particular were hated; Catholics, Lutherans and Calvinists actually united to try to destroy them. Today we tend to think of the burning of heretics as the special province of the Roman Catholic Inquisition, but this was by no means the case. Calvin had the Spanish scholar Michael Servetus burnt at the stake in 1553 for being both an Anabaptist and a Unitarian.

In England, the first Baptist Church was founded in 1611. George Fox started off the Religious Society of Friends, soon known as the Quakers, around 1650. In 1689, a year after William of Orange came to the British throne, a Toleration Act allowed freedom of worship for Presbyterians, Congregationalists, Baptists and Quakers – but not for Unitarians, and certainly not for Catholics.

It is a common misperception that the early English settlers of what would become the USA were Puritans and Quakers looking for religious freedom. The term Puritan is too loose; the Pilgrim Fathers of 1620 were Congregationalists, and that was the religion which took hold in New England. They were anything but tolerant to other religions, initially outlawing any other, though by the end of the century some areas reluctantly allowed Baptists and Episcopalians. Congregationalist Massachusetts imprisoned and whipped Quakers, even executing three in 1659. Despite this persecution, the Quaker William Penn's Pennsylvania was always tolerant of other varieties of Christianity.

The Quakers are today perhaps the most widely respected 'heretics' of all. Their basic belief is that each person should worship God in his or her own way. The authority of the Church – any Church – is rejected, and priests and sacraments, including baptism and the Eucharist, are irrelevant. There is no creed, and not really any theology; the only authority is the Inner Light of Christ, or 'that of God', in the heart of each individual believer. Like the Unitarians and the

Salvation Army, the Quakers are perhaps respected by outsiders more for their commitment to social issues – including prison reform and the abolition of slavery – than for their spiritual beliefs, though this social commitment stems from their inner spirituality.

EIGHTEENTH CENTURY

In terms of new religious movements, the eighteenth century was fairly active, as witness John Evans's *Sketch of the Denominations of the Christian World* (fifteenth edition, 1827). Only a few will be mentioned briefly here. Probably most significant, in mainstream terms, was the founding of the Methodists by John Wesley and John Whitefield in the 1740s. Like every other religious movement, this had a wide range of splinter groups – even Wesley and Whitefield fell out with each other over doctrinal differences – though most of these were reunited by the early twentieth century.

The eighteenth century is often called the Age of Enlightenment, and the intellectual rigour of its rationalist or scientific materialist ideas had an effect on religious thinking. Atheism became intellectually acceptable; and the application of reason to faith aided the growth of Unitarianism – the convoluted conundrum of the Athanasian Creed being felt unreasonable and so unnecessary – and also of Universalism, the belief that the loving God would save everyone eventually. These were more relevant to the scope of this book.

The same is true of Emanuel Swedenborg (1688–1772), who brought a mystical intellectual rigour to Christian doctrine. By going back to first principles and approaching everything from a different angle, he redefined a range of issues from the Trinity and the nature of Christ to the nature of man's relationship with God.

Finally, the Shakers were a fairly small British sect which, because of persecution, moved to America in 1774. Their teaching was Millennialist, and there is no doubt that many of the new American religions which sprang up in the nineteenth century owed a debt, directly or indirectly, to them.

NINETEENTH CENTURY

Although today's newspapers seem surprised by all the new religious movements of the last few decades, the nineteenth century was just as fertile, especially in America. Particularly for struggling frontiersmen, the Mormon promise that Americans were God's chosen people was a revelation too powerful to be ignored. Add to this the Millenarian message, that Christ would shortly return and set up his earthly kingdom for 1,000 years, and people flocked to join. The Seventh-day Adventists, Christadelphians and Jehovah's Witnesses are but three of many Millennialist religions which sprang from that same fruitful ground. Christian Science came from a different angle, making a rational science out of the formerly rather hit-and-miss nature of faith-healing.

Not all the new religious movements were born in the USA. In 1831 the Presbyterian minister Edward Irving started the Catholic Apostolic Church in London. It had the best of everything. Its organization was early Church, it was strongly Millenarian, its theology was broadly Evangelical, but its distinguishing feature was its liturgy, which borrowed from the Anglican, Catholic and Orthodox Churches. Unfortunately, it never recovered from Christ failing to return by 1855 and now has literally no more than a handful of members. Perhaps less exciting, but longer-lasting, the Exclusive Brethren began in 1840 when John Nelson Darby led a schism in the recently formed Brethren movement; their beliefs were Fundamentalist and Millenarian, and their church organization minimal.

The Salvation Army was founded by William Booth in 1877. It grew out of his Christian Mission in the East End of London, where he was appalled by both the social and the spiritual deprivation. As with the Quakers, mainstream Christianity is more tolerant of the Salvation Army than of many other Christian offshoots because of its unarguable good works. Its theology is straightforwardly Evangelical, though it does not practise the sacraments.

TWENTIETH CENTURY

Some of the new Christian-based movements founded in the twentieth century have their roots in earlier Churches. Both the Worldwide Church of God and the Branch Davidians grew out of the Seventh-day Adventists, for example, and the Fundamentalist Evangelical Churches are little different in their main beliefs from the Evangelicals of the eighteenth and nineteenth centuries. Others, although their founders may have started off in a mainstream denomination, have branched out at quite unusual angles – the Unification Church and the Family, for example.

♦

From all of these fairly recent Christian offshoots I shall look in more detail at a selection, in roughly chronological order. Some have become well-established Churches but have beliefs substantially different from mainstream Christianity. Others have fairly orthodox beliefs, but some of their practices cause concern to outsiders.

Each one sees itself as a legitimate form of Christianity (in some cases, as the only legitimate form of Christianity), but mainstream Christians regard them all with some suspicion, for one reason or another.

It should be remembered that there are many, many other Christian offshoots, with a wide variety of beliefs and practices, particularly in the USA, the West Indies and Africa.

THREE

CHRISTIAN MOVEMENTS

UNITARIANS

Historically, Unitarians differ from mainstream Christianity most particularly in their rejection of the doctrine of the Trinity and their denial that Jesus is God. Like many Christian offshoots, they claim to be more faithful to the original truths of Christianity, which they believe were lost in the many councils of the early Church. In terms of early 'heresies', they are perhaps closest to Arianism. In present-day religious terms, they would be called liberal.

HISTORY

In Christian terms, Unitarianism is essentially Arian in its rejection of the deity of Christ, though in fact pure Arianism merely states that the Son is subordinate to the Father. Despite the councils and creeds of Nicea, versions of Arianism lasted from the time of Arius himself up to at least the end of the sixth century. It was particularly strong in the Germanic lands, among the Goths and Huns, who, when they gave up their belief in the Norse/Germanic gods in favour of the new religion, were not prepared to accept the Roman version of Christianity. Attila the Hun was way ahead of his times in allowing members of his warband to follow whichever Gods they wished, so long as they didn't interfere in each other's freedom of worship or, more importantly, disrupt the warband. Arians lived and fought alongside Pagans with no difficulty; the more authoritarian Roman Christians were less tolerant, and less tolerated. The Roman Church, however, had greater secular power and Arianism (if it continued to exist at all) went underground for nearly 1,000 years.

As already mentioned, the beginnings of formal Unitarianism – in its early years known as Socinianism – can be traced to Laelius Socinus (1525–62) and his nephew Faustus (1539–1604), though non-Trinitarian ideas had been around in central Europe for some years previously. For example, the Spanish scholar Michael Servetus (1511–53), despite possessing a safe-conduct, was burnt at the stake by Calvin's supporters in Geneva; his beliefs included a rejection both of Calvinism's predestination and of the Trinity.

Laelius Socinus, who also rejected the Trinity, was appalled at the death of Servetus. His own life would be in danger if he remained in Italy, so like other non-Trinitarians, he spent some years travelling around central Europe spreading his beliefs.

Faustus Socinus was first a Catholic, then a Calvinist, before eventually following his uncle in rejecting the Trinity. He spent some years in Transylvania (modern Romania), where the term Unitarian was first used in 1600, and ended his life in Poland, where Socinianism took a strong hold. When Socinians were first persecuted and then expelled from Poland by its Catholic rulers in the middle of the seventeenth century, they went to Transylvania, Germany and the Netherlands.

In England the Act of Uniformity in 1662 imposed severe limitations on who could preach and what they were allowed to preach. Ministers had to have received episcopal ordination, to conform to the Book of Common Prayer and to take their services in accordance with the rites of the Church of England. Some 2,000 ministers refused these restrictions and went off to do exactly what they had been told not to, and their followers built churches and chapels for them. Relatively few of these dissenters were Unitarian in theology at this stage, but among them were a sizeable group who sought to reconcile the Bible with the newly emerging scientific outlook, and many of these had moved to a Unitarian position by the end of the eighteenth century under the influence of figures such as the radical Unitarian minister and scientist the Rev. Dr Joseph Priestley. Such congregations formed the basis of the Free Churches. The Church today has a coordinating body called the General Assembly of Unitarian and Free Christian Churches.

The Act of Toleration in 1689 allowed freedom of worship for Congregationalists, Presbyterians, Baptists and Quakers, but not for Roman Catholics or Unitarians. However, despite the prohibitions of the law, Arianist doctrines continued to be preached in the early eighteenth century, sometimes by Anglican priests.

Unitarians share some common ground with the Deists or Freethinkers of the early eighteenth century, the Universalists of later that century, the more secular Utilitarianists of the nineteenth century, Modernists from the nineteenth century onwards and the demythologizing work of (particularly German) biblical criticism. The Age of Enlightenment, of scientific rationalism and inquiry, and of educated egalitarianism, lies behind all of these. Whatever their individual beliefs might be, the Bishops of Woolwich and Durham mentioned on page 37 follow in the same tradition, which, in a phrase, could be summed up as not being afraid to question taught truths.

Such free-thinking always brings condemnation. Evangelicals seem to view Unitarians with particular abhorrence, seeing them not as a sect or cult (bad enough in themselves) but as a wickedly heretical movement. J. Oswald Sanders wrote 'All too many fill the pulpits of professedly evangelical churches. It appears to be a matter of policy for a fifth-column of ministers with Unitarian leanings to infiltrate the churches, with a view to future conquest.'[1] Sanders, although specifically attacking Unitarians, is really expressing the widespread Evangelical distaste for liberal theology. What seemed to worry Sanders the most was that, particularly in America, Unitarianism was adopted by a large number of intelligent, well-respected and highly influential writers, teachers and leaders of society.

Indeed, in America Unitarianism was both intellectually and socially acceptable; it had become 'the thinking man's religion'. Critics saw it more as humanism with a spiritual basis, or a religion for the religious sceptic.

Unitarianism took particularly strong hold in New England, especially in Boston. Writers such as William Channing and Ralph Waldo Emerson embraced it, and the Congregationalist Church in America split on Trinitarian–Unitarian lines. As education, morality and social activism were central to Unitarianism, Harvard College became a centre for Unitarian teachers. At least five US presidents, including Thomas Jefferson and John Quincey Adams, held Unitarian beliefs.

Another free-thinking movement, Universalism, arose in America around 1770 under the influence of a Scottish emigrant, John Middleton Murray. They believed that all would be saved and also rejected the doctrine of the Trinity. In the USA the Universalist Church merged with the American Unitarian Association in 1961, forming the Unitarian Universalist Association, with a current membership of around 200,000.

In Britain, well-known Unitarians of the past included Joseph Priestley, Charles Dickens, Elizabeth Gaskell, Mary Wollstonecraft and Josiah Wedgwood.

'While the Christian origins of Unitarianism are clear as a major strand in our development, some Unitarians trace their line of descent from the Classical world and, in particular, the philosophy of Socrates and his successors, based as it is on open inquiry,' says Matthew F. Smith, information officer for the General Assembly of Unitarian and Free Christian Churches.[2]

BELIEFS AND PRACTICES

Perhaps the most important point to note about the Unitarian creed is that there is no creed. Individual Unitarians may tend to accept much the same set of beliefs, but among these is the belief that no one has the right to impose a set of beliefs on them. As with the Quakers, freedom of belief and freedom of worship are paramount.

'The main point of division between Unitarians and mainstream Christianity is our welcome acceptance of religious pluralism encompassing a broad spectrum of views such that some members think of themselves more as religious humanists, for example, rather than Christians,' says Smith.

Despite this, there is a general agreement on a number of doctrines. Historically, the main plank of Christian-based Unitarian belief, as expressed in their name, is that there is one God, not three, or even three-in-one. They are Unitarian as opposed to Trinitarian. The Father is God, Jesus was a man and the Holy Spirit is God's influence.

They believe that the (human) Jesus of the Gospels was transformed into the God-man Jesus Christ by the Church Fathers, and that the simple Christian truths were confused and obscured by Graeco-Roman influences. They reject the dogmatism so carefully worked out by the early Church councils.

They are careful to distinguish between Jesus' deity and his divinity. Deity would mean that he was, and always had been, God, in the Trinitarian Christian sense. Divinity could mean that God indwelt him; although he was but a man, he was a good man, a holy man, a perfect man, and an example to be followed.

The idea of Jesus as an exemplar is central to Unitarianism. As one Unitarian has said, 'For me, the supreme affirmation of Christian discipleship is not "I believe" but "I follow".'[3]

Jesus's death on the cross was nothing to do with atonement, with God dying for the sake of sinful men; it was an example of love and sacrifice. 'If we speak of the "divinity of Jesus" we are saying that he had a particular quality of "holiness"; some Unitarians see Jesus as the pre-eminent spiritual teacher while others do not. This quality of "divinity" is an attribute that arguably every person can find within themselves and act upon,' says Smith.

Although undeniably there is wickedness in the world, human beings are essentially good rather than sinful, and it is up to all individuals to lead good lives in the service of others. Evangelical critics of Unitarianism say that leading a good life is all very well, but that Unitarians have it the wrong way around: good behaviour, rather than being a means of approaching God, should come as a result of repentance and faith, with the grace of God's indwelling of a person.

There is no hell, no everlasting suffering for non-believers. Opinion is divided on whether or not there is a heaven in its traditional sense. It is, in any case, more important to establish heaven on earth through right living and, for example, supporting the underprivileged.

Historically, Unitarianism has always been essentially a rationalist belief system; Unitarians place reason before revelation. The Bible is worth reading and studying, but it is not in any way the inspired and infallible word of God. It was written by a number of fallible men in particular places, times and circumstances, has been copied and edited and altered, and should therefore be interpreted in the light of reason. Parts of it are clearly allegorical and parts are the opinions of the individual human writers.

The rationalist stance has changed a little over the last few years. 'Unitarians continue to take reason seriously, but increasingly we are coming to value the intuitive and the exploration of feelings and emotions as steps towards spiritual growth. This shift of emphasis can be seen from the growing popularity of adult RE [Religious Education] programmes with a personal development focus and also through an increasing interest in New Age thought and Green Spirituality among our membership,' says Smith.

Although most Unitarians would call themselves Christians, some feel that this label is too restrictive. As with the Quakers, many Unitarians see no reason why they should not find just as much truth in the sacred texts of the other world religions – and in poetry, fiction, scientific and other writings – as they do in the Bible.

'I would tend to say that we have evolved away from the mainstream Churches over the last 50 years because we have become religious pluralists. We have become less Bible-based and Christo-centric and more concerned with each person being the authority for their own beliefs, drawing on whatever sources of inspiration they personally find helpful,' says Smith.

Stressing the Unitarian commitment to 'unity in diversity', Smith quotes from Andrew Hill's book *The Unitarian Path* (1994): 'The Unitarian path is a liberal religious movement rooted in the Jewish and Christian traditions but open to insights from world faiths, reason and science; and with a spectrum extending from liberal Christianity through to religious humanism.'

Unitarians are strongly against discrimination or prejudice of any kind, racial, sexual or religious. The Church was the first denomination in Britain to appoint professional women ministers, in 1904, and several women have been president of their General Assembly. It actively welcomes gays, lesbians and bisexuals, and fights for their legal rights and social equality.

Because of their Nonconformist roots and their historical congregational policy, every Unitarian congregation is independent and self-governing. In Britain the General Assembly of Unitarian and Free Christian Churches is a coordinating and representative body. Power is decentralized and lies with the congregations, rather than being centralized at Unitarian headquarters.

It is ironic that a Church which believes strongly that 'people of faith can and should seek to learn from one another through inter-religious dialogue and interfaith activity,' and which was a founder member in 1900 of the world's oldest surviving international interfaith organization, the International Association for Religious Freedom, 'has not found a place in the World Council of Churches because we are in conscience unable to accept the "Christ as God" formula. Although the Unitarian General Assembly was a founder member of the British Council of Churches, the Unitarian application for Observer status in the new Council of Churches for Britain and Ireland [CCBI] has attracted insufficient support among the mainstream member Churches to be accepted,' says Smith.

There are around 8,000 Unitarians in Britain.

SWEDENBORGIANS

HISTORY

Emanuel Swedenborg (1688–1772) was a Swedish nobleman, the son of a Lutheran bishop. He showed intellectual brilliance at an early age and was a doctor of philosophy by the age of 21. He worked as a metallurgist and mining engineer, but spent much of his time in pursuit of scientific knowledge, particularly concerning human physiology and astronomy. He wrote a number of well-respected scientific works. In 1736 he began recording his dreams. In 1743 he began having visions of angels and spirits, and of heaven and hell, and in 1747 he resigned his job as assessor-extraordinary with the Swedish Bureau of Mines, to devote the rest of his life to researching and writing about his spiritual discoveries. These spiritual writings attracted a large following.

He wrote his many books in Latin. The titles of two of them – *On the New Jerusalem and Its Heavenly Doctrine* and *The True Christian Religion Containing the Universal Theology of the New Church* – led to the two best-known names of Swedenborgian organizations, the Church of the New Jerusalem and the New Church. In addition to these Churches, which apparently work well together, there is the Swedenborg Society in London. Founded in 1810, its purpose is to translate and publish Swedenborg's works; it has a library and a bookshop, and also arranges lectures.

Swedenborg did not himself found a Church, or even a movement; this was done by people who had read his books. In Britain one of his earliest proponents was an Anglican priest, John Clowes, the rector of St John's, Manchester. He was the first to translate any of Swedenborg's works into English and was probably initially responsible for the movement's strength in the north-west of England. Swedenborg's ideas were then taken up by a number of Methodist ministers, one of whom, Robert Hindmarsh, founded the New Jerusalem Church in 1787.

John Wesley was impressed by Swedenborg's obvious intelligence and spirituality, and studied some of his books. As he wrote in his diary for 28 February 1770:

I began with huge prejudice in his favour, knowing him to be a pious man, one of a strong understanding, of much learning, and one who thoroughly believed himself. But I could not hold out long. Any one of his visions puts his real character out of doubt. He is one of the most ingenious, lively, entertaining madmen that ever set pen to paper. But his waking dreams are so wild, so far remote both from Scripture and common sense, that one might as easily swallow the stories of 'Tom Thumb' or 'Jack the Giant-Killer'.[4]

Wesley's conclusions were not shared by all ministers however. Over the last 200 years clergy and laity in the mainstream Churches have often joined Swedenborgian study groups and drawn inspiration from his teachings without leaving their own Church. Among those influenced by Swedenborg's work were William Blake, Robert and Elizabeth Browning, W. B. Yeats, Ralph Waldo Emerson, Immanuel Kant and Goethe.

BELIEFS AND PRACTICES

Swedenborg taught that there is only one God and that as Jesus he came to earth. This is a resurgence of Monarchianism (see p. 49). The three parts of the Trinity are God's love, wisdom and energy – 'the universal creative love, the personal revelation of that love as human, and its activity in all people and things,' says the Rev. Ian Johnson of the Committee of Ministers of the General Conference of the New Church.

The Second Coming took place in 1757 – Swedenborg saw a vision of it – and a new dispensation began then, hence the New Church. He developed a long list of correspondences between things in the physical world and their spiritual equivalents, and applied this to study of the Bible. The Bible is to be understood chiefly for its spiritual teachings and is generally not to be taken on a literal basis. Only certain books of the Bible are divinely inspired. In the New Testament these are the Gospels and Revelation, though in his later writings Swedenborg did use the Epistles (especially I John) as a source.

Swedenborg taught that the soul is immortal; after death we go to a spirit world and eventually to heaven or hell. We can choose to go to heaven 'by putting our faith in Jesus' way of love, friendship, forgiveness, helpfulness, honesty, courage and self-denial. Believing them must obviously involve practising them, obeying the Ten Commandments in the way that Jesus showed.' If instead we 'delight in pride, scorn, greed, revenge and deception' we will go to hell, but this is our own choice; 'The Lord is for ever eager to save us from such a fate, but this can only happen through our change of heart.' When our physical bodies die 'and the pressures and limitations of earthly life are removed, then our inner character will become clear to us and to everyone around us in the spiritual world. There we can continue for ever seeking our particular kind of happiness.'

To summarize the beliefs on man's relationship with God:

God is love. The whole purpose of the universe is to share heavenly joy with as many people as possible. This creating love is revealed in Jesus Christ as Divine Humanity, to show us what his love and joy are like, to make his power easier for us to share. God is wisdom. He knows what is needed for us to share his joy. He shares that knowledge with us so far as he can, through the laws, stories and poetry of many religions, and in everyday situations of life. God's love and wisdom are the life in all things, and each thing in the world represents something of his heavenly kingdom.[5]

Such teachings, and Swedenborg's clairvoyant powers, have led to his being an influence on some New Age movements. He is generally respected as a deeply spiritual mystic, even by those who don't accept all his theological teachings.

Swedenborgians have sometimes been criticized for being too intellectual. Johnson takes the point, but explains: 'The muddle of Christian tradition has needed thorough unravelling; also the idea of inner meaning requires considerable explanation and illustration for people used to literalism; but, once these barriers have been cleared away, our belief is beautifully simple.'

The heyday of the Church in Britain was around 1900, when it had some 100 churches. There are far fewer now, and the Church concentrates more on study groups and residential courses. There are several thousand members of the two main Swedenborgian Churches in America. According to Johnson, there are steadily growing movements in Africa and Asia, and some groups in former Communist countries have been 'enthusiastically revived'.

MORMONS

The Church of Jesus Christ of Latter-day Saints – or the Mormon religion – has established itself, particularly in America, as a major religion very distinct from, but with its roots firmly in, mainstream Christianity. From its beginnings in the 1820s it has grown to a current world membership of over 9 million, 170,000 of those in the UK. Non-Mormons may find it difficult to credit their beliefs, yet Mormons everywhere are well-respected pillars of society. In America they have long held major government positions: in the UK the first Mormon MP was elected in 1990.

Unless otherwise stated, references to the Mormons apply either to the common history of all varieties of Mormons or specifically to the main Utah-based Church.

HISTORY

More than with any other 'new' Christian-based religion, the story of the early Mormons can be found in history books; more than with many others, also, the founding story is a powerful myth, in the true sense of the word. We are not concerned with establishing the factual truth of this myth, only with accepting it as the basis of the religion. It should be remembered also that all history books are selective with their facts and interpretations. Pro- and anti-Mormon histories put very different slants on the same series of historical events; the 'historical truth' probably lies somewhere in between.

Because the story of the origin of the Mormons is so well known and so well documented, I shall simply sketch the outlines here.

Joseph Smith (1805–44) came from a farming family in western New York State, an area known as the 'burned-over district' because so many revivalist evangelists had set fire to people's hearts in the early nineteenth century. In 1820, at the age of 14, Smith asked God which of the many available varieties of Christianity was the true one. The main choice was between a host of different versions of Congregationalists, Baptists, Quakers and Methodists. God the Father and Jesus appeared to him in a vision, telling him that he should join none of these, because they were all wrong, but that he should wait a few years. In 1823 Smith had another vision, of the angel Moroni, who told him about some golden plates buried in a nearby hillside. In 1827 he was allowed to dig them up and begin the work of translating them, using a huge pair of eyepieces called the Urim and Thummim which enabled him to understand the text, written in 'reformed Egyptian hieroglyphics'. Smith sat behind a curtain and dictated the English text initially to his wife, Emma, and a neighbour, Martin Harris, and mainly to a young schoolteacher, Oliver Cowdery. Most of the work with Cowdery was done between April and June 1829.

When the translation was finished, the angel took the golden plates away. Martin Harris mortgaged his farm to pay for the printing and the first edition of the *Book of Mormon* was published in 1830.

The *Book of Mormon: Another Testament of Jesus Christ* tells of two migrations to the American continent, the first by the Jaredite people to central America after the fall of the Tower of Babel (*c.* 2250 BC) and the second by a group of righteous Jews whose leader was called Lehi (*c.* 600 BC). Two of Lehi's sons were Nephi and Laman. In years to come the Nephites were godly, but the Lamanites were evil, and were cursed by God so that their skin turned dark, and they became the ancestors of the Native Americans. After his resurrection, Jesus visited America and preached to the Nephites. The Lamanites wiped out the Nephites around AD 428 on the hill Cumorah near Palmyra in New York State – the hill where Smith found the golden plates in 1827. The golden plates, a history of the migrations and the American settlements, were written by the prophet Mormon and his son Moroni, who were the last of the Nephites.

The *Book of Mormon* also records in detail the appearance of Jesus in America, after his resurrection.

Because the validity of Mormonism rests so much on both Joseph Smith and the *Book of Mormon*, critics of the religion attack the credibility of both. They quote contemporaries of Smith who describe him as 'a notorious liar . . . utterly destitute of conscience', as vulgar and lewd. The Smith family, they say, were known as treasure-hunters; Joseph Smith hired himself out searching for buried treasure by peering into a magical stone, or 'peepstone'. The Mormons accept that in 1826 he was arrested as a 'glass looker' under a New York State law which made it illegal 'to tell fortunes, or where lost or stolen goods may be found'. This, critics say, is the origin of the magic eyepieces and golden plates.

Such evidence, it must be said, is largely circumstantial; it is always easy to damn someone from the mouth of his enemies.

The *Book of Mormon* presents more substantial problems. For a start, scholars of the Middle East have never heard of 'reformed Egyptian hieroglyphics'. Among the other Mormon scriptures is a small book called *The Pearl of Great Price*, which is sometimes bound in with the *Book of Mormon*. In one section, 'Extracts from the History of Joseph Smith, the Prophet', Smith tells of his friend Martin Harris taking a copy of some of the characters, and Smith's translation of them, to Professor Charles Anthon in New York. 'Professor Anthon stated that the translation was correct, more so than any he had before seen translated from the

Egyptian. I then showed him those which were not then translated, and he said that they were Egyptian, Chaldaic, Assyriac and Arabic; and he said they were true characters.'[6]

However, the *Book of Mormon* itself says, 'But the Lord knoweth the things which we have written, and also that none other people knoweth our language; therefore he hath prepared means for the interpretation thereof.'[7] If no one knew the language, critics ask, how could Professor Anthon have known that it was a correct translation?

Moreover, Professor Anthon has written:

> The whole story about my having pronounced the Mormonite inscription to be 'reformed Egyptian hieroglyphics' is perfectly false . . . Upon examining the paper in question, I soon came to the conclusion that it was all a trick, perhaps a hoax . . . It existed of crooked characters disposed in columns and had evidently been prepared by some person who had before him at the time a book containing various alphabets. Greek and Hebrew letters, crosses and flourishes, Roman letters inverted or placed sideways, were arranged in perpendicular columns, and the whole ended in a rude delineation of a circle, divided into various compartments, decked with various strange marks . . .[8]

On this incident, the Church today comments, 'There is some confusion about what happened in these interviews, but Martin Harris was unequivocally satisfied.'[9]

Critics also point not just to the large number of verses from the Bible in the *Book of Mormon* (over 27,000 words) but to the fact that they are taken from the King James Version, and ask why an 1829 translation of an AD 428 text should be in 1611 English. The *Book of Mormon* apparently also contains quotations from the seventeenth-century *Westminster Confession of Faith* and an excerpt from a Methodist book of discipline.

In addition, Mormons say that Smith's 'translation' was inspired by God and was perfect – Joseph Smith called it the 'most correct of any book on earth'.[10] Yet critics say there have been over 100 editions of the *Book of Mormon*, with a total of well over 3,000 revisions to the text. The Church points out that the vast majority of these are corrections of typographical errors, or rationalization of spelling, grammar and punctuation (the 3,000 revisions include 891 changes of 'which' to 'who').

If the *Book of Mormon* wasn't a miraculous translation from golden plates revealed by an angel, where did it come from? The theory most often proffered by critics in the past was that the historical portions were based on the manuscript of an unpublished novel called *Manuscript Found*, written by a retired Presbyterian minister, Solomon Spaulding, which had been left at a local printers where Joseph Smith's right-hand man in the early days of the Church, Sidney Rigdon, was (depending on sources) a regular visitor or even a compositor. Spaulding's widow, and others, claimed to recognize her husband's work when the *Book of Mormon* was published.

The Church points out that when a manuscript by Spaulding entitled *Manuscript Story* was eventually discovered, in 1884, it bore no resemblance to the *Book of Mormon*. Also, it says, Rigdon did not actually meet Smith until December 1830 – after the *Book of Mormon* was published. According to the authoritative *Encyclopedia of Mormonism*, 'Since 1946, no serious student of Mormonism has given the Spaulding Manuscript theory much credibility.'[11]

Some of the original papyri from which Joseph Smith translated the 'Book of Abraham' in *The Pearl of Great Price* were discovered in 1966. When translated by scholars, they were found to be standard funerary documents, bearing no resemblance to Smith's 'translation' of 'the writings of Abraham while he was in Egypt'. This discovery does not appear to have dented the faith of Mormons: 'The papyrus purchased by the Church in 1966–7 is just one of a whole bunch of papyri and, as such, neither proves nor disproves Joseph's assertions,' says Bryan J. Grant, Director of Public Affairs in the UK.[12]

There are two further arguments against the *Book of Mormon* which should be mentioned. First, there is no archaeological evidence at all of the settlements in America recorded in the *Book of Mormon*, and no genetic evidence for the Semitic origin of the Native American peoples. Second, the three witnesses quoted at the beginning of the book as having 'seen the engravings which are upon the plates', including Harris and Cowdery, all later left the Church. One of them said, 'I saw them with the eye of faith' – in other words, not as material objects.

But what is important is that millions of intelligent, well-educated Mormons believe absolutely in the miraculous origins of the *Book of Mormon*. One of the most important distinguishing tenets of their faith is that God's revelation continues in the present day; for them, the *Book of Mormon* is firm evidence of this.

◆

In 1829 John the Baptist appeared to Smith and Cowdery and conferred the Aaronic Priesthood on them, after which the two baptized each other. Later, the apostles Peter, James and John appeared to the two of them and conferred the Melchizedek Priesthood on them. These two priesthoods are still fundamental to the Church.

In April 1830 the Church, originally called simply the Church of Jesus Christ, was established, with Smith as First Elder and Cowdery as Second Elder. During the year Smith was twice tried, and twice acquitted of being 'a disorderly person'. He sensibly solved one potential problem very early on: although continuous revelation was an important plank of doctrine, and God could speak to anyone in the Church, commandments and revelations for the entire Church could only come through one man. Initially this was Smith, and then his successor, Brigham Young, and then each successive President of the Church.

The Church grew, with a number of converts from the Campbellite movement, which later became the Disiples of Christ; one of these was Sidney Rigdon. Over the next few years, as membership grew, so did opposition, and the Church was forced to move from New York State to Ohio, Missouri, Illinois and finally Utah, in the famous great trek of 1846–7.

Even as early as the mid-1830s there was dissension in the Church over the fact that its doctrines and organization were becoming increasingly complicated (Campbellites aimed for the simplicity of the New Testament Church), and over the increased involvement of Smith in temporal affairs. There was continuous friction with non-Mormon neighbours, which often led to bloodshed and death on both sides. In 1839 10,000 members moved to Nauvoo in Illinois.

Meanwhile, nine senior members led a mission to England in 1840. Thousands were converted and during the next six years nearly 5,000 emigrated to America to join the Mormons at Nauvoo. The mission was based in Preston, Lancashire, which was for a long time the centre of British Mormonism. A Mormon temple is currently being built at Chorley, near Preston.

Things were not going well in Nauvoo. Non-Mormons were unhappy about the amount of power that Smith wielded, as editor of the local newspaper, commanding general of the local militia and mayor of the town. (In 1844 he also made a bid for the presidency of the USA.) In the spring of 1844 a number of former members of the Church set up a rival newspaper, the *Nauvoo Expositor*, which attacked both Smith and the Church. Smith, via the City Council, ordered the *Expositor's* press to be smashed and every copy of the paper to be burnt. In the ensuing furore, Smith and others were put in gaol. While they were awaiting trial, Joseph Smith and his brother Hyrum were murdered on 27 June, when a mob attacked the gaol.

There followed a brief struggle for leadership between Sidney Rigdon and Brigham Young, each of whom was in a powerful position in the Church hierarchy. Young won, leading to an eventual split in the Church. Many members were already concerned at the changes to the Church in their time at Nauvoo, particularly relating to the Temple and to polygamy, and Young's leadership laid even greater stress on these. The main breakaway Church eventually became the Reorganized Church of Jesus Christ of Latter-day Saints.

Local hostility continued, and in February 1846 members of the Church began their westward journey, breaking for the following winter in Nebraska and Iowa. Then, in July 1847, Brigham Young arrived at the Great Salt Lake valley in what is now Utah.

Once they were safely established in effectively their own city and their own state, the Church sent out missionaries, particularly to Britain and Scandinavia. By the end of the century nearly 90,000 converts had moved to Utah.

Their troubles were not yet over. In 1862 Congress passed an Anti-Bigamy Act, and in 1879 the Supreme Court upheld this as constitutional. Mormons held to their belief in the practice of polygamy. In 1882 the Edmunds Act allowed up to five years' imprisonment and a $500 fine for polygamy, with lesser penalties for unlawful cohabitation. This was enforced by federal marshals searching for evidence of polygamy or cohabitation. Many Mormons, including their leaders, went underground for several years. Between 1884 and 1893, over 900 Mormons were imprisoned for polygamy-related offences. In 1887 the Edmunds–Tucker Act dissolved the Church as a legal corporation and required the forfeiture of any property worth over $50,000.

Mormons were losing the vote and being imprisoned, and Mormon property was being confiscated by the government. Faced with the options of the complete destruction of the Church for which they had fought so long and endured so much to protect, or the maintenance of a practice which had caused even internal dissension, the Church made the only realistic choice.

'Two commandments were in conflict: the need to sustain the law of the land and the need to follow what God had ordained. The prophet took it to the Lord, and the directive was that the principle [of plural marriage] should be suspended,' says Grant. In 1890 Church President Wilford Woodruff issued a proclamation, later added to *Doctrine and Covenants* (see below), which concluded, 'And I now publicly declare that my advice to the Latter-day Saints is to refrain from contracting any marriage forbidden by the law of the land.'

BELIEFS AND PRACTICES

As well as the Bible and the *Book of Mormon*, Mormons have two further books of scripture, often bound in with the *Book of Mormon*. *Doctrine and Covenants* is a compilation of revelations given to Joseph Smith and a few of his successors; new sections are occasionally added. *The Pearl of Great Price* contains two further inspired translations by Joseph Smith, a brief extract from Matthew's Gospel out of Smith's own partial translation of the Bible, and an extract from *The History of Joseph Smith, the Prophet*, in which he tells of the origins of the *Book of Mormon*.

Although the majority of Christian denominations would disagree, the Church insists that it is Christian – in fact, 'a restoration of the Church Christ organized when upon the Earth,' says Grant, who continues: 'Indeed, the name of our Church bears His name and as members we are encouraged to make Him and His teachings the centre of our lives. This should permeate our relationships with our personal families, our Church family, those that we work with, our neighbours and those in our community. In fact, everyone!'

On the surface and with a couple of exceptions, the Articles of Faith of the Church differ little from those of many other Christian Churches. The two main exceptions are Article 8, 'We believe the Bible to be the word of God, as far as it is translated correctly; we also believe the Book of Mormon to be the word of God'; and Article 10, 'We believe in the literal gathering of Israel and in the restoration of the Ten Tribes; that Zion will be built on the American continent, that Christ will reign personally upon the earth; and that the earth will be renewed and receive its paradisiacal glory.'

As we shall see with other Christian-offshoot religions, statements like Article 1, 'We believe in God, the Eternal Father, and in His Son, Jesus Christ, and in the Holy Ghost,' can mean quite different things. For Mormons, according to Grant, 'The Godhead is made up of three distinct, separate personages. God the Father and Jesus Christ have bodies of flesh and bones, while the Holy Ghost, the third member of the Godhead, is a personage of spirit.'

There has been some doctrinal confusion over the years as to whether Adam was God the Father, which critics say Brigham Young taught at one point; the Church itself has never actually taught this, regarding it as 'speculation' on Young's part.

Many anti-Mormon books take such early theological thoughts as part of Mormon doctrine. Part of the problem is that Mormons were so busy surviving in their first few decades that it took them a while to work out their doctrine in detail. It should be remembered, though, that many of the fundamental doctrines of mainstream Christianity were not properly formulated until 300 or 400 years after Christ's death.

Behind many of the Mormon beliefs which are different from mainstream Christianity lies the doctrine that our souls exist before we are born. On a planet orbiting the star Kolob, God and his many wives have children; these are spiritual beings without bodies. When a child is about to be born on earth, one of these spiritual beings inhabits the child, the spirit and the body becoming 'a living soul'.

Lucifer, who was Jesus' brother, wanted everyone on earth to be saved, without any choice; Jesus wanted us to have free will. With his death, Jesus unconditionally paid the penalty we had inherited from the fall of Adam and Eve ('original sin'); his death will also redeem us from our own sins if we believe in him and keep his commandments.

Protestant Christians believe that salvation comes through faith, and that we have faith through the grace of God. They generally condemn the idea of salvation through works, though theologically this is something of a hot potato. Mormons believe that salvation requires both grace and works – 'a revealed yet common-sense reconciliation of these contradictory positions'.[13]

Salvation actually depends on five things: belief in Christ; repentance of sins; baptism in water; receiving the Holy Ghost; and enduring to the end, by which they mean 'the member must press forward in faith, and continue in obedience to all the commandments of God'.[14]

'Receiving the Holy Ghost' is the same as the 'baptism in the Holy Spirit' found in Pentecostalist and Charismatic Evangelical Churches. It bestows the gifts of the Spirit, including prophecy, speaking in tongues, interpretation of tongues, etc.

Despite – or perhaps because of – the persecution they received through most of the nineteenth century. Mormons are very strong on religious tolerance. Article 11 states, 'We claim the privilege of worshipping Almighty God according to the dictates of our own conscience, and allow all men the same privilege, let them worship how, where or what they may.' This doesn't mean that they believe that other religions lead to salvation.

'We believe that our Church has all the truth whereas other religions have some of the truth,' says Grant, acknowledging that there are holy people in other religions. But salvation can come only through the Mormon Church. 'We believe that before the gospel was restored to the earth in 1830, man did not have the authority of God to provide the ordinances necessary for salvation.'

These ordinances include the two orders of priesthood given to Joseph Smith and Oliver Cowdery, which validate Mormon baptism and all other ordinances.

The fact that baptism is essential for salvation accounts for one of the more unusual elements of Mormon doctrine, baptism for the dead. A Mormon can be baptized on behalf of someone who is dead; it is up to the dead person whether or not to repent and thus be saved. Because Mormons quite naturally want as many as possible to be saved, each member researches his or her family history at least four generations back, so that their parents, grandparents, great-grandparents and so on may be baptized in proxy by name. The Mormon genealogical database in Salt Lake City is the largest in the world. The Church makes the information available to anyone who wishes to trace their ancestors.

Mormons are encouraged to have children, whether to increase the number of saved or to provide more bodies for the spirits born on Kolob. Obviously with polygamy a man may have many more children within marriage; Brigham Young is said to have had 56 by his 17 wives. For its own survival, the main Church very reluctantly had to drop the practice of polygamy; whether it would reintroduce it if the federal government were to change its mind is unknown. The Reorganized Church was against polygamy from the very start, but several of the more minor offshoots of the Church still practise it.

The Mormon Church is Millennial, in that it believes that Christ will return and rule on earth. Joseph Smith designated a site in Independence, Missouri, where Christ would establish his new Zion.

There is much speculation among non-Mormons as to what Mormons do in their temples. Normal services are held in normal churches, and the temples are reserved for special rites. Although non-members can be allowed in before a temple is consecrated (in the case of the London Temple, 55,000 viewed it on open days in 1992 after it had been refurbished), the temples are reserved for members 'in good standing' – about a quarter of all members, and only about 6 per cent on a regular basis. The restricted access 'is not a matter of secrecy; it is a matter of sacredness and sanctity'.[15]

'In the temples, members of the Church who make themselves eligible can participate in the most exalted of the redeeming ordinances that have been revealed to mankind. There, in a sacred ceremony, an individual may be washed and anointed and instructed and endowed and sealed.'[16]

The rites include solemnization of marriage for eternity, baptism for the dead and other ordinances. Special white clothing is worn within the temple to symbolize purity, cleanliness and setting aside the things of the world. (Although the Church is reluctant to speak of it, Mormons 'in good standing' wear a white undergarment like a long T-shirt all the time, under their normal clothing. 'Having made covenants of righteousness, the members wear the garment under their regular clothing for the rest of their lives, day and night, partially to remind them of the sacred covenants they have made with God.'[17])

Joseph Smith, and most of the early Mormons, were Freemasons, and much of the ritual within the temple is similar to Masonic rites and symbolism.

The Mormon religion lays great stress on morality and 'worthy' behaviour. Sex before marriage and infidelity within marriage are condemned, as are homosexual practices. Tobacco, alcohol and other drugs are banned for members, as are tea, coffee and cola drinks because of the stimulants they contain. Mormons do not have to be vegetarians, but meat should be eaten sparingly. These restrictions are known as the 'Word of Wisdom', a revelation given to Joseph Smith in 1833.[18] The Church claims that by following the Word of Wisdom, Mormon white males in California live eight years longer than non-Mormons, while in Utah Mormons suffer one-third fewer cancers than non-Mormons.

The Church was often accused in the past of being racist; its early leaders made a number of statements about non-white people being lower than whites. Although the First Presidency of the Church urged Mormons to work for civil rights for blacks in the 1960s, blacks were not allowed to become priests or participate in temple ordinances until 1978.

The Mormon Church was in the forefront of the fight for female emancipation, but only men may belong to either of the orders of priesthood. Boys are ordained into the Aaronic Priesthood at 12; this has levels of deacon, teacher, priest and bishop. At 18 they can receive the Melchizedek Priesthood, with levels of elder, high priest, patriarch, member of a seventy, and apostle. The majority of active adult male Mormons, including those who do missionary work on doorsteps around the world, are elders. At the top of the hierarchy is the president, who with his two counsellors makes up the First Presidency of the Church. Next comes the Quorum of the 12 Apostles, who collectively and latently hold the same authority as the president, and appoint a new president on the death of the old one. The Quorums of the seventy and the Presiding Bishopric are senior administrative levels.

The Church is organized in 'wards' – congregations of 200–600 members – led by a bishop; stakes (equivalent to dioceses), of up to ten wards, led by a stake president; regions; and areas. Missionary areas have missions, made up of districts, made up of branches, with fewer than 200 members; a branch is the equivalent of a small ward. In the UK at the end of 1993 there were 161,000 members in 41 stakes and 230 wards, plus seven missions and 114 branches; there is one Temple near London and another being constructed near Preston.

OFFSHOOTS

The Church has been plagued with schisms since it began. There are currently more than 25 offshoots, each claiming to be the only true version of the Church set up by Joseph Smith. And from the days of Joseph Smith, dissenting members have been swiftly excommunicated.

Several of the earliest breakaway groups – one headed by Joseph's brother William when Brigham Young was appointed president, and another headed by Joseph's former right-hand man Sidney Rigdon – joined together in 1860 to form the Reorganized Church of Jesus Christ of Latter-day Saints, which is by far the largest and most significant offshoot. They have always been anti-polygamy; their presidents are descendants of Joseph Smith, starting with his own son, Joseph Smith III (the prophet Joseph's father was also called Joseph); and they use Joseph Smith's *Inspired Version* of the Bible. (The main Utah-based Church prefers to use the King James Version.) Their theology is a little closer than the main Church's to mainstream Christianity. They refuse to be known as Mormons, insisting on the full name of their Church.

Another offshoot of interest is the Church of Christ (Temple Lot), founded as far back as 1852, largely in protest – once more – against Brigham Young and the growing practices of polygamy and baptism for the dead. Based in Independence, Missouri, they still own the Temple Lot, which Joseph Smith had said would be the site of New Zion when Christ returns.

A very fundamentalist polygamist offshoot began in the 1930s in Short Creek, a small town in north-west Arizona. This split in 1951, over the usual issue of disputed leadership succession. One wing, the United Order Effort, is still based around Short Creek, now renamed Colorado City. The other wing, the Apostolic United Brethren, headed by Rulon Allred, led to at least three other Churches.

The Church of the First Born of the Fulness of Times in 1955 was led by Joel LeBaron. Joel's brother Ervil left this Church to form the Church of the Lamb of God; he had Joel killed in 1972, and Allred in 1977, among several other murders. Another offshoot of the Apostolic United Brethren was the Church of Jesus Christ in Solemn Assembly, now known as the Confederate Nations of Israel, founded in 1974.

There is currently a movement of theological liberals who want to stay within the Mormon Church, while taking a more relaxed attitude towards the historicity of the origins of the Church.

EXCLUSIVE BRETHREN

The Exclusive Brethren, albeit a small Protestant denomination with straightforward Evangelical Christian beliefs, are significant for two main reasons: their exclusivity and Dispensationalism. Often known as the Plymouth Brethren, they should not be confused with the Open Brethren (or Christian Brethren), or with the much larger Church of the Brethren denomination in the USA. The term 'Brethren' used on its own below refers to both the Exclusive and the Open Brethren. The Exclusive Brethren's central body in the UK is the Bible and Gospel Trust.

HISTORY

The Brethren originated when a group of men, including a doctor, a lawyer, a missionary and a peer, started meeting together in Dublin in the winter of 1827–8. They believed in simplicity of worship, with no ritual, no set prayers and no set form of service – just a group of brothers meeting together in God's name. Like many other Churches, they wanted to return to the basic principles of the early Church, as they found them in the Bible. They were opposed to the complexities of all the Christian denominations and believed that an ordained ministry was not needed. And they believed, as did so many other new Churches in the nineteenth century, in the imminent return of Christ.

John Nelson Darby (1800–82), who was a curate in the Episcopalian Church of Ireland, joined this small group, was convinced of their beliefs and left the Church of Ireland. He moved to Plymouth in 1830 and set up meetings there. Most of the early tracts were published in Plymouth, hence the name Plymouth Brethren, which is still commonly used, although the Church dislikes it. At this time the movement was largely composed of professional and upper-class people.

Darby was an effective evangelist, and took his message to Switzerland, Germany, France and several other countries, including Australia.

His main contribution to Christian theology was Dispensationalism. This teaches that there are seven ages of man, starting with the Age of Innocence, before the Fall, and progressing through the Ages of Conscience, Human Government, Promise, Law and Grace, this last established through Christ. The seventh age, still to come, is the millennial reign of Christ. Darby was one of the first to work out the 'timetable' of the Last Things, and taught that the saved will be caught up in the Rapture before Christ's return, and so will be spared the great tribulation.

Dispensationalism in one form or another has been preached by many Evangelical Churches since then, right up to the present day. Dwight L. Moody, the influential American evangelist of the late nineteenth century, was convinced of the idea by Darby, and one of the most significant Protestant reference books of the early twentieth century, the Scofield Reference Bible, followed the teaching, and so introduced it to even more Christians. Although the Brethren at one time saw belief in Dispensationalism as a hallmark of the true believer, so many diverse Churches now teach it that it can no longer be seen as the unique touchstone of the Brethren.

BELIEFS AND PRACTICES

Theologically all Brethren are conservative Evangelical: they believe implicitly in the Bible as the inspired word of God, they are orthodox Trinitarian and they believe in the assurance of salvation by faith alone. They do not formally hold to any of the creeds, believing that the Bible is the sole source of authority for their teaching.

The Exclusive Brethren also believe in absolutely upright moral standards of behaviour and in keeping completely apart from the world. Darby's strictness on this was too much for many in the movement and in 1848 it split into two, the larger portion calling themselves the Christian Brethren or the Open Brethren, to distinguish themselves from Darby's minority group, the Exclusive Brethren, also known for a while as Darbyites. The Open Brethren are now practically indistinguishable from any other Free Evangelical Church. They welcome

Christians from other Evangelical Churches to their services, though it depends on the individual church whether they allow outsiders to join in the Lord's Supper, the communion service.

The Exclusive Brethren are another matter. They keep apart from every other Church. They hold their exclusivity as a primary virtue 'in view of maintaining suitable conditions for partaking of the Lord's Supper'.[19] They will exclude from their fellowship not just anyone who doesn't share their beliefs but any of their members who fall from the true path of absolute purity, however slightly. It is the duty of every member to point out the failings of any other member, in a spirit of loving correction. If the erring member does not repent and reform, he is 'put out' – the other members withdraw from him completely. This even applies to the spouse of an errant member. It is forbidden, for example, to eat at the same table, because this is regarded as fellowship; they 'will only eat with those with whom they partake of the Lord's Supper'.

If a member of the Church, however otherwise godly, 'should refuse to separate from someone thus disciplined, they would prove themselves also unfit for fellowship'.

It is vital that they 'abstain from all appearance of evil' or, in Darby's own translation of the Bible, 'hold aloof from every form of wickedness' (I Thessalonians 5:22). Even suspicion of errant behaviour causes a member to be 'shut up' – not admitted into church services and meetings – until the situation is clarified one way or the other.

They keep themselves separate from the corruption of the world, including what they feel are depraving influences such as television. Their children are educated in normal state schools, but do not take part in competitive sports or any extra-curricular activities, and they are strongly discouraged from making any friends outside the Church. Because they believe that student life is full of wickedness and temptation, the young people are not encouraged to go to university, with the result that there are now very few professional people in the movement. Learning practical skills, however, is encouraged.

As with the Quakers, all services are extempore, with all prayers, preaching and choice of (unaccompanied) hymns inspired by the Holy Spirit. Preachers have no formal training at all. Unlike the Quakers, women are not allowed to speak during services, in accordance with I Corinthians 14:34–5.

There are some recruits to the Church through their outdoor preaching, but the majority of members have been brought up in it. Family life is important to the Exclusive Brethren and they devote a lot of care and attention to their children, who are brought up within a consistently sound moral code. Because they have been taught almost from the cradle to keep themselves apart, and so have few if any friends outside the Church, it is reckoned to be difficult for members to leave the Church. Some do, of course, and the impression to non-members is that overall numbers are falling, though the Church disputes this. There is a curiously old-fashioned feel to the Church. For example, its tracts make no concession to the 1990s, many of them still referring to the Second World War.

For those outside the movement it might seem a harsh and unforgiving Church; for those inside, the Church is like an extended family, with members supporting each other in their desire to stay close to God and serve him unreservedly.

SEVENTH-DAY ADVENTISTS

The name Seventh-day Adventist expresses two of the main distinguishing features of this Church: they worship on the seventh day of the week and they await the second advent, the Second Coming of Jesus. Although there is one main denomination with the name, in some ways Seventh-day Adventism *per se* is less a Church than a movement. There have been dozens of offshoots, some little more than a handful of congregations, others considerably larger, like the Worldwide Church of God, and some it would prefer not to be associated with, like David Koresh's ill-fated Branch Davidians. To attempt to draw a family tree of all the offshoots of offshoots would be a fascinating but well-nigh-impossible exercise.

HISTORY

Seventh-day Adventists grew out of the Adventist movement of the early nineteenth century, though in fact anyone who believed Christ's return was imminent could be called Adventist, including the Shakers (the United Society of Believers in Christ's Second Coming) in the 1760s. A German Lutheran minister, J. G. Bengel, taught the doctrine in the mid-eighteenth century, setting the date of the Second Coming at 1836. William Miller, an American Baptist minister, attracted thousands of followers with his message, based on prophecies in Daniel and Revelation, that Christ would return in 1843. When nothing happened, he reworked his calculations, taking account of the calendraic fact that there isn't a year 0 between 1 BC and AD 1, and announced that the great event would take place in 1844, specifically on 22 October. Believers sold their properties and possessions in readiness; though apparently the oft-quoted story of them sitting on their rooftops in 'ascension robes' is without foundation. Once again, nothing happened, and the event became known as the Great Disappointment.

Adventists, or Millerites, divided into a number of Churches and movements, each coping with the Great Disappointment in its own way. Miller himself died in 1849, not endorsing any of these groups.

The Seventh-day Adventist Church was founded on three main doctrines put forward by different Adventists in the immediately ensuing years. One, revealed to Hiram Edson the day after the Great Disappointment, was that Christ had not returned to earth in 1844, but had entered his heavenly sanctuary to cleanse it and sort out the sheep from the goats in preparation for the Judgement. Another, a teaching put forward by Joseph Bates in 1846, was that Christians must obey God's law, as set out in the Ten Commandments, which include the observance of the Sabbath. (There had in fact been a few Seventh-day Baptist Churches in the USA for nearly 200 years.) The third was that in these last days the gift of prophecy would come on the Church. Seventh-day Adventists believe that the visions and teachings of Ellen G. White are a fulfilment of the biblical gifts of the Spirit.

Ellen G. White (1827–1915), then Ellen Gould Harmon, was brought up a Methodist, and joined the Millerites when she was 17. She suffered greatly from illness and injury as a child, and some critics believe that her visions were a continuation of her medical condition. Her first vision, in December 1844, convinced her that belief in the October 1844 date was not an error or delusion, despite the Great Disappointment of only a couple of months before.

Her visions, and her interpretations of them, are the basis of her several books, including *The Great Controversy* and *The Desire of Ages*. In her books she expanded on the teachings of the Church, particularly on keeping the Sabbath and on Christ cleansing the sanctuary. She also taught healthy living, instituting several dietary regulations. Her writings were regarded as prophetic and inspired, but not as replacing or even adding to the Bible.

She later married James White (1821–61), a very prominent Adventist minister. After his death she became the acknowledged leader of the movement.

This movement, initially almost a federation of independent congregations, set up its headquarters in Battle Creek, Michigan, in 1855. It didn't take the name Seventh-day Adventist until a conference there in 1860 (see p.89) and was formally organized as a Church in 1863. In 1903 it moved its centre to Takoma Park, Washington, DC.

The theology of the Church mellowed a little over the years, as Mrs White grew older. Realizing, perhaps somewhat belatedly, that some of their earlier and more extreme writings were still being quoted against them, the Church produced in 1957 a 700-page work entitled *Seventh-day Adventists Answer Questions on Doctrine*, which clarified many contentious issues.

Over the years the Seventh-day Adventist Church has met with a lot of opposition, partly because of some of its more over-enthusiastic claims of sole correctness, which have now been toned down considerably. To avoid alienating potential inquirers, for many years it deliberately adopted a policy of anonymity, presenting its books, magazines and meetings simply as Christian rather than Seventh-day Adventist. This practice attracted claims of deception and was eventually dropped.

The Church today stresses its roots among the European reformers of Christianity in the sixteenth and seventeenth centuries, rather than its American origins as a denomination: 'most teachings having been held formerly by European believers prior to the organization of the Seventh-day Adventist Church'.[20]

Less than 10 per cent of the Church's current membership lives in North America. It is still strong throughout Europe and in Britain it is particularly, but not solely, popular among the West Indian population.

BELIEFS AND PRACTICES

Evangelical anti-cult writers are divided on how close Seventh-day Adventist beliefs are to mainstream Christian doctrine. Seventh-day Adventists quite naturally become annoyed at being branded a cult when they believe in the Trinity, the full divinity of Christ, his incarnation and resurrection, the need for salvation, the indwelling of the Holy Spirit and so on. Unlike many other Christian offshoots, they have not redefined these terms in their own way and their theology, on the whole, is straightforward mainstream Christian.

Critics of Seventh-day Adventism tend to quote from the works of Ellen G. White, and from other books and articles by the Church's early writers, to prove that they are heretical. They sometimes ignore the fact the Church itself now accepts that some of these early writings were perhaps over-enthusiastic and at the very least badly phrased, and has tidied up its doctrinal statements in the last few decades.

Seventh-day Adventists attach some weight to Ellen G. White's books, but do not in any way regard them as scriptural, or even as infallible. Any revelations in the 'Spirit of Prophecy' are to be tested against the Bible, which is the sole authority. 'Seventh-day Adventists accept the Bible as their only creed and hold certain fundamental beliefs to be the teaching of the Holy Scriptures.'[21] In any case, Mrs White's visions and writings are only relevant for this Church, not for all of Christendom. There is little public emphasis on her today; the pamphlet quoted in this entry does not even mention her.

They believe that they are 'the remnant' of true believers, but they do not believe that they are the *only* true believers: 'We fully recognize the heartening fact that the host of the true followers of Christ are scattered all through the various churches of Christendom, including the Roman Catholic communion. These God clearly recognizes as His own.'[22]

They observe the Saturday Sabbath as one of the Ten Commandments, but they do not condemn as unbelievers those who worship God on Sunday; and they do not, as critics often claim, say that Sunday-worship is the Mark of the Beast. 'The majority of those in Christian churches still conscientiously observe Sunday. We ourselves cannot do so, for we believe that God is calling for a reformation in this matter. But we respect and love those of our fellow Christians who do not interpret God's word just as we do.'[23]

Although they teach obedience to the law, and are more legalistic than many other branches of Christianity, they stress that salvation does not come through keeping the law – 'by works' – but by the grace of God, through faith in Christ's atoning death.

They do have two unusual teachings about the fate of believers and non-believers. First, they believe that after death we remain in our graves, rather than going straight to heaven; when Christ returns to establish his millennial kingdom, the saved will be resurrected to everlasting life. Second, they do not believe in everlasting punishment for non-believers; eternal death means just that: final destruction. These two doctrines, of 'soul sleep' and the annihilation of the wicked, are not standard Christian doctrines, though they are held by a significant number of theologians, preachers and laity within mainstream Christianity.

The Seventh-day Adventists have been attacked for teaching that Christ possessed a sinful human nature. This, they say, is a misinterpretation (based on some admittedly clumsily written early statements) of what they actually believe, which is that Christ, being human as well as divine, had a fully human body and could be tempted in all ways. They stress that he was, however, completely sinless.

He clothed His divinity with humanity, He was made in the 'likeness of sinful flesh,' or 'sinful human nature,' or 'fallen human nature' (cf. Romans 8:3). This in no way indicates that Jesus Christ was sinful, or participated in sinful acts or thoughts. Though made in the form or likeness of sinful flesh. He was sinless and His sinlessness is beyond questioning.[24]

It should be remembered that the Early Church argued for centuries about the full implications of the God-man nature of Christ, and that mainstream Christianity has had more than one interpretation.

Since the days of Ellen G. White the Church has emphasized healthy living. As well as campaigning against smoking, discouraging the drinking of alcohol and encouraging a balanced vegetarian diet, the Church also runs many hospitals and health centres offering both conventional and alternative medicine.

The Church also believes in 'a broad education in a Christian context',[25] and in Britain runs several primary schools, two secondary schools and a higher education college affiliated to the Open University.

OFFSHOOTS

The Seventh-day Adventist Church and the Sabbatarian movement in general are responsible for a large number of schismatic Churches. Most of these offshoots have also splintered in various directions, and their beliefs and practices may be quite different from those of the Seventh-day Adventist Church.

The Church of God (Seventh Day) is made up of individual congregations which, though both Seventh-day and Adventist, didn't join the Seventh-day Adventist Church associated with Ellen G. White; apparently each sees the other as the offshoot. Its two main divisions are the General Conference of the Church of God (Seventh Day) and the General Council of the Churches of God.

The Worldwide Church of God (see p. 88) has been described as 'an offshoot of an offshoot of an offshoot of the Seventh-day Adventist Church'.

Note that a movement with 'Church of God' in its name might be an offshoot of the Seventh-day Adventist Church or of the Worldwide Church of God, or be quite separate from both. (See p. 299, note 4.)

There are also a large number of African-American Churches with origins in the Seventh-day Adventist movement.

The Branch Davidians (see p. 119) also have roots in the Seventh-day Adventist Church, though 'their teachings and code of practice were totally alien to that of ours', says Paul D. Tompkins, Communication Director of the Church.[26]

CHRISTADELPHIANS

The Christadelphians were one of the several new Christian offshoots to spring up in America in the mid-nineteenth century. They are Millennialist and Bible-believing, but their interpretation of Christian doctrine is markedly different from mainstream beliefs.

HISTORY

The Christadelphians, or Brothers of Christ, were founded in 1848 by an English doctor, John Thomas (1805–71), who had emigrated to America in 1832. He was involved in a shipwreck en route to America and vowed that if his life were saved he would devote it to religion. Although brought up a Congregationalist, he joined the newly formed Campbellites, later the Disciples of Christ, in Brooklyn, New York, in the 1830s. This was a Puritan group, with similarities to both the Baptists and the Congregationalists, but with no fixed creed. After much study of the Bible, Thomas worked out his own beliefs, leaving the Campbellites to form his own distinct brand of Christianity, which he believed was a return to the original New Testament beliefs.

In 1849 Thomas published a book called *Elpis Israel* (Hope of Israel), in which he wrote that the Latter Days had begun; before Christ's return, Israel would be restored.

The other main text of the Church is *Christendom Astray* by Robert Roberts, who took over the leadership after Thomas's death in 1871.

On several trips back to Britain, Thomas preached widely and converted many, so unusually the American and British Churches both stem from the founder himself. Christadelphianism today is probably stronger in Britain than in the USA.

With his Congregationalist background, Thomas set up no central authority, 'Each separate congregation is responsible for its own members,' says Michael Ashton, current editor of *The Christadelphian* magazine.[27] 'Fellowship between the congregations is on the basis of a shared biblical faith. There are no leaders as such, either over local congregations, over areas, countries or worldwide.

The Christadelphian magazine has been published monthly since 1864 and is, says Ashton, 'the recognized mouthpiece of our organization worldwide'.

BELIEFS AND PRACTICES

Christadelphians are ardent students of the Bible, which they believe to be the absolute word of God. Their reading plan, the *Bible Companion*, takes them through the entire Old Testament once a year, and the New Testament twice a year. All their teaching comes from the Bible, and not from the teachings and creeds of the Church Fathers.

'We do not claim to be the only group with a correct understanding of the Scriptures,' says Ashton, 'nor do we deny that other individuals not associated with us hold true Bible teaching.' On the other hand, they recognize that their interpretation of the Bible is a minority viewpoint: 'We disapprove of those Churches and organizations which claim to base their beliefs on the Bible, and yet preach a false gospel. In our opinion, all the mainstream churches in Christendom fall into that category.'

They disagree with traditional Christian belief on the nature of Christ, whom they see as 'the Son of God not God the Son'.[28] They are not Trinitarians, but they are also not, they say firmly, Unitarians. 'They [i.e. Christadelphians] really do believe that Jesus was, and is, *literally* the Son of God. They are *not* Unitarians, who think of Jesus as just a very superior man; nor are they "adoptionists", holding that God "adopted" Jesus as His spiritual Son. They believe that Jesus was God's "only begotten Son" in the way the Scriptures describe.'[29]

The Christadelphian doctrine of the atonement is fairly similar to that of mainstream Christianity – 'being himself sinless, [Jesus] was able to be offered as a sacrifice for sin'[30] – with one major difference: he could not have done this if he himself had been God.

> It was the vital atonement for sin, which makes it possible for us sinners to have hope. It is a tragedy that in popular Christianity this understanding has been perverted by the doctrine of the Trinity, which arose 300 years after the ascension of Jesus as a result of disputes within the Church. The creeds expressing the Trinity were decisions of Catholic Church Councils in the 4th and 5th centuries. Their teaching is not found in the Bible.[31]

Most Christadelphians probably have a better understanding of the Trinity than most mainstream Christians; they have to have, in order for them to refute it. They are quite correct in saying that the Bible nowhere teaches the doctrine of the Trinity; the Bible, as I have already said, is not a book of doctrine. The concept of the Trinity was formulated by the Church Fathers in an attempt to codify the God-man nature of Christ, and the relationship of the Father, Son and Holy Spirit. It is precisely because this is still a live issue today, with the Christadelphians, Unitarians, Jehovah's Witnesses and others each having their own understanding of the problem, that I devoted so much space to Early Church 'heresies'.

The Holy Spirit is seen as 'the power and influence by which God achieves His ends'[32] – or, in more detail, 'God's own radiant power, ever outflowing from Him, by which his "everywhereness" is achieved. The Spirit is personal in that it is of God Himself: it is not personal in the sense of being some other person within the Godhead.'[33]

Christadelphians do not believe in Satan as a personal devil. Such words 'represent only the evil tendencies of human nature. It is significant that throughout the Bible sinners are never encouraged to blame something or someone else for their failings, but only themselves.'[34]

Christadelphians do not believe in the immortality of the soul, or in hell, which is simply the grave, or in heaven. Eternal life for the saved and resurrected (Christadelphians, and perhaps others who have found the truth) will be on earth after Christ's return. The unsaved will simply not be resurrected. As with the Jehovah's Witnesses, the reason for wanting to be saved is more of a carrot than a stick.

The Millennialist teachings of the Christadelphians are broadly similar to those of most other Churches, whether mainstream or alternative. In their booklets there is perhaps more emphasis than usual on the importance of the Jews, who Christadelphians see very much as the Chosen People and the key to the coming millennium. They believe that we are currently in the End Times, comparing two biblical verses with current events: 'He that scattered Israel will gather him, and keep him, as a shepherd doth his flock' (Jeremiah 31:10) refers to the establishment of the State of Israel in 1948; while 'Jerusalem shall be trodden down of the Gentiles, *until the times of the Gentiles be fulfilled*' (Luke 21:24) refers to the Jews retaking Jerusalem at the end of the Six Day War in 1967. We are thus at the end of the era of Gentile times. 'The Jewish return to their homeland has occurred at a time when world statesmen vainly seek a formula for peace.

The mushroom growth of Israel has coincided with the mushroom cloud of the nuclear age. Is this a mere coincidence? Or does it portend greater things? It means but one thing: Christ is coming back to the earth.'[35] Abraham, they believe, will be raised from the dead so that he will see the Holy Land with his own eyes and inherit it as promised (Genesis 13:15–17).[36]

Long before the establishment of the State of Israel was even a possibility, an 1866 publication said, 'It is pretty certain that Jesus will return within the lifetime of the present generation.'[37] The Second Coming was forecast for 1868, then for 1910. In a somewhat more honest response than most Millennialist Churches give, Ashton now comments, 'Our eager anticipation of the establishment on earth of God's kingdom has led us in the past to some inaccurate predicting of dates. The Scriptures explain clearly that no one knows the day of the Lord Jesus' return to the earth.'

◆

Christadelphians do not believe in a priesthood. 'Each congregation elects members from its own number to act on its behalf for a set term of office (one, two or three years),' says Ashton. They will not take up arms in war, and they do not vote or take part in political affairs, but otherwise their social behaviour is standard. On morality: 'We seek to uphold the Bible standards of sexual behaviour, i.e. only in heterosexual marriage,' says Ashton. Friendly relationships with non-members are not discouraged.

It is a common criticism of the Christadelphians that they put more effort into explaining themselves to mainstream Christians than in preaching the Gospel to non-Christians. But for Christadelphians, mainstream Christians, through their acceptance of centuries of 'false' teaching, have got the message wrong. In any case, because the terminology is identical but the meaning so different, it is essential for them to explain what *they* mean, to show how their beliefs are different.

CHRISTIAN SCIENCE

Christian Science is best known for its reading rooms in many towns, for its well-respected newspaper the *Christian Science Monitor* and for its belief in healing physical illnesses by spiritual rather than medical means. It sees itself as a Christian denomination in much the same way as Methodism, the Baptist Church, etc. In fact, its theology is markedly different from established Christianity in many respects, hence – in addition to its origins in the late nineteenth century and its emphasis on spiritual healing – its inclusion here as an alternative religion.

HISTORY

Mary Baker Eddy (1821–1910), known by Christian Scientists as 'the Discoverer and Founder', was born in the village of Bow in New Hampshire, USA. Her parents were Congregationalists and she grew up in a strict Calvinist household. She was a sickly child and remained in ill-health for her first few decades. Her first husband died of yellow fever a few months after they married in 1843. Her second husband, whom she married in 1853, treated her badly and eventually deserted her; she divorced him in 1873. She married her third husband, Asa Eddy, in 1877; although she was then 56, she gave her age on her marriage licence as 40. This was some years after she had founded Christian Science, and in the five years until his death Asa Eddy helped her promote her new religion.

To avoid confusion 'the Founder' will be referred to throughout by her final married name.

Her second husband unwittingly started the process which resulted in the new religion, by introducing her to Phineas P. Quimby, a watchmaker who had set up as a mesmerist (hypnotist) and faith-healer. In 1862 Quimby, who taught that all disease is caused by faulty reasoning on the part of the sufferer, healed her of a crippling spinal disease. Quimby ascribed his healing powers to correct thinking rather than to God, but Mrs Eddy thought otherwise – though she spent two years lecturing on his work.

In February 1866, one month after Quimby's death, she slipped on ice and fell badly. A few days later she was reading her Bible and noticed the passage where Christ heals 'a man sick of the palsy' (Matthew 9:2–8). 'The healing Truth dawned upon my sense,' she wrote, 'and the result was that I rose, dressed myself, and ever after was in better health than I had before enjoyed.'[38]

This, for Christian Scientists, was the true start of it all. 'In the year 1866 I discovered the Christ Science, or divine laws of Life, Truth, and Love, and named my discovery Christian Science.'[39] She studied the Bible for three years and formulated her doctrine, then began to teach it to others. In 1875 she published the first edition of *Science and Health, With Key to the Scriptures*, which Christian Scientists read alongside the Bible in their Sunday services.

Christian Scientists today try to distance both their Founder and their religion as much as possible from Quimby.

'Her original ideas are misrepresented as coming from other sources, notably Phineas Quimby, a mesmerist with whom she had some contact before her discovery of Christian Science,' says Alan Grayson, District Manager of the Christian Science Committees on Publication for Great Britain and Ireland. 'In contrast to Quimby's method, which was based on the action of the human mind and wholly divorced from any Bible basis, Mrs Eddy's system relies wholly on the divine Mind, God, and is rooted squarely in the Scriptures, particularly Christ Jesus' example.'

However, there is no doubt that her thinking was at least initially very much influenced by Quimby. Even after his death, when she was teaching from 1867 to 1870, she apparently used as her text Quimby's manuscript, with her own handwritten annotations.

Critics have pointed out that Quimby referred to his own healing system in 1863 as 'Christian Science', and at other times as 'the Science of Christ', 'the Science of Man' and 'Science & Health', and that he called disease 'an error', which is a term often used by Mary Baker Eddy.

It has been suggested that portions of at least the early editions of *Science and Health* are based both on Quimby's own manuscripts (eventually published in 1921) and on a work by Francis Lieber, an authority on Hegel. Lieber had apparently sent a copy of his manuscript to his friend Hiram S. Krafts, who was one of Mary Baker Eddy's first students, and in whose home she lived for over a year. The Church disputes both claims, emphasizing the differences between Quimby's teachings and Mrs Eddy's rather than the similarities, and arguing that the Lieber document was actually a later forgery produced with the intent of discrediting Christian Science.

According to Mrs Eddy, 'No human pen nor tongue taught me the Science contained in this book, *Science and Health*.'[40] Quimby and Lieber might perhaps have disagreed. She also said, 'It was not myself but the divine power of truth and love infinitely above me, which dictated *Science & Health*.'[41] However, the book underwent several substantial revisions over the years, largely by the hand of a retired Unitarian minister, the Rev. J. H. Wiggin, who edited the text, rearranged the contents and corrected Mrs Eddy's grammar. He is quoted as saying later that Mrs Eddy was no scholar, and that 'Christian Science, on its theological side, is an ignorant revival of one form of ancient Gnosticism.' The current edition, with standardized page numbering, inset subheadings and numbered lines for easy reference, dates from 1907. It is alleged that the Church has attempted to destroy copies of all earlier editions.

◆

The Church of Christ, Scientist, was founded in 1879 in Boston, Massachusetts.

After her third husband's death in 1882, Mrs Eddy wrote a letter to the *Boston Post* accusing some of her former students of poisoning her husband with mentally administered arsenic. Her personal physician, Dr C. J. Eastman, who was the dean of a local medical college, performed a post-mortem at her request and confirmed her own 'diagnosis' – though Eastman was later found to have been practising with no medical qualifications whatsoever.

Mrs Eddy opened the Massachusetts Metaphysical College in Boston, where she taught around 4,000 students from 1881 to 1889, charging $300 for a 12-lesson course and also selling *Science and Health* at $3 a copy – substantial sums for a course and a book in the 1880s. Over the next few years her churches multiplied rapidly. In 1897 she ordered Christian Scientists to refrain from teaching students for a year; instead they should sell them copies of her book *Miscellaneous Writings* and her other books.

> The Bible, *Science and Health, With Key to the Scriptures* and my other published works are the only proper instructors for this hour. It shall be the duty of all Christian Scientists to circulate and to sell as many of these books as they can.
>
> If a member of the First Church of Christ, Scientist shall fail to obey this injunction it will render him liable to lose his membership in this church.[42]

This seems to be the origin of the practice, in Christian Science services, to have readings 'mainly from *Science and Health* on Sundays and equally from the Bible and *Science and Health* on Wednesdays' in testimony meetings, instead of a sermon. 'In order to move away from personal preaching, Mrs Eddy ordained these two books to be the pastor of her Church.'[43]

The compulsory purchase of reading material is also still part of Church practice. Christian Scientists today are required by a Church by-law to subscribe to the daily newspaper *Christian Science Monitor*, the weekly *Christian Science Sentinel*, the monthly *Christian Science Journal* and the *Christian Science Quarterly*, unless they would find it a financial burden to do so.

Christian Science, in common with many other new religions, does well out of its publications: Mary Baker Eddy left over $3 million, at her death in 1910, at the age of 89.

◆

Although the Church claims to have had no splinter groups, there have been a number, right from the very beginning.

A close associate of Mary Baker Eddy and a former editor of the *Journal of Christian Science*, Emma Curtis Hopkins, split away in the 1880s to form, along with Charles and Myrtle Fillmore and Ernest Holmes, New Thought, an influential religious movement which combined the ideas of Phineas Quimby and Mrs Eddy. New Thought has itself spawned a wide range of other religions, of which probably the two most significant are the Unity School of Christianity, founded in 1903 by the Fillmores, and Religious Science, founded in 1948 by Holmes. Both have themselves produced a number of offshoots.

Mrs Eddy set up a Board of Directors to run Christian Science after her death, though according to several documentary sources she expected a successor to appear within 50 years, 'the man that God has equipped to lift aloft His standard of Christian Science.'[44] There was a bitter battle of succession in the years after her death. When the Board of Directors gained legal authority from the Massachusetts Supreme Court for their directorship to be self-perpetuating, a splinter group broke away from the Church. One of the directors, John V. Dittemore, left the Board and joined forces with Annie C. Bill, an English Christian Scientist, to proclaim her the successor and to set up the Christian Science Parent Church, which published the *Christian Science Watchman*.

There have also been more recent splinter groups. The Christian Science Parent Church may long have faded away, but the Board of Directors, which still runs the Church in the absence of an accepted successor to Mrs Eddy, continues to be accused of being too authoritarian. The International Metaphysical Association promotes Mrs Eddy's teachings for 'independent' Christian Scientists who have broken away from the main Church. Another group, the United Christian Scientists, broke away in 1975 to protest against the strict rule of the Church leaders.

Part of the problem appears to be the *Church Manual*, in which Mrs Eddy laid down in immense detail, back in 1895, exactly how the Church should be administered, including the order of service which is still followed to the letter today. Many of the by-laws mention Mrs Eddy by name. For example: 'Unless Mrs Eddy requests otherwise, the First Reader of the Mother Church shall occupy, during his term of Readership, the house of the Pastor Emeritus, No. 385 Commonwealth Avenue, Boston' (Article II); 'There shall be a Board of Education, under the auspices of Mary Baker Eddy, President of the Massachusetts Metaphysical College . . .' (Article XXVIII); 'Loyal students who have been taught in a Primary class by Mrs Eddy . . . are eligible to receive the degree of CSD' (Article XXIX).

Mrs Eddy faced a lot of opposition, not all of it from people outside her Church, and the *Church Manual* includes procedures for dealing with this. The section on Discipline, Article XI, Complaints, contains Section 8, 'No Unchristian Conduct': 'If a member of this Church were to treat the author of our textbook disrespectfully and cruelly, upon her complaint that member should be excommunicated. If a member, without her having requested the information, shall trouble her on subjects unnecessarily and without her consent, it shall be considered an offence.'

In the same section, Article VIII, 'Guidance of Members', contains Section 27, 'The Golden Rule': 'A member of The Mother Church shall not haunt Mrs Eddy's drive when she goes out, continually stroll by her house, or make a summer resort near her for such a purpose.'

It is not recorded whether Mrs Eddy intended this rule-book still to be in use, unaltered in a single word, nearly a century after her death.

BELIEFS AND PRACTICES

The Tenets of Christian Science are:

1   As adherents of Truth, we take the inspired word of the Bible as our sufficient guide to eternal Life.
2   We acknowledge and adore one supreme and infinite God. We acknowledge His Son, one Christ; the Holy Ghost or divine Comforter; and man in God's image and likeness.

3   We acknowledge God's forgiveness of sin in the destruction of sin and the spiritual understanding that casts out evil as unreal. But the belief in sin is punished so long as the belief lasts.

4   We acknowledge Jesus' atonement as the evidence of divine, efficacious Love, unfolding man's unity with God through Christ Jesus the Way-shower; and we acknowledge that man is saved through Christ, through Truth, Life and Love as demonstrated through the Galilean Prophet in healing the sick and overcoming sin and death.

5   We acknowledge that the crucifixion of Jesus and his resurrection served to uplift faith to understand eternal Life, even the allness of Soul, Spirit, and the nothingness of matter.

6   And we solemnly promise to watch, and pray for that Mind to be in us which was also in Christ Jesus; to do unto others as we would have them do unto us; and to be merciful, just, and pure.[45]

Like many new variants on Christianity, Christian Science claims to have returned to what Christianity was originally all about: it is 'a church designed to commemorate the word and works of our Master, which should reinstate primitive Christianity and its lost element of healing'.[46] The Church reckons, however, that even the apostles misunderstood the message: 'Jesus' students, not sufficiently advanced to understand their Master's triumph, did not perform many wonderful works until they saw Him after His crucifixion, and learned that he had not died.'[47]

Unlike many new religions, Christian Science doesn't claim that it alone has the truth. 'Although we feel we have the clearest possible idea of this infinite spiritual truth in divine Science,' says Grayson, 'we don't feel we have a monopoly on inspired insights into God's nature, His love, and spiritual reality. Clearly then we accept – and expect! – to find holy people in many ways of life. We sincerely see the ultimate fate of members and non-members alike to be their complete salvation as a result of their realization of God's healing and redeeming love. This comes not through affiliation with our, or any, organization. It comes through the relinquishment of all within oneself which is ungodlike.'

At the heart of Christian Science is its emphasis on spiritual healing. 'The real history of our movement,' says Grayson, 'is the recent restoration and continuation of the Christian record of healing and reformation inaugurated by Christ Jesus and demonstrated by his immediate followers, as recorded with great gusto in the Bible's book of Acts. This healing element of Christianity – lost sight of in the early centuries after the crucifixion of Jesus – was rediscovered by Mary Baker Eddy towards the end of the last century, and has been responsible for countless physical and moral healings since then.'

What distinguishes the Church from others, says Grayson, is 'the commitment to Christian healing and to the direct communion of individual members with God through their own prayers and spiritual understanding. We don't, however, consider we have a monopoly on either of these things, just that the current devotion of Christian Science to both these points is at present unique.'

There is no doubt that Christian Science has over the last century brought a strong new emphasis on spiritual healing, or that through it many thousands of people have been healed, but spiritual healing is by no means as unique to Christian Science as the Church claims. Healings have taken place through the work of evangelists such as John Wesley in past centuries, and it takes only a glance at American television to show that many present-day evangelists also have a healing ministry. Particularly in the last few decades, with the growth of the Charismatic movement within the established Christian Churches, it has become commonplace for an individual or a small group of Evangelical Christians to pray for the healing of someone, and often with success. Over the same period, the Neo-Pagan movement has also laid great emphasis on healing, with equal success.

The difference with Christian Science is that healing is accomplished not by asking God to heal someone of an illness, but by believing that the illness does not exist. We only *think* that we have toothache or flu or cancer. It is an error, a lie, an illusion. Once we accept that it is an illusion, we will be healed.

The basis of the teachings of the Church is simply: God is Spirit and Truth and Love; anything which is not of spirit and truth and love is therefore not of God, and so is not real.

> If God, or good, is real, then evil, the unlikeness of God, is unreal. And evil can only seem to be real by giving reality to the unreal . . .
> The only reality of sin, sickness, or death is the awful fact that unrealities seem real to human, erring belief, until God strips off their disguise. They are not true, because they are not of God.[48]

To counter the obvious objection that the material world – rocks, trees, tables and chairs and our own physical human bodies – is demonstrably real, Christian Scientists say that 'matter is a limited, temporal, and incorrect view of present reality'[49] – a belief which is closer to Buddhism than to Christianity. Illness is clearly not of God; by ceasing to hold our erroneous belief in it, we can accept its unreality and realize that it isn't actually there.

◆

The Church doesn't concentrate only on healing physical illnesses. 'Christian Science healing involves more than mending sick bodies. It heals broken hearts and minds as well as broken homes, and is directly applicable to all of society's ills.'[50] Healing has a much wider sense: 'The word "healing" as used in Christian Science extends to the healing of family and business problems, of social injustices, intellectual limitations, psychological tensions, and moral confusions.'[51] Indeed, according to one book, 'Christian Scientists are not primarily concerned with bodily health; in fact they undoubtedly give far less attention to their bodies than do most people.'[52]

Yet spiritual healing of physical illness is still the distinctive hallmark of Christian Science. Healing is clearly important; so is general health and morality. 'When members join the Christian Science church,' says Grayson, 'they make a commitment to refrain from smoking, drinking alcohol, taking drugs, and from sexual relationships outside of a legal marriage partnership.' Like Mormons, strict members also refrain from drinking tea and coffee.

Christian Scientists:

> feel a spiritual fellowship with all who worship a supreme and righteous Deity . . . Wherever the law of God has been glimpsed and demonstrated in any degree by men of any faith, there is evidence of the essential unity of good. While this is true of non-Christian as well as of Christian religions, it should be noted that Christian Science is rooted wholly in Christianity.[53]

There are, however, some major differences between the theology of mainstream Christianity and that of Christian Science. For example: 'Distinguishing between the human Jesus and his eternal, spiritual selfhood as the Christ, or Son of God, they recognize that the Christ has been expressed in varying degree by good men and women throughout the ages and that Christianity has always reflected a generous portion of the Christ-spirit.'[54]

Jesus was man; the Christ was God's indwelling of him: 'Jesus is the human man, and Christ is the divine idea; hence the duality of Jesus the Christ.'[55] God is Spirit, so the Holy Spirit is not a distinct personage. The Trinity is therefore not a belief of Christian Science. Man is not a sinner: 'The real man is not a suffering, sinning mortal, incomplete or imperfect.'[56] Sin is not real. Hell, like sin and evil and the Devil, is non-existent. The Bible contains thousands of inaccuracies. We have seen some of these beliefs in the chapter on the diversity of early Christian beliefs.

The Christian Science Church does not aggressively recruit new members, in the way that some alternative religions do. It doesn't make it difficult for members to leave, if they wish to. It teaches high moral standards and a very genuine devotion to God, and its healing ministry can only be highly respected.

In common with some of the other religions which began in the nineteenth century, Christian Science has had a declining membership for the last few decades. This is probably due in part to the alleged authoritarian nature of its leaders and the continued use of nineteenth-century rules; but it is probably also because the Church has lost its monopoly on spiritual healing.

JEHOVAH'S WITNESSES

Most people meet Jehovah's Witnesses on their own doorsteps; door-to-door witnessing is an essential part of the religion. Their magazines *Awake!* and *Watchtower* are also well known, as is some idea of their belief in the saving of the 144,000.

The Jehovah's Witnesses are fairly open about their theology, but are rather less forthcoming about their history. Their initial response to our inquiries was to send their booklet *Jehovah's Witnesses in the Twentieth Century*, giving some very general information on their background and beliefs. A detailed letter with both straightforward factual questions and more searching questions asking for their response to criticisms, received the response, 'Although you mention that these questions give us the opportunity to rebut some criticisms made against Jehovah's Witnesses, we do not choose to do this in the way you request,' over the rubber-stamp signature 'Watch Tower B&T Society', together with a copy of *Awake!*.

The questions raised below, therefore, remain unanswered. If there are any errors, they remain uncorrected.

BELIEFS AND PRACTICES

Like many of the new religions which began in the nineteenth century, the Jehovah's Witnesses are a Millennialist Church, believing strongly in the literal return of Christ and the setting up of his kingdom on earth. Initially they believed this would start happening in 1874, and then in 1914; Christ was to return openly, and then it became invisible. Now they say that 1914 'marked the end of the Gentile Times and the beginning of the transition period from human rule to the Thousand Year (Millennial) Reign of Christ'.[57]

Other attempts to set dates – 1920, 1925, 1940, 1975 and 1984 – resulted in disappointment and sometimes loss of members on the one hand, and rapid back-pedalling of the Church leaders and subtle altering of Watchtower books on the other.

Much is made of the 'little flock' of 144,000 who will go to heaven and rule with Christ, while the 'great crowd' of 'other sheep' will remain on earth and be ruled. Critics of the religion have suggested that this careful distinction between two groups of believers (all of them Jehovah's Witnesses) came about only when the total number of Jehovah's Witnesses began to reach 144,000. All the places in heaven have now been filled – depending on the source, by 1931 or 1935. This caused some dissension in the Church when members from the 1930s onwards realized that they stood no chance of becoming one of the chosen few.

In their literature Jehovah's Witnesses give the impression that they are the only variety of Christianity to have any belief in the Last Things. In fact, the broad picture of what they (and most other Millennialist Churches) believe is not too dissimilar to what Evangelical Christians believe about the Second Coming. Some of the details and the exact order of events may be a little different, but not much more so than between any two groups of Evangelicals. It is their unwavering emphasis on God's coming kingdom to the exclusion of most other doctrine, and their persistent attempts to fix the date, that set them apart from most Christian Churches on this subject.

It is actually on other major points of doctrine that they are at odds with traditional Christian beliefs.

Jehovah's Witnesses, like most other Christian offshoots, turn to the Bible to support their beliefs. 'It is of vital importance to them that their beliefs be based on the Bible and not on mere human speculations or religious creeds,' they say.[58] As often happens, their interpretation of the Bible is quite different from traditional Christian teaching. Unlike most other Christian offshoots, the Jehovah's Witnesses have produced their own translation of the Bible, the New World Translation, which tends to support them in their doctrinal differences.

Their name is taken from Isaiah 43:10–12, which twice says, 'Ye are my witnesses, saith the LORD,' or, 'Ye are my witnesses, saith Jehovah,' in the American Standard Version. The word translated 'Lord', usually shown as 'LORD' in the King James Version, is the Jewish name for God, YHWH (written Hebrew did not use vowels), which is sometimes read as Yahweh or Jehovah. The Jews, both in the centuries immediately before Christ and at the time of Christ, were unwilling to pronounce the sacred name of God, and substituted the phrase 'the Lord' instead. Even when the tetragrammaton YHWH appeared in the Scriptures, a Jew would have read it aloud as 'Adonai', meaning 'my Lord'. (Even today, following the same sort of idea, many Jews print the word 'God' as 'G–d'.)

Jehovah's Witnesses claim that Jesus, showing his new relationship with God, named him aloud as Jehovah; most Biblical scholars dispute this. In any case, the rendering of the name as Jehovah is unknown before the twelfth century, according to some authorities, while others say it was not formulated until c. 1520. The pronunciation Jehovah comes from imposing the vowels of 'Adonai' on the consonants YHWH, with Y shifting to J, W shifting to V, and the initial (unvoiced) A of Adonai becoming an E.[59]

Jehovah may be God the Father, but Jesus Christ isn't God the Son; he is the first of God's creations, and he is God's son, but he is inferior to God. This is similar to the fourth-century Arian heresy. Jehovah's Witnesses reject the carefully formulated Trinitarian Nicene and Athanasian creeds as false, man-made doctrine not supported by the Bible. Similarly, the Holy Spirit is not a person of the godhead, but simply a term for God-in-action.

Until the 1930s, Jehovah's Witnesses taught that Christ died on a cross. In 1936 they rejected this and insisted he had died on a stake. The Greek word *stauros* does have the main meaning of 'stake', but it has subsidiary meanings including 'cross'; the Latin word *crux*, meaning 'cross' can also be translated as 'stake', depending on the context. Jehovah's Witnesses have always said that archaeology will eventually back them up. In fact, recent archaeological findings tend to support the usual concept of a cross for executions at the time of Christ.

As well as their Millennialist doctrine and their door-stepping evangelism, Jehovah's Witnesses are known for one other aspect of their beliefs: their refusal to accept blood transfusions. This is on the basis that Jewish law in the Old Testament forbids the eating of blood from living creatures. Jehovah's Witnesses, who see themselves as 'spiritual Jews', believe that they should uphold this law. (On the other hand, 'Sabbath observance was given only to the Jews and ended with Mosaic Law.'[60]) The Church's view on vaccinations and organ transplants has changed several times over the last few decades, but seems to have stabilized – officially – at being a matter for a member's individual conscience, but with a heavy weight of disapproval attached.

Less well known is their refusal to fight in war, apparently on the grounds of not taking up arms for an earthly government, rather than on the moral ground that killing people is wrong. Whatever one's own stance on this subject, their steadfastness of belief in the face of legal persecution has to be admired. But again, their literature implies that they are the only ones to be prosecuted and imprisoned for their beliefs: 'Persecution for preaching has never equalled that visited upon Jehovah's Witnesses. Many hundreds of them were executed in Hitler's concentration camps. To this day Jehovah's Witnesses are under ban in many countries, and in others they are arrested, imprisoned, tortured, and killed. This is all part of the sign Jesus gave.'[61]

One might think that this 'sign' must apply equally to everyone else who has ever been persecuted for their religious beliefs – and that includes members of many other religions over the centuries – but this is not the case. To Jehovah's Witnesses, all traditional Christian Churches, of whatever denomination, are wrong. The Church's second president, 'Judge' Rutherford, followed Charles Taze Russell in regarding anyone who is not a loyal Jehovah's Witness as an 'evil slave'. The ecclesiastical systems, Catholic and Protestant, are under supervision and control of the Devil, and form a part of his visible organization, and therefore constitute the anti-Christ.'[62]

HISTORY

Charles Taze Russell (1852–1916) was brought up in a Congregationalist household in Pittsburgh, Pennsylvania. Like many another Christian teenager he found difficulty with the idea of a God of love condemning countless millions to an everlasting hell of punishment and torment. Studying his Bible, he came to the conclusion that when it speaks of eternal death, that is exactly what it means: Gehenna, Hades and Sheol are simply words for the grave. After death there is nothing – until, for believers, the Second Coming.

Although Russell at the time, and Jehovah's Witnesses today, are loath to admit it, much of their teaching is borrowed from others. Millenarianism was rife in the USA in the second half of the nineteenth century, and Russell was strongly influenced in his beliefs on the Last Things by Jonas Wendell, among others.

Wendell dated the return of Christ at 1874. When nothing much happened in that year, Russell said that God's presence had returned to Earth; his physical return would be in 1914. (This is similar to the line taken by Ellen G. White, founder of the Seventh-day Adventists, when William Miller's date of 1843–4 passed uneventfully: the date was right, but it referred to the 'cleansing of the divine sanctuary' rather than to the physical return of Christ, which would be a little later.)

Russell's theory on the invisible return of Christ, a booklet entitled *The Object and Manner of the Lord's Return*, was first published in 1877, though later editions back date it to 1873 so that Russell could be seen to have avoided Wendell's error in advance. In 1877 he co-wrote a booklet saying that living believers would be 'caught away bodily' in 1878, in what is usually called the Rapture. When that didn't happen either, it was changed to refer to believers who died after 1878 going straight to God, rather than lingering in the grave, as they would have previously.

In 1871 the first issue of *Zion's Watch Tower and Herald of Christ's Presence* was published, and in 1881 the Watch Tower Bible and Tract Society was formed. This is still the official name of the huge publishing operation at the heart of the Jehovah's Witnesses organization.

Over the next 30 years Russell wrote six volumes of *Studies in the Scriptures*, which underlie the theology of the Jehovah's Witnesses. Christian critics of the religion make much of Russell's claim that true understanding of the Bible can come only through these volumes, not through unassisted study of the Bible itself.

> . . . people cannot see the divine plan by studying the Bible by itself . . . if anyone lays the *Scripture Studies* aside . . . and goes to the Bible alone, though he has understood his Bible for ten years, our experience shows that within two years he goes into darkness. On the other hand, if he had merely read the *Scripture Studies* with their references, and had not read a page of the Bible, as such, he would be in the light at the end of two years, because he would have the light of the Scriptures.[63]

Although they still insist on 'directed' Bible study rather than individual reading, Jehovah's Witnesses today tend to play down such claims of Russell. Indeed, they appear to find some things about him an embarrassment they would rather forget. These include his very messy divorce proceedings, which apparently showed him in a rather unfavourable moral light; his claim under oath to understand Greek, and his subsequent inability under cross-examination to identify letters of the Greek alphabet; and the fiasco of 'Miracle Wheat', which was sold by the Watch Tower in 1911 at 60 times the normal price of wheat, with claims of a miraculous yield – and was judged by the courts to be less fruitful than normal wheat.

There is also some embarrassment over failed prophecies: 1874 was forgotten before too long, to be replaced by 1914, when, initially, Christ was supposed to return.

For the origins of prophecy, Russell looked not just to the Bible but also to the measurements of the Great Pyramid at Giza, though these were altered in different editions of *Studies in the Scriptures* to reflect the changes in emphasis from 1874 to 1914. In the 1901 edition of Volume 3, the length of the entrance passage is given as 3,416 inches, 'symbolizing 3,416 years from the above date, BC 1542. This calculation shows 1874 as marking the beginning of the period of trouble.' In the 1923 edition of the same volume the length of the passage is given as 3,457 inches, and 1874 is changed to 1915.[64]

The problem with setting dates, as every Millennialist Church has discovered to its cost, is that eventually the year arrives, and the event doesn't. Now Jehovah's Witnesses admit, 'Not all that was expected to happen in 1914 did happen, but it did mark the end of the Gentile Times and was a year of special significance.'[65]

Russell died in 1916 and was succeeded in 1918, after a very bitter fight, by Joseph Franklin 'Judge' Rutherford (1869–1942). Part of the reason for the dissension was the posthumous publication of the seventh volume of Russell's *Studies in the Scriptures*, which overturned some of the previous prophecies. Around 4,000 members left the religion because of Rutherford, going off to become the Pastoral Bible Institute and the Laymen's Home Missionary Movement, and maintaining Russell's teachings. This left the remaining Church for many years trying to deny any connection at all with Russell.

Rutherford added greatly to the doctrinal writings of the Church. He also coined the famous saying, 'Millions now living will never die', still used today by Jehovah's Witnesses. This is a highly effective advertising slogan, until one realizes that it was first used in 1920; although millions of people alive then are still alive today, the years, as always, are moving steadily on.

As we have seen, the return of Christ was also expected in 1920, 1925, 1940, 1975 and 1984. In 1920 Rutherford wrote that Abraham, Isaac and Jacob would return physically to earth in 1925. A luxurious house was prepared for them, 'Beth-Sarim' in San Diego; in the meantime, Rutherford lived there.

The name 'Jehovah's Witnesses' was adopted in 1931. Rutherford was succeeded in 1942 by Nathan Homer Knorr (1905–77), the former manager of the printing works. Although, unlike his predecessors, Knorr was not a charismatic preacher, he was a tremendous administrator, responsible for the more systematic door-to-door evangelism which has resulted in the growth of the religion over the last few decades. He set up a training school for Jehovah's Witness missionaries, and was also responsible for initiating the movement's own New World Translation of the Bible, largely translated by Frederick Franz (b. 1893), who became president after Knorr's death. The New World Translation is often worded in such a way as to give scriptural support to Jehovah's Witness doctrines: for example, John 1:1 reads '. . . and the Word was a god'. Despite Jehovah's Witness claims to the contrary, most respected Bible scholars, including many of the scholars whom they themselves have quoted as supporting the New World Translation, regard it as a poor translation.

By the time of Knorr's death, the organization's governing body had become much more powerful, taking power away from the president.

After the world didn't come to an end in 1975, a large number of members, including some senior leaders, left the Church. Former members who have since written books about the Church describe it as authoritarian and often uncaring. A recurrent theme is the lack of compassion and support shown to any Witnesses with problems, whether spiritual, emotional or financial.

On the Second Coming, the official position of the Church now is to quote Jesus' warning that no one knows when he will return. 'When someone goes beyond what Jesus said . . . there will be false, or inaccurate, predictions . . .'[66] They now admit that they made a mistake in setting the date for 1914, 1925 or 1975. 'The wrong conclusions were due, not to malice or to unfaithfulness to Christ, but to a fervent desire to realize the fulfilment of God's promises in their own time.'[67] This does not, however, mean any change of emphasis for Jehovah's Witnesses. The next few pages of the same magazine list the usual signs of the times: great wars, food shortages, great earthquakes, disease and crime.

> There can be no question about it. All the things that the Bible foretold would happen during 'the final age' or 'the conclusion of the system of things', are occurring right now. We are seeing true prophecy in the course of fulfilment, and it is vital that we give heed to it . . . There are many who belittle the evidence that Bible prophecies are in the course of fulfilment . . . But today's ridiculors are mistaken. The fact is, *things have changed*. Bible prophecies *are* being fulfilled. The evidence that the end is near is overwhelming.[68]

Jehovah's Witnesses are enthusiastic and sincere missionaries for their faith. All their work is voluntary, and even elders of the Church and members of the governing body are unpaid. The loss of members after 1975 was soon countered; there are now over 4 million Jehovah's Witnesses in over 200 countries around the world.

WORLDWIDE CHURCH OF GOD – AND ITS OFFSHOOTS

The Worldwide Church of God (formerly the Radio Church of God) is best known to most people through its magazine the *Plain Truth*, its radio broadcast *The World Tomorrow* and, for long-time subscribers to the magazine, the names of its founder, Herbert W. Armstrong, and his son Garner Ted Armstrong. A lot has changed in recent years.

Several of the religious movements covered in this book have altered after their founder's death. The Worldwide Church of God is going through that period of re-evaluation as this book is being written. This provides a rare opportunity to be able to observe a Church actually going through this traumatic process of change, hence the length of this entry.

HISTORY

For around half a century the Worldwide Church of God and the name Herbert W. Armstrong were almost synonymous. Like many other Christian offshoots, the

Church was largely sustained by the vision – and the strict authority – of its founder.

Herbert W. Armstrong (1892–1986) was originally an advertising executive. He tried setting up his own business three times, but each time he failed. In the mid-1920s his wife, Loma, was convinced by a friend that the Christian day of worship should be Saturday, the Jewish Sabbath. She also took on some of the other beliefs of the Seventh-day Adventist Church. Armstrong, to prove her wrong, began to study his Bible, and was eventually convinced that she was right.

Obviously he had to join a Saturday-worship Church, but which one of the several available? In the Bible, it seemed, the only name for a group of Christian believers was the Church of God, so Armstrong checked out any denomination, large or small, with that name.

According to him, the Christian Church had lost its way in AD 69 or 70. The mainstream of Christianity had been wrong since then, but there had always been a few, somewhere in the world, who followed the true way. Among these were Constantine of Mananali around AD 650 and Sergius 100 years later. Around AD 1000 there were the Paulicians and Bogomils of Bulgaria, and a preacher called Peter de Bruys in the south of France. Even the Gnostic-influenced Cathars are claimed as forerunners of the Worldwide Church of God. The Waldenses had the truth, and so did the Lollards. There were Sabbatarians in the seventeenth century; one of these, Stephen Mumford, took the true gospel to America in 1664, setting up in Newport, Rhode Island.[69]

The Church's picking out of these particular religious movements and leaders seemed to rest on one or more of four points: their keeping of the Saturday Sabbath; the name 'Church of God'; their rejection of the standard idea of the Trinity; and their persecution by the established Church.

In every case, either mainstream Christianity destroyed the small group of true believers, or the Devil, seeing God's Truth preached, encouraged the beliefs to be watered down or distorted. This was the case in the nineteenth century with the Seventh-day Adventists (see p. 72), some of whom preferred the name Church of God. At a conference in Battle Creek, Michigan, in 1860, Ellen G. White and others voted on the name. Mrs White argued:

> The name Seventh-day Adventist carries the true features of our faith in front, and will convict the enquiring mind . . .
> I was shown that almost every fanatic who has arisen, who wishes to hide his sentiments that he may lead away others, claims to belong to the Church of God. Such a name would at once excite suspicion; for it is employed to conceal the most absurd errors.[70]

A few refused to use the new name. A church based in Stanberry, Missouri (actually one of the earliest churches in the Seventh-day Adventist movement), kept to the name Church of God and retained Saturday worship, but rejected most of the rest of Ellen G. White's theology. This church had a daughter church in Oregon, and this was the one chosen by Mr and Mrs Armstrong in 1927. By 1928 Armstrong was preaching, and in 1931 he was ordained a minister by the Church. In 1933 he gave a series of lectures around Eugene, Oregon, and in 1934 he began the two activities which characterized his Church for the next half-century: *The World Tomorrow* programme on a small, 100-watt local radio station and the *Plain Truth* magazine – 250 copies of a mimeographed sheet.

'The Work from this point grew in power and scope at the rate of 30 per cent per year over the next 35 years.'[71]

Armstrong left the Oregon Church of God when his theology – particularly on British-Israelism (see p. 95) – began to depart from theirs.

Looking back from 30 years later, Armstrong commented on the beginnings of his ministry:

Coincidence? – or DESIGN!

This brings us to a series of almost incredible facts . . .

First, Jesus Christ began His earthly ministry at about age 30. God took away my business, moved me from Chicago, started bringing me to repentance and conversion preparatory to inducting me into His ministry, *when I was 30!*

Second, Jesus began the actual *teaching and training* of His original disciples for carrying HIS GOSPEL to the world in the year 27 AD. *Precisely 100 time-cycles later*, in 1927 AD, He began my intensive study and training for carrying HIS SAME GOSPEL to all nations of today's world . . .

But *that is not all!* Consider further!

More Amazing Parallels!

. . . in the year 31 AD. For exactly one 19-year time-cycle this preaching was confined to the continent where it started – Asia. After *precisely one 19-year time-cycle*, 50 AD, Christ *opened a door* for the apostle Paul to carry the same Gospel to EUROPE! . . .

God first *opened a door* – that of radio and the printing press – for the mass proclaiming of HIS ORIGINAL TRUE GOSPEL *the first week in 1934!* The exact date was January 7, 1934. *Exactly one time-cycle later*, January 7, 1953, God opened wide the massive door of the most powerful commercial radio station on earth, and RADIO LUXEMBOURG began broadcasting Christ's Gospel to EUROPE and Britain!

What startling coincidences! – or *are* they mere coincidences?[72]

(Incidentally, this quotation illustrates Armstrong's usual literary style, with its typographical emphases.)

In 1947 Armstrong expanded into a new area, education, setting up the first Ambassador College in Pasadena, California. This was a Liberal Arts College offering 'the missing dimension in education'. A UK campus was opened near St Albans in 1960, and a third campus in Texas in 1964. Only the Texas campus still exists, now named Ambassador University.

These campuses spared no expense. The Pasadena campus had a magnificent concert hall, sculptures by top artists, fountains, sunken gardens and beautiful buildings. Armstrong believed strongly that only the best was good enough for God. He wore expensive suits and gold watches; in his travels around the world he always stayed in the very best hotels. He also had two private planes.

Yet the *Plain Truth*, the Bible correspondence course and all the other booklets sent out to millions of inquirers were completely free of charge. How was all this financed?

Armstrong believed in the American Dream. He believed in Quality. He preached Success breeding Success. It was a message familiar to, and welcomed by, American middle-class professionals (see p. 235). The principle of his 'Seven Laws of Success', similar to the 'seed-faith giving' of evangelists like Oral Roberts, was that if you give God your best, he will give you His best. Members of the Church (or 'co-workers') regularly gave a tithe, a tenth of their gross income, to the Church. They saved up a second tithe to pay for their attendance at Church festivals, and from time to time there was a third tithe, ostensibly to support needy members. For years the money rolled in, and the presses rolled out millions of copies of the *Plain Truth, The World Tomorrow, The Good News, Youth, Quest* and other magazines and booklets, in many languages.

Quest, like the Unification Movement's *The World & I*, was a glossy news-stand 'magazine of excellence' in the late 1970s. But always, the *Plain Truth* was the public face of the Church. At its height in 1988 it had a worldwide circulation of 5,813,000. Apart from one short period in 1975 when, to save money, it was produced on newsprint and designed to look like a tabloid newspaper, the *Plain Truth* has for many years been a very nicely produced full-colour magazine. *The Good News of Tomorrow's World, The Good News* and *GN* (different titles at different times) were identical in format to the *Plain Truth* but were aimed at co-workers rather than the general public, containing more deeply spiritual articles – and regular articles on the requirement to tithe.

According to an Australian investigator, the Church used powerful psychological techniques to extract more and more money from its co-workers in tithes and 'free-will' offerings. And not all the co-workers were well-to-do.[73]

The *Plain Truth* regularly showed photographs of Armstrong with great world leaders – kings, princes, politicians, prime ministers, presidents. According to some former senior members, these were intended to show Armstrong's importance by the circles in which he regularly moved; but very often, it seems, the great world leaders had no idea who this short, elderly man, asking to be photographed shaking hands with them, was. Garner Ted Armstrong disapproved of his father's many trips, calling them 'the world's most expensive autograph hunt'.[74]

On many occasions Armstrong, as Chancellor of the Ambassador Colleges, effectively 'bought' meetings and photographs by making donations to charitable causes supported by a world leader.

> While I knew his advance man, a Japanese immigrant, was giving away golf clubs, gold pen sets, free trips to the United States, and many other gifts to various of his contacts through Japanese embassies, in order to *buy* my father's way into these various meetings, my father was kept in the dark. Over $900,000 was spent in only one year by my father's advance man, arranging for him to meet various dictators, premiers and presidents, like Jomo Kenyatta, Haile Selassie, and President Marcos . . . I could not help feeling this was a terrible waste of tithe-payers' money.[75]

But so far as readers of *Plain Truth* were concerned, the photographs showed that Herbert W. Armstrong was on close terms with world leaders – and this gave him kudos and credibility.

◆

Herbert W's strong right-hand man, and the voice heard from Radio Luxembourg and many other stations on *The World Tomorrow*, was his son Garner Ted. As Herbert W. grew older, Garner Ted did more of the preaching, and took over more of the responsibility for the Church. But then things began to go wrong:

Six years ago my son Garner Ted and I often said, 'As long as we two stand *back to back* TOGETHER, no one can overthrow God's Church!' How many times we said that! And as for me, *I meant it!*

HOW was that close UNITY broken?[76]

Garner Ted began to fall out with his father. This first happened in 1972, when Herbert W. removed his son from preaching on *The World Tomorrow* for four months. He brought him back when Church revenue fell by 40 per cent. Everything was hushed up as far as possible, though the *Los Angeles Times* reported that Herbert W. had said his son was 'in the bonds of Satan', and that Garner Ted had confessed to having 'sinned against my wife, my children and the Church'.

The year 1972 was a bad one within the Church, though normal (non-member) readers of the *Plain Truth* were not aware of it. Many members believed that the year would be the beginning of the Second Coming, and were disappointed when nothing much happened. (God worked in 19-year cycles; the first began in 1934, with the launching of the *Plain Truth* and *The World Tomorrow*; the second began in 1953, with the expansion of the ministry to Europe; 1972 should have been the beginning of the next step.)

Worse was to come. In 1974 Garner Ted was in trouble again; this time there were allegations of sexual impropriety. At about the same time the Church was riven by internal disputes on two main subjects, the remarriage of divorced members, to which Herbert W. had formerly been opposed, and the dating of the Feast of Pentecost. Long-standing doctrines were being changed. Thousands of members, and some of the most senior ministers, left to found their own Churches. The Church faced public criticism for its practices, particularly Herbert W.'s authoritarian leadership, in the pages of the *Ambassador Report*, a regular newsletter produced by ex-members.

Then in 1978 Garner Ted clashed with his father for the last time, over both organization and doctrine. From Herbert W.'s point of view, Garner Ted had begun 'to water down, liberalize and secularise CHRIST'S TRUE DOCTRINES!' Worse, perhaps, 'I learned that Ted had a somewhat normal attitude of resentment against his father,' and, 'He has accused his father of senility,' and, 'His sole effort has been to DESTROY his father and GOD'S CHURCH, and draw tithe payers after him!'[77]

Unsurprisingly, Garner Ted's version of the dispute is considerably different. He had effectively been running the entire organization for several years, while his father spent up to 300 days a year on his trips. He consulted his father on major decisions, but often, after they had agreed a policy and Garner Ted had implemented it, Herbert W. would suddenly change his mind and countermand his son's actions.

'No, I did not "try to take over," but you gave the reins to me, and then continually snatched them back out of my hands until I was once more in a complete power vacuum – every decision second-guessed and suspect,' wrote Garner Ted in a long and very emotional letter to his father.[78]

In 1977 Herbert W. had major heart problems and nearly died. From then on he became more and more forgetful, and also more prone to falling out with his son. According to Garner Ted, among Herbert W.'s closest aides were several people who deliberately fed his father lies about him, which his father, confused, believed. 'To most, I am viewed as being very conservative, far-to-the-right. But to some who had my father's ear unbeknownst to me, I was being subtly painted as a "liberal".'[79]

This image of Armstrong as an easily manipulated, confused old man is supported by Roderick C. Meredith, formerly one of the Church's most senior evangelists and now leader of the Worldwide Church of God offshoot the Global Church of God:

> He did not know fully what was going on . . . He had been misguided and misinformed. When Mrs Armstrong was alive, she would spot the phonies around him and the bad guys. Once he lost Mrs Armstrong, he tended to have people, and I won't name their names, take advantage of him. As he got older, he couldn't see well or hear well, and those things happened and men took advantage of the situation.[80]

Finally, Herbert W. Armstrong threw his son out of the Church, and this time the rift was permanent. Garner Ted was not only expelled from the Church and forbidden ever to speak to any of its members, he was all but expunged from its records.

Different editions of Volume 1 of the *Autobiography of Herbert W. Armstrong* illustrate this. In the earlier editions, Garner Ted's birth is described thus: 'On the 9th day of February, a Sunday, a future servant and minister of God whose voice was later to be heard around the world, in every continent on earth, was born.' In the 1986 edition the passage reads, 'On the 9th day of February, a Sunday, my second son was born.'[81]

Young Garner Ted didn't speak until he was two and a half, when Herbert W. anointed him and prayed over him. 'Words have been pouring like a torrent out of his mouth ever since, as millions of radio listeners on every continent around the world well know! God *gave* him his voice by an unusual divine miracle. And I am *well pleased* as God was with *His* Son Jesus, that he is now an instrument in God's hands.' The miracle is mentioned in the later edition, but this comment is entirely missing.[82]

In Volume 2, which covers the period from 1938 to Armstrong's death, and which was first published in 1987, there is no mention whatever of Garner Ted's contribution to the work of the Church in the 1960s and 1970s. There is hardly a mention of him in the entire 659-page book, except for a couple of brief moral tales about fishing and smoking when Ted and his elder brother, Dick, were children. In contrast, Dick (who was killed in a car crash in 1958) features prominently in all his work for the (then) Radio Church of God. There is one brief mention in 1959, when Garner Ted made a presentation honouring Mr and Mrs Armstrong on the twenty-fifth anniversary of the beginning of their work – and after that nothing for all the years when Garner Ted was at the very heart of the Church's work.

The public were not so unforgiving, nor so deliberately forgetful. Even years after Herbert W.'s death the Church clearly still received many letters asking after Garner Ted. For some time a printed letter beginning 'Dear Friend, Thank you for your recent inquiry . . .' and signed 'Personal Correspondence Department' stated: 'In the spring of 1978, Mr Herbert W. Armstrong removed his son from all official responsibilities with the Church and its associated institutions. In the judgment of Mr Armstrong and the elders of the Church, Ted Armstrong was not spiritually qualified to continue in the ministry and leadership of the Church.' Attached was Herbert W.'s article from *The Good News*, quoted above.

Garner Ted went off to found his own Church, the Church of God International, in Tyler, Texas, taking with him a considerable number of members of the Worldwide Church of God. He rapidly set up a new radio, television and literature ministry. Explaining why he had to start a completely new organization, he wrote to his father, 'So, if I were going to continue doing God's work and keep His work alive and prevent it from being dragged down and out by the incredible internal scandals, chicanery, politics, backbiting, hatred, rancour, bitterness, vindictiveness, and spite that has become characteristic of so much of the leadership these days, I had to incorporate.'[83] This picture of his former Church is somewhat damning for a Christian organization.

Perhaps not wishing to keep old wounds alive, or perhaps accepting that there may have been faults on both sides, the Worldwide Church of God now says that Garner Ted 'helped his father in the ministry of the Church and with the radio and television program until 1978, after which he founded his own evangelistic association'.[84]

Meanwhile, Herbert W., whose beloved wife, Loma, had died in 1967, married a young divorcée 48 years his junior, Ramona Martin – partly, it seems, to act as hostess on his foreign trips – in 1977. He divorced her in 1984. Neither event was made known to ordinary *Plain Truth* readers.

Herbert W. Armstrong died in 1986, aged 94. He was succeeded as Pastor General, and as Publisher and Editor-in-Chief of the *Plain Truth*, by Joseph W. Tkach, a minister since 1963 and a firm supporter of Armstrong through all the troubles.

◆

Since Armstrong's death the *Plain Truth* has changed in character. In its heyday from the 1960s to the mid-1980s, Armstrong's distinctive style shouted from the articles, whoever wrote them. The two main themes were evolution, which Herbert W. and Garner Ted 'proved' false over and again, and prophecy, which was the central message of the Church's teachings. There were books and booklets entitled *The Wonderful World Tomorrow: What It will be Like*, *The United States and Britain in Prophecy* and *1975 in Prophecy*. We were in the End Times; Christ would return and set up his earthly kingdom very soon.

Now there is little in the *Plain Truth* which would be out of place in any conservative Christian magazine. The emphasis is on right living, on family values, on trusting God. There is no mention of unusual doctrines or of the Worldwide Church of God having the only truth. The italics, capital letters and exclamation marks have vanished. The magazine has become, in a word, bland.

On 16 May 1995 *Plain Truth* subscribers in the UK were shocked to receive a letter saying that the magazine would no longer be sent to them each month. The head office in Pasadena had ceased to provide 'a substantial subsidy'; the UK Church, already much slimmed down from its earlier glory, couldn't cope with the increased financial burden.

What had changed?

BELIEFS AND PRACTICES

Unlike many other new religious movements, the Worldwide Church of God has always been upfront about its beliefs. Every issue of the *Plain Truth* mentioned booklets which readers could send for, free of charge, on a wide variety of doctrinal subjects.

In the last few years, many of the Church's beliefs have been modified, though one or two of the fundamental points are still there. Some of these have already been mentioned. The Church still believes in the Saturday Sabbath, though its former insistence on this as a mark of the true Christian has been greatly watered down: 'Though physical Sabbath keeping is not required for Christians, it is the tradition and practice of the Worldwide Church of God to hold its weekly worship service on the seventh-day Sabbath (Saturday).'[85]

The other main practice which still exists is the Church's observance of the Old Testament feastdays. At one time this was compulsory. Now, says Joseph W. Tkach,

> The festivals are not biblically required for Christians. They are not a means of salvation; rather, they point to Jesus Christ, the real means of our salvation. For Christians, the festivals serve as memorials of God's miraculous work of redemption and sanctification through his Son, and celebrations of thanksgiving and anticipation of the glorious future inheritance that awaits believers at Christ's return.[86]

But most of the old hallmarks of the Church have gone. Armstrong preached British-Israelism, the belief that the dispersed 'Lost Ten Tribes' of Israel migrated to Europe, and in particular that biblical prophecy about the tribes of Ephraim and Manasseh referred specifically to Britain and the USA.

The theory was not original to Armstrong. It was clearly propounded by a Scot, John Wilson, in 1840, and can be traced back a couple of centuries before that. But Armstrong, having embraced it, made it his own. The *Plain Truth*, *The World Tomorrow* radio programme and numerous books preached this message over and over again.

The people (Hebrew *iysh*) of the covenant (*beriyth*) became the *British* people; Isaac's sons became the Saxons; the tribe of Dan (remembering that written Hebrew doesn't use vowels) passed through or settled in, among many others, Mace*don*ia, the Dar*dan*elles, the rivers *Dan*ube, *Dn*ieper, *Dn*iester and *Don*, and came to the British Isles, which has in Ireland *Don*egal, Lon*don*derry and *Din*gle, in Scotland *Dun*dee, *Dun*kirk and E*din*burgh, and in England, of course, Lon*don*.[87]

In addition, James VI of Scotland and I of England was a direct descendant of the royal line of Israel. The Stone of Scone was the stone which Jacob used as a pillow (Genesis 28:18), and was carried to Ireland by Jeremiah in 569 BC. The tribes of Ephraim and Manasseh, Joseph's sons, eventually became the peoples of Britain and the USA, and all the biblical prophecies about them refer to these great countries in the present day.[88]

This is only the briefest of summaries. Accepting a few initial premises and making a few conceptual leaps, the theory, considered in far more depth, has an appealing apparent logic for English-speaking Westerners. Until recently Britain had been for centuries a great world power, and many Americans tend to regard themselves as the Chosen People.

Unfortunately for British-Israelites, independent historians have always dismissed the entire theory as completely false, but this did not stop Armstrong making it the very heart of his message. It enabled him to apply biblical prophecies to Britain, the fledgeling European Community and the USA, particularly with regard to the End Times.

But now,

after having carefully researched the tenets and history of its belief that the United States and Britain are the descendants of the ancient Israelite tribes of Manasseh and Ephraim, the Worldwide Church of God no longer teaches this doctrine. While it may be an interesting theory, there is simply a lack of credible evidence, either in the biblical account or the historical record, to support a conclusion regarding the modern identity of the lost ten tribes of Israel. We recognize that there were hermeneutical and historical inaccuracies in the Church's past understanding of this issue.[89]

The central plank of Herbert W. and Garner Ted Amstrong's prophetic teaching for several decades has been discarded completely.

On Herbert W.'s 'startling coincidences' between the beginnings of the Early Church's ministry and his own, a spokesman for the Worldwide Church of God said in 1995, 'Regarding 19-year time cycles, we no longer have any formal statements or beliefs on this particular topic.'[90]

For decades Armstrong preached that Christ would return very soon. Like the Jehovah's Witnesses, he pointed to the 'signs of the times': drastic changes in the weather, drought, wars, famines, pestilences. His booklet *1975 in Prophecy* did not say definitively that Christ would return by that year, but it did say, speaking of a major drought, 'The indications of prophecy are that this drought . . . will strike *sooner* than 1975 – probably between 1965 and 1972! This will be the very *beginning*, as Jesus said, of the Great Tribulation!'[91] Throughout the booklet he emphasizes the imminence of the Great Tribulation: 'But again, I repeat – IT'S LATER THAN YOU THINK! . . . All this is now only a few years off.'[92]

Again, it depended on God's 19-year cycles. In the 1967 edition of his *Autobiography*, Armstrong says, 'Today, we are now almost eight years (written in November 1959 – but, as published December 1967, almost 15 years) into the *second* and *last* remaining 19-year cycle!'[93]

Although he immediately stresses that 'the year 1972 by no means is indicated as the year of Christ's return', many members came to believe that the Second Coming would be in 1972.

Looking back through its own history, the Church now says,

In the 1970s, growth continued, but at a slower pace, as the Church learned important lessons about avoiding predictive prophecies. Christ did not return as expected, but he did lead the Church to a deeper understanding of the Bible.[94]

The other great passion of both Herbert W. and Garner Ted was debunking evolution. They and their associates wrote dozens of gloriously illustrated articles, many of them reprinted as full-colour A4 booklets, 'proving' conclusively that evolution was a false doctrine. Titles included *Some FISHY STORIES About an Unproved Theory*, *The Amazing Archer Fish Disproves Evolution!*, *A Theory for the Birds* and *A WHALE of a TALE, or The Dilemma of Dolphins and Duckbills!*. Now the Church says:

We have firm confidence in the inspired declaration of Genesis 1:1, 'In the beginning God created the heavens and the earth.' We do not deny, however, evidence from science that indicates a long history of life on this planet. We

Above Abdu'l-Bahá
(1844–1921),
Bahá'u'lláh's son and
successor as leader of
the Bahá'í faith.

Above Ellen G. White
(1827–1915), founder of
the Seventh-day
Adventist Church.
*(Stamborough Press
Picture Library)*

Right Mary Baker
Eddy (1821–1910),
founder of the Church
of Christ, Scientist.
(Alan Grayson)

Left Two Hindu gods, Chaitanya and Nityananda, in a Hare Krishna procession. *(B. D. Das)*

Below The ISKCON Temple in Durban, South Africa.

Right The Temple of ECK at Chanhassen, Minnesota, USA.

Above Members of Osho International meditating in the walkway.

Left Osho (1931–90), formerly Bhagwan Shree Rajneesh, founder of Osho International.

Below Maitreya appearing to 6,000 people in Nairobi, Kenya, on 11 June 1988.

Above Paul Twitchell (?1909–71), founder of ECKANKAR.

Above Krishna and Arjuna, a sculpture by
Nathan David FRBS for the School of Economic
Science.

Left The Chart of Your Real Self, from the Church Universal and Triumphant. The upper figure is the I AM presence, or God; the middle figure is the Holy Christ Self, or Higher Consciousness; the lower figure shows the soul evolving through the four planes of matter.

Right Waterkin (members) of the Church of All Worlds at their 1990 reunion. Founder Oberon Zell is at the front left; the unicorn is also called Oberon.

Above Druids at a ceremony at Stonehenge include the Arch Druid of the Insular Order of Druids (holding Y staff), the Head of the Loyal Arthurian Warband (Arthur Pendragon, holding straight staff), the Arch Druid of the Glastonbury Order (wearing black cloak, at right) and members of the Druid Clan of Dana. The banner is of the Insular Order.
(Sandra D for the Insular Order of Druids)

Left Member of the Emin practising Electrobics in Trafalgar Square, London.

Below Maharishi Mahesh Yogi (b. 1911 or 1918), founder of the Transcendental Meditation movement. (*Maharishi Foundation*)

do know that only God can create life, and that the Creator has not revealed exactly how he has done this. Therefore we do not presume to speak for him on this subject.[95]

One of the most fundamental changes in belief is on the Trinity. For years the Church taught that the concept of the Trinity was invented in the first few centuries of Christianity. It limited God to three persons instead of the 'family' which Armstrong taught: 'By that doctrine, along with others, Satan has DECEIVED all traditional Christianity.'[96] Jesus is God, but the Holy Spirit is simply the power of God, an It rather than a He.

Now, however, 'The triune nature of God is an essential part of Worldwide Church of God doctrine,'[97] and the Holy Spirit is 'the third Person of the Godhead'.[98]

Although the Church always denied that it taught salvation by works, critics pointed to statements like: 'We are not justified BY THE LAW – we are justified by the blood of Jesus Christ! But this justification will be given only on Condition that we REPENT of our transgressions of God's Law – and so it is, after all, only the DOERS of the Law that shall be JUSTIFIED.'[99]

Now the Church says that it 'teaches that salvation is the gift of God, by his grace, through faith in Jesus Christ, not earned by personal merit or good works'.[100]

The Church has always been literature-oriented. Now it is having to rewrite all its literature. Herbert W. Armstrong's own books and booklets are no longer distributed, including the ones he himself considered his most significant works, *The United States and Britain in Prophecy*, *The Wonderful World Tomorrow: What It will be Like*, *The Incredible Human Potential* and, his final book, *Mystery of the Ages*, which he described as 'the largest and most important book of my life. In real fact I feel I myself did not write it. Rather, I believe God used me in writing it. I candidly feel it may be the most important book since the Bible . . . I am now in my 94th year and I feel that this book is the most valuable gift I could possibly give to you.'[101]

According to Garner Ted Armstrong, however, *Mystery of the Ages* was simply a rehash of earlier works, including portions of *The Wonderful World Tomorrow: What It will be Like*, which he had co-written with his father.

How surprised I was to see page after page, major portions of whole chapters, of my father's book, *Mystery of the Ages*, containing word-for-word excerpts from my half of that booklet.

While millions had been told my father had written a new book; imagined him, as a ninety-one or ninety-two-year-old man sitting there pounding away on a typewriter, the truth was that his books were pieced together from dozens of his old co-worker and member letters, booklets and articles, with various inserts and new material added to tie it all together. While my name does not appear as co-author of *Mystery of the Ages* I am, in fact, a co-author![102]

Armstrong died four months after *Mystery of the Ages* was published. Not much more than a year after that, Joseph Tkach had set in motion a doctrinal and a literature review.

Garner Ted Armstrong's Church of God, International, meanwhile, remains loyal to the beliefs which both Armstrongs taught for so many years. The British-

Israelite doctrine, for example, has been repackaged in Garner Ted's *Europe and America in Prophecy*.

♦

The Worldwide Church of God is honest and open about the changes in the doctrine: 'The Church needs to be prepared to make whatever changes necessary as its understanding of the Word of God increases.'[103] The 1995 edition of its *Statement of Beliefs* contains several rewordings from the 1993 edition, mainly indicating changes of emphasis. The Introduction says, 'This Statement of Beliefs does not constitute a closed creed. The Church constantly renews its commitment to truth and deeper understanding and responds to God's guidance in its beliefs and practices.'

It is strongly implied that there are more changes to come. The Church seems to be putting its past firmly behind it; it is apparent that what it believes today and what it will believe tomorrow are what count, not what it believed yesterday. It was loath to provide a list showing changes in belief on various subjects.

'I'll explain what we are trying to accomplish in terms of a lot of "folklore" that attached itself to our teachings in the past,' says the spokesman. 'If a topic is not formally documented in our *Statement of Belief* or not mentioned in our current Church literature, then it may be that we have no corporate beliefs on that subject.'

This process has not been easy for the Church. 'Changes in doctrine have caused a certain amount of upset in the Church. This would be true of any Church making major changes in their teachings,' says the spokesman. This is, perhaps, something of an understatement.

Some of the main criticisms of the Church in the past centred on its legalism, its strict observance of Old Testament law, and its teaching of salvation through a combination of faith and works. This appears to be the main change, from which many others are following: 'He has called us out of the old covenant, which Paul compares to slavery (Galatians 4:21–31), and into the more glorious new covenant,' says Tkach.[104]

The Church of God, International, however, sticks firmly to the Sabbath teaching, the requirement to observe the Old Testament feastdays – and the Old Covenant. One of Garner Ted's booklets is entitled *The New Covenant: Does It Do Away with God's Law?*. 'It is . . . ironic,' says Garner Ted, who was accused by his father of liberalizing the Church's doctrines, 'that the parent Church has become involved in many significant doctrinal changes which are *far more "liberal" than I ever thought of being!*'[105]

The changes have caused ructions in the Worldwide Church of God. There have been 'cliques and divisions, struggles for influence,' says Tkach. 'I accept some of the blame. Like all our long-term ministers, in a sincere desire to serve God faithfully, I too used to teach things that Christ has now shown me are not accurate. And brethren, for that I apologize to all . . .'[106]

Some have not been able to accept the change.

'Several of our full-time ministers have decided to step down from their pastoral duties due to their inability to lead their congregations out of the Church's historical legalism. I greatly appreciate the integrity of some of these men, who recognized their limitations and for the sake of unity in the Body of Christ, stepped aside until such time as they can fully understand and teach new covenant Christianity. I am sad for others, who are the minority as far as we can tell, who have become angry at the Church's spiritual growth and have decided to try to convince our members to follow them back into compelled Sabbath and Holy Day observance . . . Any way you look at it, this is a stressful time for the Worldwide Church of God. It is painful for all of us to set aside long-cherished beliefs and ideas. But God is always faithful, even though His children have growing to do. In His grace towards us, our Lord is bringing us out of the Egypt of legalism and into his promised land, the *true rest* of faith in our Saviour,' says Tkach.[107]

Income has plummeted – partly because many members, told that there is no longer a *requirement* for them to tithe 10 per cent of their income to the Church, have stopped giving anything at all. At the beginning of 1995 the Church had to lay off hundreds of employees. 'Unfortunately, we can barely meet the payroll we have now . . . Our financial situation is serious. We are trying to sell some property to cover our deficiencies, but I honestly don't know if we will be able to do enough,' says Tkach.[108]

Joseph W. Tkach died of cancer in September 1995. He was succeeded as leader of the Church by his son, 'Joe Jr'. According to Peter Nathan, UK office manager of the Worldwide Church of God offshoot the United Church of God,[109] Joe Jr had effectively been running the Worldwide Church of God for some years, under the figurehead of his sick father – a close parallel to the Armstrongs. The difference is that Joe Jr was not ousted; indeed, according to Nathan, he was the one to push through the changes in the Church so rapidly.

◆

At the time of writing, the Worldwide Church of God is trying to rebuild itself. Whether it will succeed, only time will tell.

As the doctrinal changes continue, the Church is getting closer and closer to mainstream Christian beliefs. The ultimate seal of conservative Evangelical approval came at Joseph W. Tkach's funeral, when Hank Hanegraaff, president of the US cult-watching organization the Christian Research Institute, embraced Joe Jr. In a Christian Research Institute newsletter dated 6 October 1995, Hanegraaff likened the transformation of the Church, 'from the status of a cult' to its present position, to the collapse of the Berlin Wall.

In rewriting their doctrines – and in turning their back on their founder's teachings and on everything that made their Church distinctive – the Worldwide Church of God has become almost indistinguishable from traditional Christianity, which Armstrong, right up to the end, condemned as 'counterfeit' and 'deceived by Satan'. 'What about those, in such churches, who profess being "born-again Christians"? They are DECEIVED! They may be ever so sincere. They do not know they are deceived and wrong in their beliefs.'[110]

◆

The Worldwide Church of God rarely bothered about having its own church buildings, preferring to rent halls for services. Without the complication of who owns local bricks and mortar, some congregations, loyal to the memory and teachings of Herbert W. Armstrong, have already broken away to form new Churches, with the old beliefs. Two main ones have formed during the recent troubles.

The Global Church of God was founded after senior evangelist Roderick C. Meredith was fired from the Worldwide Church of God in 1992. He had been about to leave in any case. 'One young smart aleck . . . one of their leaders, he said, "Mr Armstrong gave the whole Church a bucket of lies!" . . . When I realized that was their attitude, that those changes were heading in a total opposite direction from everything we had proved was the truth, then I knew it was time to leave.' He is now Presiding Evangelist of the Global Church of God, which currently has around 7,500 full members and is a conscious re-creation of the Worldwide Church of God. 'All our major doctrines are the doctrines extant under Mr Armstrong at his death in January 1986.'

The United Church of God, founded in May 1995, holds the former Worldwide Church of God beliefs but accepts that many of the problems of the parent Church stemmed from the form of leadership. It is carefully avoiding a hierarchical structure, aiming for more of a collegiate organization, says Peter Nathan. At present it appears to be closer to an association of linked congregations than a Church, though it does have paid ministers, which Garner Ted Armstrong's Church of God, International, has until now preferred not to have. The United Church of God has around 20,000 full members in Australia, South Africa, North, Central and South America, the UK and Europe. (See p. 299, note 4.)

Whether any of these, or other Worldwide Church of God offshoots, will eventually merge is an open question. Meredith regards 'other Seventh-day Churches of God, who are keeping the Sabbath and the Holy Days', as brethren, and hopes that 'God will bring together the vast majority of everyone who is faithful and zealous . . . together in one place to do one Work before it's all finished.' But he seems unlikely to join up with Garner Ted Armstrong and some other offshoots. 'I sincerely felt that some of those people had actually been put out of the Church (disfellowshipped) for very good reason. Some of these groups left while Mr Armstrong was still alive, still doing the work and still preaching the truth, and were in fact disfellowshipped properly, and I felt I had no reason to join disfellowshipped members, who left at a time that they should not have left, and left in a spirit of rebellion.'

◆

Thousands of Worldwide Church of God members have left to form new Churches holding to the old ways. It is possible that members of these Churches may together eventually outnumber those remaining in the parent Church. It is probable that some other individual ministers and members, accepting the 'New Covenant' teachings, may simply drift into other Christian Churches. Those loyal to the Church as it is now are likely to become fewer and fewer, consequently generating even less income to sustain the formerly huge organization.

A telling indicator is that circulation of the flagship magazine *Plain Truth* is now below a million, less than a sixth of what it was in 1988.

'Formerly we emphasized the role of media in communicating the Gospel,' says the Church's spokesman in explanation; 'now we have opted more for personal evangelism, open houses at our services and small group meetings. Since our practical needs are not the same, we have downsized our media operations considerably and the decline in our corporate income is partially a consequence of this basic change in method and philosophy.'

The Worldwide Church of God has changed almost beyond recognition since Herbert W. Armstrong died. He would not know his own Church today. It is ironic that among those keeping his teachings alive is the son whom he banished.

THE UNIFICATION CHURCH (THE MOONIES)

The Unification Church is officially known as the Holy Spirit Association for the Unification of World Christianity. Unofficially, its members are known as the Moonies (after their founder Sun Myung Moon), a term they dislike partly because of the bad 'cult' publicity associated with it in the late 1970s and early 1980s and partly because of the connotations of its rhyming with 'loonies'. In the mid-1990s they are very anxious to play down these images and to present themselves as a spiritually, morally, socially and culturally sound Christian Church.

HISTORY

The Rev. Sun Myung Moon was born as Yong Myung Moon in what is now North Korea in 1920. ('Reverend' is a term of respect for Moon; he has no formal theological training. Within the Church he is usually known as Father, and his wife, Hak Ja Han, as Mother.) When he was ten or 11 his family converted from their native Confucianism to Presbyterianism. At the age of 16 he had a vision of Jesus Christ, who told him he must further the building of God's kingdom on earth. He spent the next nine years in prayer and intensive study of the Bible, during which time he came to a completely different understanding of Christian theology.

During the Second World War he studied electrical engineering in Japan. He began preaching in 1945 in South Korea. In 1948 he changed his name to Sun Myung Moon, meaning 'Shining, Bright, Word', and moved back to North Korea, where the communist authorities imprisoned him for two and a half years; this probably cemented his fervent opposition to communism. He was liberated by UN troops in 1950 and resumed preaching. Apparently he had no intention of starting up a new Church, but his reinterpretation of Christianity was so radical that the mainstream Churches would not accept his teachings, so in 1954 he founded the Holy Spirit Association for the Unification of World Christianity, usually known as the Unification Church.

There is some confusion about how many times Moon has been married: two, three or even four. According to George Robertson, spokesman for the Unification Church in the UK, Moon's first marriage ended in divorce, and a later engagement failed to work out; Hak Ja Han, whom he married in 1960, is thus his second wife. They have had 13 children, one of whom has died.

In 1966 he published the text *Discourse on the Principle*, which was translated into English in 1973 as *Divine Principle*. 'While this text doesn't contain the whole revelation given Reverend Moon, it is regarded as the official teaching of the Unification Church.'[111] It is unclear whether this means that some of the revelation is for the moment being withheld from the world, or that there are further teachings not yet translated and published.

Three missionaries were sent to the USA in 1959 and the first church was established in 1961 in Berkeley, California. The Church, known as the Unified Family, grew slowly during the 1960s, despite several visits by Moon, and it was not until he moved to New York State in 1972 that it really began to pick up. In the next four years membership grew from a few hundred to around 6,000.

Progress was similarly slow in Britain. The Church was given charitable status in 1968, but it was not until 1978, when Moon sent 800 missionaries to Britain as the One World Crusade, that communities began to be set up all over the country, high streets began to see young flower-sellers in profusion (though flower-selling had been happening since 1973), and the controversy began.

The Church became the prime focus of attention of the anti-cult movements, at times even more so than the Children of God, the Hare Krishna movement and the Scientologists. Most of the usual charges against 'cults' were levelled against the 'Moonies'.

Young recruits were sent out on the streets selling flowers or candles, partly to bring in money for the Church, partly as a form of disciplinary training and partly to find new recruits. According to the cult-watchers, it was common for these recruits to spend many hours trying to reach the targets they had been set, then return to their communal homes often very late at night and work out their accounts before stumbling to bed. In the morning they might rise at 5 a.m. to perform some 'condition', a form of penance or self-denial – sometimes praying for others for a set time, sometimes taking cold showers for a week – before going out on the streets again. And however they felt, they had to look happy and enthusiastic.

On the streets they often didn't tell people they were from the Unification Church, saying they were raising money for a charity – which was quite true; what the Press labelled 'Heavenly Deception' was permissible in the service of the higher Truth. New recruits brought into a community would be 'love-bombed', hugged, surrounded by care and attention. For people in their late teens and early twenties, with all the usual personal and social problems, this in itself could be both wonderful and utterly disorienting.

For those living in the communities, lectures, study sessions and worship might go on for hours, late into the night or early morning. Meanwhile, said the cult-watchers, food was often minimal and low in protein; and discipline was strict, with 'conditions' imposed for any infringements – such as failing to achieve their targets or failing to look happy and enthusiastic. This was the basis for accusations of sleep deprivation, indoctrination, brainwashing and authoritarianism.

This was the popular image of the Moonies, regularly bolstered by the press and the anti-cult movements. George Robertson accepts that some (though not all) of it was true, but puts it down to the youthful enthusiasm and zeal typical of any new convert, and to some extent to the immaturity of both the organization and the leaders of individual communities. 'We have learned that this is perhaps not the best way to present ourselves to the world. Now we're more careful; we've grown up.' In any case, he says, most members are now married with families, living in their own homes, so since there are very few communities of that sort any more, such complaints are no longer relevant.

In 1980 the Church sued the *Daily Mail* for libel for describing it in such unfavourable terms. After a long and very expensive court case, the Church lost. Although Robertson can't brush that decision to one side, he points out that this was the only court case involving the Church in Britain. Also, the Attorney General spent four years investigating the Church and eventually concluded in 1988 that it should be allowed to continue as a registered charity. Court cases in the USA, he says, tend to be brought by individuals, usually ex-members, with a personal complaint.

Not all of them. In 1982, Moon was prosecuted for non-payment of taxes on the interest on his personal bank account; he was fined $13,000 and imprisoned for 13 months. Moon had argued that although the money was in his personal account, it was actually the Church's money and so tax-exempt. The prosecution was regarded as unfair by many other Christian Churches.

These are not the only charges which opponents have made against the Church. It has several times been criticized for its support of right-wing politicians, including General Garcia Mesa in Bolivia, General Gustavo Alvarez in the Honduras and Jean-Marie Le Pen in France. Robertson says that when the Church realized what such people actually stood for, it withdrew its support. To the outsider it seems that Moon's acknowledged hatred of communism has persistently led the Church, somewhat naïvely, to swing to the opposite extreme.

It has also been criticized for its numerous businesses, presumably on the grounds that God and Mammon shouldn't be mixed. The Church owns companies involved in pharmaceuticals, ginseng, titanium, manufacturing and military equipment; the last is quite simply because in South Korea, under permanent threat from North Korea, all manufacturing companies must produce some weaponry. It also owns the *Washington Times*, 'a characteristically right-wing paper,' according to Robertson; the editor and most of the staff are not Church members, and the paper has 'complete editorial freedom'. After several years of heavy subsidy, it is now standing on its own financial feet. The reason for all the business involvement is twofold: first, 'one should seek to bring Christian values into every aspect of life'; and second, it brings in useful money which finances the Church's evangelistic, humanitarian and cultural work.

Another criticism, similar to 'Heavenly Deception', is that the Church (or rather, the Unification Movement, which is wider than the Church) hides behind a large number of 'front' organizations which rarely state their origins openly. These include major international conferences and symposia in science, peace and religion, run by bodies such as the International Conference on the Unity of the Sciences and the Professors' World Peace Academy ('which discusses strategies to create a harmonious, peaceful world'), both promoted by the movement's International Cultural Foundation; and the New Ecumenical Research Association and the International Conferences for Clergy, both promoted by the movement's International Religious Foundation.

Robertson argues that all this is more a case of influence than subversion. 'We want to help transform the world,' he says, 'and you can't do that by sitting on your backside.' In any case, he says, most of the people at these conferences do know about the involvement of the Unification Church; there is nothing clandestine about it. 'We have learned that you do that at great cost; it doesn't accomplish anything except make people feel they've been duped, and make them angry.'

In addition to these, which tend to be academic or clergy-oriented, the Unification Movement is involved in cultural promotion. Probably the best-known outlet is the Little Angels of Korea dance troupe of 7–15-year-olds, which has performed worldwide, including before Queen Elizabeth II in 1972. The movement is also responsible for the Universal Ballet Company in Korea and a ballet school in Washington, DC. It owns a recording studio in Manhattan and sponsors the New York City Symphony Orchestra.

The Church also operates the International Relief Friendship Foundation, which has provided medical supplies, materials and help in more than 20 countries struck by war, natural disaster or famine, and sponsors medical missionaries in Kenya and Zaire.

In this context, Robertson quotes General Booth, founder of the Salvation Army: 'Soup, Song and Salvation'. The welfare, cultural and academic activities of the Church are all a wider part of spreading the message, without ramming it down people's throats – 'to entertain, to serve, and for PR,' says Robertson; 'there's nothing covert about it.'

The Church runs the Unification Theological Seminary in Barrytown, in upstate New York. In keeping with the original 'unification of world Christianity' idea, both the teaching and the teachers are multi-faith, including a Greek Orthodox theologian and a Jesuit priest; only 20 per cent of the faculty are members of the Unification Church. Although the Church has no ordained priesthood, people who have been to the seminary may call themselves Reverend if they wish.

◆

There are now around a quarter of a million members of the Church worldwide, mainly (in order) in South Korea, Japan, the USA (10,000), South America and Europe. Astonishingly there are only about 500 fully committed members in the UK, plus another 700 more peripherally involved in the Unification Movement. Why so few?

'It's a question we ask ourselves,' says Robertson. Over the years several thousand have been to Church seminars, and many people have joined the Church for a few years and then left, as in any Church. 'There's quite a turnover of membership. Living a seriously religious life is quite a difficult thing to do – a challenging lifestyle.' Even so, he seems to think the Church ought to be doing better in the UK. 'There are probably many lessons we have to learn as an organization.'

Sun Myung Moon is still actively involved in the Church he founded, and at 76 remains in good health. In the event of his death it is expected that the leadership will pass to his wife, with the support of the senior members of the Church, who are mostly Korean.

BELIEFS AND PRACTICES

Although it has moved a very considerable distance from mainstream Christian beliefs, the Unification Church still calls itself Christian. 'A Christian is someone who believes in Jesus as the Messiah (Christ anointed), who is one with God, and who makes Jesus the absolute standard for one's own life of faith,' says Robertson. 'Unificationists are Christian and so is Rev. Moon. After all, he was commissioned by Jesus Christ and has been striving to realize his will all of his life.' However, the differences from traditional Christian beliefs are quite major.

The Unification Church believes the Judaeo-Christian Bible to be inspired by God, though it does not regard it as word-for-word infallible; the Bible was written down, copied and edited by fallible men, each with their own motivations. Given equal weight to the Bible as 'a further revelation' is Moon's own book, *Divine Principle.*

> Knowing that no one can find the ultimate truth to save mankind without
> going through the bitterest of trials, he fought alone against myriads of Satanic

forces, both in the spiritual and physical worlds, and finally triumphed over them all. In this way, he came in contact with many saints in Paradise and with Jesus, and thus brought into light all the heavenly secrets through his communion with God.

The Divine Principle revealed in this book is only part of the new truth. We have recorded here what Sun Myung Moon's disciples have hitherto heard and witnessed. We believe with happy expectation that, as time goes on, deeper parts of the truth will be continually revealed. It is our earnest prayer that the light of truth will quickly fill the earth.[112]

Divine Principle covers, among much else, the purpose of creation, the real meaning of the Fall of man, a discussion of the life, work and death of Jesus, a detailed study of the history of religion from the time of Joseph right up to the present day, and an explanation of how, when and where Christ will return: as a physical man, born after the First World War, in Korea.

Until recently, although his followers always believed him to be the Messiah, Moon himself avoided answering the question directly, much as Jesus did ('Whom do men say that I am?' [Mark 8:27]). In 1992, however, he made a formal declaration that he was indeed the Messiah. Moon is not, however, God – and neither was Jesus.

The doctrine of the Church can be summed up under the headings the 'Principles of Creation', the 'Fall of Man' and the 'Principles of Restoration'. *Divine Principle* is 536 pages long, but it is possible to summarize its main teachings fairly briefly.

> God's original plan was for men and women to grow to maturity, developing a perfect relationship of love with God. Based on this spiritual maturity, all people would come to love one another as brothers and sisters . . . God-centred men and women would enter into the most intense give and take of love in the family . . . Children born to such families would experience the love of God directly from their own parents, and would themselves develop a mature love of God. The love generated in this kind of family would then be multiplied to the society, nation and world.[113]

That was the plan. It didn't happen, because of the Fall of man. The story of the Fall is at the centre of the theological differences between Unification belief and mainstream Christianity. The angel Lucifer, placed in the Garden of Eden to serve the first two people, falls in love with Eve. He tempts her and they have sex together (the 'fruit' is a symbol of sexuality). Eve, repenting her sin, tells Adam what she has done, and then has sex with him to try to put things right, when at that stage in their relationship they should still be living as brother and sister, not husband and wife. Adam and Eve had misused their love and became separated from God. 'Due to the Fall, the bond between man and God was broken, resulting in a long history of grief to man and his Creator.'[114]

According to Robertson, the Church accepts the literal existence of the original couple, though whether their names were actually Adam and Eve (Hebrew for man and woman) is doubtful.

God sent prophets to guide his people back to him. The original, ideal trinity is redefined by the Church as God, man and woman united in perfect, unsullied love. This was lost because of what happened in the Garden of Eden, so that the fallen trinity is Satan, man and woman. Jesus did not come to the earth to be crucified; he came as the Messiah to re-create the lost ideal. The plan was that he should marry and have children, re-establishing the ideal trinity through his ideal family, for all mankind. Again the plan was thwarted. Instead of that happening, he was not recognized as who and what he was, and was crucified. His resurrection brought only partial salvation to mankind.

> After the crucifixion, God gave Jesus the Holy Spirit as a mother spirit, or feminine spirit, to work with the risen Christ in Eve's place. Making restitution for Eve's part in the Fall, the Holy Spirit inspires and comforts the human heart, leading us back to God. Reflecting her feminine essence, the Holy Spirit is traditionally known as the 'Comforter'. As children are born through the love of parents, so through the give and take of love Jesus and the Holy Spirit give spiritual rebirth to all those who follow them.[115]

But to complete the job Jesus was unable to finish, it is necessary for the Messiah to come again. 'The purpose of the Lord of the Second Coming is thus to marry and establish the trinity *both spiritually and physically.*'[116] This is what Sun Myung Moon has accomplished. Through the Messiah's perfect marriage, the fallen nature of mankind can be transformed to the ideal trinity of God, man and woman again. Moon is able to pass this on to believers through the well-known mass wedding ceremonies. Each couple, blessed by God through Moon, is now in a right relationship with God (if they continue to live in the right way), and their children will be born untainted by the sin of Adam and Eve. The whole of mankind can be transformed in this way and God's original plan can come to pass. This is the aim and the sacred duty of the Unification Church.

The mass weddings have come in for a lot of criticism. Their spiritual purpose can be understood, but how can so many people be prepared to have their spouse (nearly always of another nationality) be chosen for them by someone who has never met most of them? Apparently Moon himself, even for the largest weddings, matches up the couples in most cases, praying over their photographs and being guided by God to put the right ones together. And the largest weddings are really large: the previous record of 6,516 people in 1988 was somewhat overtaken in 1992 when 30,000 couples were married in one huge ceremony – about 10,000 of them via satellite hook-up at eight locations on three continents.

Even this paled into insigificance with a ceremony at the second World Culture and Sports Festival on 25 August 1995, where 364,000 couples were blessed at 52 different locations around the world. Of these, 25,000 couples, members of the Church, were actually being married in a stadium at Seoul; the remainder were members of other religions – Christians, Muslims, Jews, Buddhists, Hindus – who were resanctifying their existing marriages. Although they weren't members of the Unification Church, and didn't necessarily believe the teachings of the Church, says Robertson, 'They felt there was a great value in demonstrating with us their belief in the potential sanctity of marriage.'

Unificationist couples are given time to get to know each other before marrying and have the option of declining their chosen partner. 'The majority of people don't, but it does happen and it's not considered anything more than their individual responsibility.' Robertson is emphatic that the Moon-type marriage is not imposed on members of the Church; 'It's a fundamental aspect of our understanding and belief.'

According to Robertson, this wedding is the ultimate sign of the believer's trust in Moon – and, of course, in God. Believers look at Moon as someone who 'has a profound relationship with God, and through his mediation they're going to get a partner that is very deeply appropriate to them'. It seems to work. Robertson claims that the divorce rate among members of the Church is only 3–5 per cent, way below that of the rest of Western society, where marriages are usually based on the often ephemeral emotion of falling in love.

Marriage, for members, is a vitally important part of God's work. The new couple are creating a new ideal family, and their children will be born without Original Sin. To symbolize the holiness of their marriage, and its place in God's plan, the newly married couple make a private and sacred ritual of their first three nights of love making. On the first night the man lies on top, symbolizing God in authority; on the second night the woman lies on top, symbolizing Eve's transgression and the victory of Satan; and on the third night the man is on top again, symbolizing God's victory over Satan and the re-establishment of God's plan.

To the outsider it may seem bizarre, but within the context of their beliefs, it makes sense. Sex is valued as an important part of a true loving relationship within marriage; having sex outside marriage is abusing it.

In this, as in other ways, the Church holds to traditional moral standards.

FUNDAMENTALIST EVANGELICALS

Scattered around Britain, America, Europe, Africa, the West Indies and elsewhere are many hundreds, if not thousands, of independent Fundamentalist Christian Churches, most of them small and many of them claiming to be the only true Church. Some of them have the word 'True' in their name: the True Jesus Church in China, the True Followers of Christ, a faith-healing Church in America, the Afro-American True Fellowship Pentecostal Church of God of America, among others.

When Herbert W. Armstrong was looking for a church to join in the 1920s, he insisted on its being called the Church of God, as he believed this was the only name ever given to the Church in the Bible (see p. 89). There are currently over 50 of these to choose from in the USA, though several add qualifying words or phrases: the Church of God (Apostolic), the Church of God of Prophecy, the Church of God (Jesus Christ the Head), several varieties of the Church of God in Christ, and the Church of God, International, founded by Herbert W. Armstrong's son Garner Ted, after his father threw him out of his own Worldwide Church of God for doctrinal differences and challenging his sole authority (see p. 90–93).

These seem to be the two main reasons why all these Churches spring up. Most are born in a schism from some other (often fairly small) Fundamentalist Church. Either the founder of the new sect (in its true sense) disagrees with his current Church on, for example, the exact details of the return of Christ, or the nature of heaven and hell, or the Trinity or the God-man nature of Christ; or else there is a power struggle between the leaders of the old and the new.

Almost all of them claim to be returning to the teachings and practices of the New Testament Church. Most of them are Fundamentalist, believing the Bible to be absolutely true in every detail, and many of them are Millennialist, believing in the imminent return of Christ and in his setting up of a literal 1,000-year reign on earth. Some of them are Pentecostalist, accepting the Gifts of the Spirit, including speaking in tongues and prophecy, and several have a doctrine on healing by faith alone.

To the outsider, indeed, most of them believe much the same. Yet many of them claim to be the only true Church.

The word 'Fundamentalist' often has similar pejorative overtones to the words 'cult' and 'sect'. Fundamentalists are seen as extremists, and a few of them are. These are the ones who are prepared in the name of Jesus (or, for Muslim Fundamentalists, in the name of Allah) to commit acts of terrorism. But the overwhelming majority of Christian Fundamentalists are simply Bible-believing Christians who believe deeply and absolutely in the fundamentals of their faith, and who love and serve God in their own way.

THE CHARISMATIC MOVEMENT

The Charismatic experience, or being 'baptized in the Spirit', once almost the sole possession of the Pentecostal denominations such as the Assemblies of God and Elim Foursquare, started spreading as a grass-roots phenomenon into the Church of England, the Methodist, Baptist and other Churches in the late 1960s, leading to such strange nicknames as Anglicostal, Pente-Meth and Bapticostal.

Christians who are baptized in the Spirit manifest the gifts of the Spirit listed in I Corinthians 12:8–10:

> For to one is given by the Spirit the word of wisdom; to another the word of knowledge . . . to another faith . . . to another gifts of healing . . . to another the working of miracles; to another prophecy; to another discerning of spirits; to another divers kinds of tongues; to another the interpretation of tongues.

To the outsider, and often to the insider, the most obvious of these is 'speaking in tongues' or *glossolalia*, in which, often in a state of ecstasy, the believer speaks rapidly in what appear to be unknown languages. Sometimes this is part of prayer and worship, and is not interpreted; other times it is a hidden prophecy, or message from God, which is then interpreted, usually by another believer.

There are many unverified cases of someone in a congregation identifying a tongue as Hebrew or Swahili or Croatian, or some other living language unknown to the speaker. There are other equally unverified cases in which the speaker is found to have been blaspheming in this language. On several occasions when linguistic experts have studied tape-recordings of speaking in tongues, they have found the 'speech' to consist of repeated random syllables with no discernible language structure.

But whatever the 'scientific' rationale of speaking in tongues might be, there is no doubt that for the speaker it is a tremendously moving spiritual experience. The rarer singing in tongues can be heart-rendingly beautiful for listeners.

EMOTIONS, HEALING AND DELIVERANCE MINISTRY

In August 1995 a Church of England minister in Sheffield was suspended from duty for allegedly committing sexual indiscretions with female members of his flock during healing services. But those who criticized him were the first to praise him for the work he had been doing for five years in the field of experimental worship. His congregations had become too large for his church, so he used a local sports centre for his weekly 'Nine o'clock Services', which were likened to Christian Rave parties. Rock music, laser lighting, videos, dancing – all were part of the service. Also, in common with a few other clergy in the 1990s (particularly some of the new women clergy), he introduced some elements which were very close to Neo-Paganism – a love, respect and almost worship of the planet itself.

He was also criticized, however, for becoming more of a personality than a priest; people came to *his* services to see *him*. The former manager of a rock band, he appeared to be attracting a cult following, in the true sense of the word.

Criticisms aside, the sort of work he was doing has been actively encouraged by the current Archbishop of Canterbury, George Carey, an Evangelical, who is keen to find new forms of worship and new means of evangelism. These include the open expression of emotion – something which is very foreign to the traditional Anglican pew-sitter.

The Exclusive Brethren might not approve, but dancing in the aisles has become a legitimate part of worship for many thousands of Christians. There's nothing new in expressing emotion in Christian worship. In his day John Wesley was frequently criticized for encouraging 'enthusiasm'. Evangelists such as Billy Graham and Oral Roberts have for years skilfully manipulated the emotions of their congregations. It's one way of drawing people to Christ, and if only a few of those who 'get up out of their seats' remain committed six months later, that's still a success in evangelistic terms.

In the last few years a new phenomenon has caught the Christian headlines: the Toronto Blessing. During services which combine worship, prayer and healing, some people spontaneously burst into tears, some into laughter – and some are pole-axed, 'slain in the Spirit', crumpling unconscious to the floor. Those who have witnessed it, even those who have experienced it, can find no explanation. In psychological and physiological terms, it is probably a form of hysterical reaction, but all involved agree that in spiritual terms it is a very real personal blessing.

Churches in which the Toronto Blessing occurs tend to have a major healing ministry. It was noted earlier (see p. 83) that one reason the Christian Science Church is waning could be that it no longer holds anything like a monopoly on Christian healing. Practically every town now has at least one perfectly standard Christian Church, of whatever denomination, in which healing services are commonplace.

The rapid spread of Christian healing in recent years could also diminish the attraction of mass-media healing evangelists such as Morris Cerullo: 'When Morris was fourteen and a half years of age through a unique witness and a tremendous spiritual visitation from God, the Messiah, in all his fulness was supernaturally revealed to him. At fifteen he was brought into the heavenlies and given a clear and unmistakable vision for his life . . . to minister God's Salvation and Healing Power.'[117]

Cerullo has been criticized for the many non-medically verified 'miracles' which happen night after night in his rallies. Many of the illnesses he claims to have healed people from had never been diagnosed, and some of the healings have turned out to be rather short-lived. He has also been criticized for 'heavenly deception' in a poster advertising a recent UK campaign. The poster showed a woman holding a baby, with the caption: 'I couldn't have a baby – Miracles can happen.' It turned out that the woman in the poster was already the mother of three children. The poster was withdrawn.

Cerullo, like many evangelists, 'binds' unGodly powers. 'In travail I would in the name of Jesus bind these powers of the enemy – the spirits of sin, the spirits of sickness, the spirit of religion, the false cults, the spirit of idol worship, and the false prophets of Baal. I was binding these things for hours in the Spirit.'[118]

The idea of sickness being caused by an evil spirit is biblical; Jesus several times 'cast out demons' from someone who was sick. Many Bible scholars, without in any way diminishing it, see this as equivalent in modern-day terminology to someone being cured of a psychosomatic illness: take away the psychological cause and the physical symptons will also go.

But today there is a new upsurge in what has become called 'Deliverance Ministry'. Some preachers specialize in casting out demons – the demon of a recurrent migraine, the demon of cancer, the demon of impure sexual urges, even the demon of smoking. While accepting the power of God to heal, many traditional Christian leaders – in addition to many doctors and psychiatrists – are becoming increasingly concerned by the practice of Deliverance Ministry. Often the 'healer' will scream and shout at the person with a problem; sometimes he will take hold of him and shake him; and there have been many documented occasions when a sick or troubled person has been pinned to the floor by three or four Deliverance adherents while the leader has interpreted his struggles to get free, or to breathe freely, as the demons fighting to maintain their hold. There have been cases, for example, when the 'victim' has shouted, 'Let me go, you bastards,' and the Deliverance 'healer' has said, 'The demon is crying out.'

The concern of both spiritual and medical critics is that Deliverance Ministry, in the name of Jesus, could do far more harm than good, and could itself create very serious psychiatric problems in those it is seeking to heal.

THE JESUS MOVEMENT

The late 1960s and early 1970s were an exciting time for the many thousands of young Christians in the Jesus Movement. 'Jesus Freaks' wore Day-glo orange Jesus stickers, wrote 'Jesus' in studs on their leather jackets, strummed acoustic guitars and sang choruses in market squares and bus stations, and preached 'the permanent revolution' to their friends, or to anyone they met on the streets. 'Hey, peace and love, man. Are you saved? Do you know Jesus? He died for you, man.' The theology was a stripped-down version of basic Evangelical Christianity. One of the most popular tracts was a little grey leaflet called *The Four Spiritual Laws*. You read it, you agreed (often under high-pressure encouragement) to its logic, you signed the back page and you were a Christian.

House fellowships proliferated everywhere. The lack of any sort of central organization or authority was one of the attractions – but also, eventually, one of the problems. Although many of the house fellowships were loosely attached to a local Evangelical church, their leaders sometimes felt they had a private hotline to God which put them outside the authority of any ordained minister. Many devout but traditional priests were challenged by house fellowship leaders as to whether they were saved. 'God has given me a message' was a frequently heard phrase, but the theology was often shaky and a surprising number of early Christian heresies began to resurface. The Second Coming was expected imminently.

Some of the Jesus Freaks eventually cut their hair and settled down to raise mortgages and children. If they stayed within Christianity, it was as 'normal' members of 'normal' Churches, and they perhaps looked back on their sticker-wearing days with a little embarrassment. Many, having dropped in to Jesus, dropped out again as soon as the initial enthusiasm waned, but others went on to join or to form other 'alternative' religious movements. Among these were the Children of God (now the Family) and the Jesus Army, which began as just two of many Jesus movements.

THE FAMILY (THE CHILDREN OF GOD)

Formerly the Children of God, and then the Family of Love, this movement has been one of the four or five new religious movements to receive the most attention, criticism and attacks, both in the press and from anti-cult organizations. The present-day Family, because of its roots, is still regularly attacked, and finds it difficult to shake off the popular perception of them. Their formal name is now simply the Family, and they describe themselves as the Fellowship of Independent Missionary Communities.

HISTORY

The first incarnation of the Family was as the Children of God, which was originally a nickname the press gave to a bunch of hippie-type Jesus people on a Californian beach in 1967–9. Other names for them – and for many similar groups in America and the UK – were Teens for Christ, Revolutionaries for Jesus, the Jesus Children, or (more broadly) the Jesus Movement. Their leader was David Brandt Berg (1919–94), an evangelist from the Christian and Missionary Alliance Church with a powerful End-Time message: Jesus would be returning very soon, so as many people as possible must be converted before it was too late.

From 1964 to 1971 Berg regularly took part in Christian radio and TV programmes, in association with Pentecostal evangelist Fred Jordan. As the Children of God grew as a movement, they would join him on the broadcasts. In 1971 Fleetwood Mac's guitarist Jeremy Spencer left the band mid-tour to join the Children of God and is still with the movement today.

In 1972 Children of God missionaries began taking their message to the UK and Europe. The Day-glo orange Jesus stickers which appeared everywhere around that time were representative of the tremendous appeal of the wider Jesus

Movement among young people. Paperback editions of the New Testament were published as *The Jesus Book*, tracts became lively rather than solemn and Christian comics began to appear. Guitars were everywhere. The Children of God were at first simply part of the same environment.

Within a year or two they were seen as something quite different. They encouraged communal living. David Berg became known as Father David, or Moses David, Mo, or simply 'Dad'. He was not merely an evangelist, but a prophet, and the Children of God were *his* followers. Wherever he was, he communicated with the Children of God by Mo Letters, often with comic-strip illustrations. But most disturbing of all, his former teaching of the value of celibacy was turned around 180 degrees. He took on a second wife, Maria (originally Karen), and told his first wife, Jane, that she could either accept the new situation or leave.

'His first wife stayed within the Family quite happily for many years and is still positive about her time in the Family,' says Rachel Scott, the Family's spokesperson in the UK.[119] 'David Berg continued to support her financially for the rest of his life, despite the fact that she has had a new husband for the last 20 years.'

Berg 'shared' the wives of some of the members of the movement. From 1976 he encouraged members to follow his example and practise sexual freedom. Some ex-members allege that at some stages he advocated lesbian and gay relationships, group sex, sexual involvement (if not actual intercourse) with children, and incest.

Scott agrees that Berg 'speculated on the possibility that homosexuality could be covered by the Law of Love [see below], but it was quickly dropped because of the way God talks about homosexuality in the Bible. I doubt it was ever practised, and the Family has had a very strong stance against homosexuality ever since.'

In the years when some individual communities got out of control there were cases of group sex, says Scott, 'and then David Berg stopped this with a letter called "Ban the Bomb" in 1983.' As for sex with children, she says, 'When it came to the attention of Family leadership that some children had been involved in sexual interaction with some adults, a message went out making sure that everyone understood that it was an excommunicable offence.'

Long before this point, in around 1972, an organization, FREECOG, was set up specifically for parents to 'rescue' (i.e. kidnap) their teenagers back from the Children of God. This was probably the first 'anti-cult' organization to be formed.

◆

Some tabloid-headline writers might be surprised to learn that the Children of God came to an end in 1978.

'In late 1977, Father David received reports that some regional leaders in the Church were misusing their authority and violating fundamental rules and principles upon which the movement had been founded. In an action that had the support of the grass-roots membership, he subsequently dismissed the entire leadership and formally dissolved the Children of God. He invited those who wished to remain in fellowship with him to form a new group, the Family of Love, with a new organizational structure. Several years later this name was shortened to the Family,' says Scott.

The sackings and reorganization occurred in February 1978. Over 300 leaders were dismissed, and 2,600 members, a third of the world membership at the time, 'chose to return to secular lives or remain independent missionaries with no further ties to Father David'.[120] It was, understandably, not a happy time, and had repercussions which continue to this day. 'A number of its former leaders, who were resentful because of their dismissal, still actively campaign against our present-day fellowship.'[121]

These included one of Berg's own daughters, Deborah (originally Linda – members usually change their names on joining, to symbolize their new lives), who was dismissed along with her first husband 'for abusing their positions of leadership in South America'. The movement now claims that her book denouncing Berg and the Children of God was actually written by her second husband, who had also been dismissed, and by 'another ex-member called Bithia, who has now retracted her writings'.

The new movement was far more loosely controlled. In an effort to avoid the authoritarian leadership which had characterized some Children of God communities – the leaders 'were sometimes hard and unloving and had lost the desire to be missionaries and were more interested in power than in spreading the Gospel,' says Scott – each local Family of Love community was self-governed, electing its own leaders and confirming them by a re-vote every six months.

However, the controversy didn't come to an end with the change of name. Indeed, in one particular respect it grew. In 1973 David Berg's wife, Maria, had begun sleeping with men, then witnessing to them. In 1978 Berg introduced the practice to the new movement as Flirty Fishing, or FFing.

Jesus said, 'I will make you fishers of men' (Matthew 4:19). Fishers need bait. Family of Love girls went out to bars and nightclubs to meet men, catch them, and draw them into the movement. Inevitably the press dubbed them 'Hookers for Jesus', and even Berg called them 'God's Whores' in one of his Mo Letters. To the outside world the practice was outrageous, but Berg argued that Christians were called upon to make supreme sacrifices for God, even laying down their lives in martyrdom; if laying down their bodies in bed brought people to Christ, it was fully justified.

> Christians were therefore free through God's grace to go to great lengths to show the Love of God to others, even as far as meeting their sexual needs . . . sex could be used as an evidence to them that we loved them with the Lord's Love, and were willing to sacrificially meet their sexual needs in order to show them that love . . . Needless to say, linking the spiritual Love of God with the physical manifestation of that love in the form of sex, in this very intimate form of personal witnessing, was, to put it mildly, not very well received by mainstream Christianity, where sex and God are seldom, if ever, associated. In fact, one might even get the erroneous impression that sex is totally of the Devil and not God's idea or design at all.[122]

Commenting on the practice of FFing, Scott says, 'Sex was offered only if the girl felt it was necessary and it was not used as a recruitment method, although some men did join as a result of their new-found faith in Jesus, and some later married the girls with whom they had fallen in love.' She also adds, 'it may be true to say that more women actually joined as a result of FFing by men.'

This new form of witnessing was fairly short-lived. Because of the threat of AIDS rather than as a response to criticism, the sexual freedom of members with each other started to be restricted in the mid-1980s, and 'FFing was officially banned as an outreach method in September 1987. All FFing abruptly stopped.'[123]

In any case, the Family say, relatively few members ever used FFing as their major form of outreach. The main methods were, and still are, creating and distributing literature and posters, and cassette tapes and videos of their own Christian music and evangelism. In some parts of the world they produce radio and TV programmes.

The Family now tend to live in small communities – effectively extended families – with their children, whom they educate at home wherever possible. There are around 9,000 members around the world, one-third of these adults. Around a quarter of their present membership were formerly members of the Children of God.

When David Berg died in 1994, his wife, Maria, took over as prophetess and leader of the Family.

BELIEFS AND PRACTICES

The Family's beliefs, with two exceptions, are those of straightforward Evangelical Christianity. They believe that the Bible is the divinely inspired word of God. They believe in the Trinity. They believe that Jesus died on the cross to save mankind from its sins and that salvation is by faith, through the grace of God. As Charismatic Christians they believe in the baptism of the Holy Spirit, and the gifts of the Spirit, including healing, prophecy and speaking in tongues. Evangelism is an essential part of their lives: 'The born-again believer's primary purpose in life [should be] to make Christ's love known to the whole world, and to seek to win others into God's Heavenly Kingdom.'[124] They believe strongly that these are the Last Days, and that Christ will shortly return to establish the Millennium. In common with many Fundamentalists, they believe in the literal biblical account of creation, not in evolution.

Unlike many Christian alternative religious movements, they have no argument with other Christian Churches. 'Basically for us, any and all who love God and love their fellow man and are trying to make it a better world for them to live in, to us are doing good.'

The two differences concern their founder and the 'Law of Love'.

'Members of the Family hold our founder, David Berg, to be a prophet whom God has ordained to proclaim the Endtime message to this generation. With David Berg's passing in the latter part of 1994, we accept his wife, Maria, as his successor and prophetess and leader of the Family,' says Scott.

The Law of Love is based on Jesus' teaching, 'Thou shalt love the Lord thy God with all thy heart, and with all thy soul, and with all thy mind. This is the first and great commandment. And the second is like unto it, Thou shalt love thy neighbour as thyself' (Matthew 22:37–9). This, they teach (in common with most Christian Churches) has replaced the point-by-point rules of Mosaic law.

'The Family holds Christ's Law of Love to be the supreme tenet upon which all Christian conduct and interpersonal relationships should be based, that all acts motivated by unselfish love for others are acceptable to God,' says Scott. (In both motivation and effect this could be seen as akin to the basic Neo-Pagan law: 'An it hurt no one, do as thou wilt shall be the whole of the Law.' Scott disagrees with the comparison: 'This is actually the opposite to the Law of Love [which] states that our actions should help someone; it is certainly not enough not to hurt someone.')

She emphasizes that the Law of Love does not mean licence: 'David Berg always stressed that this liberation is *not* a selfish, reckless freedom wherein you are free to disregard the rights or feelings of others or act unkindly, selfishly, lustfully or lawlessly towards them, for "love worketh no ill to his neighbour" (Romans 13:10).'

The controversial point is the application of this Law of Love to sexual relationships: 'We believe heterosexual relationships between consenting adults are permissible in the eyes of God regardless of marital status, providing these relationships are motivated by unselfish love, are desired by all parties, are agreed upon and hurt no one.'

Scott stresses that despite the persistent allegations, this applies to adults only: 'We have been accused of sexually abusing our children. This is an excommunicable offence. Over 600 of our children have been taken in dawn raids from our communities and have been returned when no evidence of abuse was found.'

She also points out that 'in his writings on sexual relationships, David Berg emphasized that these should remain within the legal boundaries of society'.

Perhaps partly as a response to the allegations of sexual misconduct, but mainly because of the threat of AIDS, the Family now has very strict rules on sexual relationships, which are to be only between Family members. New members must belong to a community for six months before they are allowed to share in sexual relationships. Homosexual relationships are no longer allowed, because of biblical teachings.

The whole application of the Law of Love to sexual relationships is misunderstood by outsiders, Scott says. It is 'primarily for the sake of single people within our communities who because of the fact that they cannot have relationships with people outside our communities would otherwise have to remain celibate. We do not believe this would be the loving thing to do. It is not an excuse for excess and it is carried out extremely discreetly with just two people involved.'

The Family do not actively encourage people to join their communities. Anyone who wants to must first spend some months getting to know and understand the beliefs and lifestyle, and what their commitment would entail. 'If after a time they are firmly convinced they want to join, are of legal age and free from debts, legal or military obligations that would prevent them joining, we would allow them to live in for a three-week "trial" period. The members of the Home would then vote on whether to accept them or not as a full-time member, in which case they would have another six-month probationary period before becoming a full member.'

The communities or homes are where the fully committed members (Disciples Only, or DO) live. They can range in size from four voting members (aged over 16) up to a maximum of 35 people altogether. At 16, members can vote on anything except expenditure and financial matters, which are restricted to those over 18. DO members commit everything to their home, 'forsaking all'. This usually includes giving up their job to work full-time for the community.

This work is partly internal – cooking, cleaning, repairing the vehicles, teaching the children, secretarial work and so on – and partly external – going out on an evangelization team. 'The Family ministers largely to the unchurched: individuals who cannot – or will not – be attracted to mainstream Christian denominations,' says Scott.

A community's income comes mainly from donations, both from supporters and for their posters, music cassettes and videos. From time to time a member of a community may take on a secular job to bring in more income if needed. The community itself gives 10 per cent of its income each month to World Services, the closest the Family has to a central headquarters, which is responsible for publications and for funding new 'pioneer' homes in, for example, Eastern Europe. Part of the income is also put into an emergency fund for purposes such as supporting individual members who become ill.

'The Family does not seek to establish a denomination, own property or build lavish church buildings or in any way acquire power or excessive material wealth,' says Scott. 'It considers such activities unscriptural, and believes that if mainstream Christianity were to abandon such pursuits and dedicate all their material resources to winning others to Christ and being an example of true Christian love, the world would be a far better place.'

Total membership of the Family living in communities is currently around 9,000 worldwide, of whom 6,000 are children. This figure has remained fairly steady for some years, though members obviously come and go. Apparently there are around 35,000 former members who, 'for the most part, remain on friendly terms'.

Members are free to leave their home to join another one, or to set up a new one, or to leave community life and become a TRF supporter (associate members who witness, and still send in Tithing Report Forms, but are not full-time disciples). Anyone who wishes to leave the Family altogether may do so, and if they have no money at all, their community will usually help them out, if only with their rail fare.

Scott stresses that 'for the most part all our communities are "open" to visitation by the public and anyone is free to visit'. This includes the families of members. Contrary to popular belief, members 'are encouraged to keep in contact with their relatives. In fact we like to visit the parents beforehand and encourage the new disciples to visit them whenever is reasonable, and we also encourage the parents to visit the homes.'

Although each Family home is autonomous and self-governing, the Family put together a 200-page governing charter early in 1995, which outlines the most important principles, goals and beliefs of the movement and provides a broad governing structure for the communities. The document includes a Charter of Responsibilities and Rights, and the Fundamental Family Rules. It was compiled in the year before his death by David Berg, with Maria and others, based on suggestions from grass-roots Family members. The draft Charter was then discussed in workshops around the world before being finalized. The Charter makes a major point of the rights and responsibilities of parents and children: 'The children's rights include having their spiritual, physical and emotional needs met, and to be free from any kind of abuse. They should also receive sufficient time, opportunity and materials to obtain an adequate education, including regular physical education.'

Scott also points out that 'our understanding of a nuclear family is the same as yours – Mum, Dad and the kids. Traditional family bonds are of prime importance. If there is a single mother or single father with children, we make sure that there is someone to help them with the children, and there is plenty of support from the whole community.'

As well as their evangelistic work, members of the Family help in the wider community, including giving humanitarian aid. In 1995 they set up soup kitchens for the survivors of the Kobe earthquake in Japan, and helped in the rescue after the bomb explosion in a US federal building in Oklahoma City. Their community involvement also includes prison visiting and working in homes for the elderly and for delinquent children. Their more descriptive formal name reflects how they see themselves today, as independent missionaries.

In November 1995 a British High Court Judge ruled that the three-year-old son of a Family member should be allowed to live with his mother, despite his grandmother's protests. Although the judge described some of the Family's earlier practices and teachings as 'revolting' and 'possibly blasphemous', his three-year study of the movement, culminating in a 340-page, 135,000-word judgement, concluded that the Family has changed its ways.

Scott comments: 'We are very gratified that this judgement endorses the findings of numerous other court cases around the world, that Family communities are safe and wholesome environments in which to bring up children. Hopefully this case provides a punctuation mark in our development, and that the Family can now proceed with its calling of telling others about Jesus.'

The impression given by the Family today is that they are sincere and dedicated Evangelical Christians whose only real difference from any others is that they are honest about sleeping with each other. They appear to have put the excesses of the 1970s and early 1980s behind them. They are very conscious of their bad image and now seem to make a deliberate effort to 'abstain from all appearance of evil' (I Thessalonians 5:22). They are also very tired of being attacked by the anti-cult organizations and smeared in press reports based on highly selective, inaccurate or out-of-date information from some of these organizations. 'They just take whatever sounds the most scandalous to print in their paper, and if we talk to them and tell them things from our side, they usually go ahead and print whatever is sensational anyway,' says Scott.

THE JESUS ARMY

The Jesus Army, or the Jesus Fellowship Church (its formal name), developed out of the hippie-style Jesus movement of the early 1970s. Unlike the then Children of God, born from similar roots, its emphasis has always been on militancy rather than loving. Its doctrine is straightforward Evangelical Christianity, with both a Reformed and a Charismatic element, but it is included in this book because of its very visible style.

'There is no sense in which we represent an "Alternative Religion",' says John Campbell, communications officer for the Jesus Army. 'Our beliefs are mainstream Christian, and we uphold the historic creeds of Christianity. We also recognize and respect the wide spread of "flavours" within the Christian Church at large.'[125]

They seem particularly sensitive about being regarded as any form of new religious movement and stress their theological correctness. At the foot of their letterhead are the words, 'Jesus Fellowship Church upholds the full historic biblical Christian faith, being Reformed, Evangelical and Charismatic. In particular, it upholds the doctrine of the Trinity and the full divinity of the Lord Jesus Christ.'

The letterhead itself could have sprung from the late 1960s. It is covered with reproductions of stickers proclaiming, among other things, 'Jesus Army: Love, Power & Sacrifice', 'Lift your hands. Raise the Cross. Hold the Bible. Lift up

Jesus!' 'Jesus People: Jesus Fellowship Church (Baptist)', 'Jesus Revolution: Love, Joy, Peace, Justice', and 'When you meet! Give the greet! Say JESUS!'

♦

The origins of the Jesus Army can be traced back to 1967, when Baptist minister Noel Stanton and some members of his small church in Bugbrooke, Northamptonshire, were baptized in the Holy Spirit and began speaking in tongues, healing and preaching the Gospel with new enthusiasm and effectiveness.

His church soon became too small for his rapidly expanding congregation. Money was raised and donated to buy more buildings, including an old rectory and then a farm, which became the New Creation Farm. Stanton's congregation became a community.

The Jesus Fellowship now owns 84 communal houses around the UK. It also owns a health-food company and health-food shops, building and plumbing companies, and a clothes shop. Members may continue to live in their own homes, but many choose to live in communities.

The way of life in Jesus Army communities has been described as austere and spartan, if not harsh. Rooms are often almost bare of furniture. Working hours are long and the food is apparently meagre. Everything is shared – their money, their possessions, even sometimes their clothes. TV and radio are banned, as are most newspapers. Only Christian music is allowed. Children are allowed few toys and discipline is strict, including corporal punishment, though the slipper has replaced the rod because of external criticism.

The popular Christian festivals such as Christmas are not celebrated, on the quite accurate grounds that they have Pagan origins. (One of the reasons that Christianity took root throughout Europe during the Dark Ages was its habit of taking over local Pagan festivals and sacred sites, adapting the customs of the winter solstice into Christmas, and of the spring festival into Easter, and building churches over ancient wells and springs.)

Non-members are most likely to be made aware of the Jesus Army by its brightly painted 'Battle Buses', and by the combat gear, camouflage jackets and heavy boots worn by members when they descend on a city centre. This militaristic, assertive form of evangelism is often successful, but equally often its macho style succeeds in putting people off the message being preached. The Jesus Army recruits mainly from the homeless on city streets. Unlike most new religious movements, the majority of its members are uneducated and working class.

Stanton believes that celibacy is a holy calling. Even long-married couples sleep in separate beds and are encouraged to refrain from sexual activity. Romantic liaisons between members have to be approved by the leadership.

The Jesus Army has been accused of being totally male-oriented, not only in its aggressive, thrusting approach to evangelism but also in its treatment of women. It appears to have little place for the nurturing male – or the assertive female.

The Church believes firmly in traditional gender roles in society, presumably based on Paul's rather than Jesus' teachings: women should be silent in church, the man should be head of the household and so on. Men are the leaders and the women members have very much a supporting role. They appear content to ignore the societal changes of the last few decades, ignoring the rights and status women have fought to achieve in recent years.

The Church organizes occasional 'Man Alive for God' days, when hundreds of men meet together for fellowship and worship, and to help men re-establish their manhood. They have never had an equivalent day for their women members. 'We've never found that we've been able to do that, simply because we haven't had a woman who has the vision and the calibre to lead it,' says Ed Hunt, organizer of the event.[126]

♦

The community life and the evangelistic techniques of the Jesus Army have made its original parent body, the Baptist Church, uneasy. Stanton's Church was expelled from both the Baptist Union and the interdenominational Evangelical Alliance in 1986.

The Jesus Army is, however, very careful with both members and money. New members have to live in a community for a probationary period for two years, and must be over 21, before being allowed to commit themselves to full membership. The Church keeps its running expenses and its capital completely separate, and has its accounts audited by a major financial company. Members often donate all their money to the Church's Trust Fund. If they later leave the Church, their capital is paid back, sometimes with interest.

BRANCH DAVIDIANS

Much has been written about the Branch Davidians since some 80 members of the movement died in the inferno at Waco, Texas, on 19 April 1993. It is now difficult to distinguish the facts from the somewhat sensationalist reporting in most newspapers. This is a brief entry, because we have not been able to contact any of the surviving members of the movement, who are said still to be in shock at the deaths of their leader, David Koresh, and their friends.

The history of the Church is presented here simply to show how a small Church can become, in the true sense of the term, a cult; to indicate how a religious movement can go seriously awry; and to suggest that the horrifying outcome was (despite the official verdict) perhaps as much the fault of mainstream society as of the movement itself.

The Branch Davidians began as an offshoot of the Seventh-day Adventist Church in 1935. Victor Houteff (1886–1955) taught at a Sabbath School until his apocalyptic interpretations of Daniel and Revelation caused the Church to expel him. With a dozen or so families he set up a movement called the Shepherd's Rod. In 1935 they moved from Los Angeles to set up a small community near Waco. In 1942 they were renamed the Davidian Seventh-day Adventists, after the Kingdom of David.

Houteff was succeeded by his wife, Florence, who announced that the Second Coming would be in 1959. The movement fragmented when Christ didn't return. Many members left, but several formed different groups. One of these was led by Benjamin Roden, who told his followers, 'Get off the dead Rod and move on to a living Branch,' and called his group the Branch Davidians. He died in 1978 and was succeeded by his wife, Lois.

David Koresh was born Vernon Howell in 1959. He joined the Branch Davidians in 1983 and quickly fell out with the Rodens' son George, who had announced himself to be the Messiah. George Roden was already clashing with his mother, and Howell took Lois's side. According to some reports, he also took to her bed in the hope of producing a new Messiah. He was rapidly working himself into a position of influence. In 1984 he married the 14-year-old daughter of a senior Church elder. Lois died in 1986 and George Roden forced Howell out of the community at gunpoint.

The following year Roden tried to establish his own position as leader by raising a 20-years-deceased member of the Church from the dead. Howell tipped off the police and turned up to confront Roden. After a gun battle, Roden was eventually gaoled and Howell eventually freed. He moved his own followers back to Waco, took over the movement and changed his name to David Koresh in 1990 – David after the king and Koresh after the Persian king Cyrus; Koresh was apparently also God's surname, and meant 'death' or 'destroyer'. By now Koresh was calling himself the Messiah. By now he also had two small children by two different teenage girls.

Koresh was a charismatic leader and there is no doubt that most of his followers adored him. He was handsome and sexy. He played rock guitar. He also had a brilliant mind, knew the Bible inside out and could preach for hours without notes. When he announced that he had the right to sleep with any woman in the movement in order to spread his holy seed, some members disapproved but most accepted it. He is said to have slept with at least 15 of the women and girls, some mature and married to male members, and some very young, including the 12-year-old sister of his one legal wife.

In one sense, Koresh was clearly a powerful and probably unscrupulous leader looking for a following. In another, he was at least partly the creation of the supercharged apocalyptic atmosphere of the movement he had joined in 1983. His followers were looking for a leader and the more power he assumed, the more devotion they gave him; his claim to be the Lamb of God was bolstered by their belief and support.

Koresh began the serious recruitment of new members from Seventh-day Adventist churches and colleges, including many from Britain and Australia.

Life in the Waco community was not easy. Rising at six, the members spent their days building halls and dormitories, a swimming pool, a gym and an underground storm shelter. They spent their evenings listening to Koresh's Bible expositions, which often went on till the early hours. All this on a diet which was often only cornflakes, popcorn and fruit. Male and female members, even married couples, were segregated.

The movement had taken on many of the classic features of a religious cult. Over the next year or two, several members gave up and moved out.

During this time the Branch Davidians (in common with many other American Millennialist movements) began to prepare for the coming apocalypse, stocking up with guns and military food supplies.

In February 1993, members of the Bureau of Alcohol, Tobacco and Firearms (ATF) staged a raid on Waco, looking for illegal stockpiles of weapons and ammunition. Opinions differ as to who fired the first shots, but in the ensuing gunfight four ATF agents died and over a dozen were injured. It is thought that six Branch Davidians were killed, and many were injured, including Koresh, who was shot in the wrist and the waist.

The FBI were called in and laid siege to the compound. After 51 days, with the terms of several surrender deals unfulfilled by Koresh, they ended the siege by firing CS gas (prohibited for military use by international convention) and ramming the buildings with tanks. Shortly after that the entire place went up in flames. Nine members of the movement escaped; over 80 died, a third of them British. Around 20 children were killed. The FBI claim that the members set fire to the compound themselves, but survivors claim the conflagration was sparked by the FBI's attack. Whichever is true, the effect was the same: the stockpiled weapons and ammunition exploded in a fireball.

According to members, although the movement did have weapons of their own, most of Koresh's reputed $200,000 purchase of weapons in the months before the ATF raid were for other people. Koresh was a registered arms dealer and made much of the income for the community from legal trading in weapons.

The few survivors claim that they were strip-searched, had their clothes taken away and destroyed, were manacled and paraded in flimsy orange overalls, and were kept in prison for up to 200 days without any trial.

Just how much the Branch Davidians brought their destruction on themselves is open to debate, but it is generally thought that the whole situation was badly handled by the authorities. The ATF initially claimed that Koresh was 'holed-up' inside the compound and their raid was the only way they could arrest him. Members – and local shopkeepers – say that he went into town most days and could have been picked up peacefully at any time. Without the ATF's miscalculation, David Koresh and his followers might still have been preparing for Armageddon today.

In August 1995, the ATF was cleared of any culpability.

ROMAN CATHOLIC ORGANIZATIONS

The Roman Catholic Church is often thought of by non-members as an undivided and traditionalist religion. In fact, it is neither.

Throughout its history the Church has had liberal and traditionalist movements, the latter often formed to counteract the spreading influence of the former. The Society of Jesus (the Jesuits) was founded in 1534 precisely for this reason: to maintain orthodoxy against liberalism. Several organizations with similar aims have been founded this century.

Dissent is strong within the Roman Catholic Church today. Large numbers of priests are leaving the Church, while others are staying to fight from within. Some of these rebels are more liberal than the official Church, but many are more traditional.

On the liberal side, many Roman Catholic bishops and priests in South America have embraced 'liberation theology', effectively left-wing, sometimes revolutionary politics. In Britain as elsewhere, the Charismatic revival, with its emphasis on the individual experience of Spirit-led worship, has swept through the grass-roots level of the Roman Catholic Church as much as in any denomination.

Hundreds of Catholic priests have gone against the pope's ruling and married, and not all of them have given up their calling. There are numerous splinter denominations, especially in the USA, with married priests. Most of these Churches also deny the infallibility of the pope.

On the traditional side, the sweeping changes to the Church instituted by Pope

John XXIII and Vatican II brought a reaction. Several senior clergy refused to abandon the Latin Tridentine mass in favour of the Novus Ordo, the new mass.

In both America and Europe there are several different strands of independent episcopacy. In most cases these trace their line of apostolic succession (see p. 42) back to a legally consecrated bishop who rebelled against the Church hierarchy, sometimes as far back as Vatican I in 1870, which declared the pope to be infallible. In continental Europe 'Old Catholic' Churches are quite substantial denominations, which are in communion with the Anglican Church. In Britain and America the situation is different. Some of the independent bishops have established small denominations, consecrating further bishops and ordaining priests; others have merged with branches of the Orthodox Church; and others are basically one-man bands, sometimes known as 'Wandering Bishops'.

(Old Catholic Churches should not be confused with Liberal Catholic Churches, which are basically Christian-Theosophical; see p. 172).

Within the official Roman Catholic Church there are several orders formed to maintain the purity of the faith against both internal and external liberal influence. Probably the best known of these, after the Jesuits, is Opus Dei ('The Work of God'). This was founded in 1928 by a Spanish priest, Monsignor Josemaría Escrivá de Balaguer y Albas (1902–75), who took the first step to becoming a saint when he was beatified in 1992.

Over the last 15 years there has been a great deal of controversy over Opus Dei. Many articles and at least one book have described it in terms usually reserved for a cult. It is said to be politically right-wing and authoritarian; to impose strict forms of behaviour, such as members sprinkling holy water on their beds at night to encourage chastity, strict penances, such as wearing a *cilice* or spiked bracelet, and strict mortifications, such as lashing oneself with a cat-o'-nine-tails until the blood runs. It has rules and regulations for its members and censors what they may read and what they may do. It separates children from their parents, and men from women. It is dedicated to the holiness of its members and is condemnatory of anything they do which it decides is wrong. Members find it very difficult to leave the organization. If they manage to do so, they are shunned by their former friends still within it. If they have put any money into the organization, they are unable, under its constitutions (which have never been published), to reclaim any of it. Opus Dei has been criticized for its business dealings and for the wealth of property it has accumulated. It has been described as a secret society, a Church within a Church, with a disproportionate amount of power in the Vatican. Like many other religious movements, it claims to have the only truth: once you are a member, salvation can be found only within the organization.

These are the criticisms, but the 80,000 members of Opus Dei – including an archbishop, 15 bishops and 15,000 priests – see it differently. For them, Opus Dei is a society which helps them in their daily commitment to Christ within the orthodoxy of the Roman Catholic Church. They study the Church's doctrines in more depth and are encouraged to pray. They find ways to live a fully religious life in their daily working life, rather than having to keep the two separate. They do vital social work among the inner-city poor. Far from being any sort of cult, they point out, Opus Dei is fully a part of the Roman Catholic Church, and has the personal blessing of the pope himself.

Opus Dei is not the only ultra-orthodox movement within the Church. Three others which have caused concern in recent years are the Focolare, founded in 1943, the Neocatechumenate, founded in 1964, and Communion and Liberation, also founded in the 1960s. Like Opus Dei, each is outside the normal diocesan structure of the Church and has been criticized for being its own uncontrolled master, and for bringing division within individual congregations. Each, from its own point of view, is promoting true spirituality, religious orthodoxy and conservative morality.

The criticisms levelled at them are very reminiscent of those levelled at alternative religious movements, and the responses to those criticisms strike a similar note.

PART THREE

✠

EASTERN
ORIGINS

FOUR

EASTERN MOVEMENTS

Mention Eastern-inspired new religions, and most people think of saffron-robed young men and women chanting 'Hare Krishna' in the High Street, or the Beatles sitting down with the Maharishi Mahesh Yogi among heaps of flowers. Most of the Eastern religions which were so prominent in the 1970s have changed considerably in the last few years. In some cases the founder has died and without his presence the followers have re-formed themselves in a different style; in other cases the Eastern origins have been all but forgotten.

This chapter covers several movements which are partly Esoteric but are included here because they are inspired, at least in part, by the East.

THE APPEAL OF THE EAST

What is the appeal of Eastern-inspired religions? They often involve strict discipline and obedience, hardship, giving up everything you have, rising hours before dawn, wearing very noticeable clothing and chanting mantras for hours on end.

This in itself is the appeal to many of the devotees. They want to give up control of their own lives; they want someone else to tell them what to do, to make all the decisions for them. There's an element in all of us which longs to let go and give it all away. As the world becomes ever more complicated and decisions ever more difficult, it can be a tremendous relief to hand everything over to someone else. There is a parallel in the mundane world: on leaving the army or prison, many people find it very difficult to adapt to a world where *they* now have to make all the decisions, where there is no fixed structure for them to live within.

And the discipline, the clothing and the way of life of an initiate in an Eastern religion are actually not too dissimilar to those of monks and nuns through 2,000 years of Christian history. When Pope John XXIII's Vatican II initiated sweeping changes in the Roman Catholic Church, including considerable freedom of choice, many monks and nuns found it difficult to adapt. A lot of people like to know exactly where they stand. Hare Krishna devotees and Christian monks and nuns alike find peace in submission.

Another factor is more spiritual. The East is old, and old is original, and original is true. The logical gaps in that sentence are easily ignored. Many members of new religions are searching for Truth with a capital T. They find it in the religions of the East. After all, you can't get much older than Hinduism, and therefore more original, and therefore more true. Holy men traditionally come from the East, and Hinduism has had a lot of holy men in its 4,000- or 5,000-year history. An elderly man, sitting cross-legged with a blanket around him, uttering gnomic statements in an ancient language, must be holy. He has seen through the complexity and falseness of modern life, has found an inner core of stillness deep within himself, and is in tune with God, or the gods, or the immutable laws of the cosmos.

That is, of course, a simplistic account of the spiritual fascination of the East for the intelligent Western seeker, but it contains an element of truth. Look into the depth of peace in an Eastern guru's eyes and you will see there something that we all want. Few Western religions can offer it. For those disenchanted with the faith of their fathers, the very genuine spirituality of Eastern religions is most attractive.

ISKCON

ISKCON, the International Society for Krishna Consciousness, is better known as the Hare Krishna movement. Their popular image is of groups of young people dressed in saffron robes, dancing in the streets, playing cymbals and chanting 'Hare Krishna, Hare Krishna, Krishna Krishna, Hare Hare; Hare Rama, Hare Rama, Rama Rama, Hare Hare.' After the death of its founder in 1977, the organization went through several years of turmoil, from which it now appears to have emerged.

HISTORY

ISKCON was founded by A. C. Bhaktivedanta Swami Prabhupada (1896–1977), who was born Abhay Charan De, in Calcutta. He became a follower of the Gaudiya Mission, a Hindu revivalist group, and in 1933 was charged by the leader, Bhakti Siddhanta, to take Krishna conciousness to the West. He spent the next 30 years working as a sales executive for a pharmaceutical company and translating Hindu scriptures into English. The movement uses his translation of the *Bhagavad-Gita*, with his commentary, believing all other translations to be badly flawed, 'motivated', while his is pure. He became a sannyasin in 1959, renouncing his earlier life, possessions and family for his new spiritual life. For various reasons, including immigration laws and lack of funding, he was unable to go to America until 1965. When he did, with his robe and sandals, begging bowl and little else, he quickly found acceptance among the hippies of the Bowery district of New York, and shortly after in the Haight-Ashbury district of San Francisco. He founded ISKCON in 1966.

In 1968 six American ISKCON members came to Britain and the following year, fresh from the Maharishi Mahesh Yogi's transcendental meditation, the Beatles' lead guitarist, George Harrison, helped in the recording of the song 'Hare Krishna Mantra', based on the Hare Krishna chant. Performed by Radha Krishna Temple, the American 'missionaries', and reaching Number 12 in the charts in October that year, the song brought the fledgeling movement tremendous publicity. Harrison bought a country mansion in Letchmore Heath, Hertfordshire, for the movement's use, and later sold it to them for a token £1. Bhaktivedanta Manor is still the UK headquarters of ISKCON.

Over the next few years the movement spread rapidly, in America, England and elsewhere. At that time it particularly attracted ex-hippies, ex-dropouts and ex-drug-takers, all of whom seemed to find fulfilment in the vastly different lifestyle. Bhaktivedanta Manor, meanwhile, became both a Hindu temple and a theological college, training priests in the movement.

Before his death, at the age of 82, Prabhupada set up the international Governing Body Commission to run ISKCON. The idea was that there would be no one successor stepping into his shoes. It had 29 members, 11 of whom were gurus, with both spiritual and administrative control over different territorial zones around the world. The gurus were all sannyasin, who had taken final and irrevocable vows of chastity and renunciation. They were able to initiate new disciples on Prabhupada's behalf, effectively acting as him. Very quickly they became higher than the other members of the Commission.

'That was really an error, to do that,' says Bhagavat Dharma, Communications Manager for ISKCON in the UK.[1] 'Looking back, we can see now that Prabhupada wanted the governing body to have authority, without anyone above them.' But instead, the gurus had absolute power.

At one point there was a nearly 90 per cent failure rate of those who had taken sannyasa vows. 'The gurus found themselves in impossible situations, really; they had thousands of disciples; the elevation they received in some cases went to their heads. They were unable to carry the responsibility that Prabhupada carried, basically. Some of them deviated, in various different ways.'

A German devotee, Hansadutta, began stockpiling guns in Berkeley, California. In 1980 he started shooting out the windows of liquor stores. 'This got him, and the movement, into an awful lot of trouble. He was the first one to really go off the rails. According to our scriptures, the guru should be worshipped as being as good as God, and here was this man breaking the law. No one really knew what to do, so we just patched it up.'

In 1982 the guru for England, Jayatirtha (originally named James Immel), began taking LSD and having sex with some of his female disciples – both strictly forbidden for any devotee, let alone a guru. His dancing was particularly ecstatic and for a long time his followers believed him to be tremendously spiritual. The Governing Body Commission confronted him with his behaviour in Mayapur in 1982 and he left ISKCON, taking his disciples who were with him across the Ganges to a Gaudiya temple, until they were asked to leave. Jayatirtha called his disciples from England to join him and eventually they ended up in Nepal. 'That seriously disrupted the movement here,' says Bhagavat Dharma. 'Some of the repercussions are still going on.' Gradually his disciples began to realize Jayatirtha was taking drugs and most of them left him, apart from those who were taking drugs with him. Jayatirtha merged Prabhupada's teachings with a version of Christianity and became a New Age guru. Some of his followers now live in the US; others live in Glastonbury.

In 1987 one of his disciples, John Tiernan, who was psychologically disturbed, cut Jayatirtha's head off with a meat cleaver in a shop on Finchley Road, London. Tiernan was committed to a mental hospital for a while, but has now been released. According to Bhagavat Dharma, he is doing what he used to do very well as a Hare Krishna devotee, selling Hong Kong paintings.

Hansadutta and Jayatirtha were not the only gurus to cause the movement problems. Several were found to be homosexual, which is counted as illicit sexual activity because it doesn't lead to procreation. It is claimed that the leader in Japan, Guru Kripa, taught his followers to be pickpockets, and ended up being gaoled in the Netherlands for smuggling gold and gems.

Prabhupada's first initiated disciple, Kirtananda (Keith Ham), 'was from the beginning a controversial figure. He was sort of in between the Beat generation and the hippie generation. He went to India in 1963 to look for a guru. He didn't find one that he was happy with, came back to New York and met Prabhupada. But he never really accepted the authority or discipline of Prabhupada, and there were a few times when he fell out with him or walked away from him. But Prabhupada was a very broad-minded, compassionate and encouraging person, so he would accept him back and give him another chance.'

Kirtananda set up a community called New Vrindavan, with a 'Palace of Gold', in West Virginia. His father had been a Baptist minister, and he also introduced Christianity into the beliefs, along with Buddhism. In 1987 both Kirtananda and New Vrindavan were expelled by the Governing Body Commission. 'He had been involved in criminal activity, particularly fraud, and there were also some murders on the property at New Vrindavan. ISKCON were aware of that and worked with the police to bring him to prosecution.' He was found guilty of fraud, but is currently appealing against his conviction. New Vrindavan itself is in the process of coming back within ISKCON. Its leaders have recently taken new vows to follow Prabhupada and have been reinitiated into ISKCON.

Jayatirtha's successor as guru in Britain was another very early follower, Bhagavan. He had previously been in charge of central and southern Europe, particularly Italy, and had been extremely successful. He was apparently very intelligent, an extremely good organizer and manager, and he printed and distributed millions of Prabhupada's books. After Jayatirtha's downfall in 1982, Bhagavan was asked to take over Britain and South Africa. A lot of the older devotees didn't like his style, which tended to be autocratic, and left to go to the USA. Under Jayatirtha and especially under Bhagavan, some 30 million books were distributed in Britain alone.

Bhagavan also fell from the straight and narrow. He began having an affair with his secretary, which was not acceptable behaviour for a sanyassin. When this was discovered, the two of them left the movement, in 1986.

'It was too much for one man, what he was trying to do,' says Bhagavat Dharma. The same applies to the others who went awry, he says: 'In one sense it was the system rather than the individuals. Of course you can't condone criminal activities, but the sexual relationships, the drug-taking – the system put too great demands on individuals.'

Ravindra Svarupa, who joined ISKCON in 1971 and is now both a guru and chairman of the North American Governing Body Commission Continental Committee, puts the blame on the immaturity of both the individuals and the organization: '[Prabhupada's] early followers were young, immature, untrained and inexperienced. Many of them had suffered mental, moral and spiritual disorders as a result of their sojourn in the counterculture . . . The movement's early explosive growth created a further problem. New people, without much material or spiritual maturity or even training, had to assume positions of leadership and responsibility.'[2]

Within ten years of Prabhupada's death, six of the original 11 gurus (including both gurus responsible for Britain) had left or been expelled.

ISKCON has had to do a lot of soul-searching in recent years. 'We're going through the process of admitting to ourselves that we've made mistakes,' says Bhagavat Dharma. Since 1984 a 'reform movement' within the organization has been analysing what went wrong and finding ways to stop it happening again.

The basic problem was that 'the conception of guru was implicitly based on a traditional model of an inspired, charismatic spiritual autocrat, an absolutely and autonomously decisive authority, around whom an institution takes shape as the natural extension and embodiment of his charisma'.[3] How could this be squared with a modern committee-led management structure?

Members saw the guru more as an acharya – a pure devotee, God's direct representative, a model to be followed, literally, 'one who teaches by example'. Traditionally, as in the Shankaracharya of the North (see p. 149), the acharya was the appointed successor to the originating leader of a movement and his successors; it was a position of great honour, great responsibility and great power. The 11 territorial gurus saw themselves in the same light.

But Prabhupada's intention had been that there should be no spiritual successor to him, no acharya; the gurus should teach, and initiate new devotees, but otherwise should be responsible to the Governing Body Committee. The reform movement eventually managed to bring this about: the territorial zone system was scrapped, and the number of gurus increased. There are currently around 50, and devotees anywhere in the world can now choose to be a disciple of any one of them. In the Soho Street temple in London, for example, there are disciples of maybe ten different gurus.

In addition, one senior member of ISKCON is a trained management consultant. His job in the movement is to help them with management techniques.

◆

While all of this internal confusion and reform was going on, ISKCON was facing a new problem. Bhaktivedanta Manor had become a major temple and Hindus from all over Britain – not only ISKCON members – were coming to it for the main spiritual festivals. On two days a year, at Krishna's birth celebration, the roads in the small village would be clogged with cars and coaches bringing thousands of the faithful, and the locals objected. ISKCON offered to build a relief road at their own expense, leading directly to the Manor and bypassing the village. In May 1996 ISKCON won a public inquiry and the Manor was granted permission to build an access drive, and to be a public place of worship.

BELIEFS AND PRACTICES

Unlike many other forms of Hinduism, Krishna Consciousness teaches a relationship between individuals and a personal god, Krishna, who was the eighth incarnation or avatar of Vishnu – though ISKCON sees Krishna as the original form of Vishnu. Rama was another avatar of Vishnu, as was the Buddha.

There is Truth in all the great scriptures, but the oldest surviving scripture, the Vedic Hindu *Bhagavad-Gita*, is the literal words of Krishna. This is a small section of the vast *Mahabharata*, and records the conversation between Krishna and a young warrior, Arjuna.

Krishna is regarded as the Supreme Godhead; this is effectively a monotheistic form of Hinduism, known as Vaishnavism (worship of Vishnu). Krishna is omniscient, omnipresent, omnipotent and eternal, and the sustaining energy of all creation. But he is also personal, rather than unknowable, which the more mystical Hindu movements teach. He cares individually about every *jiva*, every living entity. Unlike the teaching of Shankara, for example, which is that the *atman*, or higher soul, of every person is the same, ISKCON teaches that every person is an individual.

The last incarnation, of avatar, or Krishna was as a Bengali saint, Chaitanya Mahaprabhu (1486–1533). There was a long-established tradition of Vaishnavism in both the north and the south of India. Chaitanya began a reformed branch of this known as Gaudiya Vaishnavism, or Vaishnava Bhakti (loving devotion and complete surrender to Krishna), specifically related to Krishna as a young man. Chaitanya's devotion and worship consisted of singing the names of Krishna, and ecstatic dance. One of several stories of his death is that he danced into the sea and was drowned; another, a little more prosaic, is that he injured his foot dancing and died of the subsequent infection. ISKCON believe he was absorbed back into the deity form in the temple.

Bhakti Hinduism has been a widely respected form of the religion since Chaitanya's death. Krishna Consciousness, far from being a new religious movement, is simply a modern version of a 500-year-old tradition, concentrating its attention on the West rather than the East.

ISKCON devotees believe that by living a life of deep spirituality they can achieve pure, blissful consciousness in this current life. The ultimate purpose of man, in this or any other world, is to serve God, and chanting the Hare Krishna mantra, repeating the names of God, helps them to attain a deep love of God. All the souls in the original spiritual world are in love with Krishna, says Bhagavat Dharma. 'Krishna is eternally enjoying Himself, with His cow-herd boyfriends and His cow-herd girlfriends, in His spiritual world; He is always happy, He is always having fun, in the spiritual world.'

♦

Devotees don't have such an easy time. Those who choose to live in the temples have to chant the Hare Krishna mantra 1,728 times a day – once per bead, for 16 rounds of 108 beads – to purify their consciousness. This is known as *japa* and takes about two hours a day, first thing in the morning. Prabhupada's guru used to chant 64 rounds; cutting it to 16 was Prabhupada's concession to the West, says Bhagavat Dharma. That is one of the few concessions, however.

At their initiation, when they take their vows, devotees are given Indian names; Bhagavat Dharma is actually a Geordie.

Their appearance is quite conspicuous. Some shave their heads, though this is no longer very common among those not living in a community, or ashram. All wear the *sikha*, a small plait or pigtail, to show that they are an individual – they haven't shaved *everything* off, as a Buddhist might. They usually wear a *tilaka*, a white stripe of clay from a sacred lake in India, on their forehead, and on seven other points of their body; this is sometimes called 'the footprint of Lord Vishnu' and marks the body as the Temple of God. Men wear *dhotis* – saffron for celibate men, white for married men – and women wear saris. They see this as spiritual clothing, not as Indian cultural trappings – and in any case, says Bhagavat Dharma, in the spiritual world people wear *dhotis*. India is the closest to the original spiritual culture.

Those living in an ashram – far fewer than in the 1970s – have to get up at 4 a.m. for worship. All members have to give up meat, fish and eggs; alcohol, tobacco, drugs, tea and coffee; gambling, sports, games and novels; and sex except for procreation within marriage – which means only on the two or three days a month when the woman is fertile, and not while she is pregnant or lactating.

'The scriptures teach that the pleasure to be obtained by spiritual activity, compared to the pleasures of the material world, of which sex is the highest pleasure, without a doubt, is like an ocean compared to the water in a calf's footprint,' says Bhagavat Dharma.

The movement is currently conducting a survey to find out how strictly members actually practise this. There is a core who follow it strictly, but other members probably follow it to varying degrees.

It's a demanding lifestyle. Outsiders might wonder why people join. In ISKCON's heyday, in the late 1960s and early 1970s, many members were ex-hippies. The new spiritual awareness and identity gained from ISKCON, underlined by the strict asceticism of the lifestyle, came as a welcome clarity after their search for something similar through sex and drugs and rock'n'roll. But it was this very background which contributed to the disastrous events in the years following Prabhupada's death.

'The difficulty for ISKCON was exacerbated from the beginning, however, by the marginal social position of most of the early recruits. They were very young and very alienated, and in joining ISKCON they became double dropouts – from mainstream society into the counterculture, from the counterculture into ISKCON,' says Ravindra Svarupa.[4]

The public image of ISKCON has modified a little over the years. Devotees may still sell books on the streets, but they haven't sold records since Jayatirtha's time as UK leader, and much of the fund-raising necessary to support the temples is now from the Hindu community. The money doesn't support only the temples. ISKCON runs a charity, Food for Life, which distributes free food where there is need; the Russian invasion of Chechnya in 1995 was one recent example.

Chanting in the streets is also seen less often, though the London temple chants on Oxford Street most lunchtimes and the temples in cities like Manchester and Liverpool do so once a week.

The chanting with drums and cymbals – *sankirtan* – is an essential part of their teaching. 'Just by chanting the name of God you can realize God. ISKCON is a movement for spreading that teaching. If a person chants sincerely, their heart becomes purified. In this material world we are trying to find enjoyment, just as we see Krishna enjoying himself,' says Bhagavat Dharma. The reason mankind is in such a mess is that 'each one of us trying to be a Lord of the Material World breeds conflict and hypocrisy because of the identification of the *jiva* with something material'. But unlike Buddhism, which seeks to negate such desires, Krishna Consciousness transforms them: 'The only permanent, non-conflicting identity is as a servant of the Living God; the desires become purified, and find an attachment to God.'

The movement appears to be maturing and developing. It is now far more oriented towards study than in the past, and the temples aim to educate the devotees about Vaishnavism, rather than simply teach them by rote.

Like many religious movements, ISKCON has been criticized for its treatment of women. In fact, it was some years ahead of the Church of England in having women priests – another of Prabhupada's few concessions to the West. Some of the temple presidents in Germany and in Northern Ireland, and a vice-president in London, are women. There are no women gurus, but there is apparently no reason why there should not be in the future.

It's difficult to say exactly how many members ISKCON has now. There is, says Bhagavat Dharma, a high attrition rate of members, but there are also many still around from 25 years ago, and many others, no longer active members of ISKCON itself, who still keep in touch and attend reunions. In Britain there are around 300 devotees living in temples and currently only a further 1,000 initiated members, but they might attract 30,000 to a festival at Bhaktivedanta Manor.

ELAN VITAL (DIVINE LIGHT MISSION)

Like several of the other religious movements which were popular in the heady days of the 1960s and 1970s, Elan Vital has moved on from its origins. Originally the flamboyant and definitely Eastern-inspired Divine Light Mission, it has matured into something new, changing its name to reflect its current emphasis and approach and, presumably, to distance itself from the past. It is included in this section because of its origins, rather than its current teachings.

HISTORY

There were several popular Eastern gurus in the late 1960s, including the Maharishi Mahesh Yogi, Bhagwan Shree Rajneesh and the Guru Maharaji. The first two, with their long beards, fit the Western conception of an Eastern guru; the third was, when he sprang to prominence in 1971, a 13-year-old boy.

Maharaji was the son of Shri Hans Ji Maharaj, who began the Divine Light Mission in northern India in 1960, based on the teachings of his own Hindu guru of enlightenment through knowledge. When his father died in 1966, the eight-year-old Prem Pal Singh Rawat or Pratap Singh Rawat-Balyogeshwar stood up, announced that he was the new guru and started teaching. As Guru Maharaji he embarked on a world tour in 1971, quickly establishing a large following in Britain and America. In 1973 he held what should have been a huge event in the Houston Astrodome. Millennium '73 was intended to launch the spiritual millennium, but the event was a washout in its effects and its attendance, and was a financial disaster. In 1974, at 16, Maharaji married his 24-year-old secretary Marolyn Johnson.

At about this time he fell out with his mother, Mata Ji, who had until then really been running the organization along with one of Maharaji's three older brothers, Bal Bhagwan Ji, who (after legal battles) still heads the Divine Light Mission in India. Press reports at the time said that she disapproved of Maharaji's lifestyle, which included Rolls-Royces and luxury homes.

According to Glen Whittaker, National Organizer of Elan Vital in the UK, 'He did her the disservice of marrying an American woman he loved (rather than taking an Indian bride), and behind this the subtext of her declining influence over the way the teaching was promoted as Maharaji became adult and made it increasingly clear that the Knowledge was not an Indian teaching, but universal.'[5]

Maharaji had seen that the Indian influences on his Western followers were 'unnecessary and in fact a hindrance to the wider acceptance of his teaching'. Over the next few years the style of the teachings changed, dropping the Hindu terminology and ideas and focusing entirely on the Knowledge. In the early 1980s Maharaji changed the movement's name to Elan Vital to reflect the change in emphasis. He dismantled the structure of ashrams, or communal homes, and also appears to have renounced his almost divine status as guru. Teachers of the Knowledge, formerly called mahatmas, became simply instructors.

The British organization Elan Vital was founded in 1991, 20 years after Maharaji first took Britain by storm. It was registered as an educational charity in 1992.

BELIEFS AND PRACTICES

Elan Vital has now dropped all of its original Eastern religious practices: 'Although Maharaji is originally from India, there is no connection between what he teaches and the religions or religious background of that country. In particular, the teaching does not concern itself with such concepts as reincarnation, heaven or life after death. Maharaji only encourages people to experience the present reality of life now.'

Unusually, the fact that Maharaji came from a line of 'Perfect Masters' is no longer relevant to the reformed movement. 'This is not where the authority comes from, nor the recognition of Maharaji as the master by his student; this comes rather from the nature of the teaching and its benefit to the individual.'

Maharaji himself has put his early life behind him. 'In a simple metaphor explaining his position, he will . . . say, although the service history and list of previous owners of a car is useful to have, what is more important is does it work and is it in good enough condition for you and what you need it for now.'

The Divine Light movement used to be criticized for the devotion given to Maharaji, who was seen to live a life of luxury on the donations of his followers. Clearly conscious of past criticisms, Whittaker is emphatic that Maharaji now earns nothing from Elan Vital or any other movement promoting his teachings.

'He lives as a private individual in the United States with his wife and four children and spends most of his year on teaching tours in various parts of the world.' He speaks at around 250 meetings a year 'on his own experience of life, its nature and purpose, often with humour and perception. He speaks essentially of an experience of stillness, peace and contentment it is possible to achieve within, and his Knowledge consists of techniques to go within for this purpose.'

At the heart of Elan Vital is this Knowledge – loosely, the joy of true self-knowledge. 'In brief, his view is that each individual should seek to know his or her true self. In his talks, he explains the rationale for the need to know oneself and to explore the clues which point to that within us which is worthy of our knowledge, and which, when experienced, brings with it a feeling of well-being, of happiness, of being in harmony with one's own source . . . For those who wish to pursue his teaching in a practical way he is able to direct them in certain simple techniques of inner stillness, which when practised allow the sense of well-being, of inner satisfaction, to be experienced; this teaching is given the name "Knowledge".'

The Knowledge includes four secret meditation procedures: Light, Music, Nectar and Word. 'That which we seek is already within us. The process of reaching it is one of learning to experience what is already there. It is one the individual has to perform for him- or herself, with the guidance and help of the teacher.' The emphasis is on individual, subjective experience rather than on a body of dogma, and in its Divine Light days the movement was sometimes criticized for this stressing of emotional experience over intellect.

The teachings could perhaps best be described as practical mysticism. 'It is important to understand that his teaching is practical and pragmatic. He will speak of the great value of trust in that power which gives life, and orders life most perfectly, but only in terms of a real experience. He does not refer to "God", but to the god within you, or the divinity within, as the power that gives existence. He has sometimes referred to the existence of two gods – the one created by humankind and the one which creates humankind. But though such references obviously infer an acceptance of a creative, loving power, he distances himself and his teaching strongly from the concept of religion. He regards himself as an educator.'

In the UK Elan Vital is a very small operation, with only three or four full-time staff, depending very much on volunteer help and funding. As a charity, it 'provides the legal framework and support structure for the personal teaching between master and student to take place'. It presents video screenings of Maharaji's talks in some 100 towns around Britain and arranges for his teaching tours.

'When visiting Britain in person, Maharaji is also able to instruct people who wish in the techniques of Knowledge. This process is sometimes called "receiving Knowledge".' It is not clear whether it is possible to receive Knowledge from anyone other than Maharaji.

There are perhaps 10,000 people in the UK who 'practise the techniques of Knowledge'. Outside India there are around 75,000 altogether, with a further 250,000 in India. Whether those in India follow the teachings of Maharaji, or those of his father's original Divine Light Mission, now run by his brother, is not known.

Those in the West do not see themselves as members of a religion: 'We are simply people who appreciate and practise the teaching of a unique individual, who asks nothing of us other than that we enjoy our life to the full,' says Whittaker. Not only that, but, 'Beyond the intrinsic merit of the teaching, it differs from many other teachings which might seem similar from the outside by being free of charge at every stage.'

ECKANKAR

ECKANKAR[6] claims to be the root religion: 'ECK is the ancient teaching that is the source from which all religions and philosophies spring.'[7] It has Hindu and Sikh roots, and so is included in this section, but it is an Esoteric movement in as much as it concentrates mainly on the individual's relationship with God (SUGMAD) through the spirit of God (ECK).

ECKists experience ECK through light and sound in their 'spiritual exercises, dreams and everyday life'. They also explore heavenly worlds through 'soul travel', in which they meet the Masters and learn from them. There is always a Living ECK Master, currently Harold Klemp, who speaks on ECKANKAR at seminars around the world, and whose inner being, the Mahanta, meets and guides other ECKists on the other planes.

HISTORY

Born in Kentucky, Paul Twitchell (?1909–71) claims to have learned the technique of Soul Travel at the age of three from his elder sister, who had been taught it by their father, who had learned it from an Indian guru, Sudar Singh. Twitchell first met Sudar Singh in Paris when he was quite young.

Twitchell's family don't confirm this version of the story.

It is significant that Twitchell was adopted. Writing of an eighteenth-century ECK Master, he says, 'He came into this world . . . in the usual manner of the ECK Masters – very mysteriously. Few know how they are given birth, but always some family adopts them during their infancy and while raising them, one member of the family who is adept at Soul Travel teaches them at an early age.'[8]

In 1944, Twitchell says, he met a Tibetan Master, Rebazar Tarzs, in his soul body, who taught him about ECKANKAR. Twitchell was at that time in the US Navy. Later, like L. Ron Hubbard, the founder of Scientology, he 'made his living by writing for pulp magazines'.[9]

Before founding ECKANKAR, from 1950 to 1955 Twitchell was a member of the Self-Revelation Church of Absolute Monism, a Hindu movement led by Swami Premananda. He was apparently required to leave the Church because of misconduct, and in 1955 he joined Scientology, becoming one of the very first to go Clear. Also in 1955 he joined Ruhani Satsang, a Sant Mat movement founded by Kirpal Singh (see p. 142). Twitchell's second wife, Gail, was initiated in 1963, but then he fell out with Kirpal and they left the movement the same year.

The ECKANKAR explanation is that Twitchell met Rebazar Tarzs and other Masters of the Vairagi. Then, 'while they trained Paul to become the Living ECK Master, he explored a wide range of spiritual traditions under different teachers'.[10]

Twitchell founded ECKANKAR in the USA in 1965, at the same time declaring himself to be number 971 in an unbroken line of Living ECK Masters stretching back many thousands of years. His lectures and books on self-realization and God-realization, particularly *The Tiger's Fang* and *The Spiritual Notebook*, publicized the new movement, which grew rapidly. It was registered as a non-profit-making religious organization in 1970.

After Twitchell's death from a heart attack in 1971, leadership passed to his appointed successor, Darwin Gross (Living Master number 972), despite some dissension among senior members of the movement, several of whom left. Gross later married Gail Twitchell, who had supported his succession, though they were divorced in 1978. Gross moved the Church's headquarters to California, and membership continued to rise, despite adverse publicity about much of ECKANKAR's teachings having been 'borrowed' from Ruhani Satsang and other Sant Mat movements.

Gross's leadership was apparently controversial, and in 1981 he handed the Living Master's 'rod of power' to Harold Klemp (number 973). Gross remained as president of the ECKANKAR corporation until 1983, but in 1984 Klemp declared that Gross was no longer to be recognized as an ECK Master, and his books on ECKANKAR were banished from the movement. Gross, a former musician from Oregon, returned there to set up a new movement, Sounds of Soul, with other ex-ECKists. Gross's movement is now known as Ancient Teachings of the Masters (ATOM).

Klemp moved the headquarters to Minneapolis in the 1980s. He has gone on to write the overwhelming majority of the inspirational and teaching books of the movement, leading to the suggestion by some critics that he is the St Paul to Twitchell's Jesus. Eve Illing, the regional ECKANKAR cleric for the UK, who joined ECKANKAR only two months after Twitchell's death, disagrees with this interpretation: 'ECKANKAR is a living, evolving religion in which the message of a past ECK Master is always secondary to that of the current Living ECK Master.'[11]

She outlines their different roles: 'It was Paul Twitchell's mission to put spiritual truths that had always been handed down from Master to pupil into book form for the growing number of seekers. Harold Klemp has continued this, but part of his mission has been to establish a seat of power in the building of the ECK Temple at Chanhassen, MN, USA. Also he has established the RESA (Regional ECK Spiritual Aide) structure which puts a regional representative of the Living ECK Master in each area. Sri Harold has also done much to show how the spiritual principles can be applied in everyday life through divine love and service to all.'

Klemp's pre-eminence is emphasized in two talks transcribed in one of his books.

> We must be careful that we in ECK don't create gods out of past Masters, no matter how much we love and revere them, no matter how important they have been to the history of ECK. As soon as we start to look to a past ECK Master for our present guidance, we become no different from an orthodox religion . . . The Living Word refers to the Mahanta, the Living ECK Master of the times. Whenever we look to a past master for our present spiritual guidance, we take a detour.'[12]

Although Twitchell's founding role and his teachings are of immense importance to the movement, the man himself now seems to be down-played. 'To say he had a checkered life is an understatement. In many ways he was quite a rascal.'[13]

ECKANKAR claim 'tens of thousands of ECKists in over a hundred countries'. It is not known how many there are in the UK.

BELIEFS AND PRACTICES

In *The Spiritual Notebook*, Twitchell defines ECKANKAR as 'the ancient science of Soul Travel'.

> The term 'bilocation', which is the ability to be in two places at the same time, is no longer in the vocabulary of ECK. This word has been dropped from our terminology because it sounds too much like astral projection. The expression 'Soul Travel' is used instead, as it gives more depth and breadth to the teachings of ECK.[14]

Soul Travel, ECKists explain, is the ability to expand one's consciousness, which may include the inner self travelling independently of the body, on the Astral and higher spiritual planes. Some of these travels are experienced during sleep, and one of the earliest parts of ECK training is in recalling and recording one's dreams.

On these planes one can meet both the Living ECK Master and other Masters. Both Gross and Klemp had been practising Soul Travel before they encountered

ECKANKAR. Both recognized Twitchell's photograph on the back of his books as someone they had met on the other planes.

(According to one source, Jesus and St Paul became ECK Masters. Twitchell wrote that the Living ECK Master at the time of Christ was Zadok, who worked with a group who had broken away from the Essenes – 'a secret, mystical organization which exists to this day in the Middle East'. Jesus apparently 'studied for some time under the great Zadok. The ECK Master gave Jesus the basic fundamentals of ECKANKAR, who [sic] used them in His own teachings. Out of His knowledge of ECK came what we know today as Christianity.'[15])

There are a dozen known planes between the Physical and SUGMAD, 'the Ocean of Love and Mercy'. Each has its temple, its Guardian and its unique sound. Above the Physical plane is the Astral plane. According to ECKANKAR, this is as far as most occultists ever reach. Its Guardian is Gopal Das, and its sound is the roar of the sea. Next comes the Causal plane, where the memories of all our past lives are stored. This plane can be recognized by the sound of tinkling bells. Beyond that is the Mental plane, which is the source of all religions and philosophies. Its sound is running water.

Although ECKANKAR does not have a dualist belief, it teaches that the Mental plane 'is the home of the Kal Niranjan, the God of the lower worlds and ruler of the negative forces. He is known by many names, including Satan, the Devil, Asmodeus, Beelzebub and Ahriman, to name a few. The negative power is often known as the Universal Mind, which many sects and religions worship as the true God power.'[16]

The illusions of the physical world include religions, philosophies and the ideas of social reformers. The entire material universe is really a prison in which mankind is trapped. According to Twitchell, the ECK Masters 'come from outside this prison to liberate all souls from Kal's possession for ever. It is with the help and grace of these Masters that we leave this dark land of illusion and begin the journey homeward again.'[17]

The top level of the Mental plane is the Etheric plane, which is the source of unconscious, primitive thought.

We now step out of the lower planes into the pure spiritual worlds: the Soul plane, Alakh Lok (plane), Alaya Lok, Hukikat Lok, Agam Lok, Anami Lok and the SUGMAD World. There are apparently other, unnamed planes before reaching SUGMAD itself.

The *chela*, or student of ECKANKAR, rises through various levels of initiation, becoming able to access successively higher planes. After the second initiation, to the Astral plane, the ECKist has avoided the necessity for any further physical incarnations. He can also teach ECKANKAR classes. Higher initiates, those who have reached the Soul plane and above and who have had additional training, are the clergy of ECKANKAR.

'The function of ECK clergy is much the same as in other religions, e.g. ECK wedding ceremonies, memorial services, worship services, etc.,' says Illing. Clergy can be male or female. However, 'Living ECK Masters up to this moment in time have always been male.'

As with other Esoteric religions, or any movement with a series of initiations, there is a clear 'spiritual career path' with many levels.

'The goal of every ECKist is to experience life to the fullest. That is spiritual mastery. Some of us may eventually serve on earth as "guardian angel" ECK Masters, while others will pursue specialized interests in the spiritual worlds.'[18]

Twitchell was given the ECK rod of power by the Tibetan Master Rebazar Tarzs, and this has since been handed on, first to Gross and then to Klemp.

> The departing Master always leaves on . . . October 22nd, and in turn his successor always accepts the Rod of ECK Power on the same day, at midnight, at the full of the moon in the valley of Shangta, in northern Tibet, near the Katsupari Monastery. The ritual takes place at the site of the ancient Oracle of Tirmer under the direction of the ancient sage Yaubl Sacabi, whose age is beyond the imagination of the normal senses. The Adepts of the ancient Order of the Vairagi meet at the time of the handing of the mantle of spiritual power from the departing Master to his successor.[19]

These meetings are not in the physical, material world – that is, Twitchell did not physically go to Tibet when he became Living Master, and again when he handed the rod on to Gross – but on a higher plane, through Soul Travel.

It is not always clear whether the Vairagi ECK Masters whom Twitchell met early in his spiritual career were earthly people or purely on the spiritual planes. According to Eve Illing, most of the Vairagi Masters 'exist in the various levels of heaven'. It appears that Twitchell may have met Rebazar Tarzs, who was over 500 years old, in physical form, but he met Fubbi Quantz (over 1,000 years old) and Yaubl Sacabi (possibly over 2,000 years old) at Golden Wisdom Temples (see below).

Twitchell writes, 'All ECK Masters, like Rebazar Tarzs, Fubbi Quantz and Yaubl Sacabi, may live on for years in their physical bodies, far exceeding the normal lifetime of man. Then they will retire and give up their duties to another. However, they will still stand in the background, watching and helping the world unfold spiritually toward its higher destination.'[20]

It might seem strange, then, that Twitchell died when he was only around 60, especially as he says:

> Usually the ECK Master does not die, in the same way we know human death, but merely moves out of this arena of action into another. The living ECK Master turns over the Rod of Power to his successor at a particular time and then withdraws into the other worlds. Sometimes he stays around, like Rebazar Tarzs, Fubbi Quantz and Yaubl Sacabi.[21]

Rebazar Tarzs was apparently born in 1461 in Tibet. 'He stayed on earth for seventy-five years teaching ECK, then he retired in the same body to the mountainous vastness of the Himalayas.'[22]

Twitchell is apparently now working in the heavenly worlds. 'I have no scientific proof myself of this, nor do I know what work he is doing, but I have met him briefly in the inner worlds,' says Illing.

The Adepts of the ancient Order of the Vairagi are 'ECK Masters who are the guardians of the *Shariyat-Ki-Sugmad* in the Temples of Golden Wisdom'.[23] These Temples include 'the Katsupari Monastery in Tibet (Fubbi Quantz, guardian); the Gare-Hira Temple at Agam Des in the Himalayas (Yaubl Sacabi, guardian); the House of Moksha, the Temple on Retz, Venus (Rami Nuri, guardian); and the Temple of ECK, in Chanhassen, Minnesota (Harold Klemp, guardian)'.[24] According to Illing, these guardians 'once served as Living ECK Masters on Earth'.

There are also 'nine secret ECK Masters who are responsible for the hidden knowledge of the spiritual worlds . . . These Masters are responsible for the collection of the secret knowledge and its placement into the greatest of sacred books, the *Shariyat-Ki-Sugmad*.'[25] There are 12 volumes of the *Shariyat* on the higher planes, of which the first two have been transcribed by Twitchell and published by ECKANKAR.

◆

ECK, the power or Spirit of God, can be experienced directly through the senses of light and sound. This experience is the focal point of the religion, the proof to its members that it works.

> The Light and Sound of God – the Holy Spirit. The two aspects through which God appears in the lower worlds. The Holy Spirit can appear to us as Light, which is a reflection of the atoms of God moving in space, or as Sound, which is the Audible Life Current that carries Soul back home to God. The spiritual exercises of ECK show people how to look and listen within themselves for these qualities of Divine Spirit for uplift and guidance.[26]

The Light and Sound may be seen or heard with the physical eyes and ears, but are usually experienced in a different way. ECKANKAR, like many of the Esoteric religious movements, trains its members in the techniques of visualization, sometimes known as guided meditation; in sleep it is known as lucid dreaming, in which the dreamer takes control of the dream. 'Dreams play an important role in the spiritual unfoldment of the ECKist. They are a look into the heavenly worlds. In many cases, the dream becomes a teaching tool.' In fact, 'The ultimate purpose of dreams is to bring the individual closer to the Light and Sound of God'.[27]

This is how visualization works:

> Begin to visualize a growing, golden light surrounding you. It may be very subtle at first. It embraces you, flows with you. Soon you are riding currents of light into the vastness of the cosmic sea . . . Ever so lightly, you sense a breeze. You hear the sound of a wind from deep within. It creates tiny ripples on the surface of the sea. Suddenly you realize you're experiencing the Light and Sound of God. You can stay here for a while if you choose, basking in this radiant, soothing ocean of Light and love. When you're ready, slowly come back . . .[28]

ECKANKAR often borrows the phraseology of other religions (though ECKists see it the other way around) to describe the spiritual benefits of their own. 'Rami Nuri, the great ECK Master in charge of the third section of the *Shariyat-Ki-Sugmad*, at the Temple of Golden Wisdom on Venus, said, "He who drinks of the stream of ECK can never thirst, but in him is a well of water springing up into life everlasting."'[29] Cf. John 4:14. The ECK Master Gopal Das is quoted in the *Shariyat-Ki-Sugmad* as saying, 'Those who follow the ECK take nothing for granted, for they must prove it themselves. Only then will they know that God so loved them that He sent a living ECK Master to bring Souls home to Him.'[30] Cf. John 3:16.

Much of the criticism of ECKANKAR focuses on whether their beliefs are original, truly revealed to Twitchell by Tibetan Vairagi Masters, or whether he cobbled them together from bits of other religions. But in one way, it could be asked, does this really matter? Many of the Esoteric and Neo-Pagan religions are openly eclectic, with the philosophy, 'If it works, use it.'

For its members, ECKANKAR works. 'I have been studying the ancient teachings of ECKANKAR for 23 years and for me they have fulfilled my dreams and answered my questions about Life,' says Illing. 'I am truly grateful for having been shown how to live a balanced life and how to find my own answers.'

The point only becomes important if the religion claims uniqueness in its origins, its vision and its teachings, beliefs and practices, which was certainly the case in the early days of ECKANKAR.

> But each of those who leave the path of ECK, or refuse to accept the living ECK Master, will come to grief upon the rocks as surely as a captain wrecks his ship on the reef by not listening to the pilot. Again and again I have pointed out that there is no other path than ECK . . . anyone who tries another path is trying to start on a lower rung . . . The Order of the Vairagi is the only pure line of spiritual Masters in the world.[31]

Emphasizing that only ECKANKAR has the truth, Twitchell also wrote:

> only by the use of ECK can we take the straight road to this absolute kingdom. All other practices leave us in the lower worlds, because the vehicle they use is not purely spiritual. The ECK makes use of a true spiritual entity, and consequently gets us access into the pure spiritual regions. Whoever is properly initiated into the mysteries of ECK by a perfect Adept may easily scale spiritual heights that are inaccessible to those who follow any other path to God.[32]

Paradoxically, despite this belief that it is the only true path. 'There is no desire to convert people to ECKANKAR.'[33]

For several years ECKANKAR simply ignored the mounting evidence that Twitchell had borrowed from other sources, even directly plagiarizing other people's books (including Sant Mat writer Julian Johnson) in his own. The official explanation since the mid-1980s is that fragments of the Truth are to be found, often distorted, in all the world's religions, and that Twitchell had drawn these together. Nevertheless, it has also been shown that in some of his books on ECKANKAR Twitchell ascribes quotations to various named Masters which, in earlier articles, he had ascribed to L. Ron Hubbard, Kirpal Singh and the leader of the Self-Revelation Church of Absolute Monism, Swami Premananda.

Effectively, ECKANKAR is one of many modern Western versions of the Sant Mat tradition of northern India. Of the three religions Twitchell was involved in before founding ECKANKAR, Ruhani Satsang is the most significant. The teachings of ECKANKAR are generally similar to those of Kirpal Singh, and several of the teachings Twitchell ascribed to Rebazar Tarzs (a name not recognized by other Sant Mat movements, which also do not recognize ECKANKAR's lineage of Masters) were actually taken from Kirpal Singh.

There is a large range of esoteric Hindu/Sikh-inspired movements in the Western world, many of them ultimately stemming from the Sant Mat tradition. In the West, these are constantly splintering to form new movements, each one claiming to be the true successor to one of the others. For example, Radhasoami Satsang Beas, Kirpal Singh's previous movement, was itself one of several splinter groups from Radhasoami Satsang, which was founded in 1861 by Soamiji Maharaj. When Kirpal Singh lost the leadership succession in Radhasoami Satsang Beas in 1951, he founded Ruhani Satsang, which itself has spawned at least four other movements, one of them ECKANKAR.

From an outsider's point of view, such constant splits in this type of religion are inevitable because of the essentially subjective nature of the spiritual experience. When the leader of a movement dies, it is quite possible that two or more senior members of the movement, in their individual Soul Travels, will be 'told' by the Masters that they have been appointed to take over.

Quotations from three of the other offshoots of Ruhani Satsang will illustrate the similarities to ECKANKAR.

- Sawan Kirpal Ruhani Mission: 'We can attain self-knowledge and God-realization through mystic experiences on the path of the Masters.'
- Sant Bani Ashram: '... initiation into the path of Surat Shabd Yoga [i.e. the yoga of the celestial sound], a path of love and discipline that embraces the essence of the teachings of all True Masters'.
- Kirpal Ruhani Satsang, founded by Kirpal's disciple, 'the present Living Master, Sant Thaka Singh Ji', is 'devoted to communicating the truth about human existence, its nature and purpose as expressed by the Masters of the Yoga of Inner Light and Sound'.

In response to this, Eve Illing says, 'I can only say my truth is that the teachings of the Light and Sound of God are the root religion, the source of all teachings. There was no one name for this path before 1965 when Paul Twitchell was given the word ECKANKAR by the Vairagi Masters to be able to identify these ancient teachings by name.'

ECKANKAR itself has produced at least one offshoot – in addition to Darwin Gross's movement – the Divine Science of Light and Sound, founded by a former ECKANKAR leader, Jerry Mulvin, in California in 1980.

OSHO INTERNATIONAL/ RAJNEESH

Osho International used to be known as Rajneesh. Its guru Bhagwan Shree Rajneesh changed his name to Osho shortly before he died. Since the troubled times of the mid-1980s, and since Osho's death in 1990, the movement has seemed to become more relaxed, but it was dogged by controversy through the 1970s and 1980s.

HISTORY

Rajneesh (1931–90) studied philosophy at university in Jabalpur, India, going on to teach philosophy there. Finding the university too restrictive, in 1966 he began lecturing and preaching around India, promoting meditation and free love. In 1969 he settled in Bombay, then moved to Poona in 1974, attracting large numbers of followers to his ashram and upsetting the local authorities in each case. He left Poona in 1981 and moved to the USA, setting up a large community in a 325-square-km (126-square-mile) ranch in Oregon, where his followers, or sannyasins, built the 'city' of Rajneeshpuram.

He was criticized for a wide range of things over the years, perhaps the most obvious being his ostentatious wealth. He preached his message only to the well-off. The poor have enough to do simply surviving, so have no time and energy left for spiritual development. The well-off, in contrast, have the time – and the money – to go to spiritual retreats, meditation classes and so on. His followers brought money with them, and were encouraged to bring more – living in the ashrams was never cheap – and the money was openly spent on gold, jewellery, at least 11 Rolls-Royces and four aeroplanes. It also got him into trouble with the tax authorities, first in India and then in the USA.

Rajneeshpuram was a centre of controversy. There were accusations that the work was effectively slave labour, as his devoted followers built the city for little or no pay. There was conflict with the local towns of Antelope and The Dalles, whose residents objected to the influx of Rajneesh's followers, especially when they began to buy up more property and allegedly tried to rig local elections by bussing in followers to vote, and by giving local people food poisoning on election day. The 'city' became an armed camp, with its own security guards.

The focus of hatred for both the local people and the authorities was not so much Rajneesh himself as Ma Anand Sheela, an Indian woman who had been Rajneesh's secretary and was now the leader of the religion and the community. She was supposedly acting as Rajneesh's spokesperson – he took a vow of silence for several years – but was actually in complete control. When matters came to a head in 1985, Rajneesh denounced Sheela and expelled her. Sheela fled to Germany and Rajneesh also tried to leave the country. He was arrested when his plane stopped to refuel.

Rajneesh was fined an amount which is variously quoted as $40,000, $400,000 or $4 million, given a suspended gaol sentence and flung out of the USA. Sheela was extradited from Germany and given a 20-year gaol sentence, of which she served four years. The charges against Sheela and other senior members included attempted murder, firearms offences, immigration offences and financial irregularities, among others.

Two British women were senior in the organization: Sally-Anne Croft was in charge of finance and Susan Hagan ran the Rajneesh Investment Corporation, which included overall responsibility for the construction of Rajneeshpuram. Both were charged, with others, with conspiracy to murder a local federal attorney. They managed to return to Britain, and spent several years fighting extradition back to the USA, claiming that they were innocent but would probably be found guilty simply through association. In July 1995 their fears were proved correct; in October they received prison sentences of five years. The evidence for their guilt rested almost entirely on the testimonies of other senior ex-members, who had used plea-bargaining to reduce their own sentences.

In failing health, Rajneesh himself eventually returned to India, where he died in Poona in 1990. He claimed that he had been poisoned by the American authorities. Some say that he was poisoned by Sheela or others in the organization; and there are persistent rumours that he died from AIDS.

Since his death, Osho International has re-established itself in Rajneesh's original commune in Poona, India, setting up a 'multiversity' and continuing to pass on Rajneesh/Osho's teachings.

BELIEFS AND PRACTICES

The name Bhagwan is variously translated as 'the Blessed One', 'god-man', 'master of the vagina' and, it seems, 'cunt-cock'; according to Rajneesh himself, it was coined from words for the female and male genitalia. Rajneesh used the name as a 'challenge', but at the end of 1988 he announced that he had tired of the joke. For a few days he was called Gautama the Buddha, and then Shree Rajneesh Zorba the Buddha, but when both names brought complaints he dropped them and eventually took the name Osho, meaning 'friend', by which the whole movement is now known. If nothing else, it separates the present-day movement from the tarnished image of the earlier Rajneesh organization.

As a youth and as a student, Rajneesh was argumentative and disruptive, challenging and questioning everything he was taught. The philosophy he later taught sprang from this: one must challenge everything traditionally taught by religions from both the East and the West.

It is intentionally difficult to pinpoint the beliefs in Rajneesh/Osho. There was a book, *Rajneeshism: An Introduction to Bhagwan Shree Rajneesh and His Religion*, but it was withdrawn only two years after its publication in 1983. Rajneesh's teachings often appear contradictory, but he explained:

> This is one of my basic insights: that in life there are no contradictions. All contradictions are complementaries. Night is complementary to day, so is summer to winter, so is death to life. They are not against each other. There is nothing against, because there is only one energy, it is one God . . . Opposites are just like wings of a bird, two wings – they look opposite to each other but they support each other. The bird cannot fly with one wing.[34]

His teachings are a mixture of homespun philosophy and deep spiritual insights. His followers tend to be intelligent, middle-class people. It has been said that although he preached a non-intellectual message, his followers needed to be intelligent in order to understand the message that they must lay their intellect to one side.

> My message is very simple. That's why it is difficult to understand. I teach the obvious; it is not complex at all. Because it is not complex there is nothing much to understand in it. It has to be lived, experienced. My message is not verbal, logical, rational. It is existential, so those who want to understand it intellectually will only misunderstand it.

For Rajneesh, God is not 'somewhere out there'; he is everywhere, in everything, and every part of life can be communion with God.

> My trust is total. I trust the outer, I trust the inner – because outer and inner are both together. They cannot be separated. There is no God without this world; there is no world without God. God is the innermost core of this world. The juice flowing in the trees is God, the blood circulating in your body is God, the consciousness residing in you is God. God and the world are mixed together just like a dancer and his dance; they cannot be separated, they are inseparable . . .

> I teach the whole man. I am not a materialist or a spiritualist. My approach
> is wholistic – and the whole man can only be holy.

(As a philosopher Rajneesh may well have known that the English words whole,
holy, health and hale – as in 'hale and hearty' – all come from the Old English
root *hal*, *halig*, meaning 'whole', while the word 'holistic' comes from the Greek
root *holos*, also meaning 'whole'.)

Through all his teachings Rajneesh was opposed to doctrine and indoctrination.
Spirituality may be learned, but it cannot be taught, at least not as a set of rules.

> The people who are with me are not my followers. They are my lovers, but not
> my followers. They are my friends, but not my followers. They are my
> disciples, but not my followers. And what is the difference between a disciple
> and a follower? A follower believes; whatever is said, he makes a dogma out of
> it. The disciple learns, experiments, and unless he finds the truth himself he
> remains open. I am not giving any dogma to my friends here, to my
> sannyasins. All that I am doing here is helping them to understand themselves.
> All I am doing here is helping them to be themselves . . .
>   . . . man has not to follow anybody. Understand certainly, learn certainly,
> listen certainly, remain open. But follow your own inner spontaneity, follow
> your own being . . .
>   I am not the leader and they are not the followers. And I am not creating
> a cult, I am not creating a church. The sannyasins are just a commune
> of friends, not a church. We don't have any dogma that everybody has to
> believe in.

That was certainly the theory, though the practice under Ma Anand Sheela may
have been somewhat different.

♦

Although there is no argument that things fell apart seriously in the early and
mid-1980s under Ma Anand Sheela, and that at various times in his career
Rajneesh was chased by the authorities for non-payment of tax, most of the other
criticisms of the movement could be seen more as a matter of perception than
anything else. Briefly, they can be listed as sexual orgies, rape, other violence,
mind-control, authoritarianism and deliberate reduction of self-dignity. There has
no doubt been some truth behind all of them, at some point, but it is a truism
that what appeared a good idea at the time can change its appearance markedly
when portrayed by a disaffected ex-member.

Guided meditation could perhaps be seen as mind-control; submerging oneself
in God might lead to a reduced sense of the importance of self; while there is a
fine perceptual line between the necessary discipline of living in a religious
commune and authoritarianism.

Rajneesh did encourage people to scream and shout, to flail around, to express
their anger and frustrations. Sometimes this became uncontrolled violence,
causing physical injuries, but Rajneesh put a stop to this as early as 1979.

Within the ashram he also promoted free love, encouraging people to view sex
as a powerful affirmation of spirituality. Although this belief is common to both
Tantric Buddhism and some areas of Neo-Paganism, it was viewed with a certain

mixture of horror, disgust and prurience by mainstream religious society in both the West and the East.

Western religions, Rajneesh said, taught that sex was sinful, while most Eastern religions insisted on celibacy for their gurus. Both condemned him for his many 'energy-giving sessions' with young, attractive, female sannyasins, though for them sex with Rajneesh/Osho was the highest honour.

Rajneesh roundly condemned both Western and Eastern religions.

> The East is against love. That's why Eastern spirituality is sad, dull, dead. No juice flows through the Eastern saint. He is afraid of any flow, any vibration, any streaming of his energy. He is constantly controlling himself, repressing himself. He is sitting upon himself, on guard. He is against himself and against the world. He is simply waiting to die, he is committing a slow suicide . . .
>
> The Western man has lost all idea of who he is. He has lost track of consciousness, he is not aware. He has become more and more mechanical because he denies the inner. So laughter is there but laughter cannot go deep, because there is no depth. The depth is not accepted. So the West lives in a shallow laughter and the East lives in a deep sadness. This is the misery, the agony that has happened to man.

At the same time he absorbed into his own teachings much of both Western and Eastern spiritual teaching.

> We are experimenting in a multi-dimensional way. We are experimenting with Tao, we are experimenting with Sufism, we are experimenting with Jainism, Hinduism, Islam, Christianity. We are experimenting with Tantra, Yoga, alchemy; we are experimenting with all the possibilities that can make the human consciousness rich and a human being whole . . .
>
> I am not against anything. I am for all. I am utterly for all, I claim the whole human heritage, and whatsoever is good in any tradition is mine[35] and whatsoever can make man richer is mine. I don't belong to any tradition, all traditions belong to me.
>
> So this is a new experiment. It has never been done before in such a way. This is the synthesis of all the paths.

This synthesis is seen most clearly in two aspects of Osho International: meditation and courses.

One of the central meditational practices of the movement is the Mystic Rose. This involves laughing for three hours a day for the first week, crying for three hours a day for the second and sitting in silence for three hours a day for the third week. Another, usually done first thing in the morning, is Dynamic Meditation: 'Osho's basic and most popular meditation, consisting of five phases including breathing, catharsis and jumping up and down on one's heels shouting the Sufi mantra "Hoo", "Hoo", "Hoo". In the Dynamic Meditation a Gurdjieff "stop" exercise is followed by the deep relaxation needed to be a witness of oneself, watching whatever is happening within and without.'[36]

Many other forms of meditation are taught, but the primary principle is that meditation should be a part of every aspect of life: 'Work and relaxation are not contradictory but integral to the transformative process.'[37]

The commune, or multiversity, in Poona offers courses in meditation, dance, mysticism, tantra and a wide variety of spiritual, psychological and alternative healing practices. It also publishes hundreds of pamphlets and books, mostly transcribed from Osho's spoken teaching.

The commune discourages visitors from bringing children with them. Those under 12 are allowed in only during the lunch-hour and must be accompanied by an adult; those between 12 and 18 are told that 'the commune exists for people who want to meditate'[38] and have to participate in meditation themselves. It also discourages anyone who is physically or psychologically unfit, sensibly warning that for such people 'coming here can be unsettling and may aggravate the condition'.[39]

There is one other requirement of interest. The commune is 'an AIDS-free zone' and the brochure insists that 'all visitors who wish to participate in its activities' take an AIDS test on arrival.

SCHOOL OF ECONOMIC SCIENCE

The perhaps misleadingly named School of Economic Science (SES) is not a religion *per se*, but at the heart of its teachings is a very distinctive religious philosophy which, although it has both elements of Christianity and some Esoteric origins and beliefs, is largely Eastern. The School is included in this book partly because of its spiritual teachings and partly because it has been branded as a 'cult'. It is a particularly good example of how tabloid sensationalism can create considerable amounts of smoke from not very much fire.

HISTORY

When founded by Andrew MacLaren, the School was for the teaching and study of economic and political theory. MacLaren, who was a Labour MP for most of the years from 1922 to 1945, held deeply rooted beliefs on taxation reform, on the basis of taxing land rather than income. He began the SES in London in 1937. Over the years his son Leon, a barrister who had also tried, unsuccessfully, to enter Parliament, took over the running of the school. Andrew MacLaren died in 1975, aged 91. (All further references to MacLaren are to the son.)

Leon MacLaren (1910–94) shared his father's zeal for social justice, but 'realized that the laws governing human nature needed to be discovered before meaningful change could occur for the well-being of society,' according to David Boddy, spokesman for the School.[40] This led him into a study of philosophy (which means 'the love of wisdom'), and this deepened into a search for spiritual wisdom, with study of Plato and his successors, the Bible and Christianity, the wisdom of great poets such as Shakespeare, and the Upanishads, part of the Hindu scriptures.

Then as now, the School taught orally in small groups, following the Socratic tradition of dialogue between teacher and students, rather than establishing a set course with a curriculum, textbooks and examinations.

In the 1950s MacLaren joined the Study Society (formerly the Society for the

Study of Normal Psychology), which had been founded in London by Dr Francis Roles on the basis of P. D. Ouspensky's teachings (see p. 177). Ouspensky and Gurdjieff had taught, along with much else, that the study of religious or esoteric philosophy should be on the basis of a teacher and his disciples. Although MacLaren was a teacher in his own School, he was looking for someone who could effectively become his, and the School's, guru.

In 1960 the Maharishi Mahesh Yogi came to Britain, and members of the Study Society, including MacLaren, went to hear him and were introduced to Transcendental Meditation. Both the Society and the School realized the value of this and began to teach it. In 1961 MacLaren organized a major meeting for the Maharishi in the Albert Hall.

Dr Roles and other members of the Study Society returned to India with the Maharishi, and there met Sri Shantanand Saraswati, the Shankaracharya of the North in India. Saraswati and the Maharishi had been fellow students of the previous Shankaracharya, Guru Dev (1869–1953).

Shankara (sometimes spelt Samkara) was a Hindu philosopher who is generally thought to have lived from AD 788 to 820, though many scholars place him a century earlier. He was the founder of Advaita Vedanta, one of the most important Hindu philosophical systems.

He established four monasteries – or perhaps four schools of learning – of Advaita in the north, south, east and west of India, in Badrinath, Srngeri, Puri and Dwarka respectively; some believe he established a fifth at Kanchi or Conjeeveram. The schools of thought have been passed on through the centuries by each teacher, or acharya, to his successor, up to the present day. According to Boddy, the now elderly Saraswati has appointed his successor as Shankaracharya of the North, and has stepped into an honoured semi-retirement. His own followers remain with him rather than his successor, until his death.

Roles returned fired with enthusiasm, and shortly afterwards Leon MacLaren went to India to meet the Shankaracharya. On his return, the Society and the School jointly set up the School of Meditation, specifically to study and teach the principles and practical use of meditation. MacLaren, having found the teacher he was looking for, began to pass on the Shankaracharya's teachings in the SES.

Every two years from 1965 MacLaren went to India to talk with the Shankaracharya through an interpreter, for a couple of hours a day for a week. The conversations, taped and transcribed, form the material for the senior students at the School, as well as the basis of the more introductory teaching.

Throughout the 1960s and 1970s the School grew steadily, acquiring thousands of students, and through bequests acquiring some very desirable properties, and establishing daughter Schools around England and abroad. There are currently branches in Bath, Colchester, Stourbridge near Birmingham, Leeds, Manchester and Edinburgh, and courses are held in around 30 other towns and cities. Associated Schools around the world, under a variety of similar names such as School of Philosophy and School of Practical Philosophy, are based in the USA, Canada, Australia, South Africa and several European countries, among others. These are separately financed and separately governed by their own constitutions, though they are supplied with the Shankaracharya's teachings by the SES.

◆

Controversy hit the School in 1984, with the publication of a book called *Secret Cult* by Peter Hounam and Andrew Hogg. Hounam and Hogg were journalists on

London's right-wing *Evening Standard* newspaper, and according to Boddy their original story in the paper, in 1983, was largely politically motivated. They had discovered that the chairman of the Liberal Party and several Liberal parliamentary candidates were involved with SES, and splashed this in their story, with a lot of pejorative information about the 'cult'. This was on the day before the 1983 general election, which resulted in a landslide victory for the Conservatives under Margaret Thatcher. What Hounam and Hogg apparently hadn't realized at the time of their original political exposé was that David Boddy (who has now been with SES for 22 years) was, until 1983, Director of Press and Public Relations at the Conservative Party's Central Office, and a close adviser to Margaret Thatcher. 'That really upset them, when they found that out,' he says. 'It blew their whole story.'

Boddy is still angry about Hounam and Hogg's book, and about the 'severe misunderstanding, and in some cases libel and slander' which have occurred since its publication. The book has, however, had one beneficial result. Hounam and Hogg wrote: 'In many ways the SES is its own worst enemy, for without the secrecy that surrounds the cult, there would be no need for an exposé such as this.'[41]

'In retrospect,' says Boddy, 'we may well have been mistaken in not describing fully enough our activities, the things we stand for and the way we work. This led to the accusation of secrecy . . . At the time Hounam and Hogg published their book, we took guidance from Shankaracharya. Amongst the advice given was to examine whether there was a need for change. What was quite clear was the need for new openness.'

Part of the problem, he says, is the difficulty of 'explaining subtle and spiritual matters to people whose interest is more centred on materialism and sensationalism'. Any mystical religion or philosophy requires progressive understanding, step by step; but people want to 'know the end of the philosophy without working from the beginning. That is not possible. It is rather like an O-level physics student expecting to sit in on a couple of advanced classes and coming out with a Ph.D.'

Although the School also teaches economics, art, music and languages, among other subjects, it now makes it clear to all students from the first lesson that its principles are based on a particular spiritual philosophy, and its introductory booklet, *The School*, openly states that MacLaren 'sought guidance from the Shankaracharya of the North, one of the great spiritual leaders of India and successor to the first Shankara, who wrote the famous commentaries on the *Gita* and other Vedic masterpieces. From the first contact to this day the Shankaracharya has poured wisdom and guidance on the School.'

Leon MacLaren died in 1994, aged 84, having appointed 38-year-old Donald Lambie, also a barrister, to succeed him as senior tutor. This succession was approved by the 200-strong Fellowship of senior members of the School.

There are currently around 4,000 students in the UK. The foreign Schools, which are independent, though receiving the Shankaracharya's teachings via the 'mother' School in London, have a further 8,000 students.

BELIEFS AND PRACTICES

The underlying spiritual philosophy stems from a form of mystical Hinduism. The main Hindu scriptures are the Vedas, some 8,000 poems, hymns and stories – 'in a sense, embodying the knowledge of how things work,' says Boddy. Advaita, or Unity, the Shankaracharya's philosophy taught by the SES, comes from the end of the Vedas, hence Vedanta (*anta* meaning 'end'). According to Boddy, though, the Shankaracharya speaks of Advaita Vedanta 'not in any religious form, but as a philosophy of unity in which all religions can unite. He has stressed the philosophic, as distinct from the religious, nature of Advaita Vedanta. To put it another way, the philosophy of Unity is no more Hindu than the teaching of Jesus Christ is Middle Eastern.'

The basic belief of Advaita Vedanta can be expressed very simply: the Atman (individual Self) is identical to the Brahman (universal Self) – or, in Christian terms, 'I and my Father are one' (John 10:30).

'The essence of his teaching is that there is a Self in everyone, which is the same Self: Atman, or Param-Atman, or Absolute. The essence of any true religion is its acknowledgement of the God, or the Absolute, or the Atman. Shankaracharya would say that the philosophy transcends any particular or narrow religious view, and is really talking about the nature of the human race and the nature of creation, and above all, the all-pervasive nature of this consciousness. So if you said to him, "Are you a Hindu?" he would say, "No, I am myself."'

The description of the single unified Self or consciousness is best embodied in the Upanishads, which are studied by the School.

'People will come to know the truth about themselves, which is what we mean by "the Knowledge"; and that truth about themselves is that there is a single Self, and there is an identity between everyone. They will come to it either through their hearts, in a sort of devotional way, or through their minds, or through their actions. The School adopts a composite approach, coming at it differently according to people's natures.'

Boddy stresses that neither Leon MacLaren nor the Shankaracharya are anything other than men; MacLaren never even called himself a teacher, while 'the Shankaracharya is the same as you or me, but has developed this clarity of mind and purity of heart which enables him to recognize this true expansiveness of God, or Absolute, whereas you and I probably have further to go.'

The School regards Shankaracharya as 'a Realized Man, of high consciousness'. They follow his teachings because, they say, 'His wisdom, which we've followed, works.'

Like most varieties of Eastern religion, the SES holds the doctrine of reincarnation. 'The way you spend this life is very important as to the way you will spend any future lives. The completion of your journey through humanity would be to reach the supreme unity with God, the actual Realization that you are not different from your Self.'

Unlike some Eastern religions, the School does not teach the unreality of the material world; it does, however, stress the reality of the Self or Absolute, of pure consciousness.

'This consciousness permeates all,' says Boddy. 'The material world is totally supported by pure consciousness, and we teach the value of discriminating the pure consciousness, which does not change, from that which always changes. For example, the human body is born, grows, decays and departs, and throughout this whole process the consciousness remains the same. However, it is very important that people do not negate the value of the material world, but instead come to see it for what it really is, namely a passing show in a glorious play, all within the vision of the Absolute. Shankaracharya encourages full participation in the world whilst continuing to recognize and acknowledge the single consciousness which is not affected by the drama.'

Strangely, the School takes no interest in the other three Shankaracharyas, and is unaware of whether they have any equivalent Western schools. They all teach Advaita philosophy, and the essence of their teaching will be broadly the same, says Boddy, because it comes from the same source, the Shankara, but the style of the teaching may be different. Each Shankaracharya presents the teachings in his own way. The current Shankaracharya of the West, for example, has a great interest in medicine, while the old Shankaracharya of the South, who has recently died and been succeeded by one of his disciples, was particularly interested in mathematics. But whatever their personal interests, their work is the education of people in Vedanta. Boddy sees no merit in examining and comparing their teachings; once a disciple has chosen a teacher, he should stick with him. 'You find a teacher, you trust that teacher because his wisdom works, and you follow him through. It saves an enormous amount of anxiety.'

◆

The School teaches practical philosophy, rather than an academic course in philosophy, and meditation is an important part of this. After the introductory philosophy course, taken by over 80,000 students over the years, and the following two terms, those who continue at the School normally take a course in meditation, and are encouraged to practise meditation to a simple mantra every morning and evening. 'The process of meditation takes you from an agitated mind to a state of stillness, and that which takes you there is the mantra,' says Boddy. Everyone uses the same mantra, though if anyone comes to the School from Transcendental Meditation, they are allowed to keep their own mantra.

Vegetarianism is encouraged on health grounds: a healthy body, a healthy mind and a healthy spirit. The Shankaracharya's teaching is, 'They should eat that which does not produce clouds of heaviness in the mind or body, and they should only eat as much as the body requires.'

This is part of the teaching known in the School as Measure. The same applies to sleep: students are encouraged to get up when they first naturally wake up, rather than drowsing in bed, which is not considered to be healthy. 'Measure simply means knowing when to stop. The idea is that you stop eating before your stomach fills up; that you stop working before the body is exhausted . . . The idea of Measure is to learn to take on some degree of self-discipline so that the body and mind do not get over-used, and so that you can come to rest in the innermost part of your being, which is known as the Self or Absolute. The essence of a measured life is to start each day at rest in meditation, and to bring each day to a conclusion with another period of rest and meditation.'

They accept that not everybody can live up to this ideal. Although it would be difficult to progress very far in the School's teaching without regular practice of meditation, a few minutes instead of the recommended half-hour, or once a day instead of twice, is considered better than none at all. Similarly, vegetarianism is not compulsory; quite a few students have progressed through the School without becoming vegetarians. 'The wise have said, "Don't eat meat," but they're not going to jump up and down with a meat-axe if you do!' says Boddy.

He suggests that it is a fairly typical outsider's misunderstanding of the application of Measure which has led to some of the criticisms of the SES. For example, the School's teaching that most healthy adults do best on around five hours of deep sleep can give rise to the usual 'cult-attackers'' accusations of sleep-deprivation.

The accusation that they discourage the eating of cooked food seems to stem from the fact that at their weekend and week-long residential courses, the meals tend to be bread, cheese, salad and fruit. This, Boddy points out, is simply because this is easier, and cheaper, to prepare for 100 people than a four-course banquet would be. Any special dietary requirements for cooked food are provided for.

Hounam and Hogg also accuse the School of putting pressure on people who have signed up for a course one night a week to come in on extra nights as 'volunteers' for menial work such as serving coffee and sweeping up the rooms. According to Boddy, it is not a case of pressure, but 'encouragement is given to people to work with and for fellow students, and with and for the communities in which they live, without seeking any personal reward or gain. This aspect of service to fellow human beings is an important one for a man or woman seeking the truth about themselves and their fellow humanity.'

In fact, apart from two office staff, all the School's work is done on a voluntary basis, including the teaching, and also including Boddy's work as media spokesman, and Donald Lambie's as senior tutor. 'So far as the tutors are concerned, there is a very important principle here: nobody gets paid for imparting knowledge.' The standard courses are put on in the evenings not just to enable students to attend after work but also because the tutors all have full-time day jobs, many of them as teachers, doctors or lawyers, or running their own businesses; both teachers and students tend to be professional people. 'In addition, nobody is allowed to profit commercially or financially from any association that they have in the School.'

Most of the tutors teach one night a week, and attend their own group another night. Before being invited to be a tutor, people have usually been in the organization for 15 to 20 years, and will have contributed to the work of the School in one way or another during those years.

According to Boddy, people give their time to the School because they believe in what it's doing – and on matters like sleep, vegetarianism and meditation, if students accept the teachings, they are prepared to accept the changes to their way of life. 'People throughout the ages have always taken to a discipline, to meet this inner development,' he says. 'At the end of the day, people have got to take a look at themselves and ask, "Is my life more fulfilled, is it happier?"'

◆

As well as the adult courses, the SES runs separate junior and secondary schools, the St James Independent Schools for girls and boys. Around half of the 600 pupils come from homes with no connection with the School, but the parents are now made fully aware of the association – all the teachers, apart from a few specialists, are SES members. In the past, Boddy admits, this may not always have been made clear. The pupils come from a variety of religious backgrounds, and the schools have a close relationship with the local Anglican Church, where the children worship.

'In many ways St James is very traditional,' says Boddy, 'but in other ways it is highly innovative.' In addition to normal academic courses up to A-level, the schools teach Latin, Greek, Sanskrit, calligraphy and philosophy from a very early age. Each lesson starts and ends with a few moments of silence, to dedicate the lesson to the Absolute and focus the minds of teachers and pupils. From the age of ten, with parental consent, pupils may be taught meditation. There is also a strong emphasis on sport through team games. 'The children are given the finest material to develop body, mind and spirit. They sing, they learn their tables by heart, and they are taught the virtues of politeness, courtesy, truthfulness and honesty.'

These traditional moral values are a feature of the School as well as of the children's schools. The family unit is seen as vitally important to society. Sex outside marriage is regarded as wrong, as is homosexuality. Women members are referred to as 'ladies' and are encouraged to dress decorously, in long skirts. Boddy stresses that this is not a case of treating women as second-class citizens; rather, 'the first responsibility of the men is to regard the lady with great honour and as a goddess'. Generally, woman is seen as the nourisher and man as the protector. 'The word "lady" seems to embody the qualities which Shankaracharya has indicated that we as men should see, to move away from seeing them as sex objects. There is a tremendous equity between man and woman; and a husband and wife, the two of them together are an individual unit.' But although women are treated with the greatest respect, the School's teaching is the same as St Paul's, that 'the head of every man is Christ, and the head of the woman is the man' (I Corinthians 11:3).

Within the School, slightly more than half the tutors, and around half the students, are women. For the first few years, both men and women tutors take mixed-sex groups; the more senior and more specialist groups tend to be single-sex, with a tutor of their own sex, though 'of course [they] come together from time to time,' says Boddy. Around 30 per cent of the Fellowship are female.

Both the SES and the children's schools teach the basics of Sanskrit: the concepts, grammar and common terms. Some of the members are able to translate from Sanskrit, and a very few are able to speak the language. The point is that Sanskrit is one of the oldest languages and underlies most Western languages. 'It is a fantastic foundation to grammar. If you can crack Sanskrit grammar, which is very simple and very beautiful, you can then move through to Greek, Latin and English with a great deal of facility.' Also, it is the language of the Vedas and Upanishads.

Spiritual study in the SES is not restricted to the East. In a recent project over several years, members have prepared a new translation from Latin, in five volumes, of the letters of Marsilio Ficino (1433–99), the founder of Renaissance Neo-Platonism and leader of the Platonic Academy in Florence. Ficino is most significant for his own translations of the works of Plato, Plotinus and Hermes Trismegistus, after whom Hermetic Philosophy is named. They are also working on a fresh translation of the works of Hermes Trismegistus, which were probably penned by a number of Greek and Egyptian esoteric philosophers between 300 BC and AD 300.

Unlike the Esoteric Schools of the Western Mystery Tradition, however, the SES has no interest in anything remotely occult. The Shankaracharya, when asked, said, 'Those who are interested in self-realization don't get diverted by such mystical powers, but keep their attention on discovering the unity of consciousness alone.' Marsilio Ficino and Hermes Trismegistus are studied 'solely for what they have to say – which is a lot – about the philosophy of unity,' Boddy stresses.

The teaching from both Eastern and Western traditions, he says, is because, 'If you strip away the coverings you'll come to the same essential truth in them all; and where that essential truth is proclaimed, or thought to be proclaimed, we will go and study it.'

In line with the practical application of philosophy, the teachings are applied to all aspects of life. For example, the School is very keen on the arts, teaching fine art, music and literature. People have different talents, but 'everybody is here to express their full personality and self' – or to learn to be excellent at whatever it is they can be excellent at. The SES organizes the annual Art in Action Festival at Waterperry House in Oxfordshire.

'The Shankaracharya puts it like this,' says Boddy. 'You participate completely in your life in the world, with your family and your job, but you come to an inner stillness which lets you meet your true happiness, and at the same time will allow you to be more efficient and more effective in what it is you do. To play this full role in the world, you need to have your intellect fed, your emotions fed and engage in service.'

The 'spiritual career path' in the School is a case of personal development, rather than attaining knowledge. According to Boddy, students 'are encouraged to realize their true natures, and to ask the question, "Who am I?" They are encouraged to connect more fully as their studies progress, with the power of consciousness through attention and efficiency in all actions. They are discouraged from acquiring "bodies of knowledge".' As students progress through the School, Boddy says, they don't so much learn deeper truths as gain a deeper appreciation of the same truth, which they were presented with on the first night.

The SES does not claim to have a monopoly on the truth. 'There are some for whom this is entirely appropriate, and there'll be some for whom another way is entirely appropriate. The important thing is that people go to it in the way which is most natural to them.'

NICHIREN SHOSHU/ SOKA GAKKAI

Nichiren Shoshu, a recently revived offshoot of Buddhism, is also often known by the name of its lay organization, Soka Gakkai.

HISTORY

Nichiren Shoshu owes its origins to the Japanese Buddhist monk Nichiren Daishonin (1222–82). Like many another before and since (cf. Joseph Smith, founder of the Mormons), he was confused and unsettled by the large number of varieties of religion available to him. Instead of opting for any one of them, he devoted several years to careful study of the writings of Gautama, the Buddha, and eventually came to the conclusion not only that all the current variants of Buddhism were both wrong and corrupt but also that he had rediscovered the true essence of Buddhism.

Buddha's purest teachings, Nichiren found, were summed up in the Lotus Sutra, which he wrote six years before his death. All of Gautama Buddha's other teachings, which led up to and underpinned this, were 'provisional' and were superseded by the Lotus Sutra. Nichiren taught his followers that by chanting just the title of this Sutra they would implicitly be chanting the whole Lotus Sutra, and thus would attain enlightenment.

Nichiren persistently warned that Japan would suffer both internal strife and invasion by the Mongol leader Kubla Khan, because it had turned from the true way. He was branded as a heretic for his denunciation of all the traditional forms of Buddhism, was persecuted by the authorities, beaten up and very nearly executed. After a dozen years of persecution, he was eventually pardoned in 1274 and settled down to write doctrinal theses.

> Since the ruling authorities seemed determined to continue to rely on adhering to provisional teachings, and convinced that he had done all he could to warn the nation's leaders, Nichiren Daishonin now turned his efforts towards ensuring the correct transmission of his teachings to the future. In keeping with an old Chinese maxim that a sage who warns his sovereign three times and is not heeded should retire to a mountain forest, he left Kamakura for good and went to live in a remote hermitage in the wilderness of Mount Minobu. Here he gave lectures on the Lotus Sutra and devoted himself to writing and training his disciples.[42]

Over the years Nichiren's version of Buddhism split in many directions: by this century there were around 40 different Nichiren sects. One of these was founded by Nikko Shonin, who had left Nichiren's temple at Minobu after falling out with other disciples and had built a temple at Kitayama. Eventually, in 1913, Nikko's version of Nichiren's version of Buddhism, which was battling against not only all the rest of Buddhism but also the other Nichiren sects, set itself up firmly as the Orthodox Nichiren Sect, or Nichiren Shoshu.

In 1930, two devotees of Nichiren Shoshu, Tsunesaburo Makiguchi (1871–1944) and Josei Toda (1900–58), founded a lay movement, Soka Kyoiku Gakkai, the Value-Creating Education Society. During the Second World War the Japanese government demanded religious unity and insisted that every home should have a Shinto shrine for the worship of the Emperor. Nichiren Shoshu refused both demands, and Makiguchi and Toda, among other leaders, were imprisoned. Makiguchi died in prison, but Toda, on his release, put all his energies into reviving the lay movement. Seeing its purpose as more universal than just education, he dropped 'Kyoiku' from the name. In 1951 he announced his goal of 750,000 new members in the next seven years; he just lived to see this accomplished.

Under his successor as president of Soka Gakkai, Daisaku Ikeda (b. 1928), the movement continued to spread around the world. American servicemen stationed in Japan – particularly those who had married local women – took it back to America with them. There are now several temples in America, where the movement is generally known as Nichiren Shoshu rather than Soka Gakkai. Soka Gakkai International (SGI) was founded in 1975, with Ikeda as president, and is affiliated to the United Nations as a Non-Governmental Organization.

Nichiren Shoshu and Soka Gakkai were brought to the UK by a British businessman, Richard Causton, who had worked in Japan. The headquarters of the UK organization are in a Tudor stately home in Berkshire, purchased with a £6 million interest-free loan from the Japanese headquarters. There is as yet no British temple, but there are 4–5,000 British members.

BELIEFS AND PRACTICES

Traditional forms of Buddhism turn their back on the world, describing its pleasures and pains as illusory. Nichiren Shoshu believes in a living, working faith which affects every part of our everyday lives in a contemporary world. They spell out the difference from normal Buddhism very clearly:

> Early forms of Buddhism taught that everything in the universe is impermanent, and that suffering results from first desiring, and then trying to cling to, what is essentially unstable and transient. As nothing can last forever, one should try to eradicate this suffering by eliminating one's desires and illusions and so achieve a state of total selflessness, or *nirvana*. Indeed, *nirvana* was often viewed as being a state of life achieved beyond this world, after death.
>
> Later Buddhist teachings pointed out the limitations of this view of suffering and desire. Not only is wanting to achieve the state of *nirvana* a strong desire in itself, but to totally eradicate desire ultimately means to eliminate life, as a fundamental desire of all living things is to carry on living.[43]

Nichiren Daishonin taught that 'earthly desires are enlightenment (*nirvana*)'. His followers believe they can attain Buddhahood

> by transforming illusions and earthly desires into enlightened wisdom rather than extinguishing them; *nirvana* is, therefore, nowhere else but in this world. Thus earthly desires and enlightenment are not different in their fundamental essence. It follows that enlightenment is not the eradication of desire but a state which the entity of life can experience by transforming innate desires from influences which are negative to desires which are positive.[44]

The main religious practice of Nichiren Shoshu is the chanting, every morning and evening, of the phrase '*Nam myoho renge kyo*'. *Nam* is a Sanskrit word meaning 'devotion', and the remainder of the phrase is the title of the Chinese translation of the Lotus Sutra. *Myoho* means 'the enlightenment of the law', *renge* means 'lotus' and *kyo* means 'sutra', or the teaching of a Buddha. The whole phrase, then, means 'devotion to the enlightenment of the law of the Lotus Sutra'.

This is chanted in front of the *gohonzon*, a 25 x 50 cm (10 x 20 in) scroll given to each new devotee. On the *gohonzon*, which means 'object worthy of honour and fundamental respect', is written '*Nam myoho renge kyo Nichiren*', along with names of enlightened ones. Each *gohonzon* is hand-copied by a high priest of Nichiren Shoshu. The original, written by Nichiren, is in a shrine at the head temple at the foot of Mount Fuji. Both *gohonzons* and high priests go back in an unbroken line, like an apostolic succession, to Nichiren himself. As well as chanting the phrase, a member will also recite part of the second and all of the sixteenth chapter of the Lotus Sutra. The entire ritual is known as *Gongyo*, or 'assiduous practice'.

◆

If it is possible to have materialistic Buddhism, that is what Nichiren Shoshu and Soka Gakkai could be said to represent, aiming mainly at the middle classes, at professional people who either have or would like to have power, position and wealth.

The movement has been criticized for its materialistic philosophy, summed up as, 'Chant *"Nam myoho renge kyo"* and ask for a new car.' They stress, however, that although you might get a new car, you might not, but instead could receive an inner peace and understanding of why you don't actually need a new car.

According to the movement, there are nine consciousnesses or levels of perception. The first five are the five senses. The sixth integrates the information received from these so that we can make physical judgements. The seventh makes moral and value judgements. The eighth stores our karma, everything from past lives and our present life that makes us who we are. The ninth and deepest level is the very essence of life.

> Because this level of consciousness might be described as pure life force, and is unaffected by cause and effect, tapping it by chanting Nam Myoho Renge Kyo enables one to purify all of the other eight consciousnesses. In other words, when one chants Nam Myoho Renge Kyo, the pure life-force of the ninth, or Buddha, consciousness permeates our entire being. Therefore one sees, hears, smells and tastes more clearly; one's sense of touch becomes more sensitive; one begins to perceive and make judgements about both the physical and the abstract world with greater clarity. One also begins to become aware of, and cleanse, those aspects of one's karma which cause unhappiness and which are therefore detrimental to the functioning of the pure Law of life, since they are a hindrance to developing one's full potential or purpose in life.[45]

Soka Gakkai is the lay movement – members who remain in the outside world, in normal jobs, rather than, for example, training for the priesthood. It describes itself as 'a movement for culture, education and peace: its activities both on a local and global level always aim to "create value" through the active support of these three pillars of civilization'.[46]

Members live in society, and it is their duty to work within society – in part, simply by being who they are. 'The ultimate purpose of those who practise the Buddhism of Nichiren Daishonin is to reveal the creative potential of their lives for the benefit not only of their personal fulfilment but also, and equally, of the development of society.'[47] And to change society, they first must change themselves. 'Buddhism teaches that if you want to change your life, it is no use blaming your circumstances. On the contrary, you must change that aspect of yourself which has given rise to the circumstances in which you find yourself. When you change, your environment will automatically change with you.'[48]

The motto of SGI-UK is 'Trust through Friendship, Peace through Trust'. The entire movement is dedicated to world peace. Their aims are:

1 To contribute to peace, culture and education throughout the world based upon Nichiren Daishonin's Buddhism.
2 To contribute to world peace, specifically through deepening the links between the ordinary citizens of different countries of the world.
3 To further the study and practice of Nichiren Daishonin's Buddhism, which declares absolute pacifism, and, upon this basis, to contribute to the above fundamental aims as excellent citizens in accordance with the culture and laws of the individual countries.[49]

Nichiren Shoshu and Soka Gakkai have at times been criticized for their recruiting techniques, which have been known to be somewhat heavy-handed. Evangelism is known as *shakubuku*, meaning 'break through and overcome'. Members are encouraged to apply whatever pressure they can on their family and friends to join. The movement gained a reputation in Japan for actual physical violence – a strange attribute for a pacifist religion.

Other Buddhist movements criticize Nichiren Shoshu because, just like Fundamentalist Evangelicals in Christianity, it claims to be the only legitimate version of Buddhism; all the others are wrong, and must be shown to be wrong. From the viewpoint of mainstream Buddhism, it is Nichiren Shoshu which is heretical.

There is now a rift between Nichiren Shoshu and Soka Gakkai. The huge temple complex at the foot of Mount Fuji – the largest temple in Asia, and possibly in the world – is no longer used by Soka Gakkai. In 1992, after a long-running power struggle, the high priest of Nichiren Shoshu excommunicated Daisaku Ikeda and every Soka Gakkai member for 'refusing to change their ways'.

The Soka Gakkai movement is extremely wealthy, owning large amounts of property in Japan. Former members claim that it puts tremendous pressure on members to contribute to its funds. Further criticism is raised by Soka Gakkai International's close links with the Mitsubishi Bank.

Daisaku Ikeda founded the Soka University in Japan in 1971. The movement's money has made it a highly successful and influential establishment. In the USA, which has 150,000 Soka Gakkai members, there is a campus in California. As founder of the university, Ikeda often awards honorary degrees to royalty and politicians, including, among many others, Nelson Mandela and Mikhail Gorbachev. Critics claim that he uses these hand-shaking occasions for photo opportunities to show that he is on familiar terms with great world leaders, so increasing his own standing (cf. Herbert W. Armstrong, see p. 91) – even though he might never have met them before and they might have no idea who he is.

In its efforts for world peace and cultural reformation, Soka Gakkai also seeks political power. Just as the religious right (the 'moral majority') exerts an increasingly strong influence on the Republican Party in the USA, Soka Gakkai, although legally separate, had strong links with the third main political party in Japan, Komeito (Clean Government Party), which merged with another party in 1994 to become the Shinshinto Party. Critics claim that Soka Gakkai, through its power over its members, controls 6 million votes – 10 per cent of the Japanese electorate. In the 1995 elections, Shinshinto gained 40 seats in the Japanese upper house of parliament.

PART FOUR

✠

ESOTERIC AND NEO-PAGAN MOVEMENTS

FIVE

BACKGROUND

While there is some overlap between Neo-Pagan beliefs, witchcraft or Wicca, Druidism, Esoteric and occult beliefs, magical groups and Satanism, there are also many differences. Careless journalists who lump them all together and equate, for example, Tarot-reading with witches with black magic with Satanists, haven't done their homework – or, if they have, have decided not to let the facts get in the way of a good story. Fundamentalist Christians who do the same have other motives: any belief which isn't of Christ must necessarily be of the Devil – 'He who is not with me is against me' (Matthew 12:30) – so all Neo-Pagans are equivalent to Satanists, whether they say they are or not.

After a brief examination of Satanism, the majority of this part covers Esoteric and Neo-Pagan movements, which have been divided into two chapters with the caveat that there is sometimes considerable crossover. For example, although the Esoteric movements are usually either Eastern-based or Judaeo-Christian in origin, some of them are closer to Goddess-worship, which is essentially Neo-Pagan. Similarly, although the Neo-Pagan movements are mainly based on Celtic, Norse or Native American traditions, some of the more academically oriented also study Tarot and the Cabbala, which are essentially Esoteric. Any simple categorization is bound to have its inadequacies, in just the same way as the political labels Conservative and Labour, or Republican and Democrat, each covers a wide range of beliefs which sometimes overlap.

I am avoiding the word 'occult' altogether, partly because of its general pejorative overtones and partly because it means 'hidden' or 'secret' and since many 'occult' teachings are now widely available, the term no longer really applies.

In addition to the specific groups considered here, there are of course millions of individual people who belong to no movement but who read Tarot, or have their horoscope interpreted or their palms read. There are also many who use aromatherapy, reflexology, acupuncture, homoeopathy, herbal remedies, yoga, meditation and a host of other alternative medical or psychological methods. The New Age (or Aquarian) movement which encompasses all of these and more is too huge to be included in this book, although it does, of course, overlap strongly with the Neo-Pagan revival of the last three decades.

One term which both Esoteric and Neo-Pagan movements have in common is magic, a word which immediately summons up Denis Wheatley-type images, giving opponents an easy rod with which to beat both types of movement. Speaking very broadly, Esoteric groups with a Judaeo-Christian lineage tend to practise what might be called high ritual magic, while Neo-Pagans generally practise a more nature-centred magic, though this also often involves ritual. Generalizing again, perhaps Esoteric magic tends to be more cerebral and Neo-

Pagan magic more emotional. But what do they actually mean by 'magic'?

For a Neo-Pagan, magic might mean healing someone of a headache by drawing power into them, or it might mean encouraging plants to grow healthily. Blessing a new child or a home, or any positive activity might also be called magic; it is a dedication to the Goddess and/or God. But Neo-Paganism also shares with Esoteric religion the main purpose of magic, which is more a reworking of the inner person than of the outer world. The alchemical transformation of base metals to gold was always an analogy for the transformation of the soul.

All magic involves the will and the imagination, or controlled visualization: adepts picture what they desire to occur, realistically or symbolically, and will it to be. Part of the work of most Esoteric schools is training in visualization techniques and in concentration of the will.

Does magic actually work? The short answer has to be yes, so far as those who use it are concerned. Whether a sceptical observer could be persuaded is another matter, and is perhaps irrelevant. If someone believes that magic works, then it *does*, at least for that person. With the examples of magic we have just mentioned, there can be little doubt that healing often works, and whether it is through a Christian's prayers and the Holy Spirit's work, or a Neo-Pagan asking the Goddess, or a channelling of natural power, the headache is still gone. As for encouraging plants to grow healthily, some people naturally have 'green fingers', which could be seen as a form of magic – certainly so far as those people who can't keep a plant alive for more than a week are concerned.

As for the transformation of the soul so that someone becomes more spiritual and a better person, prayer, devotion, meditation, mysticism, miracles and magic could all be seen as different names for much the same set of interrelated causes, processes and effects. Too much concentration on the precise definition of labels isn't really all that useful.

In general, the groups in this part of the book were extremely helpful and were far more forthcoming about their beliefs and practices than several of the better-known Christian movements. Because of past media distortion and deceptive practices employed by some previous 'investigators', some of the schools of magic were initially quite understandably wary; most were eventually far more open than might have been expected.

One group, however, wrote: 'It is hard to imagine that any *genuine* magical organization, being of necessity secretive and élitist and only admitting those who knock loudly on their door, would agree to be included in such a publication. There are those who seek publicity; I prefer to avoid it where possible, and would ask you not to include any mention of us.' I will respect that and not name them.

The point is well made, though, that few of the groups, organizations, movements or schools in this part go out actively recruiting new members. Some do advertise in New Age magazines or bookshops, or take a stand at Mind-Body-Spirit fairs, but the high-pressure sales techniques often employed by 'sects and cults' are alien to the entire philosophy of most Esoteric groups.

People who are interested in joining them, one way or another track them down and ask (usually very politely) if they might be allowed to find out more about them. In the case of what could be called the Eco-Pagans, they are generally welcomed with open arms; in the case of the schools of magic, they might be required to prove their sincerity over the first few months, and to spend their first year or more on an introductory, probationary course, before being invited to go on to deeper study – or not.

I acknowledge the help of Stewart Farrar, for several pre-publication chapters of his excellent book *The Pagan Path* (Phoenix Publishing, USA); Shan, Clan Mother of House of the Goddess, for her *Pagan Index*; and Chris Bray for *The Occult Census*.

All the organizations listed here have given permission for their addresses to be quoted. Several of them have post boxes, mainly, in the UK, BM names. This is not so much from any desire for secrecy but more that, in a world of religious intolerance, they want to protect themselves against possible physical attack. British Monomark (BM for personal and BCM for business post boxes) is a long-established London company which offers secure post boxes to anyone who needs one. The address used during the research for this book was a BM box; some of the movements covered in the book have been known to be unfriendly to investigative writers in the past. Several of the cult-watching organizations use BM boxes for the same reason. Many Neo-Pagan and Esoteric organizations use them because of the occasional threat from Fundamentalist Christians.

This threat can be all too real. One Neo-Pagan healer, not even a fully practising witch, known personally to the author, was publicly denounced by name as an enemy of Christ by a minister who had never met her in a Church of England service at which she was not present. She learned of this when some of her workmates ostracized her. Neo-Pagans have received death threats from Christians. Shortly after a TV documentary in 1989, which apparently painted a somewhat one-sided view of Chris Bray's activities, his Sorceror's Apprentice esoteric bookshop in Leeds was firebombed by Fundamentalist Christians. A few years later an esoteric bookshop in Lincoln was also firebombed.

The overwhelming majority of Fundamentalist Evangelical Christians, whatever their views of Neo-Pagan and Esoteric faiths, would be horrified at this. Present-day witches shiver when they speak of the 'burning times', the literal witch-hunts which lit up Europe only a few centuries ago. With the rise in Fundamentalism, some fear they will see those days again.

The main problem, as mentioned above, is that for Fundamentalist Christians anyone with any form of Esoteric or Neo-Pagan belief is by definition a Satanist. (This has logic only if one first redefines 'Satanism' to mean 'anything which isn't Evangelical Christianity' – which would then include Hinduism, Buddhism, Judaism, Islam and, for the hardcore Fundamentalists, Roman Catholicism.)

One obvious recent example was when Neo-Pagans came in for a lot of misrepresentation during the Satanic ritual abuse scare in the early 1990s. It was hardly surprising that Fundamentalist Christians leapt on the bandwagon; what is less well known is that the bandwagon was the creation of Fundamentalist Christians in the first place.

Before examining Esoteric and Neo-Pagan movements, then, I shall first take a brief look at Satanic ritual abuse, and at Satanism itself.

SATANIC RITUAL ABUSE

In February 1995 eight children were returned to their families in Ayrshire, Scotland. They had been 'taken into care' by social workers five years earlier, after some of the parents had been accused of abusing them. The parents were completely innocent of any such behaviour.

In the early 1990s Britain was shaken by case after case of so-called Satanic ritual abuse. In Orkney and in Cleveland, children were taken away from protesting families. Apparently when one home was raided by police and social workers, the Satanic evidence included an inverted cross, a full-length black cloak and a recording of disturbing, obviously occult music. The inverted cross was later revealed to be a wooden kite, the cloak a normal clerical cloak belonging to the local priest and the disturbing music was Holst's *The Planets*. No evidence was ever found of any abuse, ritual, Satanic or other.

A lot of distress was caused to children and their parents. A fair amount of distress was also caused to thousands of practising Neo-Pagans who, in the headline-conscious eyes of journalists, were synonymous with witches, who were synonymous with Satanists. Some claimed that it was hardly possible for them to brew a pot of herbal tea without people believing that they buggered babies. The air was thick with accusations, Christian spokespeople and social workers monopolized radio interviews – but almost no one was actually prosecuted.

Suddenly it all faded away. Even the then chief constable of Greater Manchester, James Anderton, widely referred to at the time as 'God's spokesman', said there wasn't enough evidence to sustain a prosecution. Some social workers were reprimanded for being over-zealous, and the children were eventually returned home.

◆

The entire concept of Satanic ritual abuse was based originally on the unsubstantiated claims of first one, then several women to have been 'teenage breeders' of babies for sacrifice by Satanic cults. The usual pattern was that, under counselling or therapy, the woman would come out with more and more detailed accounts of horrific tales which had lain buried in her subconscious for years.

(In later cases in the USA, stories obtained under hypnotic regression have led to the sometimes successful prosecution of quite a large number of men for sexual offences. In many of these cases there was no evidence apart from the formerly repressed memories. In some cases there was actually evidence counter to the 'memories': for example, the woman who claimed to have been raped many times, but was later found still to be a virgin. Psychiatrists, doctors, social workers and the police are now becoming a little more wary of the dangers of False Memory Syndrome, whereby an already disturbed person can be led, through hypnosis or 'counselling', to remember in graphic detail events which never occurred. In passing, False Memory Syndrome also throws some doubt on hypnotic regression into past lives.)

In the 1980s these stories were believed by a few child-care specialists, and a small group of Fundamentalist Christians in America passed the idea of Satanic ritual abuse across the Atlantic to British social workers.

An extremely detailed British government report in 1994 concluded that there has been no evidence whatsoever for Satanic ritual abuse. Some paedophiles, for their own perverted fun, might sometimes cloak what they do with some form of ritual trappings, but this is not the same thing as genuine believing Satanists abusing children as part of their religious rites.

Yet the suspicion lingered that there is no (unholy) smoke without (a witch's) fire, that there must have been something in all those true-confession stories of being a teenage brood-mare of babies for sacrifice – after all, there *are* people who believe in witchcraft.

But witchcraft is not the same thing as Satanism; they are quite different religions. The original Paganism was pre-Christian. Neo-Paganism usually stems from the mythic roots of one's own country (in the case of Britain, Neo-Paganism is Celtic in nature). High ritual magic is a mixture of Judaeo-Christian, Greek and Egyptian Esoteric theology, while Satanism, where it actually does exist, is not just a perversion but an inversion of Christianity.

SATANISM

Satanism is effectively an offshoot of Christianity. It has nothing whatsoever to do with Neo-Paganism. In fact, Satan, or the Devil, is part of the Christian religion. As many of the Christian sects point out, the biblical evidence for him as a personal being is slight, though it is there. The Devil is a carry-over from Gnostic dualism, which has some of its roots in Zoroastrianism. This taught the neat contradiction, still present in Christianity, that although there is only one God – monotheism – he has an evil opponent; this is not quite but almost dualism, the difference being that Christianity has changed the Devil from an evil God into a powerful but limited fallen angel.

Most good Bible dictionaries[1] reveal that there is no simple identification in the Bible of the Devil equals Satan equals Lucifer. Instead there is talk of demons and devils, and also of 'the satan' meaning 'the adversary or accuser' as in a court of law. The terms often seem interchangeable. William Smith says, 'We can only conjecture, therefore, that Satan is a fallen angel.'[2] The identification of Lucifer with the Devil has been claimed to be a mistake made by St Jerome in the fourth century, which is still with us. Lucifer, far from being a proper name, is simply Latin for 'light-bearer' or 'light-bringer', a term sometimes applied to the morning star, the planet Venus. (In Victorian times matches were known as lucifers, without any demonic inferences being drawn.) The 'name' appears only once in the Bible, in Isaiah 14:12. Allegorically, according to the Evangelical *New Bible Dictionary*, 'the true claimant to this title is shown in Revelation 22:16 to be the Lord Jesus Christ in His ascended glory,'[3] and not the Devil at all.

The popular image of the Devil with horns, a tail and cloven hoofs is entirely medieval in origin – and here is, indeed, the one connection with Paganism. Christianity, as we saw earlier, deliberately borrowed Pagan festivals and customs (which is why some of the Christian offshoots refuse to recognize Christmas and Easter) and Pagan holy places to build its churches, in order to make conversion easier during the Dark Ages. (There is a good argument for suggesting that the continued veneration of the Blessed Virgin Mary is a natural consequence of the persistence of Goddess-worship.)

By the Middle Ages Christianity was well established throughout Europe, but there were always a few pockets of Paganism stubbornly refusing to be wiped out. It was quite a brilliant move on the part of the Church to take the Horned God of the Pagans, whether the Greek Pan or the Celtic Cernunnos, and superimpose his physical appearance on to the Christian Devil. This then meant that anyone showing evidence of worshipping the Horned God wasn't just a follower of another religion, bad enough in itself, but a worshipper of Satan, and thus by definition blasphemous and evil – and accessible to the Inquisition.

So began the confusion in the popular mind between Paganism and Satanism which still exists today.

Incidentally, the above argument, though appearing to be a useful apologia for Paganism, is supported by the Rev. J. Gordon Melton, a conservative Evangelical Wesleyan Methodist minister, and one of America's most respected authorities on alternative religions. He also argues that practically everything we know about 'Satanism' comes from the pens of Christian writers: 'Though none had ever seen a Satanist ritual or met a real Satanist, these Christian writers described their practices in great detail. That is to say, the Satanist tradition was created and sustained by generation after generation of anti-Satanist writers.'[4] Satanic ritual abuse was simply a recent version of the same process.

♦

Present-day Satanists, few as they are, fall into several categories. Many are groups of teenagers who, inspired by the lyrics and stage trappings of a few heavy metal bands, have read Aleister Crowley, or more likely have read about Crowley, because his own works are pretty inaccessible. Then, reading a few Denis Wheatley novels, they have tried their own re-creation of black magic rituals. If they are particularly unpleasant youths, they might sacrifice a cockerel or a cat. Few are likely to go as far as attempting sex magic, though they might talk about it. If they were to attempt it with an unwilling participant (i.e. rape), they would probably find any magical effects rebounding negatively on them.

Some supposed Satanists, as mentioned above, are the very small minority of paedophiles who dress up their perversion with pseudo-Gothic religious trappings, either to instil more fear in their victims, or to increase their own sense of 'fun', or perhaps, following some warped psychological reasoning, to excuse to themselves their own actions. Such people are not Satanists, though they might actually practise more genuine evil than those who really are.

There is apparently a small subset of people interested in Esoteric studies, who seem to use the word Satanism as a synonym for their seeking after knowledge. Although this might seem a strange definition, it fits in with the Garden of Eden story of the tree from which the serpent persuaded Eve to eat the fruit: 'For God doth know that in the day ye eat thereof, then your eyes shall be opened, and ye shall be as gods, knowing good and evil . . . the woman saw that the tree was . . . a tree to be desired to make one wise' (Genesis 3:5–6). But they are not truly Satanists either, in the sense of worshipping the force of evil.

There are, however, some who proudly and openly take the name of Satanists, and who have created their own Satanist religion. Probably the best-known recent Satanist of this type is Anton LaVey, author of *The Satanic Bible*, and founder of the Church of Satan in San Francisco. His aim was to make carnal desires a proper object of celebration. 'Satanism is a blatantly selfish, brutal religion,' says Burton H. Wolfe in his Introduction to LaVey's book. LaVey lists nine Satanic statements, including:

1 Satan represents indulgence, instead of abstinence!
4 Satan represents kindness to those who deserve it, instead of love wasted on ingrates!
5 Satan represents vengeance, instead of turning the other cheek!
8 Satan represents all of the so-called sins, as they all lead to physical, mental or emotional gratification![5]

LaVey courted publicity and was often photographed performing rituals over a 'living altar' – a naked woman.

The Church was thought to have folded in the mid-1970s, but it is possible that it became less centralized and more low-key. A breakaway group, the Temple of Set, was founded by Michael Aquino in 1975.

This entry should not be read as a whitewash of Satanists or Satanism. There is no doubt that there are people who call themselves Satanists, some of whom genuinely worship Satan, and some of whom practise evil. But there are probably many more who practise evil without taking the name of Satanists.

SIX

ESOTERIC MOVEMENTS

The wide range of Esoteric groups which have grown up over the last century or so have many differences, but also have a number of things in common. Some are a synthesis of Western (Judaeo-Christian) and Eastern (Hindu, Buddhist or Sufi) thought. Others could be described as mystical, magical, Judaeo-Christianity. Many believe in secret Masters (sometimes called the Great White Brotherhood: the word 'white' does not refer to race, but to the aura of white light which apparently surrounds these Ascended Masters), who have tremendous powers and who have guarded the true religious teaching, the origin of all world religions, for thousands of years. They tend to be a form of Gnosticism, in that they emphasize secret knowledge, restricted to a select few (their own members).

Their originators were often both brilliant and highly unorthodox in both their thought and their lifestyles. Their beliefs and practices can be described as occult (hidden), esoteric (within, i.e. only for the initiated) or hermetic (after Hermes Trismegistus, but also implying 'sealed', as in an hermetic seal). They also usually include both magic and mysticism. They are highly complex, and progressive, in that the teachings build up on each other in steps.

Most present-day Esoteric movements are eclectic, borrowing from several traditions, including slightly older movements. Schisms and offshoots are frequent, partly perhaps because of the unorthodox nature of both the beliefs and the believers. The entries which follow – a small but probably representative selection – can be only brief summaries, giving a broad indication of those beliefs and practices which are known to outsiders.

THEOSOPHY

The Theosophical Society is associated with two people in particular, Madame Blavatsky (1831–91) and Annie Besant (1847–1933). Important in its own right in its day, it is more significant now for other movements which owe it a debt, and for two of the most important Esoteric teachers of this century, Rudolf Steiner, and Krishnamurti, who both had links with Theosophy.

HISTORY

Madame Helena Petrovna Blavatsky (usually known as HPB) claimed psychic abilities even as a small child in her native Russia. The surname Blavatsky came from her husband, whom she married at the age of 17; he was 40. The marriage was never consummated and she left her husband after a few months, though they never divorced and she kept his name.

Like several others (for example, Gurdjieff), she travelled to the Far East, claiming to have studied with the Secret Masters in Tibet for a while. The years 1848–58, when she was travelling and studying, she called 'the veiled time' of her life. She went to Cairo and founded the Société Spirite. She was well practised in the usual late-nineteenth-century arts of table-tapping, clairvoyance and levitation. Both then and later in her life she was accused of fraudulent mediumship.

In 1873 she emigrated to New York and the following year met Colonel Henry Steel Olcott, who had similar Esoteric interests. In 1875 they founded the Theosophical Society, along with William Q. Judge, and in 1877 HPB published her first book, *Isis Unveiled*, which told of the Masters and their secrets. By 1878 the Society was faltering, and HPB and Olcott travelled to India in the hope that the source of Hinduism and Buddhism might revive it. The Society's headquarters were moved to Adyar, near Madras, where HPB continued to receive communications from the Masters on the spirit level. In 1885 she moved to Germany, where she wrote her second book, *The Secret Doctrine*. This set out the Theosophical beliefs on the evolution of the universe and mankind, and on reincarnation, and attempted to build bridges between religion and science, and between the occult traditions of the East and the West. She wrote two more books, *The Key to Theosophy* and *The Voice of the Silence*, before her death in 1891. *The Theosophical Glossary* was published posthumously in 1892. She claimed that parts of her books were 'dictated' by the Masters, though critics have accused her of plagiarizing other people's books.

◆

The second major name associated with Theosophy is Annie Wood Besant. She was a freethinker and a radical, a colleague of Charles Bradlaugh and a member of the Fabian Society. A feminist campaigner, she was once unsuccessfully prosecuted for selling a leaflet on birth control. She wrote a review of *The Secret Doctrine*, met HPB in 1889 and became a supporter of Theosophy, turning her London home into the UK headquarters. After HPB's death, Besant and Judge took joint control of the Theosophical Society, until they fell out in 1894. By this time, even though Judge had been there since the beginning, Besant had established a power base, and took over the British, Indian and some of the American organizations. Judge died in 1896 and Olcott in 1907.

HPB had been a mystic and perhaps something of a fraud. Besant, on the other hand, had no great psychic abilities, but was a great intellect, and was responsible both for the continued growth and influence of the Theosophical Society and for something of an improvement in the respect given to it. She herself was held in great esteem in India, and was heavily involved in education and politics, founding several schools (one of which is now the University of Benares), establishing the Indian Home Rule League and becoming president of the Indian National Congress. Olcott also founded a number of schools in India and Ceylon (now Sri Lanka). Besant was also heavily involved in the Boy Scout movement, and in Co-Masonry, a version of Freemasonry which admitted women as equal to men.

The separated wife of an Anglican clergyman, Besant became closely associated with another, the Rev. Charles W. Leadbetter, and together they changed the emphasis of the Theosophical Society more towards Esoteric Christianity rather than Esoteric Buddhism.

Annie Besant wrote many influential books, including *Esoteric Christianity*, *Introduction to Yoga* and a translation of the Buddhist scripture the *Bhagavad-Gita*. She also co-wrote several books with Leadbetter. She died in 1933.

Leadbetter wrote a number of significant books of his own, and in 1916 became the founder and a bishop of the Liberal Catholic Church, which split off from the Dutch Old Catholic Church when the latter's archbishop, Arnold Harris Matthew, also a former Anglican clergyman, announced that Theosophy was incompatible with it.

It was Leadbetter who in 1908 first discovered the 14-year-old Jiddu Krishnamurti (1895–1986; Jiddu is the surname) – the boy apparently had a remarkable aura – and announced that he would become the Maitreya, the long-prophesied fifth Buddha (Gautama was the fourth), the living incarnation of a Master and the new World Teacher. Besant and Leadbetter promoted Krishnamurti, initiating him into the Great White Brotherhood in 1910, and founding a separate organization for him to head, the Order of the Star in the East, in 1911. Krishnamurti wrote of his acceptance by the other Masters of the Great White Brotherhood in his book *At the Feet of the Master*, though some critics believe the book was actually 'ghosted' by Leadbetter.

Krishnamurti became increasingly uncomfortable with the role which had been thrust upon him, and in 1929 he disbanded the Order of the Star of the East, resigning from the Theosophical Society the following year. He continued teaching throughout his long life, but insisted that the Truth could not be apprehended through any religion or organization; it must always be an individual, personal discovery through complete self-knowledge.

Despite this, and the fact that he never wanted any followers, there are now several schools around the world presenting his teachings.

BELIEFS AND PRACTICES

The word 'Theosophy' comes from the Greek *theos*, God, and *sophia*, wisdom. Many of the concepts of Theosophy have been around for well over 2,000 years, since Pythagoras and others. The German mystic Jakob Boehme (1575–1624) gave them a wider audience. The word is generally used to describe mystical philosophies which seek to explore the relationship between mankind and the universe or God.

From the start, the threefold aim of the Theosophical Society was to form a universal brotherhood of man, irrespective of race, religion or social class; to study the ancient religions, philosophies and sciences; and by investigating the laws of nature, to reveal and develop the divine psychic powers latent in man.

To understand the strong appeal that Theosophy had to intellectuals in its heyday, it is necessary to see it in its historical setting. In 1859 Charles Darwin's *The Origin of Species* had introduced Western society to the theory of evolution, and had driven an apparently immovable wedge between science and religion (the reverberations are still echoing through American courts, where Fundamentalists have successfully fought for rulings that evolution cannot be taught in schools unless creationism be taught alongside). Science had stripped God of his role as creator; intellectuals were torn between being Godless scientists or irrational believers.

Theosophy neatly took the concept of evolution and projected it forwards instead of backwards. Not only was the human race still evolving, but each individual person, progressing from life to life through reincarnation, was evolving to a far higher state. The Masters had long held secret knowledge, which was now available to all, to help us progress more rapidly until we too could become Masters.

Add to this the lure of the mysterious East, the thrill of HPB's spiritualist manifestations and the ideas of social reform, and the whole package became a powerful and very attractive mixture at the turn of the century.

The diversity of ideas which the Theosophical Society encompassed were both its strength and its weakness. There were many who disliked Madame Blavatsky's showmanship, though her demonstration of psychic or spiritualist abilities, genuine or not, undoubtedly attracted many others. Later there were some, including Rudolf Steiner, who were put off by Annie Besant's championing of the young Krishnamurti as the coming World Teacher – but again, the publicity brought Theosophy to a wider audience. And then there were many, including Colonel Olcott, who thought the most important parts of Theosophy were its social and educational work, and its scholarly work in bringing Eastern texts to the attention of the West.

With the exit of Krishnamurti, the Theosophical Society lost its impetus. There are still Theosophical Societies in Britain, America and around the world, but the fire has gone out of the movement and they appear to be little more than study groups, custodians of interesting libraries. What is far more important, though, is the legacy of the Theosophical Society, in both individual people and later movements. Krishnamurti became a widely respected mystic and teacher. Rudolf Steiner, once head of the German Society, went off to found Anthroposophy. P. D. Ouspensky was influenced by Theosophical teachings. The poet and mystic W. B. Yeats was a member for a few years, before moving on to the Order of the Golden Dawn. There were many others.

Beyond that, many of the Esoteric movements which are thriving today have borrowed liberally from Theosophical teachings, particularly in respect of the Great White Brotherhood. The idea of the Secret Masters was not original to the Theosophical Society, but they greatly fleshed out and popularized the concept. The Master Koot Hoomi in particular not only gave HPB much of the content of her books but later inspired Alice Bailey (founder of the Arcane School) in the writing of her own books of mystical teaching, and also Robert and Earlyne Chaney, who founded the Astara Foundation in California in 1951. This was a school of the ancient mysteries and a centre for psychic research, and perhaps one of the closest of all the Theosophical Society's successors to the original.

ANTHROPOSOPHY

Rudolf Steiner (1861–1925) had an interest in both Esoteric wisdom and social reform for some years before he joined the Theosophical Society. His unusual intelligence was recognized quite early; he was only 22 when he was invited to edit the scientific works of Goethe for a standard edition. He joined the Theosophical Society around 1900 and became leader of the German organization in 1902.

His leaving stemmed from two causes. In 1912 he expelled a particularly troublesome member, only to have his decision overridden by Annie Besant. But he had been moving in his own direction away from the Society's particular combination of beliefs and practices for some time. Besant's championing of the coming World Teacher in Krishnamurti was the last straw, and in 1913 he broke away, setting up his own Anthroposophical Society and taking many of the German Theosophists with him.

Steiner also belonged for a while to the Rite of Memphis and Misraim, a quasi-Masonic occult order, and probably also to the Ordo Templi Orientis (O.∴T.∴O), a quasi-Rosicrucian German occult society founded in 1906, which studied and perhaps practised sex magic. It is likely that Steiner didn't join these so much to gain secret knowledge as to find others who shared his own ideas. Also in 1906 he started giving a series of lectures in Paris, which drew many people interested in his teachings on clairvoyance.

He delivered over 6,000 lectures in 25 years. Most of his many books are effectively barely edited lecture notes, rather than cogently argued texts, which tends to make them difficult to understand. In the next few years he influenced education, agriculture, architecture, the arts and politics, among other areas of life.

◆

While Theosophy is God-wisdom, Anthroposophy is man-wisdom. Rather than evolving forwards to become God-like Masters, Steiner taught that man used to have these powers but has lost them, and must strive to regain them. Buried deep within us are these lost secrets. Through meditation and study we can find our lost nature and achieve spiritual growth on four levels: the senses, imagination, inspiration and intuition.

Anthroposophy is closer than Theosophy to Christianity, and there are still specifically Christian groups which study Steiner's teachings. Steiner taught that Christ's life, death and resurrection were supremely important. Christ can help man ascend to the higher spiritual levels he once knew, but Lucifer and Ahriman are two evil powers holding man back, Lucifer through internal pride and Ahriman through the external material world.

It should be noted that Steiner continued to use the word Theosophy, but his use of it is quite different from that of the Theosophical Society. 'Rudolf Steiner, however, uses the term independently and with different and much wider connotation . . . Ultimately it leads us back to St Paul who says (I Corinthians 2:6–7): ". . . We speak the wisdom of God (Greek 'Theosophia') in a mystery, even the hidden wisdom which God ordained before the world into our glory."'[1] Loosely, then, Anthroposophy could be seen as a form of esoteric Christianity.

Like Theosophy, Anthroposophy seeks to unite science and religion. As Anthroposophy developed, its teachings spread into various areas of life, including education and agriculture. In the latter case, Steiner introduced a spiritual and scientific basis to what would now be called organic farming, with 'natural' times for sowing and harvesting, and no chemical fertilizers. In the case of education, he was in the forefront of 'child-centred' education, Anthroposophical theories concentrating on 'awakening what is in a child' rather than forcing knowledge into a child. Over 500 Waldorf schools now teach according to Steiner's principles, and are very highly regarded. His methods, including the use of guided movement to music, are particularly effective with retarded children.

Anthroposophy is important partly for this social legacy, but also because its ideas have influenced other forms of Esoteric Christianity.

MAITREYA/BENJAMIN CREME

Christ is alive and well and living among the Pakistani community around Brick Lane, London, according to Benjamin Creme. This was Creme's message in 1982, as perceived by Evangelical Christians, who were greatly offended by it. In fact, Creme was speaking of Maitreya, the most senior of the Masters, or the Great White Brotherhood, who have usually been based in the Himalayas. Maitreya had 'overshadowed' Jesus, making him the Christ; now he would be returning in his own right.

♦

Creme's teachings are based on Alice Bailey's developments from Theosophy. Bailey (1880–1949) joined the Theosophical Society in California, where in 1919 she met the American secretary of the Society, Foster Bailey, whom she later married. Alice Bailey claimed she was contacted by several Masters, including Koot Hoomi and Djwhal Khul. She began 'channelling' messages from them, and writing books from their messages. She fell out with Annie Besant, Madame Blavatsky's successor in the Theosophy Society, who clearly saw her as a threat. Eventually she and Foster Bailey left the Society.

In 1922 they founded the Lucis Trust to publish her books (she wrote 20 in all), and in 1923 they founded the Arcane School to teach their followers. Bailey's teachings were basically Theosophical, with an emphasis on the imminent coming of the Maitreya Buddha, which could be seen as the second coming of Christ, or as another avatar of Krishna, or as the Jewish Messiah, or as the Muslim Imam Mahdi. Maitreya is all of these.

After Alice Bailey's death, her movement splintered into several offshoots. The Arcane School itself continued under her husband until his death in 1977.

Benjamin Creme (b. 1922) studied the works of Blavatsky, Leadbetter and Bailey, among many others, in his youth. In 1957 he joined the Aetherius Society (see p. 202), but left them in 1959 after disagreements.

He was contacted by a Master in 1959 and told of the Maitreya's imminent return, and of his own importance in spreading the word. Nothing much seems to have happened until 1972, when he received further messages. In 1974 he began to set up an organization of followers, with whom he learned to transmit spiritual power. Later that year, Maitreya himself spoke through him. Creme began to publish books containing messages from Maitreya.

In 1982 he announced that Maitreya was living anonymously in the Asian community in east London and would reveal himself to the world shortly; the media must be ready. Sensing a good offbeat story, a number of journalists searched the Brick Lane area, but no one could point them at the returned Christ. Creme lost both credibility and supporters, and gaimed some serious enemies among Evangelical Christians. An Evangelical book, *The Hidden Dangers of the Rainbow* (1983), attacked all New Age and Esoteric movements – especially Creme and the Maitreya – as a Satanic conspiracy. It was one of the first of several such books attacking the New Age by conservative Evangelicals, and did much to promote the illogical belief that members of New Age movements, Neo-Paganism, Wicca and Esoteric religious movements are all Satanists (see p. 163).

According to Creme:

On 31 July 1985, largely through the efforts of one freelance journalist who had actually seen Maitreya in His local area in 1984 and who was convinced of the truth of Creme's information, an internationally representative group of 22 influential journalists met in an Indian restaurant in London's East End, hoping that Maitreya or an envoy would approach them there.[2]

They were to be disappointed.

In an unusual twist on the urban myth about the vanishing hitchhiker, Creme claims that Maitreya has hitched lifts with Evangelical Christians, told them they would shortly see Christ, then vanished from their cars.

His most publicized appearance, however, was at a healing meeting in Nairobi, Kenya, on 11 June 1988. He was seen by 6,000 people, photographed and reported in the *Kenya Times* and on CNN and BBC news. Since 1992, says Creme, Maitreya has appeared – and disappeared – in front of many groups of Christians, Jews, Muslims, Hindus and Buddhists 'from Mexico City to Moscow, from Geneva to Johannesburg; in North Africa and the Middle East, India and Pakistan'.[3] At several of these meetings he spoke to the assembled people for 15–20 minutes before vanishing again. In July 1994 he finally turned up in London, addressing a group of 300–400 Christians for 17 minutes.

These appearances are all a prelude to the Day of Declaration, when Maitreya will appear on radio and television all over the world and speak to everyone, telepathically, in his or her own language.

Maitreya's message (as with the Aetherius Society, the Raelian movement and others) is simple:

Share and save the world . . . Take your brother's need as the measure for your action and solve the problems of the world. There is no other course.

GURDJIEFF AND OUSPENSKY

HISTORY

Georgei Ivanovitch Gurdjieff (*c*.1874–1949) was a powerfully charismatic teacher, a clever businessman (some called him a shyster) and an unpredictable, even volatile personality (he has also been called a charlatan and a showman). Born of Greek parents in Armenia, he spent some years wandering the Far East, including Tibet, where he claimed to have studied under Masters of ancient wisdom, learning, among much else, the techniques of hypnotism and yoga. (It should be noted that a number of authorities present Gurdjieff's early travels more as myth than as history.) On his travels, at times working for a railroad company, he set up stores, restaurants and cinemas, and traded in expensive carpets, making a small fortune. At the same time he was seeking after deep philosophical and religious wisdom, and gathering a band of like-minded seekers around him. By the time he had moved to Moscow, and later in St Petersburg, he was lecturing on what he had learned. But Russia, being in the middle of a revolution, was not the safest place for a wheeler-dealer and unorthodox philosopher, and he moved to France, where in 1922 he bought an estate at Fontainebleau, setting up his Institute for the Harmonious Development of Man. He moved to Paris in 1933.

One of his earliest followers was the Russian mathematician P. D. Ouspensky (1878–1947), who had earlier been greatly influenced by Theosophy. He later wrote a book on Gurdjieff's teachings, to some extent codifying and clarifying them. Most movements today with a background in Gurdjieff's teachings are actually Gurdjieff–Ouspensky (G–O) offshoots.

What makes for a powerful synthesis between the two is that Gurdjieff was intuitive and unpredictable, encouraging the unexpected and the out-of-balance, while Ouspensky was rational, logical, methodical and looked for a systematic approach. It is likely that the force of Gurdjieff's personality was sufficient to carry his seemingly haphazard teachings and practices during his lifetime, but that in the absence of his physical presence it is necessary to have some rational justification for them.

Among many other things, Gurdjieff has been criticized for imposing quite unsuitable exercises – most of them exhausting and some actually dangerous – on his followers. The writer Katherine Mansfield, for example, went to Fontainebleu suffering from tuberculosis. He ordered her to ignore her illness and made her sleep above the cowshed; she died shortly afterwards, aged only 35.

Gurdjieff's own books are *Beelzebub's Tales to his Grandson*, *Meetings with Remarkable Men* and *Life is Only Real when I Am*; Ouspensky's book on Gurdjieff's teachings is *In Search of the Miraculous*.

BELIEFS AND PRACTICES

Gurdjieff's teachings could be described as a sort of Esoteric Christianity, or as a blending of the West and the East, or as a combination of religious thought and philosophical psychology (or perhaps psychological philosophy).

The two main states of consciousness are to be either awake or asleep, though most people, Gurdjieff said, more or less sleepwalk their way through their waking life. He put forward two other states of being: self-consciousness and objective consciousness. Like some of the Personal Development movements covered later in this book, Gurdjieff's philosophy points out that most of us are not really in touch with ourselves, with the entirety of our inner being, our 'I', and so are cut off from anything approaching full use of our abilities. Ouspensky likened this to people living in the basement of a house, without ever realizing that there are other floors upstairs. Life passes us by, and we are mere observers of it, like an audience at a play, rather than being up there on the stage, a combination of participants, scriptwriters and directors. Even if one changes the analogy to make us the actors, we are confined to a script, having grown into roles imposed on us by upbringing and strengthened by unthinking habit. Our several 'brains', our Instinctive, Moving, Emotional and Intellectual Centres, are out of kilter with each other.

We can be woken up only by performing arduous physical exercises, which break our deeply ingrained habits. Gurdjieff made his followers perform tasks well below their intellectual or social level; part of his teaching on Esoteric development was unquestioning submission to a teacher – a Man Who Knows. He encouraged his followers to dance themselves into a frenzy, something like the whirling dervishes of the Sufi religion. His methods also included rhythmic exercises to music, breathing exercises, fasting, sleep deprivation and mental training. The emphasis on music came from a new interpretation of Pythagoras's Esoteric teaching on the music of the spheres and the numerical or numerological significance of rhythm and the functions of parts of the body.

By performing these exercises one can reach a higher level of consciousness, become truly self-aware and tap one's reserves of spiritual and psychic power. Either from Pythagoras or perhaps from the mathematician Ouspensky, Gurdjieff developed a Law of Seven to do with music, and a Law of Three to do with the working of the universe (active, passive and neutral), the human body (carnal, emotional and spiritual) and food. He devised a symbol called the enneagram, a circle divided by nine points, which joined up to illustrate his teachings.

Many of his followers, including Ouspensky, deserted him, but most continued to follow what he taught – the movement without the man. Today's movements which follow Gurdjieff's teachings (sometimes called the Fourth Way School, moving on from the three old ways of the fakir, the monk and the yogi) tend to concentrate more on their mystical aspects rather than the punishing physical exercises he required.

Gurdjieff–Ouspensky movements usually include study of the Cabbala among their teachings and this is often linked with a deep study of Tarot (Ouspensky's book on Tarot is still widely available).

SUBUD

HISTORY

Subud began in Java, Indonesia, in 1924, when Muhammad Subuh Sumohadiwidjojo (1901–87), a clerk in a local treasurer's office, unexpectedly had a series of powerful religious experiences in which he experienced the inner power of God. By the 1930s he realized that he should pass on this experience to others, and in 1933 he set up Subud, which is apparently not related to his name but is an abbreviation of the Sanskrit words *susila*, *buddhi* and *dharma*, meaning 'to follow the Will of God, with the help of the Divine Power that works both within us and without'.[5] Over the next 20 years he worked quietly, spreading Subud slowly in Indonesia. Eventually some Europeans came into contact with Subud.

Gurdjieff, in common with other Esoteric teachers, had spoken of One who is to come. For some it was the Maitreya; for Gurdjieff it was the Prophet of Consciousness; the Ashiata Shiemash. A group of Gurdjieff's followers invited Subuh to England in 1956, believing him to be the Prophet foretold by Gurdjieff. First in Britain, then in America and Australia, Subud spread rapidly, until today it is represented in over 70 countries and has around 10,000 members.

Muhammad Subuh, known to his followers as Bapak (an affectionate and respectful Indonesian term for 'father'), died in 1987.

BELIEFS AND PRACTICES

Subuh discovered not only that he could enable others to receive the spiritual energy he had first encountered in 1924 but that those who had received it from him could pass it on to others. The basis of Subud is the *latihan kejiwaan*, Indonesian for 'spiritual exercise', usually just known as the *latihan*, or exercise. Some three months after first attending Subud meetings, a new member stands in a group with several others, including some experienced 'Helpers', and the *latihan* occurs. The first time is known as the Opening.

The experience is different for different people, and this is part of the basis of Subud. Some will experience joy, others peace; some will laugh, others cry; some feel an inner vibration, others a quiet simplicity; some will dance, others will pray. Every one of these is equally valid.

The *latihan* lasts for about 30 minutes and is usually done twice a week with the group. Once members are experienced, they can do an additional *latihan* once a week on their own, at home.

> The effects of doing the latihan vary greatly. People usually have a feeling of well-being and relaxation after doing latihan. In the longer term, the process for some brings a peaceful, gradual development. For others it initiates dramatic changes in their lives. For everyone the pace of development depends on their own inner capacity, but in time each one is put increasingly in touch with his/her own nature and talents, and as well experiences spiritual comfort, guidance in life and an inward security.

The experience of *latihan* is apparently not always pleasant; the power of God is acting directly on the inner person and may well be purging out the dross within. 'Sometimes difficulties must be faced as the purification begun by the latihan takes its course.'

Subud says firmly that it is not a religion in its own right; it has no priests, no rituals, no dogmas or doctrines. Members are actively encouraged to continue to belong to the religion they came from. Because they are directly in touch with the Power of God, or the Holy Spirit, or the Great Life Force, they become brothers and sisters together, irrespective of whether they are Christians, Muslims, Buddhists, Hindus or anything else.

> Therefore, in the latihan of Subud we do not have a teaching; there is nothing we have to learn to do, because all that is required of us is complete surrender . . .
>
> So this divine power, which works in us during the latihan, will bring to each person what is already in himself . . . the latihan of two people can never be the same, because everyone is different from everyone else. It is clear, then, that there cannot be a theory or spiritual teaching in Subud because each person is different. Whatever he needs and whatever he receives will differ from what somebody else needs and receives . . .
>
> Every person will find for himself the right way towards God, and what may be the right way for one may be completely wrong for another . . . You must become your own self and you must develop your inner self if you want to find the way to God. You must not follow or imitate anyone else, because you must find your own way to God . . . it is God who will lead you towards

himself and what really happens in the latihan is that you will be introduced to your real inner self – to the real I.[6]

Like a number of other religious movements, from the Quakers to the Bahá'ís, and from the Soka Gakkai to the Theosophists and Anthroposophists, Subud is very strong on the brotherhood of all mankind. It has a number of subsidiary organizations involved in welfare, education and community work. Susila Dharma International, the charitable arm of Subud, is accredited as a Non-Governmental Organization to the United Nations' social arm, ECOSOC. Most Subud members donate a portion of their income (usually 3 per cent) to the movement, and they are actively encouraged to set up businesses which will donate a portion of their profits to support Subud, particularly in its charitable work.

ROSICRUCIANS

There are many different Rosicrucian organizations in Britain, Europe, the USA and around the world, with widely differing teachings. Some are far more secretive than others, reserving their membership to Freemasons of the highest grades. Others have a more open membership, but paradoxically are perhaps more difficult to join. Others, like AMORC (the Ancient and Mystical Order of the Rosy Cross), advertise widely and claim a quarter of a million members of their correspondence courses. Some trace their lineage back – legitimately or not – to the earliest 'history' of the Rosicrucians; others are clearly far more recent.

I shall look briefly at the origins of the Rosicrucians, and at just one modern example which is more overtly religious than some others.

♦

In the early seventeenth century three mysterious works were published in Germany: *Fama Fraternitas* or *The Praiseworthy Order of the Rosy Cross* (1614); *Confessio Fraternitas* or *The Confession of the Rosicrucian Fraternity* (1615); and *Chymische Hochzeit* or *The Chymical Marriage of Christian Rosenkreutz* (1616). These told the life story of Christian Rosenkreutz, who was born in 1378, travelled in the Middle East and died aged 106 in 1484. When his tomb was discovered in 1604, his body had not corrupted. Rosenkreutz set up a fraternity, the Spiritus Sanctum or House of the Holy Spirit, dedicated to the well-being of mankind, social reform and healing the sick. This reformation of the whole world was to be accomplished by men of secret, magical learning.

The documents are now thought to have been written by a Lutheran priest, Johann Valentin Andreae (1586–1654), who created the symbolic myth of Christian Rosenkreutz in an attempt to stimulate others to take up Rosicrucian ideals. Within a couple of years, other Rosicrucian writings appeared, including one by the influential physician, alchemist and Hermetic philosopher Robert Fludd (1574–1637), and Rosicrucian societies began to spring up around Europe. There was a resurgence of interest in the nineteenth century, particularly in Britain and America. New societies included the Fraternitas Rosae Crucis (1858), the Societas Rosicruciana in Anglia (1865), the Rosicrucian Fellowship (1907), the Societas Rosicruciana in America (1907), the Ancient and Mystical Order of the Rosy Cross (1915) and Lectorium Rosicrucianum (1924).

Lectorium Rosicrucianum was originally founded in the Netherlands under the name Rozekruisers Genootschap (Rosicrucian Fellowship) by two brothers, Z. W. and J. Leene; the latter used the nom-de-plume J. van Rijckenborgh. It was linked for a while to the Rosicrucian Fellowship in America, but broke this connection in 1935. After the war it re-formed as Lectorium Rosicrucianum, the International School of the Golden Rosycross. It has centres in Britain, America and over two dozen other countries, and its magazine, *Pentagram*, is published in ten languages.

Its teachings are a version of Gnostic Christianity (see p. 50), stressing 'the living spiritual core in the original revelations of all the great world religions and mystery schools' and imparting 'the inner knowledge which points the way to soul-rebirth and ultimately the re-establishment of the link with the Spirit of God'.[7]

Gnosticism generally teaches the contrast between the spiritual world (good) and the material world (evil). Lectorium Rosicrucianum teaches that there are two nature-orders, 'the familiar one containing both the living and the dead . . . characterized by pairs of opposites and by perishability' (which it calls 'dialectics') and 'the original divine nature-order. Although this interpenetrates our nature-order completely, it is not perceptible to dialectical sense organs because it is separated from our nature-order by an enormous difference in vibration.' The divine nature-order is also known as the Kingdom of Heaven, and the human heart contains a remnant of it, a Divine Spark (cf. Church Universal and Triumphant, p. 194) or Rose of the Heart, which causes us 'to seek out the original state of being "with the Father", the state of being immortally at one with God'.

Following insight into the difference between the two nature-orders, and the desire for salvation, one can achieve the rebirth of transfiguration through self-mortification, the 'total self-surrender of the I-personality to the actualization of this salvation'. This is followed by a new mode of life, 'under the direction of the aroused spirit-spark-atom, the newly born soul', and fulfilment, 'the resurrection in the original field of light'.

In common with other Rosicrucian movements, Lectorium Rosicrucianum places a great deal of emphasis on symbols, including the golden rose on a golden cross, the circle containing a square and an equilateral triangle – 'the Circle of Eternal Love containing the Trigonum Igneum or Fiery triangle and the Square of Construction', and the Pentagram, 'ever the symbol of the reborn, new Human Being'.

In addition to *Pentagram* Lectorium Rosicrucianum, like many other Esoteric schools, provides a wide range of books on its beliefs in English and other languages, including *Elementary Philosophy of the Modern Rosycross*, *The Universal Gnosis*, *The Egyptian Arch-Gnosis* and *The Secrets of the Brotherhood of the Rosycross*, all by J. van Rijckenborgh.

◆

Although Rosicrucianism is not, in itself, a religion, we can see from this example that it contains very powerful religious ideas, There are clear links and cross-influences between the Rosicrucians, the Illuminati, the mystical side of Freemasonry, alchemy, Hermetic Philosophy, the Western Mystery Tradition, Theosophy and Esoteric Christianity.[8]

ORDER OF THE GOLDEN DAWN

Like Theosophy, the Hermetic Order of the Golden Dawn (OGD) is important for the people associated with it during its relatively short existence, and for its continuing effect on later movements.

It is now generally accepted that, from a critic's viewpoint, the OGD was founded on a lie – in fact, a series of lies. An apologist might say that, like most Esoteric organizations, it was eclectic: it borrowed some of its teachings and rituals from various places, and created others out of whole cloth – from scratch. As for the invention of a German 'predecessor', it was necessary for it to be able to claim authority. In any case, such a practice is hardly new: the early Christian Church was littered with Gospels and Epistles supposedly written by the apostles; the Athanasian Creed was certainly not written by Athanasius, but it reflected his beliefs, and giving it his name ensured that people would take notice of it.

The Hermetic Order of the Golden Dawn was the creation of Dr William Wynn Westcott, Dr William Robert Woodman and Samuel Liddell 'MacGregor' Mathers. It was the brainchild of Westcott, who in 1887 was given a manuscript of around 60 pages containing (in an artificial language) fragments of 'Golden Dawn' rituals which clearly owed much to Freemasonry, with large elements of the Cabbala, astrology, alchemy and related subjects. Westcott asked Mathers to flesh out the fragments into full working rituals, and recruited Woodman, who was Supreme Magus of the Societas Rosicruciana in Anglia, to be the third leader of the new organization.

The lie came in with Westcott's invention of Fräulein Sprengel, Chief Adept of a non-existent German occult order, who granted a charter to the OGD, which thus became the British branch of an ancient continental order whose teachings went back into the mists of antiquity. It had a provenance; it therefore had authority.

By 1888 the OGD was up and running. It was a secret society very like the Freemasons and the Rosicrucians in that it awarded 'degrees' as members progressed up the ladder, but its main emphasis was the study of magical theory and ritual. There was plenty of material they could study: French writers such as Éliphas Lévi, Papus and Etteilla had produced books on the mystical meanings of Tarot and the Cabbala, and much else, and there were Mathers's 'ancient' rituals to be learned.

The main degrees were Neophyte 0=0, Zelator 1=10, Theoricus 2=9, Practicus 3=8 and Philosophus 4=7. But for a few (and unknown to the rest) there was an inner circle, the Ordo Rosae, Rubeae et Aureae Crucis, 'the Rose of Ruby and the Cross of Gold', based on the Rosicrucian symbolism of Christian Rosenkreutz. This had three degrees: Adeptus Minor 5=6, Adeptus Major 6=5 and Adeptus Exemptus 7=4. The outer order studied only the theory of magic; the inner circle taught practical ritual magic, and was probably the most intensive and all-embracing Esoteric school of its time.

Beyond this was an even higher order, the Mysterious Third Order of the Silver Star, or Argenteum Astrum (A∴A∴). This had three more degrees: Magister Templi 8=3, Magus 9=2 and Ipsissimus 10=1. The adepts of this order were beyond mere humanity, existing purely as spirits on the astral plane.

Members of the OGD included the poet W. B. Yeats, the influential esoteric historian A. E. Waite, the tea heiress Annie Horniman, the actress Florence Farr and, to the dismay of many of these, Aleister Crowley. In 1891 Dr Woodman died suddenly. From 1892, when the Ordo Rosae, Rubeae et Aureae Crucis was introduced, to around 1896, the OGD flourished under Mathers and Westcott. Then things started going wrong.

Annie Horniman fell out with Mathers and resigned in 1896. The following year Dr Westcott was told that his membership of a secret society which practised magic did not look good for a man in his position as a senior London coroner. He resigned, leaving the OGD entirely in Mathers's hands.

Aleister Crowley joined in 1898. By the next year he had risen to Philosophus, the highest degree in the outer order. Mathers had moved to Paris, setting up a temple there. Crowley went to Paris, where Mathers initiated him in the first grade of the Ordo Rosae, Rubeae et Aureae Crucis, but when he returned to London in 1900 the other members refused him access to papers he was entitled to have. Crowley tried to take possession of the London temple. Around the same time Mathers revealed the truth about the non-existent Fräulein Sprengel, which understandably created a storm throughout the OGD. Both Mathers and Crowley were expelled.

W. B. Yeats took over, Annie Horniman returned and together they tried to sort out the mess. The OGD as a major force was finished, though remnants of it continued. A. E. Waite took over the London temple and changed the emphasis from ritual magic to a more spiritual – and more Christian – 'mystical path'. Later members, under Waite, included the Christian occult novelist Charles Williams and the mystic, poet and academic Evelyn Underhill.

Those who wanted the original emphasis on magic formed a new order, Stella Matutina, the Order of the Morning Star. These included Yeats, two people who were to become important in the continuing British Esoteric tradition, Dion Fortune (see p. 186) and Israel Regardie – who later published a four-volume work on the teachings of the OGD – and one who was more famous as a children's novelist, E. Nesbit.

The OGD's reputation often suffers from its brief association with Crowley. Because he is known to have been heavily into sex magic, it is wrongly assumed that the same applied to the OGD. Although the theory of sex magic might have been studied, it never formed part of the Order's practice. In fact, both Mathers and his wife were revolted by the very idea of physical sex; they never consummated their marriage. Annie Horniman has been described as a prude, although, in contrast, Florence Farr had liaisons with, among others, Yeats and George Bernard Shaw.

◆

Aleister Crowley (1875–1947) also fell out with Mathers and went off to form his own order, called Argenteum Astrum (A∴A∴), the Order of the Silver Star, and to become renowned for his sex-magic exploits and his outrageous behaviour. He later became British leader of the Ordo Templi Orientis (O∴T∴O).

Crowley is often credited with what has become the Wiccan rede, 'Do what thou wilt shall be the whole of the law' (now usually prefixed by 'An it hurt none . . .'). In fact, it originated from François Rabelais,[9] nearly four centuries before Crowley used it in his *Liber Legis* or *Book of the Law* (dictated by Aiwass, a spirit speaking for the Egyptian god Horus, through Crowley's wife, Rose Kelly, in 1904). Largely, it must be said, because of Crowley's own hedonism, this maxim has been much misinterpreted. It never meant, 'You're free to do whatever you like', a recipe for self-indulgence. The point of the precept is that for the Esoteric adept one's will should be totally in line with the will of God, so that one acts always within the will of God. It was also intended by Crowley to be half of a greeting; the response should be, 'Love is the law, love under will', which fills out the meaning considerably.

Although few would dispute Crowley's unpleasant, at times disgusting, character and behaviour, many serious Esotericists say that his written work, particularly *Magick in Theory and Practice* (1929), contains much of value.

BUILDERS OF THE ADYTUM

The Builders of the Adytum (BOTA) is an American offshoot of the Order of the Golden Dawn (OGD). It was founded, originally as the Shrine of Ageless Wisdom, by Paul Foster Case (1884–1954), who had been interested in the Esoteric since his childhood.

Case received messages from 'the Master R', who is usually equated with the Comte de Saint-Germain. The Masters wanted Case to establish an Esoteric school to bring the hidden teachings to America. Case joined the Chicago branch of the OGD, rose through the ranks and then took the teachings into his own school in the early 1920s. After his death, he was succeeded by Dr Anne Davies, who further extended his teachings until her own death in 1975.

Most of the books supplied by BOTA are by Case or Davies, but they also recommend Dion Fortune's *The Mystical Qabalah*. The School offers correspondence courses in Tarot, the Cabbala, alchemy and other related subjects.

> Hitherto, the great practical secrets have been guarded carefully from spiritual dilettantes and have only been given to duly initiated men and women under the strictest pledges of secrecy. In the past, this secrecy has been necessary because of the ecclesiastic and legal restrictions upon freedom of thought and worship. Today such close secrecy is no longer necessary. Much may now be given out openly which formerly could be imparted only in private and by word of mouth.[10]

After 'associate members' have taken the introductory courses, they may be admitted into a group known as a Pronaos, practising ritual magic.

As with similar schools, the philosophy is practical. The aim is that as the member 'continues with the process of self-unfolding, he gradually increases mastery of himself, first in small things, then in greater'. Progress can be made only if there is sincerity, desire and willingness to work.

> For you to be successful in our Work, your personal goals must correspond to those of the Order: personal enlightenment, self-transmutation, and service to Life. To only desire healing and wealth is not enough and will surely result in failure . . . BOTA does not offer to remake your world for you. It does offer you the keys to knowledge that will enable you to do it for yourself, with the inner help that linkage with a true Mystery School confers.

'Adytum' is Greek for 'the innermost part of the Temple, the *Holy of Holies, that which is not made with hands'*. The name Builders of the Adytum 'indicates that we propose to help you build the *Inner Temple* wherein conscious contact with the Higher Self may be made and your true spiritual heritage may be realized'.

There may well also be physical improvements in a member's life, such as health and wealth, as a result of their studies, but these should not be the reason for joining. However, if they are as powerful as BOTA indicate, they should certainly not be dismissed.

> The practical work of BOTA, which includes study, meditation, imagery and ritual, initiates a series of subtle but important changes in your inner world, not the least of which is an expansion of your conscious awareness. Even a slight increase in this area has a remarkable effect on your mental/emotional capacities. Your intelligence increases and you become more aware of your motivations. You become more observant, which improves your memory. Your ability to anticipate future effects of present causes is enhanced, improving your discrimination in making choices. Objectivity is increased, aiding the ability to think more logically and clearly, which increases control over your environment and helps you define your goals . . .

The list is remarkably similar to L. Ron Hubbard's claims about a 'Clear' (see p. 253–4), except that his techniques are psychological, while those of BOTA and other mystery schools are spiritual. Their expression here is also akin to the goals of the 'self-improvement' courses and seminars, which have always had a great appeal in America (see p. 235–6).

But the main aim is to enable the initiate to be raised to a higher state of consciousness. Other terms used include 'an awakening' and 'illumination', or an awareness of the God within.

Unlike the Society of the Inner Light (see p. 188), BOTA's teachings are not tied to a particular national mythos and its members are not tied to a particular nationality. They are international, with centres in Europe, South and Central America, New Zealand, Canada and throughout the USA. Unusually, members are not required to relinquish membership of any other orders.

Like most Esoteric groups, BOTA teach both Cabbala and Tarot. The Cabbala's Tree of Life is used symbolically to represent the relationship between God and man. As Tarot expert Rachel Pollack has said, 'Tarot has come into being as a lively pictorial version of the inner knowledge found on the Tree.'[11] BOTA say of Tarot, 'The particular potency of this system lies in its use of symbols, which are a universal language that directly instructs subconsciousness with its pictorial wisdom, regardless of language differences . . . It was originally devised as a means of conveying universal principles regarding Man's structure, place and purpose in the Cosmos, through the use of symbols.' In common with most Esoteric schools, they use Tarot for study, meditation, imagery and ritual, rather than for fortune-telling or divination.

Like several other OGD offshoots, they have published their own design of Tarot, the images symbolizing the deep Esoteric truths taught by the movement. The cards are black and white, and members are encouraged to colour them to bring out the personal interpretation of the symbolism and the member's own relationship with them.

There are now several Esoteric Tarot packs claiming to stem from the teachings of the OGD. These include the well-known Rider Tarot, designed to the instructions of A. E. Waite, Aleister Crowley's Book of Thoth, Robert Wang's Golden Dawn Tarot (based on Israel Regardie's pack, which was based on a pack painted by Mathers's wife to his instructions), Godfrey Dowson's Hermetic Tarot, and the Morgan-Greer Tarot, which is based on the interpretations of Waite and Paul Foster Case. Considering that these all stem from the same root, their images and symbolism are often markedly different, though the BOTA pack, drawn to the instructions of Case, is very similar to the Rider-Waite pack, and is presumably a copy of Mathers's pack.

The OGD and some of its offshoots were closely linked with Freemasonry and Rosicrucianism, and much of the symbolism is similar between all of them. Interestingly, the Masonic Tarot, a French pack, is quite different from the OGD-offshoot packs.

SOCIETY OF THE INNER LIGHT

HISTORY

Dion Fortune (1890–1946) was born into a Christian Science family as Violet Mary Firth. She took her pseudonym from her family motto, *Deo, non Fortuna* (By God, not by chance). She had visions from her childhood and joined the Theosophy movement briefly. From Theosophy she took the idea of the Masters, but saw them as spiritual rather than physical beings.

In an early job, when she was 20, she felt that she was under psychic attack from a female superior and set out to discover how she could defend herself. One of her most significant works is *Psychic Self-Defence* (1931). She studied psychology, particularly the works of Freud and Jung, and worked as a lay psychoanalyst.

Her visions continued. In one she met Jesus and the Comte de Saint-Germain, and learned about her past lives. She joined the Order of the Golden Dawn (OGD) offshoot Stella Matutina in 1919, and in 1922 founded her own order in Glastonbury, initially called the Christian Mystic Lodge of the Theosophical Society, within the OGD umbrella. When she fell out with Mathers's wife, this was renamed the Fraternity of the Inner Light in 1928, and became an independent order with a London headquarters.

From 1927 to 1939, when he divorced her, she was married to a Welsh occultist, Thomas Penry Evans. With Evans as her priest, she developed her study and practice of magic, a blend of Esoteric Christianity, Cabbalism and Tarot, with some strong Neo-Pagan elements. Her 24 books, including six occult novels, are read and recommended today by both Esoteric and Neo-Pagan movements, though the Society of the Inner Light stresses that she was never a witch, and down-plays the Neo-Pagan aspects of her work.

When Evans left her she apparently went into a decline, though she continued her researches into Arthurian and Grail material. She was also instrumental in mounting a magical defence of Britain during the Second World War. It is claimed that, through spirit-contact with certain members, she continued to run the Society of the Inner Light for several years after her death from leukaemia.

BELIEFS AND PRACTICES

The Society has changed the emphasis of its teachings over the years. It was strongly influenced for a while by Alice Bailey's teachings on the Secret Masters. It picked up on the Alexander Technique for improving physical posture. It even dabbled briefly, 'for purely practical reasons', with Scientology's E-meters. However, its founder's teachings continued to be of prime importance.

For public consumption the Society of the Inner Light is 'a registered charity based on the Christian religion'.[12] In fact, it is a school within the Western Mystery Tradition.

> The principle aim of the Western Esoteric Tradition is expansion of consciousness. It deals with the 'ground of all being', unmanifest, beyond time and space, which differentiates countless modes of being in evolving through a manifest universe. The purpose of these modes of being is to realize the Divine Intention . . .[which] is concerned with the true purpose and destiny of each one of us. To achieve this we train our members in the Qabalah, Bible and with ritual, as well as daily usages, including meditation.[13]

Its main source books are Dion Fortune's *The Mystical Qabalah* and *Cosmic Doctrine*. As with other British Esoteric schools, there is a great emphasis on mythology, particularly Celtic and Arthurian mythology. Fortune herself was closely linked with Glastonbury.

Following initial training, the Society teaches three different paths: the Mystic, the Hermetic and the Path of the Green Ray.

> On the Mystic Path the ego casts everything aside that separates it from God. It seeks to know even as it is known; and as the mind cannot know God, it even casts away the mind to enter into the Divine Union. All that is not God to it is dross; and it purges and repurges the soul until nothing remaineth but pure spirit. This is a steep and narrow way, though swift and sure.

The Path of the Green Ray seeks God in nature, in his works.

> For the god within, being lifted up and exalted to ecstasy with a divine inebriation, perceives the God Without in hill and herb and elemental force . . . it is an inebriation of the soul, not of the flesh. An inebriation of colour, sound and motion that lift the senses out of the flesh into a wider vision, for Dionysius is a Messiah as well as the Christ, and the soul can transcend the mind by sublimating the senses as well as by renouncing, and some find God on this Path as truly as by the Way of the Cross.

The Hermetic Path is a middle way between the other two: 'Use the mind God gave you to reach up and realize the things of the spirit upon the one hand, and reach down and control the things of the senses on the other, and thus you shall stand equilibrated between them, as the Initiated Adept.'

♦

Like most other Esoteric schools, the Society stresses the difficulty of the work, almost to the point of actively discouraging people from becoming members. It also lays great stress on moral living, courteousness, good citizenship, self-discipline, responsibility and other similar virtues.

Two former members of the Society of the Inner Light, who have produced very significant books in the Esoteric tradition, are W. E. Butler and Gareth Knight.

The Society is quite specifically British in emphasis, though it does have an overseas membership. Candidates for its four-year course must ideally have been:

> A. Born and raised in the United Kingdom. B. Raised with experience in the British tradition: i.e. fairy tales, nursery rhymes, and folk stories; full knowledge of the legends and myths of our history . . . The candidate must have: C. A good knowledge of British history with no conflicting beliefs from other religions or cultural training or experiences. D. A love of all things British.

This emphasis is reminiscent of Mathers, who was involved for a while in extremely patriotic semi-political movements, such as the restoration of the Royal House of Stuart. The Society says that its emphasis is for 'practical and technical reasons'.

SERVANTS OF THE LIGHT

The Servants of the Light (SOL) is a 'School of Occult Science' founded in 1972 by W. E. Butler (1898–1978) and based in Jersey. The Helios Course, which led up to its formation, began in 1968. Butler was a former member of Dion Fortune's Fraternity/Society of the Inner Light, and an ordained priest in the Liberal Catholic Church (founded by the Rev. Charles W. Leadbetter, who helped turn the Theosophical Movement more towards Esoteric Christianity). Butler has written a number of significant works on the Western Mystery Tradition. SOL is now run by Dolores and Michael Ashcroft-Nowicki.

SOL is organized on standard lines of progression from Novice upwards. The Entered Novice takes a 50-lesson main course. The first six lessons are based on *The Art of True Healing* by Israel Regardie, a former member of the Order of the Golden Dawn (OGD) and the remainder on *Practical Guide to Qabalistic Symbolism* by Gareth Knight, another former member of the Society of the Inner Light. By the tenth or twelfth lesson, if progress is satisfactory, the Novice becomes a Fellow within the Fellowship of the SOL. This is the First Degree.

If a Fellow wishes to progress to the Second Degree, he or she must attend three practical (i.e. ritual) workshops, at Beginners, Intermediate and Advanced level, over a period of 18 months. At some point during this time the Fellow may be offered initiation, and at the end of the main course may enter the Second Degree, becoming a Frater or Soror of the Fraternity of the SOL. Fraters and Sorors help to teach Novices and lead Fellows in their ritual work.

Beyond this is a Third Degree, by invitation only, initiates of which are called Councellors (*sic*).

Servants of the Light, like most Mystery schools, has outer and inner levels. The outer level (i.e. visible to the outside world) comprises the First and Second Degrees. From these are drawn the members of the Inner Court. SOL is a 'contacted' school:

> by contacted, we mean those schools that are in close psychic touch with the overshadowing Hierarchy on the Inner Planes. It is in this Inner Group that the real power resides; and from there it is mediated in various ways to its counterpart on the physical level. The SOL *is* so contacted, and its inner powers are slowly becoming available to those who come within its sphere of influence.[14]

The main emphasis of the teaching for Novices and Fellows is on the Cabbala, whose Tree of Life:

> has been described as 'the Mighty, All-Embracing Glyph of the Soul of Man and the Universe'. Without this composite system, it is probable that the Western Tradition would have been entirely destroyed. Owing to its simplicity, however, the glyph is easily committed to memory; and because of its profundity, from this sparse simplicity can be derived a complete and satisfying philosophy and knowledge of life in both its inner and outer aspects.

SOL see the Cabbala as:

> the foundation of the Western Mystery Tradition . . . The great body of philosophy to be found in the religion texts of the Jews, including the Old Testament of the Bible, particularly the Pentateuch. It can also be seen in the vast complex of astrological, alchemical and occult symbology that has come down to us, as well as in the Rosicrucian and Masonic myth – including the Tarot, which is indigenous to the West.

The Western Mystery Tradition, sometimes called the Hermetic Tradition, also has clear links with Egyptian and Greek thought from around the time of Christ – the Gnostics and Neo-Platonists. SOL's 'contact' is from the ancient Esoteric School of Alexandria, from the Temple of On, or Heliopolis.

SOL also encourages its members to become familiar with mythology, particularly but (unlike the Society of the Inner Light) not solely Celtic mythology and the Arthurian cycle – the Matter of Britain. 'Any mythological knowledge you acquire will not be wasted. The ability to cross-index the legends and god forms can be of immense value in the understanding of the ancient past.' During the course students must make a detailed study of at least two pantheons in addition to their native tradition.

The School sees:

> an urgent need for seekers of all ages to resume the Quest of the Grail. The need for sound esoteric training is more urgent than it has ever been. We do

not claim, as others do, that the occult way holds all the answers to the world's ills; but we do claim that it has a part to play in the eventual victory over them. We believe, sincerely, that the ancient traditions hold a timeless key which may be applied to modern life and its problems. We aim to train dedicated men and women who will help others to achieve the inner serenity that is their birthright.

The SOL have added to the number of Esoteric Tarot packs with their own Servants of the Light Tarot. For once this doesn't claim to be a copy of Mathers's pack, or even to contain the true symbolism of the OGD. Instead, Dolores Ashcroft-Nowicki has worked together with two artists to produce a pack which reflects the Esoteric teachings of the School. Her book *Inner Landscapes* uses the SOL Major Arcana for 'pathworking', or guided meditational journeys.

There are around 2,000 members worldwide, making SOL one of the largest and most influential Esoteric movements.

THE LONDON GROUP

Like the Servants of the Light, the London Group was founded by a former senior member of the Society of the Inner Light, in 1975. It is also, in its initial training programme, or Outer Court, a correspondence school, and, despite its name, it is not limited to London.

The London Group offers two introductory courses, to be taken consecutively: first, basic occult tenets and introduction to the Cabbala; and second, introduction to the modern mysteries, particularly the practical use of symbols and ritual. The second part also outlines the structure and methods of a modern occult group. If students progress satisfactorily, they may then be invited to take a Threshold course to prepare for entry into the Fraternity. The fees, at £20, £12 and £6 for the three parts (1995 prices) are considerably lower than those of the Society of the Inner Light (£100) and the Servants of the Light (£334), though these are for longer, more detailed courses.

The Group stresses the practical nature of its work. 'Our keynote is "action". We have no room for armchair philosophers. We welcome innovation and use many techniques to help individuals become truly "themselves".'[15] The primary goal is personal regeneration, with the clear understanding that this will benefit others:

> The principles learnt are lived out in the daily life of its members . . . like yeast working in a mass of dough, right thinking and a right ethic based on Cosmic Law, are set to work in the world. It is surprising just how much even a single such archetypal "pattern" can help to redress the chaos so prevalent in the world today . . . There has never been a greater need for sane, well-balanced men and women than there is today.

The London Group, like its forerunners, is based firmly in the Western Mystery Tradition. 'A notable feature of all the religions of the past is that each had an inner and an outer aspect. The outer form became the Race religion, whilst the inner form contained deeper teaching which offered a direct path to personal experience of the inner realities and an opportunity to help in the spiritual evolution of the Race.'

It is not known why the founder left the Society of the Inner Light to found a new School, but there is perhaps a clue in the statement that 'the London Group passes on that tradition in a modern form suitable for the use of twentieth-century men and women'. It also gives the impression of being a little more flexible than some of the other Schools:

> We welcome enquirers of all denominations and beliefs, for this Age is the Age of synthesis. There is room for many viewpoints . . . There are many ways of service and many groups seeking to put esoteric ideals into practice . . . if this group does not seem to meet your needs, then at least we may have helped you to realize more clearly what it is that you *do* need! There is no 'one perfect way'; but there *is* a best way for each individual.

THE I AM MOVEMENT

The I AM movement, with its various offshoots, has its roots in Theosophy. It was founded in 1931 by Guy and Edna Ballard. The previous year Guy Ballard (1878–1939), who had read widely in Theosophy and other Esoteric religion, was on a walking holiday on Mount Shasta in California, looking for a supposed Esoteric Brotherhood of Mount Shasta, when he met the Ascended Master the Comte de Saint-Germain, a historical eighteenth-century alchemist who features in a number of Esoteric movements. Saint-Germain had apparently been scouring Europe for centuries, looking for someone to whom he could give the Great Laws of Life. Finding no one worthy, he had turned his attentions to the USA.

The Ballards began to make regular contact with Saint-Germain and other Masters. They set up the Saint Germain Press to publish their books on I AM, including *Unveiled Mysteries* (1934) and *The Magic Presence* (1935) under the pseudonym Godfre Ray King, and *I AM Adorations and Affirmations* (1936). They began teaching classes and training other teachers in their message across America. By 1938 it was estimated that they had had up to a million students. After experiencing problems with hecklers at their open meetings, they started to hold membership-only classes.

After Guy Ballard's unexpected death in 1939 the movement ran into a series of difficulties. Apparently he had taught mastery over death and many members felt cheated. Like many other religious leaders, the Ballards had become wealthy through their movement; some ex-members accused them of using the US postal service for fraudulent purposes – obtaining money for a false religion. Unusually, the validity of the teachings of a religion were tested in court. From 1942 to 1954 the movement was unable to use the normal mail and had to distribute its books and magazines by Railway Express. In 1957 it was finally granted tax-exempt status as a religion. Edna Ballard died in 1971, leaving the leadership in the hands of a Board of Directors.

♦

The movement teaches that the omnipotent, omniscient and omnipresent creator God ('I AM' – Exodus 3:14) is in all of us as a spark from the Divine Flame, and that we can experience this presence, love, power and light – the power of the Violet Consuming Flame of Divine Love – through quiet contemplation and by repeating 'affirmations' and 'decrees'. By 'affirming' something one desires, one can cause it to happen. In a sense the I AM movement overlaps with the Personal Development or Human Potential movements, because of this 'positive thinking' aspect of its teachings.

The Ascended Masters are religious adepts who have (like Buddhist *Bodhisattvas*) stepped off the wheel of reincarnation and now devote themselves to the guidance of mankind; they are the same as the Great White Brotherhood. Because Jesus is one of the Ascended Masters, the movement calls itself Christian. The Ballards and their son Daniel (who later left the movement) were the only Accredited Messengers of the Ascended Masters – they received over 3,000 messages between them – though all believers may experience the Christ Self within them. It is the duty of believers to use the divine power wisely, for harmony and purity. Its misuse has been the cause of discord and death through the centuries.

The teachings of the Ballards were not new, but the publicity they gave to them encouraged their spread through the developing New Age movements, many of which have taken up the idea of the Masters.

CHURCH UNIVERSAL AND TRIUMPHANT

The Church Universal and Triumphant (CUT) and its publishing wing, Summit Lighthouse, have much in common with the I AM movement – they even recognize Guy Ballard as an Ascended Master – though they are quite independent. They are also one of the most prominent modern versions of Gnostic Christianity. In recent years they have come in for much criticism from the anti-cult organizations, particularly the Cult Awareness Network, which ran public lectures against the Church in America.

HISTORY

Mark L. Prophet (1918–73) had been involved in an I AM offshoot, the Bridge to Freedom (later the New Age Church of the Christ, and now the Bridge to Spiritual Freedom), for some time before he founded Summit Lighthouse in Washington, DC, in 1958 to publish the teachings he had received from the Ascended Masters. Prophet, incidentally, was genuinely his family surname. In 1961 he met Elizabeth Claire Wulf (b. 1939), who had been raised a Lutheran, had joined Christian Science in her early teens and started reading I AM literature when she was 18. She was trained by Mark Prophet and by the Ascended Master who had appointed him a Messenger, El Morya, who had been King Arthur, Thomas à Becket and Sir Thomas More in three of his incarnations (she herself had apparently been the New Testament Martha, and Guinevere; Mark Prophet

Above   The Mormon Tabernacle Choir at the Tabernacle, Temple Square, Salt Lake City, Utah.

Right   Sun Myung Moon (b. 1920) and his wife, Hak Ja Moon, at a Unification Church ceremony.

Above Sun Myung Moon (b. 1920),
founder of the Unification Church.

Above   Joseph Smith
(1805–44), founder of
the Church of Jesus
Christ of Latter-day
Saints.

Left   The First Church
of Christ, Scientist,
Boston, Massachusetts.

Top right   A. C.
Bhaktivedanta Swami
Prabhupada
(1896–1977), founder of
the International Society
for Krishna
Consciousness.

Right   Maharaji (b.
1958), founder of Elan
Vital, formerly the
Divine Light Mission.

Below The Lectorium Rosicrucianum Renova Temple at Bilthoven, The Netherlands.

Left Masonic and cabbalistic symbolism in *The Open Door*, the brochure of the Builders of the Adytum.

Right Esoteric Christian and other religious symbolism on the brochure of the Society of the Inner Light.

Left Martin Cecil (1909–88) and Lloyd Meeker (1907–54), founders of the Emissaries.

Right Elizabeth Clare Prophet (b. 1939), Messenger of the Church Universal and Triumphant. *(Kali Productions)*

Left   A model of the Embassy the Raelian movement intend to build for the Elohim.

Below   Raël (Claude Vorilhon) (b. 1946), founder of the Raelian movement.

Two cards from the Emin Gemrod Mosaic (Tarot):

Right The Empress: 'Follow you the ways of the great Mother, who has a great wisdom, and who spreads a great wonder and experience before you. Learn her signals and laws, for to do so is to make full and sound the heart of your destiny, which can be certain.'

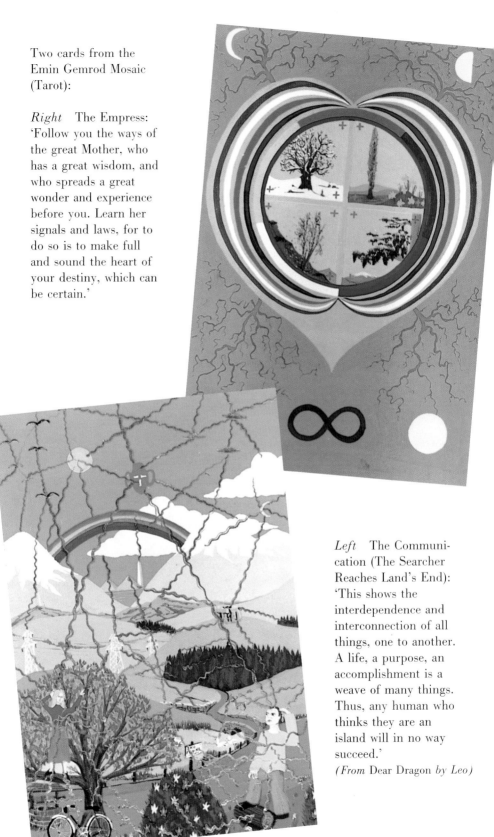

Left The Communication (The Searcher Reaches Land's End): 'This shows the interdependence and interconnection of all things, one to another. A life, a purpose, an accomplishment is a weave of many things. Thus, any human who thinks they are an island will in no way succeed.'
(From Dear Dragon *by Leo)*

had been the Church Father Origen). She married Mark in 1963, and a year later she too became a Messenger. The Ascended Master Saint-Germain instructed them to form the Keepers of the Flame Fraternity to teach others about the Masters.

On Mark's sudden death from a stroke, Elizabeth Prophet took over the organization. The following year she set up CUT, and Summit Lighthouse became its publishing house. She has grown in importance as the Church has grown. Within the movement she is known formally as Guru Ma and usually as Mother, though not as Ma Prophet, her popular name in the US press.

Over the years CUT has been based in several areas, outgrowing each one and moving on to the next. Mark Prophet was living in Washington, DC, when he founded Summit Lighthouse. In 1962 they moved to Fairfax, Virginia, and in 1965 to Vienna, Virginia. In 1966 they moved to a mansion in Colorado Springs, which became the world headquarters of Summit Lighthouse. During these years the two Messengers travelled around America and Europe spreading their teachings. They also set up 'the Motherhouse' in Santa Barbara, which housed Summit University for a few years. Other centres were set up around America. CUT leased a Church of the Nazarene college campus in Pasadena, California, in 1976, then moved yet again the following year, buying from the Claretian Fathers an estate in the Santa Monica Mountains near Malibu which they renamed Camelot.

In 1981 the Church bought its present home, the Royal Teton Ranch in Paradise Valley, near Livingston, Montana, next to the famous Yellowstone National Park. Along with many other organizations, it bought caravans and kitchen equipment from the Rajneesh community when that broke up in 1985. It moved its headquarters to the Royal Teton Ranch in 1986. The ranch is now a 1,000-hectare (24,000-acre) site. Many members live there in trailer caravans; others have bought plots of land to build their own houses.

The Church has been at the centre of controversy for some years, first because it bought up large areas of land, which local people found worrying, especially after the political takeover-attempt at Rajneeshpuram (see p. 144); then because it built nuclear fallout shelters against the threat of a disaster; and then for supposedly stockpiling weapons – Mrs Prophet's current husband, Edward Francis, was gaoled for a short time for illegal arms activity. He is her fourth husband. Her first, before Mark Prophet, didn't join in her belief in the Ascended Masters; she also had a brief third marriage after Mark's death.

Elizabeth Clare Prophet has continued to receive messages from the Ascended Masters, particularly Saint-Germain, 'the Knight Commander of the Keepers of the Flame Fraternity',[16] and Lanello, the Ever-Present Guru – the Ascended Master name of her late husband. The weekly *Pearls of Wisdom* magazine contains messages from the Ascended Masters. Her many books, incorporating these teachings (and the teachings given earlier to Mark Prophet), have gained a wider circulation than the Church itself, becoming influential in more general New Age circles.

BELIEFS AND PRACTICES

Although some of its teachings derive from the I AM movement, and ultimately from Theosophy (though 'Theosophy has a far more intellectual approach,' says Murray Steinman, the Church's director of media relations[17]), CUT has its own distinctive theology, which in recent years has embraced large elements of Gnostic Christianity. It identifies itself as firmly based in the Judaeo-Christian tradition.

Jesus Christ and Saint-Germain – together with all of the heavenly hosts: Ascended Masters, Elohim, archangels, angels and servant-sons of God, who comprise the Spirit of the Great White Brotherhood (the multitude of saints robed in white witnessed by Saint John) – have come forth from the inner Mystery School at the end of Pisces and the beginning of Aquarius to teach us how to call upon this name of the LORD, alchemical formulas whereby we may put on our individual Christhood even while we overcome personified evil and the *energy veil* of our negative karma, the so-called sins of our past lives.[18]

In common with the I AM movement, CUT teaches that there is an element of the Christ, a divine spark of the God flame, within each of us.

The fundamental principle of the teachings of the Ascended Masters is that all sons and daughters of God have a divine spark which is their potential to become, or realize, the Christ within and ascend to God as Jesus did. This concept is at the heart of the major religions, East and West. And it was part of Jesus' original teachings to his disciples which were either destroyed or obscured by Church Fathers.[19]

His teachings were also corrupted by the New Testament writers. Jesus studied in India and Tibet between the ages of 12 and 30; two of CUT's publications are *The Lost Years of Jesus* and the four-volume *The Lost Teachings of Jesus*. The first is based on old Buddhist stories of Saint Issa, who travelled to the East and studied under Masters there before returning to Palestine to take up his ministry. 'Then it was that Issa left the parental house in secret, departed from Jerusalem, and with the merchants set out towards Sind, with the object of perfecting himself in the Divine Word and of studying the laws of the great Buddhas.'[20] *The Lost Teachings* incorporates some of the ideas of such non-canonical works as the Secret Book of James and the Gnostic Gospels of Philip, Thomas and Mary Magdalene, but are actually 'a reconstitution of Jesus' basic message through the Messengership of Mark and Elizabeth Prophet, which they have written down,' says Steinman. CUT emphasizes particularly the Book of Enoch, another of the many books which never made it into the Bible.

The Church does not accept all the Gnostic teachings, says Steinman, but 'a lot of the things we totally agree with, like where Jesus is saying in the Gospel of Thomas, "If you drink from the same stream that I have, you will be just like me, we'll be twins";[21] that's essentially our core teaching, that you can become like Jesus. If you miss that point, then you're missing the point of his message.'

Jesus was not God the Son, in the traditional Christian sense; he was a man in complete touch with the Christ-consciousness within him. He ascended to God immediately after leaving his human body and is now one of the Ascended Masters. Jesus and Mary Magdalene were married; it is not known whether the Church believes they had children. Mary Magdalene, who was Jesus's twin flame, is now the Ascended Master Magda. The Virgin Mary is venerated as the perfect expression of the Mother aspect of God. The Statue of Liberty is symbolic of the Goddess of Liberty. In this Aquarian Age the Church places equal emphasis on the masculine and feminine aspects of both God and individual people, whether they are female or male.

Saint-Germain is a very significant figure. Before becoming an Ascended Master he lived on earth as (among others) the prophet Samuel, Mary's husband Joseph,

Merlin, Roger Bacon, Christopher Columbus and Francis Bacon. He is 'Chohan (Lord) of the Seventh Ray of Freedom, Hierarch of the Aquarian Age, sponsor of the United States of America; initiator of souls in the science and ritual of alchemy and transmutation through the violet flame by the power of the spoken Word, meditation, and visualization.'[22] Saint-Germain inspired the American Constitution and the Declaration of Independence.

The Church teaches that we can step off the wheel of reincarnation – in ascension – by becoming united with our Christ-consciousness through study and prayer and, as in I AM, through affirmations and decrees. Affirmations affirm the person's relationship with God; decrees use the name of God (I AM) to make statements of power such as, 'I AM the light of the heart, shining in the darkness of being, changing all into the infinite mind of Christ', or, 'I AM a being of violet fire, I AM the purity God desires.' Ascension is not physical, but 'a spiritual acceleration of consciousness which takes place at the natural conclusion of one's lifetime when the soul returns to the Father and is freed from the round of karma and rebirth'.[23]

But CUT does not claim to be an easy short-cut to God. 'The path to the summit of being is steep. With fellow seekers and with the Ascended Masters who have gone before us we can make our way through these hitherto uncharted paths, and reach the summit of being.'[24]

Central to the Church's teachings – and its art – is 'the violet flame':

> the gift of the Holy Spirit known to mystics throughout the ages but
> introduced at large by Saint-Germain early in this century. When invoked and
> visualized in the giving of dynamic decrees, this seventh-ray aspect of the
> sacred fire transmutes the cause, effect, record and memory of negative karma
> and misqualified energy that result in discord, disease and death. Those who
> correctly call forth the violet flame daily, experience transformation, soul
> liberation, and spiritual upliftment.[25]

The Tenets of the Church – in effect an expanded creed – set out the beliefs and spiritual obligations of full members of the Church. They include:

> We proclaim the Church Universal and Triumphant, founded by Almighty
> God upon the rock of the Christ consciousness, to be the true Church of Jesus
> the Christ, Gautama the Buddha, and all who have ever become one with the
> Christ and the I AM THAT I AM in the ritual of the ascension . . .
>
> We acknowledge and adore the one supreme God, the Creator of heaven and
> earth, and the individualization of the God flame in the I AM Presence as the I
> AM THAT I AM, the Source of life for each individual soul. We give
> allegiance to the Word that was made flesh, the only begotten of the Father,
> the eternal Logos, who is the universal Christ individualized as the Christed
> Self of the sons and daughters of God and the children of God . . .
>
> We accept the message of salvation and the statement of cosmic law
> contained in all of the sacred scriptures of the world according to the
> interpretation of the Holy Spirit given to the messengers Mark L. Prophet and
> Elizabeth Clare Prophet. We accept the progressive revelation of God as
> dictated through his emissaries, the ascended masters, to their messengers
> Mark L. Prophet and Elizabeth Clare Prophet and their appointed
> successors . . .

> We accept the example of the Virgin Mary in her ensoulment of the Mother ray as the supreme definition of our own opportunity to prove the Mother as the God flame wherever we are . . .[26]

CUT believes that it is 'a very valuable path for some people,' says Steinman, but it does not believe that it is the only path. Neither is it dogmatic in its teachings. Apart from the fully committed communicants, members are not required to believe every aspect of the Church's teachings. It also believes that it is more important to look for the similarities between religions than to emphasize the differences. In keeping with this philosophy, its doctrines are still developing, as it explores the mystical paths of all the world's religions. It has already examined Hinduism, Buddhism and others, and is currently looking into the Cabbala.

According to Elizabeth Clare Prophet:

> The Ascended Masters present a path and a teaching whereby every individual on earth can find his way back to God. I do not claim to be a Master but only their instrument. Nor do I claim to be perfect in my human self. I am the servant of the Light in all students of the Ascended Masters and in all people. My books and writings are intended to give people the opportunity to know the Truth that can make them free – so they can find God without me. My goal is to take true seekers, in the tradition of the Masters of the Far East, as far as they can go and need to go to meet their true Teachers face to face.[27]

Elizabeth Clare Prophet, like her late husband, is a Messenger of the Ascended Masters. The Church sees this as similar to the prophets of the Old Testament, who delivered messages from God.

> She is fully conscious and in possession of her faculties, yet in an exalted state, while delivering the words of the heavenly host as 'dictations'. Her work is not a form of psychism or spiritualism in which a discarnate entity from the spirit world takes over the body of a channeller. Rather it is a conveyance by the Holy Spirit of the sacred fire and the teaching of immortal beings who with Jesus have returned to the heart of the Father.[28]

There have been many criticisms of the Church, both by some of their neighbours in Montana and by the anti-cult movements. A member of the Church was recently kidnapped in Belgium for deprogramming. She managed to get away after a few days, and the police eventually arrested her mother, brother and the deprogrammers.

Any Church which builds nuclear bunkers is bound to face criticism. CUT is both survivalist and intensely patriotic, and has been accused of being ultra-right wing. Apparently at the time of Waco its leaders sought (and obtained) assurances from the FBI that they would not be attacked next.[29]

On the charge of being right-wing, Steinman accepts that they espouse conservative morality and think that 'civil defence and strategic defence are a good thing', but he points out that on other topics, particularly environmental issues and their stand against pesticides, they tend to be conservationist, and that in their criticism of nuclear power plants they are positively liberal. They follow what the Ascended Masters tell them on different issues, so their stance is more spiritual than political, he says. He also suggests that middle-class Americans in general tend to be more patriotic and more conservative than their British counterparts. It is often said, incorrectly, that Mrs Prophet forecast the end of the world – or at least a cataclysmic disaster – for April 1990. In fact, she had been told by Saint-Germain to have the underground shelters ready by then – not just for sheltering members of the Church, but also for protecting all the world's spiritual teachings in the event of a major attack.

On the firearms story, which brought the Church a lot of bad publicity, the facts – as established in court – are that the Church itself owns no weapons; individual members may own whatever weapons they want for sporting purposes or for self-defence. Edward Francis, Mrs Prophet's husband, with another Church member, tried to buy guns to defend the Church's fallout shelter if necessary against local right-wing extremists. The weapons would have been quite legal if Francis hadn't made the mistake of trying to buy them under a false name – ironically to avoid publicity. 'Obviously we screwed up. It was a huge mistake and it was ill-conceived,' says Francis,[30] who is vice-president and business manager of the Church. Mrs Prophet had not known of the firearms purchase in advance.

Mrs Prophet has also been criticized for her love of expensive clothes and jewellery. Her response is that the clothes were a gift and the jewellery is a focus of spiritual power, and belongs to the Church, not to her.

The Church has also, like many other alternative religious movements, been accused of brainwashing its members, a charge which it strenuously denies. An independent study of the Church, sponsored by the Association of World Academics for Religious Education (AWARE), concluded that there was no evidence of anything approaching brainwashing. The members are predominantly white middle-class adults; three-quarters are between 30 and 60; a quarter have an advanced degree. They are generally of above average intelligence. Politically they do tend to be right of centre; half describe themselves as conservative and a further 8 per cent as very conservative; a quarter say they are moderate, and only 4 per cent say they are liberal. But as for CUT being another Waco-in-the-making, as some cult-watchers assert, the study found that adult members 'scored lower than the normed population on the Aggression subscale'. Using a number of different indicators, the study concludes that CUT has the characteristics of a denomination rather than those of a cult; as with mainstream denominations, for example, it is quite possible to be a 'nominal' member. Part of the study concentrates on the children in the Royal Teton Ranch: 'contrary to the claims of critics, they found the children bright, well taken care of, loved, and well educated'.[31]

In common with its spiritual great-grandparent, the Theosophical Society, CUT places great value on education, running a Montessori school to offer quality education to children from pre-school to high school age.

Although the Church makes use of music, it is opposed to rock music. 'We don't think that rock music is all that healthy for you,' says Steinman. 'Rhythm and music are extremely important as an expression of sound, and we see sound as the creative power of the universe – "In the beginning was the Word". Where the rhythm becomes destructive, that's where we draw the line.'

Communicants of the Church pledge to abstain from alcohol, tobacco and drugs. Other members might smoke or drink, though 'we don't think it's a good idea for them to do it,' says Steinman. The Church recommends a macrobiotic diet without much red meat, but Steinman suggests the most important thing in diet is balance and common sense.

◆

Like many other religious movements, the Church doesn't give membership figures. There are practical reasons for this. It has a core membership of communicants, who have committed themselves completely to the Church, pledging acceptance of the Tenets and tithing their income to the Church. Keepers of the Flame are 'signed-up members', but are not necessarily deeply committed. In addition, there are thousands of people around the world who, having read Mrs Prophet's books, accept much of the teaching, but are not actually members of the Church. Having said that, there are about 700 residents at the Royal Teton Ranch. CUT also has around 120 groups in the USA, and groups in about 40 other countries, as well as individual members in another 20 countries. Some communicants live in communities, but the majority live and work in the outside world. In the UK, there are groups in London, Leeds, Litchfield and Solihull.

Elizabeth Clare Prophet was trained by Mark Prophet and by El Morya, and had been a Messenger for ten years when Mark died. The Board of Directors actually run the Church and will continue to do so after Mrs Prophet's eventual death. No one has been trained as a Messenger to succeed her. The Church expects the Holy Spirit to direct them on this when the time comes.

Guy and Edna Ballard's son Donald had been appointed a Messenger, but later left their I AM movement. The Prophets had three daughters and a son before Mark's death; two of these have now left the Church. Mrs Prophet, remarkably, had a fifth child in 1994, her first by Edward Francis, whom she married in 1981.

THE EMISSARIES

The Emissaries are not really either Esoteric or Neo-Pagan, but they could fairly accurately be called one of the earliest New Age movements. They live in a dozen small communities – from 20 to 150 people – in the USA, Canada, the UK and elsewhere, with a further 150 centres for meetings. The UK community at Mickleton House, near Stratford-upon-Avon, calls itself a 'centre for personal renewal and honouring the sacred in all things'. One reason for their inclusion in this book is as an example of how even a closely knit spiritual group can have problems – and work to solve them.

HISTORY

The Emissaries were founded in Tennessee in 1932 by Lloyd Arthur Meeker (1907–54), the son of a farmer and minister. He had searched through philosophies and religions for a purpose to his life, finding nothing to satisfy him.

> He finally looked to himself and came to the profound realization that he was completely responsible for the state of his world and the quality of his experience in it. He knew he could not continue like the mass of humanity, victim or victor in the world of circumstance. He saw and experienced a life of peace and value.[32]

Meeker wrote widely under the name Uranda and his ideas began to spread. In 1940 he met Martin Cecil, later the seventh Marquess of Exeter (1909–88), who took Meeker's mass of ideas and developed them into a more systematic and comprehensible system. Their writings and the transcripts of their talks are now collected in a set of volumes called *The Third Sacred School*.

By 1948 the Canadian headquarters of the movement was at Cecil's cattle ranch, 100 Mile House, in British Columbia, which eventually became a thriving Emissary community. The international headquarters, established by Meeker in 1945, is Sunrise Ranch in Colorado.

When Meeker died in a plane crash in 1954, Cecil took over the organization, which was then known as the Emissaries of Divine Light. This was later shortened to their current name, the Emissaries. Other early names for the movement included the Foundation of Universal Unity, the Ontological Society and the Integrity Society.

BELIEFS AND PRACTICES

It is difficult to pin down the Emissaries on exactly what they believe. It's been described as a combination of Gurdjieffian self-awareness and the Christian ideal of loving one another. This sounds vague, but:

> the philosophy was – and is – one of a very practical spirituality, based on the recognition that God works through the individual – you and me, here and now. This means that we each have a personal responsibility for letting Divine action happen in the world through us, by consciously letting our inner connection with the source of all things direct all our daily actions and interactions. In other words, don't blame anyone else for what's happening to you.[33]

Meeker had expressed it in more Esoteric terms: 'You are the means by which the invisible becomes visible.'[34] But the purpose of the Emissaries, again in his words, is more straightforward: 'to assist in the spiritual regeneration of the human race'.[35]

It all comes down to the individual's relationship with the Divine: 'Divine Action, as it appears through the actions and interactions of the individual, is anything that springs from the desire to bring unity rather than separation, to participate rather than isolate, to create rather than destroy, to understand with the heart rather than attack with the mind.'[36]

It is the very individuality of each human being which displays the power and diversity of God; and in a community of such people the whole is greater than the sum of its parts.

> When a group of conscious people each agree to commit themselves to surrendering to the inner impulse, the intensity of the group energy is magnified . . . This means that Divine energy has a bigger area available, which means that more of it can be made manifest than if the same number of people were surrendering in separate places, unknown to each other.[37]

By 'group energy' or 'Divine energy' the Emissaries mean something almost tangible. At one time they called it 'Pneumaplasm' (Spirit Substance), but now it is simply known as Substance.

As well as appreciating the spiritual value of living in a community, Emissaries teach a practice called Attunement, 'a gentle, meditative technique for aligning subtle body energy with universal energy for increasing Divine Awareness within,' says Kate Hall, events manager and visitor contact at Mickleton House.[38]

The heart of the beliefs, in Meeker's words, is that:

> God is not just one Being, but God *is* one Being. The Body of God is made up of many God Beings. But we do not have a multiplicity of gods, just one God. All the parts of God are perfectly co-ordinated, perfectly cohesive, and every part of the Body of God is an individualized God Being. That individualized aspect of God is in you, in your body. So it is with every man, woman and child on the face of the earth, good, bad or indifferent.[39]

'To Emissaries,' says Hall, 'this is known as Divine Identity, or True Identity. Most people are not in touch with their own True Identity, but most Emissaries believe that we can begin to become more conscious of our True Identity by choosing to act with greater awareness of the effect of all our actions, great and small, and by consciously taking full responsibility for our behaviour and how it affects everyone around us.'

To put it another way, if we are created in God's image, then we can each manifest the divine nature on Earth. If hate, fear, anger or other negative emotions or influences get in the way, the divine nature is distorted. We have the choice, however, of accepting divine control, of letting the divine nature and the divine design remanifest through us in a process known simply as healing. This is what Emissaries aim for, to experience reality (God) and to manifest divine truth and love in a distorted world.

Hall lists the main spiritual principles that Emissaries recognize:

> **Love:** To the degree that individuals fail to let love permeate themselves and all their thoughts, words and deeds, they function outside the realm of the Divine.
> **Trust:** Trust in the Divine process – that no matter how it looks, everything is happening for a reason.
> **Thankfulness:** Be truly thankful for all your blessings, whatever they are.
> **Acceptance:** Accept that everything is just as it is meant to be, without judgement, condemnation or resignation.
> **Forgiveness:** Letting go of our negative feelings towards others and allowing healing to happen. As we each heal our own lives, so the whole world may become healed.

It could perhaps be said that Meeker was a hippie, at least in his ideals, 30 years before anyone else. As Hall says, 'Scratch a middle-aged Emissary and you may well find a Sixties hippie, still full of those peace and love ideals, underneath.' She makes it clear that she is referring to the values of the idealistic youth of the 1960s, not to their supposedly common lifestyle of sex and drugs and rock 'n' roll.

The majority of current members are between 35 and 50, and come from the professions, the arts, media and small businesses. 'Recently more and more young people are joining in as well, most of them with strong and committed concerns about the environment and the state of the planet.'

♦

For 30 years the Emissaries were guided by Martin Cecil. Every community, at its Sunday morning service, would read a transcript of a talk he had delivered the week before to the main community in Colorado; it was a link between all the groups. He died in 1988, aged 79, and his son Michael (b. 1935) took over. He had different ideas from his father's about how the Emissaries should be organized.

His decision was the logical development of the basic philosophy; it all comes down to the individual, working in harmony with other individuals in a community. He removed his own 'father-figure' central authority over all the communities and said that each one should not only be self-governing but also set its own aims. Although, with seven other trustees, he has the title of spiritual leader, the new style is 'one of shared responsibility and personal empowerment'.

This set in motion a troubled time, 'a painful but vitally necessary growing up process for all the Emissary communities and a personal maturing process for everyone living in them,' says Hall.

The UK community at Mickleton fell from over 60 members to less than 30. It was only in 1994 that it began to reconstruct itself, finding a workable balance between the individual and the collective.

'As a group we have now realized that some people have a strong compulsion to give unstintingly of themselves, of their own volition, over many years, without thought of their own welfare. The result was that others naturally took advantage of this, and after many years these people woke up to find that they were burned out. We have now devised a code of ethics that prevents this kind of abuse of people's natural generosity.'

It took two years of 'sometimes painful processing', but now 'at Mickleton the worst of the transition from hierarchy to consensus and group autonomy is over . . . Now our numbers are growing again, as new people are attracted to the timeless ideal of discovering how to live and work together practically, in true spiritual community with each other.'

Now, as well as being a community of like-minded believers, Mickleton House offers courses to non-members in a variety of New Age-type subjects, including Dowsing, Tai Chi, Sacred Dance, Women's Earth Mysteries, 'Mayan Essence Self-Alignment' and Archetypes. According to Kate Hall, 'We feel a natural identification and affinity with the Findhorn Community' (see p. 231). Although there are no formal links, 'Our approach to everything is more similar to their approach than any other group I know of.'

THE 'FLYING SAUCER CULTS'

Idaho businessman Kenneth Arnold has a lot to answer for. To be more accurate, the blame should attach to the reporter who misquoted him in 1947 as saying he had seen 'flying saucers'. Within a year or so, flying saucers (or, more correctly, Unidentified Flying Objects) were everywhere.

As UFOs are now part of the global subconscious, it was inevitable that someone would bring the imagination of science fiction to bear on such Bible passages as Ezekiel's vision: 'The appearance of the wheels and their work was like unto the colour of a beryl; and they four had one likeness; and their appearance and their work was as it were a wheel in the middle of a wheel' and 'I heard also the noise of the wings of the living creatures that touched one another, and the noise of the wheels over against them, and a noise of great rushing' (Ezekiel 1:16, 3:13).

Erich von Daniken also has a lot to answer for, with books such as *Chariots of the Gods* and *In Search of Ancient Gods*, which sparked off a host of imitators. But (to misquote the title of a similar book) he was not the first.

There are many religious movements linked to UFOs and extraterrestrial beings, some more serious than others, and some very serious indeed. Some, particularly perhaps in California, spring up, flourish for a year or two and fade away; others are longer-lasting. One, British in origin, has been around since 1955 and shows no sign of vanishing into the deep blue sky.

Many outsiders who are quite prepared to accept the sincerity of Moonies and Mormons throw their hands up at the thought of 'crackpots' seriously believing that alien beings have come in flying saucers to bring mankind a message from the gods. But this is really no more unbelievable than the basis of many other religions. As the White Queen says to Alice, 'Why, sometimes I've believed as many as six impossible things before breakfast.' Most people, if they are prepared to be honest, do so – at least by lunch.

I shall be looking at the science fiction content of Scientology later (see p. 252). For now, out of the many available candidates, I shall look at just two of what are sometimes rather unkindly referred to as 'the saucer cults'.

It is important to accept that the members of these movements believe in the extraterrestrial origin of the messages given to them, just as Mormons believe in Joseph Smith's golden plates, and Christians believe that the creator of the universe became a man for 33 years. They should not be dismissed as 'UFO nuts'. Their belief is genuine and their religions are worth as much attention as all the others in this book.

For those who question either the rationality or the truthfulness of these movements and their founders, it should be pointed out that there are now many thousands of people who say they have talked with aliens, or have been abducted by them. They don't just claim this; they believe it. For them it is as much a fact as the colour of their car or the name of their home town. So far as other people are concerned, they might well be deluding themselves, but they're not doing it deliberately. Psychologists and sociologists have a number of theories, but all agree that such 'abductees' are utterly sincere. So are those whose religion originates in messages from extraterrestrials.

Alternatively, people have been having profound religious experiences, and visions, for millennia. Receiving messages from aliens could be seen as simply a modern rendering of the same thing (see p. 289).

Those are the cynics' interpretations. It could, of course, be possible that extraterrestrials *have* spoken to the founders of these movements. Certainly, no one can prove otherwise.

THE AETHERIUS SOCIETY

HISTORY

His Eminence Sir George King, born in Shropshire in 1919, founded probably the first and certainly the longest-lasting of the 'saucer cults' in 1955. His titles, which take up several lines, include among others Metropolitan Archbishop of the Aetherius Churches, Grand Master of the Mystical Order of St Peter, and Doctor of Science, Theology, Literature, Sacred Humanities and Philosophy – though according to Dr Richard Lawrence, Executive Secretary of the Aetherius Society,[40] he doesn't usually make use of most of his titles and degrees.

His consecration as a bishop was from the Liberal Catholic Church, a Theosophical-Christian organization entirely unconnected with the Roman Catholic Church. His knighthood is from the Byzantine Royal House in exile, and is not recognized by the College of Arms, though it is legally recognized in France and Italy, and does appear on his British passport.

King began practising yoga in 1944, and 'developed his latent powers to such an extent that he attained the much sought after deep trance state of Samadhi in which many of the hidden secrets of the Cosmos were revealed to him'.[41] In May 1954 he heard a voice saying, 'Prepare yourself! You are to become the Voice of Interplanetary Parliament.' At that time he had never heard of the Interplanetary Parliament (see p. 204), and didn't know anything about UFOs, but he realized he had been given a significant message. From the following year he began receiving 'Cosmic transmissions' – over 600 to date – with messages from the Masters on other planets.

The first Cosmic Master to speak to him, from the planet Venus, used the pseudonym Aetherius. In 1955 King founded the Aetherius Society, and began writing and lecturing on what the Masters were teaching him, starting at Caxton Hall in London.

He receives most of the messages when he is on his own or with a few members of the Society. When he is receiving a Cosmic transmission in public, King sits on stage wearing dark glasses and goes into a trance state. First a voice known as Mars Sector 6 (or sometimes Mars Sector 8) speaks through King, giving interplanetary news or warnings of impending troubles on earth. Then Aetherius, or one of the other Masters, speaks through him, delivering spiritual and moral teaching and messages of hope and encouragement.

The Aetherius Society does not publish membership figures, but it is believed to have several thousand full members around the world, mainly in Africa, Britain and the USA. George King now lives in Los Angeles.

BELIEFS AND PRACTICES

The beliefs of the Aetherius Society include aspects of Christianity and Buddhism, among others. Their religious services use both Christian prayers – including a new version of the Lord's Prayer – and Buddhist mantras. They believe in reincarnation based on the Law of Karma – or, in Paul's words, 'whatsoever a man soweth, that shall he also reap' (Galatians 6:7). We progress, life by life, towards perfection. 'Man came forth from God and all things are a part of God. There is nothing but God in the Cosmos, in varying stages of evolution. Everyone will eventually become a Master and will continue evolving from there.'[42] Masters can be male or female.

In common with many other Esoteric religious movements, including Theosophy, ECKANKAR, Benjamin Creme/Maitreya, the I AM movement, the Church Universal and Triumphant and others, they believe in a living spiritual hierarchy of Masters, the Great White Brotherhood. Jesus, Buddha, Krishna and the other great religious teachers were all Masters.

Specific to the Aetherius Society is the belief that each planet in our solar system is akin to a classroom, where we learn certain life-lessons before progressing to the next planet. 'A person may have to live on a Planet for thousands of lives before he has learned the required lessons and can pass the "examination" so that he can graduate to the next higher Planet – the length of time spent in "school" varying with each individual lifestream, depending on how much effort he puts into living by God's Laws.'

The solar system is ruled by a Cosmic Hierarchy, or Interplanetary Parliament. 'This is made up of very highly elevated Masters and is based on the Planet Saturn. This Hierarchy, in turn, is responsible to the Lords of the Sun for the evolution of every lifestream in the Solar System.'

Of the great Cosmic Masters who have come to earth, Jesus and Buddha came from Venus, and Krishna came from Saturn. 'They all taught the same principles or Laws of God. Therefore, man's great major religions sprang from the same source (Masters from other Planets) and the principles were identical.'

Some of these Cosmic Masters speak through Sir George King. In 1958, for example, the Master Jesus gave some new teachings entitled the Twelve Blessings, which he has urged mankind to accept as their Bible.

A few Masters live on Earth. Before long another great one will come, whose 'magic will be greater than any upon the Earth – greater than the combined materialistic might of all the armies. And they who heed not His words shall be removed from the Earth' – not to be destroyed, but to go to another planet to continue their evolutionary process elsewhere, says Lawrence. The coming Master will appear openly, in a flying saucer. There will also be a millennium of peace, but it seems that this depends largely on man's own efforts, rather than being imposed from above.

The Aetherius Society's belief in cooperation with people from other planets is quite sincere. 'We're not out to change existing religions so much as to add a cosmic dimension to them,' says Lawrence.

◆

The Aetherius Society is happy to call itself New Age. It teaches and practises spiritual healing, alternative medicine, yoga and dowsing, among others. Healing is 'the transfer of Prana, the Universal Life Force, from the Healer to the patient. This energy, which flows freely throughout space, when channelled into a person suffering from disease can bring about a state of balance within that person.'[43] Anyone can heal; it is not a special gift, but the birthright of every person on earth.

The basis of all the Society's teachings is 'service to others'. The most unusual aspect of this work is known as Operation Prayer Power. A group of members invoke spiritual energy by chanting mantras and prayers. This energy is focused and transferred to trained prayer team members, who then pour it into 'a specially designed radionic apparatus' known as a Spiritual Energy Battery. These batteries can store vast amounts of spiritual energy indefinitely; the energy can later be released, specifically to help in times of crisis, such as a war or earthquake.

The Great White Brotherhood is engaged in a battle with evil forces, and the Aetherius Society has a part to play in the fight. It regularly engages in 'Spiritual Pushes' in which, by praying and meditating, they are able to draw Prana down to earth from a huge spaceship, *Satellite Three*, in close orbit around the earth. The spaceship is shielded so that it doesn't show up through telescopes or radar.

In addition to charging Spiritual Energy Batteries, members of the Aetherius

Society took part in Operation Starlight, climbing 18 mountains around the world between 1958 and 1961 so that the Cosmic Masters could charge them with spiritual power. Members now make regular pilgrimages to the peaks of these mountains, where the movement's symbol is painted.

◆

Among the evils which the Aetherius Society campaigns against are pollution and nuclear power. They can justifiably claim to have been several years ahead of today's ecology movement.

The Society's literature quotes various prophecies made by the Cosmic Masters through George King which have since come true. In 1958, for example, their magazine *Cosmic Voice* gave details of an atomic accident in Russia which was not known about in the West until 1976. Reporting on this in 1978, the *New Scientist* apparently said it had 'been scooped by a UFO'. Also in the 1950s King was receiving messages warning of the long-term genetic effects of radiation.

However, such problems are symptoms rather than causes. 'The Aetherius Society believes that the only major crisis on Earth is the spiritual energy crisis. If that is solved, all other crises will also be solved,' says Lawrence.

THE RAELIAN MOVEMENT

HISTORY

On 13 December 1973, a 27-year-old French journalist, Claude Vorilhon (now known as Raël), was contacted by a being from another planet. Then, and in later meetings, he was given messages to pass on to mankind. On 7 October 1975 he was taken in their spacecraft to their planet.

Mankind is now sufficiently developed to understand that we were deliberately created by a race called the Elohim who are some 25,000 years more advanced than we are. In Genesis the word Elohim is translated as 'God', but in Hebrew it is actually a plural noun; according to Raël it means 'those who come from the sky'. (Raël means 'the messenger of those who come from the sky'.) Mankind was created, by manipulation of DNA, in the image of the Elohim.

> Leaving our humanity to progress by itself, the Elohim nevertheless
> maintained contact with us via prophets, including Buddha, Moses, Jesus and
> Mohammed, all specially chosen and educated by them in order to
> progressively educate humanity by delivering this message, adapted to the level
> of culture and understanding at the time. They were also to leave written
> references to the Elohim so that we would be able to recognize them as our
> creators and fellow human beings when we had advanced enough scientifically
> to understand them.[44]

We are now, apparently, at that point. The Elohim have appeared to Raël as the prophet for our age, have explained themselves in late-twentieth-century scientific terminology, and will shortly be returning physically to earth to greet all of us. However, knowing that earth has many different nations, and not wishing to be identified politically, morally or culturally with any particular one of them, they have instructed Raël to build an embassy in internationally recognized neutral territory, where they can meet representatives of governments. 'When they land, the only philosophy they wish to endorse is their own, so therefore they will only arrive at an embassy built by the movement they created.'

Because 'it is the mission of Israel to welcome the messenger (Messiah) of the Elohim,' says Giles Dexter, secretary of the British Raelians, 'the Elohim have requested that the embassy should be built on a piece of land given to the Raelian movement by the State of Israel'.[45] Failing that, it will be built in a neighbouring country – Jordan, Syria, Lebanon or Egypt.

A Frenchman was chosen for the Elohim's message because France is 'a country where new ideas are welcomed and where it is possible to talk about such ideas openly'. Raël himself was chosen because his father was Jewish and his mother Catholic: 'We considered you an ideal link between two very important peoples in the history of the world.' Also, the world entered 'the Age of Apocalypse' with the first nuclear bomb in 1945; Raël was born in 1946.

Since its formation in 1973, the Raelian Movement has spread into over 50 countries and now claims around 40,000 members. Its writings have been translated into over 20 languages so far. Raël himself now lives in Québec, Canada.

BELIEFS AND PRACTICES

The accounts of Raël's meetings with the Elohim, and their message for the world, are contained in his books *The Book That Tells the Truth* and *The Extra-Terrestrials Took Me to Their Planet* (now available in English in one volume, *The Message Given to Me by Extra-Terrestrials – They Took Me to Their Planet*); further books are *Let's Welcome Our Fathers from Space*, *Sensual Meditation* and *Geniocracy*.

Raelians say they are not ufologists. They find evidence on our own planet to confirm the messages given to Raël by the Elohim. They don't demand blind faith: 'The Elohim invite us to verify their work of creation referred to in our ancient texts, by our own scientific development, and by our opportunity to rationally understand the universe.'

Apart from spreading the message, and raising funds to build the embassy, Raelians aim:

> to build a society adapted to the future, not the past. This is done through courses of Sensual Meditation held all over the world, enabling individuals to regain control over their lives by questioning all their habits, beliefs and attitudes and implementing choice to retain only what is useful to their development. As each individual becomes more happy and fulfilled, so humanity as a whole becomes more happy and fulfilled and the society of the future begins to develop.

This philosophy applies to all areas of life, including education, love, sexuality, work, leisure and self-development.

In some ways this echoes the ideas of, for example, the Transcendental Meditation movement, which believes that a small number of people meditating together can affect the wider world.

Sensual meditation is a set of techniques to help us 'link with the infinity that we are a part of'. It enables people to:

> understand how our minds and bodies function; question the Judaeo-Christian inhibitions of guilt and the mysticism of Eastern traditions; develop our minds and discover our bodies; and reprogramme ourselves by ourselves into what we really wish to be. Sensual Meditation enables us to love ourselves better and to better love others, to discover our individuality and our common humanity.

Some of the meditation techniques are intended to be used with a partner of the opposite sex. 'No specifically sexual techniques are taught at the seminars,' says Dexter, 'though individuals are encouraged to experiment sexually if they wish, and to develop their sensuality.'

This is a key part of Raelian teaching. 'Sex is an important source of pleasure, which along with "choice" and "infinity" (correctly identified) is a very important element of Raelian philosophy. The messages state "Pleasure is the fertilizer which opens the mind. A life without pleasure is like an uncultivated garden."

The movement has a completely free attitude towards sexual relationships, which depend entirely on individual choice. They have monogamous heterosexual couples, others 'who prefer to have different partners', homosexuals, transexuals . . . 'In sexuality, as in all other things,' says Dexter, 'the promotion of choice is all-important; and furthermore, that sexually as in every other way (race, appearance, etc.), we more than tolerate, we love the differences . . . A varied community is essential for the equilibrium of the whole.'

The Raelian Movement holds major 'Courses of Awakening' in France, Canada, Japan, Korea and Australia, and smaller courses in Britain, the USA and other countries. The aim is 'to create a world of leisure, love and fulfilment where we have rid ourselves of the moralistic social inhibitions which paralyse our joy for life, so that everyone has the courage to act as they so wish, as long as this action does not harm others'. This last sentiment is the same as one of the main principles of Wicca: 'An it harm none, do as thou wilt shall be the whole of the law.'

The symbol of the Raelians, worn as a pendant by members, is a six-pointed Star of David made up of two triangles, the one pointing upwards representing the infinitely large, and the one pointing down representing the infinitely small. A swirling design inside the star represents infinity in time. The symbol can also be used as a focus for telepathic contact with the Elohim.

(The swirl has replaced the swastika, which was originally in the centre of the star. 'This was done out of respect for the victims of the Nazi holocaust and to facilitate the building of the embassy in Israel, despite the fact that the Elohim's symbol is the oldest on earth and that traces of it still remain in Israel today.'[46])

Infinity is an important concept in the Raelian movement. They believe that the subatomic particles of atoms are themselves galaxies, containing stars, planets and people, and that our own galaxy is a tiny particle of an atom of a living being on a planet revolving around a sun in a galaxy. This is a concept which has been covered in science fiction, but is not generally accepted in human science, though the Raelians say that the Elohim have proved it to be true.

As in many other religious movements, full members tithe a tenth of their income. In Britain a third of this goes to the British Raelian Movement, and the remainder to the international movement.

The geniocracy of Raël's fifth book is a proposed political system to be run by the most intelligent for the benefit of all. Some critics have alleged that it is implied, if not actually stated, that these will be of the white races, and that the Raelian Movement is therefore white supremacist. Dexter strongly denies this: 'The messages clearly state, "Do not suffer racist fools" . . . There are people from all the different races of the world in the Raelian Movement, whose aim is to break down barriers between peoples of different ethnic and cultural backgrounds, and create a family of humanity.'

The aims of the Raelian Movement are similar to those of many others; the difference is that their revelation came from extraterrestrials rather than from Ascended Masters or God.

SEVEN

NEO-PAGAN MOVEMENTS

The word 'Pagan' originally meant 'country-dweller'. The sophisticated, cosmopolitan, educated Romans applied the term to anyone (usually on the fringes of the Empire) who held to strange, primitive beliefs – the uneducated barbarians. Stripping off the pejorative overtones, 'Pagan' simply means someone who follows the old native religion of their land, rather than an imported religion. Usually, but not always, this includes worship either of the Earth Mother Goddess (but see pp. 211 and 212), with or without her consort, or of a pantheon of gods – or both. (Hinduism can technically be called a Pagan religion, and overlaps with Hindu ideas can sometimes be found in Western Paganism, but for the purposes of this book Hinduism and its offshoots are treated only as Eastern religions, and Paganism refers only to Western Paganism.)

'Heathen', similarly, meant 'people who live on the heath', again in distinction from sophisticated city-dwellers.

'Neo-Paganism', to quote Oberon Zell, founder of Church of All Worlds, who is said to have coined the term, is 'a revival and reconstruction of ancient Nature religions adapted for the modern world'.[1]

Probably the largest area of Neo-Paganism encountered in Britain and Europe is one form or another of Wicca, though there are also, among others, Druidism, Shamanism and Norse religion. In North America the revival of ancient cultural traditions, including those of Native Americans, was well under way before Wicca started to make inroads there in the 1970s. Also, as we will see later in this chapter, Wicca is largely the legacy of one British man in the 1950s, whereas North American Neo-Paganism, to quote Zell, 'emerged in the 1960s, and was strongly affected by the whole hippie consciousness – sex, drugs, rock 'n' roll, communes, hair, etc.'.

Because nearly everything that can be called Neo-Pagan is eclectic, borrowing from several sources, there are overlaps between the various forms of Neo-Paganism. There are links between some forms of Wicca and Druidism, and between both of these and Shamanism. Some followers (and self-acknowledged re-creators) of the Norse religion prefer the term Heathen, to distinguish them from the more Goddess-based Wicca-type Neo-Paganism.

There is a wide variety of books available on all aspects of Neo-Paganism and related subjects. On the Celtic, Arthurian and Western Mystery Traditions, prominent writers include Caitlín and John Matthews and R. J. Stewart, among many others; on Wicca, writers include Janet and Stuart Farrar and Marian Green; on the Northern (Norse/Germanic) Traditions, Kveldulfr Gundarsson/Stephan Grundy, Nigel Pennick and Freya Aswynn; on Druidry, Ross Nichols and Philip Carr-Gomm; and on Shamanism, Joan Halifax and Kenneth Meadows. This is by no means an exclusive list of authors, but includes some of those whom the present author has found useful, sound and readable.

◆

One of the most important facets of Neo-Paganism for the non-Pagan to understand is its diversity.

'The trouble with general Paganism and Wicca, from the point of view of an encyclopedia, is that they are non-hierarchical and do not have organizations that are religion-based beyond their own small groups; it is therefore advisable to talk to as many people as possible . . . Beware of those who claim to speak for all witches!' says Elen J. Williams, secretary of the Pagan Federation.[2]

Oberon Zell says much the same: 'We have met dogmatic and non-dogmatic Christians from the same church. The same goes for Pagans. Some may be dogmatic about the form of their practice, while others are not. Some people believe that magic is stronger when actions are repeated the same way each time. Others make their rituals completely new each time. The general structure of Neo-Paganism, however, is so varied as to be impossible to dictate to any large number of people. As the saying goes, ask two Pagans a question and get three different answers.

'We generally believe the world is to be discovered, not dictated. We are not arrogant enough to think we have all the answers, and believe flexibility is essential in reflecting an organic, Nature-based religion. Dogmatism stagnates. Only flexibility allows evolution to occur.'

This seems to be a fairly general view in the Neo-Pagan world – though, as he says, not everyone will agree . . .

◆

In the following pages I shall look at a small handful of the many hundreds of different Neo-Pagan and Heathen groups. This doesn't claim to be a representative sample, because that probably wouldn't be possible even if several dozen different groups were covered. But those which have been included here should give some idea of both the diversity and the commonality of Neo-Paganism today.

It should be stressed that the individuals quoted – Oberon Zell, Shan, Philip Shallcrass, Freya Aswynn and others – are speaking for themselves and their own movements, and not on behalf of Neo-Paganism as a whole. Even those who offer introductory courses to the whole movement are speaking from their own perspective.

WICCA

Wicca is simply another name for witchcraft, often used to avoid many of the negative connotations of the latter word. Wicca is usually traced back to a Saxon root meaning 'to bend', sometimes to a word meaning 'wit', as in knowledge or understanding, and sometimes, though with less justification, to a word for 'wise', as in 'wisewoman' (it should be remembered that in France, a midwife is still known as a *sage-femme*). Some, instead of witchcraft or Wicca, prefer to call it 'the Craft'.

The term 'witchcraft' covers a wide range of things. A news story in 1995 reported that over 100 women had recently been burnt to death – often with a petrol-soaked tyre around their necks – in the Transvaal in South Africa; they had been accused by neighbours of being witches. It has been suggested that in the famous Old Testament injunction, 'Thou shalt not suffer a witch to live' (Exodus 22:18), the word 'witch' might be better translated 'one who poisons wells', which would make some sense for nomadic peoples living in a desert.

Today's witches rarely match the popular image of the toothless old hag living in her hovel. They live in the country and the town, in all Western countries. They are likely to be well educated, and many of them are professional people. Old and young, they are as likely to be men as women. Male witches are called witches; terms such as 'warlock' and 'wizard' belong only in fantasy novels.

One point must be made clearly here, once again. Witchcraft has nothing to do with Satanism; witches do not worship Satan. Again and again during the research for this book, witches (and other Neo-Pagans) said that this is still the most common misunderstanding they have to cope with. Medieval witchcraft, with all its demonic trappings, rather than being any sort of reality, was very largely the creation of the two Dominicans who around 1486 wrote the *Malleus Maleficarum* ('The Witch Hammer'). The book, which becomes the textbook of the Inquisition, is full of accounts of how succubi and incubi pass semen between men and women. It also puts the burden of witchcraft largely on women: 'They are more credulous . . . naturally more impressionable . . . they have slippery tongues . . . they are weak . . . since they are feebler both in mind and body, it is not surprising that they should come more under the spell of witchcraft . . .'[3] Modern witches would tend to disagree.

The book's authors, both men, both highly educated Dominicans, displayed a fear of women which was fairly common at that time, especially among educated religious men. Women, it was believed, had the power to emasculate men, not just metaphorically but physically; the book contains numerous accounts of men claiming a witch had stolen their penis. Here is an early account of multiple Bobbittism:

And what, then, is to be thought of those witches who in this way sometimes collect male organs in great numbers, as many as twenty or thirty members together, and put them in a bird's nest, or shut them up in a box, where they move themselves like living members, and eat oats and corn, as has been seen by many and is a matter of common report? It is to be said that it is all done by devil's work and illusion, for the senses of those who see them are deluded in the way we have said. For a certain man tells us that, when he had lost his member, he approached a known witch to ask her to restore it to him. She told the afflicted man to climb a certain tree, and that he might take which he liked out of a nest in which there were several members. And when he tried to take a big one, the witch said: You must not take that one; adding, because it belonged to a parish priest.[4]

The serious reason for including this marvellous passage is that many men today believe that they are being emasculated not only by feminism, with its creation of the New Man, but also by Wicca, with its emphasis on the Goddess. There are all-women areas of Wicca, but most Wicca, and most of the wider world of Neo-Paganism, is now taking great care to let men realize that the religion is for them as well. Outsiders may notice only the Goddess, because of the difference from the male Judaeo-Christian God, but a lot of Neo-Pagans worship both Goddess and God.

To quote Shan, Clan Mother or Priestess of the House of the Goddess, 'So what does this mean for men? It means a third way, neither bully nor wimp, but powerful, wild, loving, sexual and supportive with room for doubt and uncertainty. This is very much the cutting edge of the Craft today.'[5]

To return to the medieval persecution of witches, there is an interesting argument that the Inquisition could not have had so much 'success' in identifying witches if ordinary people had not been willing to turn in their neighbours; and that the reason for grass-roots public opinion turning against the formerly respected wise-women or herbalists could perhaps be to do with the Black Death, which swept Europe between 1347 and 1350, killing as many as a third of the population. If people asked their local herbalist for a potion against the Black Death and were given, for example, an infusion of willow-bark (the forerunner of aspirin), it would have had little effect against the plague. If you ask for help and your loved ones die, you are apt to lose faith in – or even to blame – the person whose help you sought.

THE RECENT BEGINNINGS

To some extent modern witchcraft is the creation of a retired British civil servant, Gerald Gardner. Before him, however, and providing at the time the powerful backing of academic study, came the anthropologist Dr Margaret Murray. Murray argued persuasively in *The Witch-Cult in Western Europe* (1921) and *The God of the Witches* (1931) that the medieval witches didn't worship the Devil, but were followers of an old, pre-Christian Pagan religion 'which appears to be the ancient religion of Western Europe'.[6] Murray called this worship Dianic, after the goddess Diana.

Murray has been criticized on many academic grounds. Richard Cavendish, the eminent historian of the Esoteric, states, 'This brilliant and ingenious theory is unfortunately full of holes and has been demolished time and again.'[7] This didn't stop the Oxford University Press splashing on the US paperback of *The God of the Witches*, 'The findings she sets forth, once thought of as provocative and implausible, are now regarded as irrefutable by folk-lorists and scholars in all related fields.'

Other scholars now point out that there is actually no evidence whatsoever for a religion of *one Goddess*; early Pagan religions were pantheist rather than female monotheist. Murray, they say, came up with her theory, then selected evidence to support it.

Whatever the factual truth, Murray's thesis – with the added weight of Robert Graves's *The White Goddess* (1946), a study of the Moon Goddess in many different cultures, which perhaps contained more poetic than historical truth – has become accepted wisdom for many of today's Neo-Pagans, making it possible for them to say they are re-creating the old religion, not creating something which is solely 'New Age'.

Present-day Dianic Wicca stems very much from Murray's thesis. It is a religion of the Goddess, and very much a religion for women. It has been argued that Dianic Wicca, and similar religions, are historically more a spiritual expression of the feminist movement than anything else.

Other Neo-Pagans say the validity or otherwise of Murray's ideas doesn't actually matter to them, readily accepting that their religion is a modern synthesis from many roots.

♦

Other books significant in the development of modern Wicca were Charles Leland's *Aradia, or the Gospel of the Witches* (1899), based on the teachings of an Italian hereditary witch called Maddalena – which very likely sparked off Murray's own research; Robert Graves's *The White Goddess*, and to a much lesser extent the fictional and non-fictional works of writers like Dion Fortune, Montague Summers, Charles Williams and Denis Wheatley, which were actually more to do with the occult than with Paganism, but which at least kept Esoteric religion in the public eye.

Gerald Gardner (1884–1964) had a lifelong interest in folklore, magic and the Esoteric. He belonged to a Rosicrucian group, and was an initiate of Aleister Crowley's Ordo Templi Orientis. When he discovered a coven of witches in the south of England in 1939 he was delighted and joined them. In 1951 Britain repealed its witchcraft laws and in 1954 Gardner published *Witchcraft Today*.

Most British, European and American witches owe a considerable debt to Gardner. His re-creation of witchcraft was a blend of folklore, Masonic rituals and Crowley-type magic, and had quite a major sexual element; Gardner was into both naturism and flagellation. His handwritten *Book of Shadows*, containing ritual and ceremony borrowed from a number of sources, has formed the basis for much of what came after him – though some of the more overtly sexual parts have been quietly dropped by many of his successors.

After Gardner came Alex Sanders (1926–88) and his wife, Maxine, who popularized witchcraft in the 1960s. They had a flamboyant style, which may or may not have been good for the 'new' religion but certainly caught the headlines. Alexandrian witchcraft is a much freer and more open version than Gardnerian. Maxine Sanders, who separated from her husband in 1973, is now a widely respected leader of Wicca.

Today's Wicca, as Stewart Farrar (who was initiated by the Sanders in 1970) points out,[8] has roots in both the old Pagan religions and the nineteenth- and early-twentieth-century occult revival. Many groups, some calling themselves covens, others not, have developed their own rituals and their own sets of beliefs over the last few years, based in part on earlier traditions.

'There were really many "old religions" such as various Celtic cults, Nordic ones, Isis, Mithras, and so on,' says Shan from House of the Goddess.

The 'Old Religion' is actually a bit inaccurate, but a very affectionate name for the Craft. We often argue among ourselves about how much of the Craft nowadays is a modern invention, how much ancient tradition. Some of us say almost all of it is modern – but fine, it works. Some think it's a mix. Some say most of it has been handed down to us.[9]

A lot of Neo-Pagans share Shan's free approach. Others insist on the importance of the ancient origins of their beliefs, while a few, the comparatively rare 'hereditary witches', believe that their own family tradition and bloodline are vital.

Most agree that Neo-Paganism's strength lies in its diversity. For example, Chris Bray of Sorceror's Apprentice hates the term Wicca, but says, 'Of course Neo-

Pagans can have Paganism any way they wish within reason; what I will not allow them to do is monopolize it with another exclusive priesthood.' And though there is sometimes rivalry, mutual criticism and acknowledged bitchiness between different traditions and groups of Pagans, Wiccans or witches, there is probably far more commonality between them, and mutual support in the face of opposition, than there is between the many variations and offshoots of Christianity.

◆

Many Wiccan groups hold to 'The Charge of the Goddess', which is, as Shan says, 'the nearest thing the Craft accept as a statement of faith common to all'. The Charge was written by Gardner and Doreen Valiente, with some sections taken from Leland's *Aradia*, and so perhaps going back hundreds of years. There are many different versions of the 'Charge' today. Here I present enough extracts to demonstrate its style and content, the roots of Goddess worship under many different names and the life-affirming nature of Wiccan belief.

THE CHARGE OF THE GODDESS

> *Listen to the words of the Great Mother, who of old was called Artemis, Astarte, Athene, Dione, Melusine, Aphrodite, Cerridwen, Diana, Arianrhod, Isis, Brighde and by many other names . . .*
>
> *Whenever ye have need of anything, once in the month, and better it be when the moon is full, then shall ye assemble in some secret place and adore the spirit of me who am Queen of all Witches . . .*
>
> *And ye shall be free from slavery; and as a sign that ye be really free, ye shall be naked in your rites; and ye shall dance, sing, feast, make music and love all in my praise. For mine is the ecstasy of the spirit, and mine also is joy on earth, for my law is love unto all beings.*
>
> *Keep pure your highest ideal; strive ever towards it, let naught stop you or turn you aside; for mine is the secret door which opens upon the door of youth, and mine is the cup of the wine of life, and the cauldron of Cerridwen, which is the holy Grail of immortality.*
>
> *I am the gracious Goddess, who gives the gift of joy unto the heart of man . . .*
>
> *Nor do I demand sacrifice; for behold, I am the Mother of all living and my love is poured out upon the earth . . .*
>
> *I am the beauty of the green earth, and the white moon among the stars, and the mystery of the waters, and the desire of the heart of man.*
>
> *Call into thy soul; arise, and come unto me; for I am the soul of nature who gives life to the universe . . .*
>
> *Let my worship be within the heart that rejoices; behold, all acts of love and pleasure are my rituals. And therefore let there be beauty and strength, power and compassion, honour and humility, mirth and reverence within thee . . .*
>
> *If that which thou seekest thou findest not within thee, thou wilt never find it without thee. For behold, I have been with thee from the beginning; and I am that which is attained at the end of desire.*
>
> *Blessed be.*

HOUSE OF THE GODDESS

House of the Goddess is 'a modern Pagan clan and temple, founded 1984/1985 by Shan, its Clan Mother. The original inspiration was Dianic (Kindling Coven) and the temple was built and consecrated by women. A year later, the Goddess required the temple to serve both women and men.'[10]

The temple is 'a big, comfortable wooden hut' in the garden of a suburban terraced house in south London. Shan works as a healer and counsellor, in addition to being Clan Mother, which involves her, among other things, in conducting Neo-Pagan weddings, divorces, baby-welcomings and funerals. She specializes in Circlework, which is her own introduction to Neo-Paganism for groups of six to ten newcomers who want to learn something about it, but who might not want to commit themselves yet to a more formal group.

> While the value of common sense, and spirituality or magic in everyday life is a Circlework basic, the more profound reaches of philosophy and mystery are given their due honour. The great cycles of history, the purposes of the Goddess for women and men, safe and rightful use of power, the nature of magic itself, and initiation, usually arise as discussion topics quite naturally. Types of Paganism, the eight festivals, eco-magic, and any other topic can be included if a particular person asks.
>
> Each Circlework is strikingly different, because I build it around who's there. The first steps are fairly structured and predictable to provide a safe, solid start. After that it depends on what you want. I teach through a lot of chat, cups of tea and coffee, discussion as a sharing, pieces of trying things out, and sometimes a suggested exercise from my inner toybox. You are always free to hold back or plunge in as it suits you.

The Circlework course takes six evenings, or a weekend and a half, and is moderately priced. The idea is that the Circlework 'graduate' can then approach any other Neo-Pagan tradition, if they wish, with a solid introductory background; or they can build on what they have learned to work out their own independent path; or if they like the House of the Goddess and want to go further, they can take more structured training lasting at least a year, before formal initiation. Or, as Shan says, 'you can decide that your interest in Paganism is satisfied, and move on to other things'.

CHURCH OF ALL WORLDS

A number of new religions – Scientology, the Aetherius Movement, the Raelians, even the Mormons – have what outsiders might see as science fictional elements to their mythology. The Church of All Worlds (CAW) is perhaps the only religion for which a science fiction novel is a prescribed text. It was founded in 1962 by Oberon (Otter) Zell – then plain Tim Zell – and three college friends. Although a form of Neo-Paganism, it bases much of its teachings and ritual on Robert A. Heinlein's classic *Stranger in a Strange Land*. 'Thou art God,' its members say to each other. A question in the *CAW Membership Handbook*, 'Does CAW accept the divinity of Jesus?' is answered, 'Certainly. Why should he be left out? We accept the Divinity of every living Being in the universe!'

CAW has no particular dogma or creed: 'We are essentially "Neo-Pagan", implying an eclectic reconstruction of ancient Nature religions, and combining archetypes of many cultures with other mystic, environmental and spiritual disciplines . . . Some of our individual paths include Shamanism, Witchcraft, Vodoun, Buddhism, Hinduism and Sufism, as well as science fiction, transpersonal psychology, bodywork, artistic expression and paths of service.'[11]

As with many Neo-Pagan groups, CAW's beliefs are spiritual, environmental, social and personal. 'We concentrate on healing the separations between mind and body, men and women, civilization and nature, Heaven and Earth. We are fairly all-embracing in promoting general Pagan and Gaian lifestyles and values. We advocate basic feminist and environmentalist principles, including freedom of reproductive choice, ordination of women as priestesses, sacred sexuality, alternate relationships, gay and lesbian rights, legalization and utilization of hemp products, protection and restoration of endangered species, wilderness sanctuaries, green politics, space exploration and colonization, etc. We are also engaged in restoring ancient Mysteries and rituals, such as the Eleusinia and Panathenaia.'[12]

The Church has a path of progression from Seeker, an ordinary member, to Scion, those who help run subsidiary branches, to Clergy, ordained priests and priestesses. It generally takes a few years of training and personal spiritual development before anyone is ordained.

CAW has developed slowly and gradually, with a number of ups and downs over the years. Compared to many religious organizations, it is refreshingly honest about its failings. 'We try to learn from our mistakes and not make them again,' says Zell. 'Most of our most glaring mistakes have been due to either ignorance or arrogance. Mistakes of ignorance can be cured with additional knowledge. Mistakes of arrogance have been far more painful, and humbling. We have had to eat considerable crow as we have evolved over the years. We will probably continue to make mistakes, for we are fallible creatures (a pack of monkeys, actually!) and sometimes our mouths overload our brains. Hopefully we will also continue to get better, but I seriously doubt we will ever attain infallibility!'

Membership is currently around 650, 'and growing rapidly,' says Zell. There are over three dozen 'nests' or branches scattered across the USA and Australia. CAW incorporated in 1968, 'becoming the first of the Neo-Pagan Earth religions to obtain full Federal recognition,' he says. It was also the first legally recognized Neo-Pagan religion in Australia. It has 'proto-nests' in Germany, Switzerland and Austria, but nothing as yet in the UK.

Some of the terminology and symbolism is borrowed from Heinlein – nests, grokking, water-sharing – or other science fiction writers (Zenna Henderson's 'The People' stories are another favourite), and there is a relaxed attitude to sexuality and social nudity, but CAW appears to be somewhat more than a bunch of spiritually minded hippies living in a commune.

The mission of CAW is 'to evolve a network of information, mythology and experience that provides a context and stimulus for reawakening Gaia and reuniting her children through tribal community dedicated to responsible stewardship and the evolution of consciousness.'

Linked organizations are heavily involved in ecology, particularly forestry, scholarly research into history and mythology – and the development of a 'living unicorn', from a goat rather than a horse.

From the start CAW has aimed for communal living, even if a community is only a handful of people. Living in a community, there is more opportunity to put their beliefs into practice.

> Since we are concerned with the emergent evolution of a total new culture and lifestyle, and since we perceive no distinction between the sacred and the secular, we consider every activity to be essentially a religious activity. For us, recycling is as much a religious duty as prayer and meditation . . . We recognize that the essence of a religion is in the living of it.[13]

But specifically religious or spiritual activities are an important part of their lives. 'The religious aspects include maintaining household altars and shrines (in a Pagan household, every horizontal flat space becomes an altar, just as every wall becomes a bookcase!), meditations, conversations with the Gods, to rituals and celebrations, especially those of the great Sabbats of the Wheel of the Year. These latter often include great theatrical productions, with sets, costumes, props and music, wherein people take on the personas of Gods, Elementals, and other Archetypal beings.'

For non-Neo-Pagans, the belief in and practice of magic is one of the more worrying aspects of Neo-Paganism. For Fundamentalists, it brands Neo-Pagans as evil. What Zell says about magic is fairly typical of many Neo-Pagan groups: 'The practice of magic is a major component of virtually all Pagan traditions, including CAW. We define magic as "probability enhancement". I don't think it is possible to separate out the magical from the religious, as it all seems a continuum. Magical practices run the gamut from simple "Kitchen Witch" spells and charms – mostly concerned with individual healings, blessings, transformations, and other small workings, through "Circle Work", involving raising group energy for healings, community service, weather working, etc., to larger group workings to save the planet – protecting endangered forests, people and species, etc.'

One point which separates them from many Neo-Pagan groups, particularly in the UK, and which most Christians (except the Family) would condemn as sinful, is their free approach to sexuality. If any two people – or three, or four – want to make love, that's entirely up to them. But the Church is very aware of the possibilities of abuse and of misinterpretation. 'It is *absolutely unacceptable* to attempt to pressure, cajole or coerce another into any sexual activity that they do not wish freely and wholeheartedly to participate in . . . A loving touch, hug or a massage is not an invitation to coitus, so if your attempts at intimacy or caring make someone uncomfortable, *stop!*'[14] Any form of 'sexually charged interaction', let alone lovemaking, with youngsters under the age of consent is forbidden.

CAW is by no means a typical Neo-Pagan group, but most of its principles, and its eclectic approach to building up a belief system, are broadly the same as those of many other Neo-Pagans, and it appears to be well respected within Neo-Paganism at large.

ASSOCIATION OF
CYMMRY WICCA

Another of the well-organized American groups, the Association of Cymmry Wicca, is a wider movement based on the Church of Y Tylwyth Teg, founded by Rhuddlwm ap Gawr in Georgia, USA. This traces its origins back through the Llewellyn family to a Druid-based Welsh Wicca centuries old. 'Our records show that in AD 1271 Prince Llewellyn . . . commanded those trusted scribes and clerks who owed allegiance to him, to begin the task of compiling what was left of the known family mystical knowledge into ordered volumes. It is said that his Druid Bard was the first to collect *The Thirteen Treasures*,' says Gawr.[15]

The family absorbed the teachings of other Pagan groups, and of the Knights Templar, over the centuries. 'For over 700 years, the Llewellyn family kept the ancient knowledge as a secret tradition. But in 1965, the family, seeing a gradual drop in numbers of those of its members who were still keeping the ancient traditions, began inducting members from the outside world.' Gawr was inducted, and in the following two years set up the American branch of Y Tylwyth Teg in Maryland and Washington, DC, and the Association of Cymmry Wicca.

'When Rhuddlwm first met Sarah Llewellyn in 1965, there were less than a hundred practitioners of *The Welsh Tradition of Dynion Mwyn* in England, Wales, Scotland, Canada and America. Today, there are literally thousands.' Gawr gives current membership figures for the Association of Cymmry Wicca (1995) as 9,764 in the USA, 3,237 in the UK and a total of 15,433 throughout the world; ten years ago the comparable figures were 2,914, 910 and 4,147 worldwide, and 20 years ago 316 in the USA, 46 in the UK and a world total of 392. The growth in 20 years has been impressive. To keep track of this many people, most of whom will be in small groups, requires some organization.

One of the problems faced by all Neo-Pagan groups is finding the right balance between relaxed spontaneity (which can quickly become disorder, if not chaos) and practical organization (which can just as easily become dogmatic and prescriptive). Over the decades, many groups have disintegrated because they have refused to become institutionalized. But especially in the USA, if Neo-Pagans want the legal freedoms and tax advantages of being a religion, they have to become incorporated, which involves statements of belief and practice, structure and hierarchy, rules and regulations, constitutions and by-laws. The religion becomes a Church, and has to take on many of the attributes of organized religion which are alien to many Neo-Pagans.

Rhuddlwm Gawr appears to be a natural organizer. Although *The Sword of Dyrnwyn*, the newletter of Y Tylwyth Teg, is as chatty and friendly as most science fiction fanzines, to which it bears a marked resemblance, the Church itself appears to be very structured. Its main community, Camelot-of-the-Wood, situated secretly somewhere in the North Georgia mountains, has set up the Bangor Institute, a spiritual training college. This in turn is composed of a School of Natural Therapeutics, a School of Human Behaviour, a School of Spiritual Consciousness, a School of Natural Healing and a Research Center. Camelot has a Council of Elders, elected Planners and appointed Managers.

After a provisional year, a new member 'signs a contract with the community agreeing to accept the community by-laws and behaviour code . . . Clothing and personal effects remain the property of the member unless they are shared. Resources may be held outside the community for a period not to exceed one year, but one cannot benefit from their use while a member.'

These may be thoroughly sensible rules for the running of a close-knit community, but some Neo-Pagans might be a little uneasy about the amount of organization.

DRUIDRY

There are currently around two dozen different Druid organizations in the UK, according to Philip Shallcrass, Chief Druid of the British Druid Order. As with Wicca and other areas of Neo-Paganism, they have very different approaches to their beliefs and practices, but 15 of the different groups have come together since 1989 in the Council of British Druid Orders. This entry gives a brief overview of the recent history of Druidry, some of the Orders and some of the major beliefs.

The traditional derivation of the word 'Druid' is from the Greek *drus*, the Irish *daur* and the Welsh *derw*, each meaning 'oak', and the Indo-European word *wid*, which is to do with knowing (cf. wit, wise and wisdom, from the same root, and the Sanskrit *veda*). A Druid was one who knew or understood the oak, or perhaps the wise man of the oak – the oak standing for all trees. Interestingly, in both Irish and Welsh the words for 'tree' and 'knowledge' are etymologically connected. It was not that the Druids worshipped the oak, or any other tree, but they had a close relationship with nature, their worship took place in groves and they seem to have seen trees as symbolic of wisdom and solidity. 'Although the oak seems to have been favoured by the Druids of Gaul, those of Ireland certainly seem to have preferred the yew or ash as their primary sacred trees,' says Shallcrass.[16] However, most modern Druids, he says, do regard the oak as especially sacred.

Shallcrass also points out that many scholars have now discarded the 'oak' derivation 'in favour of derivations from either an early Celtic intensive prefix *dru*, which would give the meaning of druid as "very wise one", or from an Indo-European root, *dreo*, meaning "true", which would give the meaning "true [or truth] knower".'

The main problem with re-creating the old religion of the Druids is that little or nothing was written down by the original Druids – or if it was, it is long lost. Nearly all that we know about the Druids is from other writers of their time, such as Julius Caesar, Cicero, Pliny and Tacitus, whose reports are likely to be antagonistic, and might well be inaccurate.

Present-day Druids have had to re-create the religion from what is known or surmised about the religious and philosophical beliefs of the Celts. Love and respect for nature were and are clearly central. So is the emphasis on oration and song; many of the original Druids were respected as tale-tellers and bards.

It was this latter aspect which was largely at the heart of the Druid revival of the eighteenth and nineteenth centuries. Bardic schools existed in the Celtic fringes of the British Isles up to the seventeenth century, and Pagan 'folk' custom (including, for example, well-dressing, May Day, Hallowe'en and decorating houses with greenery at midwinter) have continued in one way or another right up to the present day. Some of the earlier Druid revivals were therefore more cultural and artistic – and more Romantic – than spiritual. The Welsh Eisteddfod, for example, originally a serious bardic assembly, became essentially a music festival with ritual robes.

The revival of Druidry can be traced to several people in the seventeenth and eighteenth centuries. The antiquarian John Aubrey first associated Stonehenge and Avebury with the Druids in the 1690s. Influenced by Aubrey, William Stukeley also studied Stonehenge seriously. John Toland's *History of the Druids* was published in 1726. Later in the eighteenth century a Welsh stonemason, Edward Williams, took the name Iolo Morganwg, and researched and wrote much about Welsh bardic tradition. The historian Stuart Piggott is derisory about Iolo Morganwg 'furthering his nonsense'[17], and even Philip Shallcrass describes him as a 'scholar, forger and genius.'[18] He not only originated many 'early' Welsh documents but also created the 'ancient' Gorsedd, or bardic religious ceremony at Primrose Hill, London, in 1792 and at the Eisteddfod in 1819.

Although most of Iolo Morganwg's work can justifiably be called fraudulent, it was largely responsible for inspiring nineteenth- and twentieth-century interest – and somewhat more scholarly inquiry – into the Celts, and specifically the Druids. In addition, his work should not be dismissed out of hand simply because much of it stemmed from his own imagination. In all areas of Neo-Paganism, the creative use of the imagination is an important part of symbolism, ritual and magic. No one would argue that the entire Arthurian mythos should be thrown away on the grounds that the majority of it is fictional rather than factual. It is not the factual basis of mythology which is important; rather, it is the truths contained, often symbolically, within the myths. The same argument could be applied to Iolo Morganwg's work.

◆

Present-day Druidry includes the Ancient Druid Order, said to have been founded in 1717, which holds regular ceremonies at Stonehenge, Primrose Hill and Tower Hill. The Ancient Order of Druids, founded in 1781, also holds some ceremonies, but is largely (like the Freemasons, the Rotarians and so on) a fund-raising organization for those in need. The United Ancient Order of Druids developed out of it in 1833.

Most of the other orders are far more recent. One of the most respected, the Order of Bards, Ovates and Druids (OBOD), an offshoot of the Ancient Druid Order, was founded in 1964 by Ross Nichols (1902–75), whose *Book of Druidry* (HarperCollins/Aquarian Press, 1990) is an imaginative but very spiritual exploration of Druid beliefs. It has a fairly eclectic membership, which includes both Neo-Pagans and Christians. The British Druid Order was founded in 1979 as a specifically Neo-Pagan-oriented Druid group, whose teachings are based on the *Mabinogion* and other early British/Celtic texts. The Secular Order of Druids, founded in 1986, is heavily oriented towards environmentalism, and to supporting the civil rights of Druids to meet at places like Stonehenge in the face of police opposition.

Some groups, such as the Breton Druids and the Cornish Druids, are more cultural in their emphasis. Others, like the College of Druidism, based in Edinburgh, are more shamanistic, while others, like the Insular Order of Druids, based in Portsmouth, are in many ways closer to Wicca. The Druid Clan of Dana, based at Clonegal Castle in Eire and in London, is a well-organized and rapidly expanding Neo-Pagan Druid movement, and part of the Fellowship of Isis (see p. 231); it publishes the magazine *Aisling*. The Loyal Arthurian Warband, led by the colourful self-styled King Arthur Pendragon, campaigns for environmental and animal rights, and against new road building, nuclear and chemical weapons, and the Criminal Justice Act.

The Gorsedd of Bards of Caer Abiri, founded in 1993, holds open celebrations of the eight Druid festivals within the stone circles of Avebury in Wiltshire. 'The Gorsedd well represents the current ecumenical trend in Druidry in that it brings together members of several different Druid orders as well as followers of other Pagan and non-Pagan faiths. Its rituals combine modern Druidic practice with the Iolo Morganwg tradition and elements from the other faiths represented among its membership,' says Shallcrass.

Druidry is just as widespread, and just as diverse, in the USA. To take one example of many, the Henge of Keltria is a Neo-Pagan Druid movement based in Minneapolis. Its major beliefs are worth quoting, as a general summary of what many of the more modern Druid orders believe:

We believe in Divinity as it is manifest in the Pantheon. There are several valid theistic perceptions of this Pantheon.
We believe that nature is the embodiment of the Gods.
We believe that all life is sacred, and should neither be harmed nor taken without deliberation or regard.
We believe in the immortality of the spirit.
We believe that our purpose is to gain wisdom through experience.
We believe that learning is an ongoing process and should be fostered at all ages.
We believe that morality should be a matter of personal conviction based upon self-respect and respect for others.
We believe that every individual has the right to pursue enlightenment through his or her chosen path.
We believe in a living religion able to adapt to a changing environment.
We recognize that our beliefs may undergo change as our tradition grows.[19]

The eight festivals celebrated by modern Druids are the same as those of modern Wicca: Samhaim (Hallowe'en), the winter solstice, Imbolg (Candlemas), the spring equinox, Beltaine (May Day), the summer solstice, Lughnasad (Lammas) and the autumn equinox.

Most of the Druid orders are deeply concerned with the environment. OBOD, which offers a correspondence course in Druidry, is probably speaking for most orders when it says:

More than ever, we need a spirituality that is rooted in a love of nature, a love of the land. Druidry and the teaching programme of OBOD is based upon this love for the natural world, and offers a powerful way of working with and understanding the Self and Nature – speaking to that level of our soul and of our being which is in tune with the elements and the stars, the sun and the stones. Through the work of the Druids we are able to unite our natural, earthly selves with our spiritual selves while working, in however small a way, for the safeguarding of our planet.[20]

Many of the Druid orders contain three grades or groupings of members. These focus on different talents and interests, and although they are not necessarily progressive levels, as in the Esoteric Mystery Schools (see, for example, p. 188), those at the third level would normally have passed through the first two. In OBOD, for example, Bards are the keepers of tradition, those who remember and relate the stories, poems and myths; the Ovates are trained in prophecy and divination, and are the seers and shamans of the movement; and the Druids are the teachers, counsellors and judges – philosophers rather than priests, they will tend to be the older, more experienced members of the order.[21]

The British Druid Order also has three roughly equivalent grades: Bard (Poet/Seer), Ofydd (Philosopher) and Derwydd (Druid).

> The essence of the Order's teachings lies in working with the spiritual energy known to the British tradition as Awen. The feminine noun Awen literally means 'flowing spirit' or 'fluid essence'. The Bards of medieval Wales saw it as their primary source of inspiration, and as a gift of the ancient pagan Goddess Ceridwen, 'the Bent White One', who they referred to as Patroness of the Bardic Order.
>
> In the Bardic grade this 'flowing spirit' is directed into creativity on many levels, particularly in the traditional areas of poetry, music and storytelling, but also in all other arts and sciences.
>
> In the Ofydd grade, Awen is used to create windows, or gateways, into unseen worlds, leading to the development of the gift of seership, and knowledge of the Faery realm, the Otherworld, and its inhabitants.
>
> In the Derwydd grade, Awen is related to Earth energies, or Dragon Lines, which run through the landscape, accumulating at sacred sites. The task of the Druid is to learn to work with this energy for the benefit of the land and its inhabitants, human and animal, physical and non-physical.
>
> In all this work, we call upon the aid of the Ancestors, who are both our physical forebears who have passed on, and our spiritual Ancestors, the Druids of all past ages, and also the Gods themselves. Much of our strength and wisdom comes from them, and they give it freely and joyously, because we are part of the same golden chain of age-old tradition.[22]

Present-day Druidry, in all its varieties, is clearly part of the Neo-Pagan revival, but is usually quite distinct from the more Wiccan varieties of Neo-Paganism, though the two traditions generally seem to have respect for each other. According to Shallcrass, Ross Nichols, the founder of OBOD, was a friend of Gerald Gardner, who effectively founded modern Wicca; Gardner, who was a great eclecticist, joined OBOD shortly before his death in 1964.

THE NORTHERN TRADITION

Part of the Neo-Pagan revival of recent years has been a renewed interest in the gods and goddesses of native traditions. These include not only the Celtic and Native American, but also the old Norse and Germanic religions – the Northern Tradition. For many people this goes little further than using runes instead of (or as well as) Tarot cards, for divination, meditation and magic; but for some, the religion itself is being revived and reinterpreted for a modern world.

Heathenism, or the Northern Tradition as it is alternatively known, is perhaps the most diverse of all faiths under the pagan umbrella. It has a structure unlike any other pagan religion but at the same time, a sort of nomadic looseness at worshipper level. Heathens may invoke many gods and goddesses, and yet some may worship only one, such as the shamanic wind god Odin. Heathenism is one religion or many related religions according to your point of view.[23]

As with Neo-Paganism, there are several different movements in the Northern Tradition. These include the generic term Odinism, Asatru, the Elder Troth or Ring of Troth, the Odinic Rite and Odinshof, each of which has its own emphasis. All follow the Northern European traditions of the Norse, Germanic and Anglo-Saxon peoples, practised from around 2,000 years ago, and supplanted by Christianity from around 1,000 years ago.

Elder Troth, or the Ring of Troth, is 'a religious organization dedicated to the promotion and practice of the native heathen folk-religion of Northern Europe,' says Freya Aswynn, Drightinne in the Rune Gild and an Elder in the Ring of Troth. 'The religious organizations I represent are relatively young and modern; however, the religion itself is old, not new age as some other forms of contemporary Paganism. We therefore distinguish ourselves by naming ourselves Heathen rather than Pagan.' 'Heathen' originally meant 'the beliefs of the people of the heath', as 'Pagan' originally meant 'the beliefs of the country people'.

Aswynn stresses the immediacy of religion to her Norse ancestors. 'For them there was no separation between sacred and profane, spiritual and secular. Their faith was intricately interwoven into everything they did, from working in the fields to naming their children. Theirs was a life where the gods and goddesses were never any further away than their own shadow.'

These gods and goddesses include the entire Norse pantheon, known to us through the poetic or *Elder Edda* and the prose or *Younger Edda*. The German equivalent is the *Nibelungenlied*, on which Wagner's Ring Cycle was based, and which inspired J. R. R. Tolkien's *Lord of the Rings* and related books.

Asatru is the American movement often known as Odinism in Britain. It is named after the Asa or Aesir, one of the two main families of Norse gods; the other family were the Vanir.

'Modern-day Asatru is a religion based on reconstruction from historical sources. It is a polytheistic faith encompassing belief in a multitude of different gods and goddesses. Within Asatru there is the emergence of a sister tradition named Vanatru, centring mainly on the Vanir. This branch takes especial interest in the feminine mysteries and female ancestor work.'[24]

The religion has a strong ethical side similar to that of most Neo-Pagan movements:

Modern concerns of Asatru are environmental issues and the re-establishing of family values. Unlike many other ethnic peoples, we have lost the sense of kinship, community and extended family. Many old people are freezing or starving. Young people drift towards a life of drug abuse, crime, and general uselessness – with little but the dole queue to look forward to. We offer change. We want to give back – especially [to] the young – a pride in ancestors and their achievements. We aim to instil responsibility, respect and care for our elders, and stress the value of education for our youngsters.[25]

The Norse peoples, and their gods, lived life to the full. They were a hot-tempered bunch, but honourable within their own rules. 'The concept of Honour is the most vital element of Asatru ethics. Others are Courage, Truth, Loyalty, Self-discipline, Hospitality, Industriousness, Independence and Endurance. We strive to express these nine virtues in our lives and dealings with people. Forgiveness, loving your enemy and turning the other cheek are tactics with no place in Asatru,' says Aswynn.

The Odinic Rite also places strong emphasis on honour and self-discipline. 'Each time that we speak out against tyranny, are hospitable to guests or help to protect the environment we are performing a religious act.'[26]

The Odinic Rite, like other Northern Tradition movements, places great emphasis on the family and the extended family, including close friends. It is organized in Hearths, groups of ten to 12 people who usually meet in members' homes.

> Odinism is the organic religion of the peoples of Northern Europe. Our ancestors . . . reflected their awareness of a unity in which the cosmos is one with man and nature . . . Odinists aim at creating a restored order based on the idea of respect for all life and on the explicit recognition of spirituality within ourselves and in the world in which we live, to extend our views of nature so that it is seen as a true manifestation of the spirit.[27]

The Rune Gild was founded in the USA in 1980 by Edred Thorsson, author of *A Book of Troth*. The most influential academic leader is Kveldulfr Gundarsson, author of *Teutonic Magic* and *Teutonic Religion*. (His *Rhinegold*, under the name Stephan Grundy [Michael Joseph, 1994], is an extraordinarily readable modern novelization of the same saga.) Freya Aswynn's *Leaves of Yggdrasil* is a very personal and powerful study of the runes, the Norse gods and magic.

The structure of the various organizations is democratic, but with leaders.

> One of the weaknesses in some previous attempts at reviving the Elder Troth has been the lack of a wise and learned priesthood, a body of persons qualified and certified as experts in the lore and work – in theory and practice – of the Elder Troth. Too often, uninformed anarchy led to dissolution, where a little help from those more experienced and knowledgeable may have brought success. As long as the Troth remains an amateur pastime of the untrained enthusiast, it cannot achieve its destiny.[28]

Like most other Neo-Pagan movements, the revived Norse religions do not actively recruit new members. 'They find us,' says Aswynn. 'People join us because they want to work with others to contact the gods and goddesses. What they get out of it is a closely knit artificially 'constructed "Tribal Family" where we support each other in everything. We are mostly bound together by personal friendships between us and our enthusiasm for our gods.'

Odinshof does not limit itself strictly to the Norse religion. 'The philosophy of the 'Hof is to look back over 2,500 years or so and gain insight from most periods since then,' says Martyn Taylor, co-founder of Odinshof in 1987.[29] Like most of the other new religious movements of the Northern Tradition, its numbers are small. Its members:

want to promote the cult of Odin (Odintru) and learn spiritual truths ('dharma'). Odinshof members do not reject anything from the past but believe strongly in the 'now' . . . The backbone of the Odinshof is its membership, whether they be working alone or attached to an official hearth or loose group (sometimes called a kindred). Some members feel the need to progress to the level of being at one with Odin – to be 'an Odin'. These are potential Grimserular, or shaman-priests . . . A Grimesruli is seen by the Odinshof as a healer, pathfinder, runemaster and teacher, all rolled into one.[30]

The roots of Norse religion go back at least 2,000 years. The god most closely associated with the runes is Odin or Woden, the Allfather. The myths tell how Odin hung upside-down from the great World Tree Yggdrasil for nine days and nights, impaled on his own spear, in order to gain wisdom.

The Norse were a very down-to-earth people. The mystical, the magical and the religious were seen as a fundamental part of everyday life. The runes were associated with wisdom and well-being, with words and deeds, with the gods and with magical power. They were both practical and mystical. If a particular combination of runes brought good luck or protection, it made sense for a warrior to carry it with him.

Although people might initially be attracted to Odinism by the use of runes, there is much more to the religion than that.

> Those who believe that runes and runology are the be-all and end-all of Odinism have a too narrow vision of the runes, a shallow knowledge of their mysteries and ignorance of the meaning of religion. The runes are the essential mystical ingredient of the Odinic Rite and are its spiritual mainstay. But they are not its sum total . . . The Odinist religion is our way of life, our inherited culture and our patrimony.[31]

Like most mythologies, Norse mythology includes creation myths and end-of-the-world myths. It has interrelated families of quarrelsome gods, who from time to time had dealings with humans; and these gods swap responsibilities to some extent over the centuries as the mythology evolves. These are a few of the better-known gods and goddesses:

- Odin (Woden), sometimes known as the Allfather, was foremost among the gods. He is generally pictured with a wide-brimmed hat sloping over his blind eye, in the company of two ravens, his messengers. He was known for his wisdom, but also for his unpredictability. Like many gods, he had a trickster side to his personality.
- His son Thor was the god of weather, particularly thunder, and is often seen wielding a hammer, which he frequently used to slay giants. He was also the god of the peasants and common people, which might account for the fair way in which Norse rulers treated their people.
- Tyr or Tîw was the original god of war; some of his attributes were later taken on by Odin.
- Frey, one of the most important gods, was a fertility god, and also the god of summer.
- Frey's sister (and at one point wife) Frija or Freya was the goddess of sexuality and beauty.

- Often confused with Frija, especially in the Germanic versions of the myths, is Frigga, goddess of fertility, but more in the sense of motherhood. She was one of Odin's wives.
- Balder, son of Frigga and Odin. He was the most beautiful of all the gods, an expert in herbal medicine and also in the runes – indeed, he had runes carved on his tongue.
- Loki, the god of lies, deceit and trickery – and of fire and leisure. Through his treachery, Balder was slain.

There are several dozen other gods and goddesses, in addition to giants, dwarfs and heroic humans, entwined in Norse mythology. Four of them live on today wherever the English language is spoken around the world, in the days of the week: Tuesday is named after Tyr or Tîw, Wednesday after Woden or Odin, Thursday after Thor, and Friday after either Freya or Frigga.

◆

As Christianity made inroads into northern Europe, the power of the old gods waned to some extent – but not entirely. For some centuries the two religions existed side by side, and there are many examples of gravestones or crosses with the crucified Christ on one side and scenes from Norse mythology on the other. Very often the inscriptions were in runes, rather than in the Roman alphabet. Runes continued to be used for writing, and for more esoteric purposes, for many more centuries, despite the efforts of the Catholic Church to stamp out their use. As late as 1639 there was an edict in Iceland forbidding their use, and it is said that even towards the end of the nineteenth century pastors in remote rural parts of Scandinavia were required to be able to read and write the runes.

Many elements of the Old Norse language survive today, obviously in the Scandinavian languages, but also in English, Dutch and German. There are still a few valley sheep-farmers in south Cumbria who speak between themselves a variant of Old Norse. The closest present-day language is Icelandic. In English, the occasional use of 'Ye' to mean 'The' is a reminder of the rune Thorn, which is pronounced 'Th' but looks something like a 'Y'.

◆

Do the modern-day successors to Sigismund and the other great Norse heroes actually believe in Odin, Thor, Balder, Frija and the rest of the gods? 'We have no fixed doctrine at all,' says Aswynn. 'Most of us believe on the whole in an objective existence of our gods as spiritual beings, whereas others in our religion perceive the gods more as Jungian archetypes. Most people have a favourite god or goddess they are devoted to in particular.' Thus there are Odinists, Thorians, Tyrians and others.

The Odinic Rite explain it a different way:

> We know that our gods exist: we can see, feel and sense them. They are manifested in various forms: in the summer and the winter, sunshine and storm, hill and river and plain. Because it is in keeping with our culture and our tradition Odinists give names to the gods who show themselves to us in this way: Thor, Frey, Balder, Odin and many others . . . There is nothing unusual or illogical in this Odinist use of an ancient mythology. All religions

are mythical in their development. It is not the myth that we believe in but the gods whom the myth helps us to understand.[32]

Believers in the Norse/Germanic religions are conscious that they have some seriously bad press to overcome. In the 1930s and 1940s Adolf Hitler deliberately drew on Norse/Germanic sources to provide a religious, mystical and magical basis for Nazism. The SS used the rune Sigel as their symbol. The swastika is one of the oldest religious symbols in the world, but has probably been irreparably polluted by its adoption by Nazism.

'Unfortunately,' says Freya Aswynn, 'some in the past have sought to use the revival of our native folk religion to advance their racial and political agendas. Such activity is not tolerated in the Ring of Troth. The peoples of the North did not achieve great things by fearing, distrusting or hating everyone unlike themselves; rather they attained greatness through their ability, where necessary, to learn from others and to borrow, adapt and improve ideas and technologies which suited their own needs. If the Germanic peoples had hated and feared all that was new and different they may not have achieved all that they have.'

A press release on Asatru looks at it from a different angle: 'Attempts to call and control the Northern gods were made in the '30s and '40s. However the gods had their own agenda, and seeing the subversion of the runes and other sacred signs, extracted the penalties of the perpetrators – who lost!'

Their efforts to distance themselves from Nazism are made more difficult by two things: the fact that the Norse religion *is* an ethnic tradition, and the recent rise of neo-Nazism, which is once again appropriating some of the symbols and which lays claim to the same ethnic heritage.

◆

Odinists, like Wiccans, have sometimes been accused of being too much in love with a rose-tinted past. They disagree. 'It is not a spare-time religion providing an escape route from the problems of modern life by invoking visions of the romantic past but an opportunity for the individual to grow in self-reliance, to grow closer to nature in the practice of the ancient rituals of our ancestors and to secure the future.'[33]

Odinshof also stress the practical, everyday nature of their beliefs:

There is a danger of members becoming too reliant on written texts and not spending time being involved with hearth activities or out of door rituals. 'Armchair Heathens' do not change society for the better. Again, Tacitus said, 'The Germanic-speaking tribes do not think it is in keeping with the divine majesty to confine gods within walls or to portray them in the likeness of any human countenance. Their holy places are woods and groves, and they apply the names of deities to that hidden presence which is seen only by the eye of reverence.'[34]

Like the other Norse movements Odinshof is dedicated to nature, and in particular to maintaining areas of wildwoods. It helped campaign against the proposed road through Oxleas Wood in London. In 1992 it set up a charity called Land Guardians to purchase and maintain a wildwood.

PAGAN FEDERATIONS

In general, Neo-Paganism glories in its diversity. Shamans, witches, Druids and others have different approaches, often based on different national traditions, and within each broad group there are many different emphases. This is both a strength and a potential weakness: the lack of any central organization stops the movement becoming dogmatic and authoritarian, both of which are alien to the Neo-Pagan way of thinking, but it can also mean that individual groups, influenced by a strong local leader, might wander off in strange directions.

Inevitably, umbrella organizations have arisen over the years. In Britain there are two main ones: the Pagan Federation and PaganLink. The Pagan Federation, officially launched in 1971, 'works to make Paganism accessible to people genuinely seeking a nature-based spiritual path'.[35] A large part of its current work is informational, and it has become effectively the mouthpiece of British Neo-Paganism to the outside world. It has established links with the Home Office, the police, social services, the press, libraries, teachers and Members of Parliament. It is working towards establishing the same rights for Neo-Pagans as for members of any other religion, including, for example, hospital and prison chaplains, and weddings and funerals.

Initially the Pagan Federation was almost exclusively Wiccan, but by the 1980s, according to Janet and Stewart Farrar and Gavin Bone, it was 'facing increased criticism for its lack of democracy, and its inability to cater adequately for members who followed other paths than Wiccan'.[36] It was also very much centred on the south-east of England, which was a source of irritation to Neo-Pagans elsewhere in the country. In the early 1990s, recognizing these weaknesses, it expanded its work to give more emphasis to non-Wiccan Neo-Paganism, and made real efforts to make itself more democratic.

Until then for non-Wiccans the PaganLink, which began in 1986, was a better umbrella. Initially it was less centrally structured than the Pagan Federation, acting mainly (as its name suggests) as a link between different groups scattered around the country. By 1988 it was well enough organized to run its first national festival, though it is still at heart a contact network. The purpose and aims of PaganLink are 'to make Pagan and magical ways accessible to anyone who is seeking them . . . to promote links between the various paths . . . to enable us to learn from each other . . . to share energies towards our common aim of manifesting our spiritual and magical nature in harmony with the Earth'.[37]

The two organizations, recognizing each other's areas of expertise, apparently work well together. There is a lot of overlap of both aims and members, and there has been occasional talk of a merger.

◆

The United States has several different nationwide federations of Neo-Pagans. It also has far more formally organized Churches or denominations, with branches scattered across the country. To the outsider there might be some confusion between the two, especially as the prominent leaders of Churches are also the prominent leaders of the federations.

The recently formed Universal Federation of Pagans, for example, was proposed in 1991 by Otter Zell of the Church of All Worlds, along with Rhuddlwm Gawr of the Association of Cymmry Wicca – both widespread Neo-Pagan Churches with many branches – with the aim of creating a federation of Neo-Pagan religions 'which could unite in a common cause rather than wasting energy in conflict'.[38] Although over 120 Neo-Pagan leaders from all over the world apparently became trustees, the 'co-facilitators' and 'incorporators' appear to be largely from Cymmry Wicca, and the Federation was legally incorporated in 1993 in the state of Georgia, the home state of Cymmry Wicca.

Similarly, the Covenant of the Goddess is a legally recognized Wiccan Church, but its attitude to its member congregations is more like a federation. The Preamble to the Covenant charter says: ' . . . we are not the only members of our religion. If the members of a local congregations choose not to join this Covenant and the Church thus created, their choice creates no presumption that they are not members of our religion.'[39] In many ways the Covenant is like the Congregationalist Church in Christianity. 'There is no sovereign authority in our religion outside each local congregation.' The Covenant only has as much sovereignty over congregations 'as the Church will need in order to function effectively as an instrument of their joint will'.[40]

♦

The Isle of Avalon Foundation isn't a religion in itself, or even a federation as such. It is more of a study centre, a clearing house for teaching about Neo-Pagan and New Age ideas, set in Glastonbury. Unlike the Association of Cymmry Wicca's spiritual training college, Bangor Institute, the Foundation is not tied to one particular Pagan Church.

The Isle of Avalon Foundation was set up as the University of Avalon in 1991, 'with the vision of creating a recognized University of the Spirit in Avalon within the temenos of Glastonbury, known for centuries as the Isle of Avalon. We are a University in the original sense of the word – meaning an educational establishment concerned with exploring the whole of creation, encompassing spiritual as well as material values and systems.'[41]

The British government didn't see it the same way. The Foundation was told that it couldn't use the name because it was not an officially recognized university offering academic degrees. In April 1995 it changed to its current name, and reassessed its aims and ideals: 'Isle of Avalon Foundation is a spiritual education centre whose main purpose is to make available to visitors and residents the transformative energies of Avalon and the experience of people who live in Glastonbury and elsewhere on the planet.'[42]

They offer talks and courses on, among others, Personal Development, Music and Magic, Healing, Runes, Numerology, Dowsing, Shamanism and the teachings of Dion Fortune. The aim is to develop courses at beginner, intermediate and advanced (Mystery School) levels in seven faculties, similar to the Schools of the Bangor Institute: Consciousness, Health and Healing, Human Potential, Planet Earth, Sacred Arts, Sacred Sciences and Spiritual Revelation.

♦

Federations and other umbrella groups serve a number of functions: exchange of views, mutual support, general friendship, central information point for the media and official bodies, centralized research and publication and so on. The Neo-Pagan movement in general is still quite young, and a lot of its vigour seems to come from its diversity. A possible danger, which the leaders of the federations are clearly aware of, could be a shift from what is essentially a mutual support group to a structured, centralized authority which decides who may and who may not join, with a too rigid codifying of what is or is not a valid and acceptable form of Neo-Paganism. If this were to occur, most would see it as being against the overall free spirit of Neo-Paganism.

OTHER MOVEMENTS

The movements already covered in this chapter are only a small sample of the huge diversity to be found within the Neo-Pagan field. Many important ideas and movements have not been mentioned. What follows is a brief glance at just a few of them.

NEW AGE

There is, first of all, a tremendous overlap within what is usually called the 'New Age' between Esoteric and Neo-Pagan beliefs. A glance at the 'Mind, Body, Spirit' shelves in a general bookshop, or at the contents of a specialist Esoteric bookshop, will reveal books on healing, spiritual environmentalism, crystals, channelling, Tarot, astrology, mythology, the Goddess, reincarnation, Hermetic philosophy, Rosicrucianism, the Order of the Golden Dawn and Esoteric Christianity – to name but a few subjects – stacked side by side. Some books buyers may be interested in only one particular subject, but probably most will have an interest in several, which will overlap in different ways for different people.

SHAMANISM

Shamanism is part of many Wiccan and Druidic movements, but is really an individual, even solitary path. The modern shaman, like the shaman of early religion, usually works alone. He or she is able, through trance or visions, to enter the spiritual world and communicate with the beings there, working magic or bringing healing back to those in their care. Because it is based on individual experience, there is no single set of beliefs – each shaman finds their own way – but an increasing number of courses in learning how to be a shaman now exist. One of these, based in London, is Eagle's Wing, the Centre for Contemporary Shamanism. It offers evening classes, weekend workshops and year-long part-time courses.

> Shamanism is the oldest tradition on Planet Earth of healing, maintaining balance and harmony in society and the individual, and keeping our connection with Mother Earth and All Creation. A shaman knows that all things are alive, lives both in this world and the spirit world, and has understanding of the inner realities. What I like to call contemporary shamanism is the application of these ancient timeless ways to our situation of the present, be it urban, suburban or whatever. Our outer world may be different, but our human inner landscape has the same components it always did.[43]

FINDHORN COMMUNITY

The Findhorn Community began in 1962, when Peter Caddy, the former manager of a nearby hotel, moved with his wife, Eileen, their children and a friend, Dorothy Maclean, to the Findhorn Bay Caravan Park on the Moray Firth in Scotland. They began a garden using no artificial fertilizers and, following the guidance of God, found themselves communicating with the nature spirits of the garden. They became experts in organic gardening. Within a few years the garden had grown, the community had grown and its fame had spread around the world. Here were people living in harmony with their environment, and living deeply spiritual lives. 'The role of Findhorn, since its inception, has been to demonstrate communion and cooperation with nature, based on a vision of the life and purposeful intelligence inherent in it.'[44]

The community has now spread into several nearby buildings, including the hotel (now Cluny Hill College), plus the caravan park and the Isle of Erraid. It has an educational programme and regularly hosts environmental conferences. Around 200 people now live at Findhorn and the community attracts over 4,000 visitors a year.

FELLOWSHIP OF ISIS

The Fellowship of Isis was founded in 1976 in Eire by the Rev. Lawrence Durdin-Robertson, his wife, Pamela, and his sister Olivia. They worship the Goddess, but differ from many other Neo-Pagan organizations in emphasizing Egyptian as well as Celtic roots. Their priesthood, they claim, 'is derived from an hereditary line of the Robertsons from Ancient Egypt'.[45]

Because they venerate all goddesses (and also gods), members include people from a variety of religions, including Hindus, Buddhists, Christians and Spiritualists. 'The good in all faiths is honoured . . . The Fellowship accepts religious toleration, and is not exclusivist. Members are free to maintain other religious allegiances.' They claim a membership of 12,500 in 81 countries, with over 450 Iseums (Hearths of the Goddess) in 37 countries. The Fellowship has three 'daughter' societies: the Order of Tara, which has chivalric titles, the Druid Clan of Dana, which works on the development of psychic gifts, and the College of Isis.

In common with Esoteric Mystery Schools, the College of Isis offers a correspondence course – 'a structured Magi Degree Course in the Fellowship of Isis Liturgy. There are 32 working degrees, the 33rd relating to spontaneous mystical awakening.'[46]

In contrast with Esoteric Schools:

> There are no vows required or commitments to secrecy. All Fellowship
> activities are optional, and members are free to resign or rejoin at their own
> choice . . . The Fellowship reverences all manifestations of Life . . . [and]
> believes in the promotion of Love, Beauty and Abundance. No encouragement
> is given to asceticism. The Fellowship seeks to develop friendliness, psychic
> gifts, happiness, and compassion for all life.

UNIVERSAL LIFE CHURCH (BRYTHONIC)

The Universal Life Church (Brythonic), founded by David Brock in Portland, Oregon, in 1985, is one of many examples of a currently small religious movement which may or may not grow into something larger. It calls itself Meso-Pagan rather than Neo-Pagan. It is a 'synthesis of late Zoroastrianism, Cabala (which *may* be late Zoroastrianism with a Semitic veneer) and Wicca (reconstruction of Celtic and pre-Celt system, seen in a Zoroastrian framework),'[47] says David Brock, Magister (High Priest) of the Church. As with most other Esoteric and Neo-Pagan religions, it is a modern reconstruction, 'since both original Zoroastrian and Wiccan data have been lost and need to be rediscovered'. Its members are 'of white ancestry and straight sexually . . . homosexuality is opposed to Ahura-Mazda's natural order'.

◆

This last point is one of the few fundamental bones of contention within the whole wide spread of Esoteric and Neo-Pagan movements. Generally, though by no means in all cases, Esoteric movements emphasize the magical polarity of heterosexual male and female, while Neo-Pagan movements welcome people of all sexual orientations. Hoblink is a British organization specifically for gay and bisexual Neo-Pagans.

PART FIVE

✠

PSYCHOLOGY AND SELF-HELP

EIGHT

PERSONAL DEVELOPMENT MOVEMENTS

In earlier decades books such as this sometimes included Marxism or humanism as secular equivalents to religion, in that they performed many of the same functions, and sometimes shared some of the same characteristics. In the last few years there has been a clear societal change. On the one hand, the significance of Marxism, humanism and rational scientific materialism has waned, and on the other, there has been an increased interest in 'personal development'.

In Britain advertisements in magazines offer 'The Realization System: Private Lessons in Practical Psychology'. For £180, paid in easy stages, a correspondence course (says the promotional letter) 'will start to build the structure of a new and dominant YOU, a serene and successful YOU, a more courageous and capable YOU, a happier, healthier, more wonderful YOU . . . A triumphant YOU born of Greater Self-Knowledge which THE REALIZATION SYSTEM will bring you, just as it has done for countless others in all walks of life.' Although it says that it is not in any way a religion, later in the course the student is introduced to the concept of 'the Universal Creative Mind' of which we are all a part.

Personal development isn't new. Samuel Smiles wrote his famous *Self-Help* in 1859, with the aphorisms 'He who never made a mistake never made a discovery' and 'The shortest way to do many things is to do only one thing at once.' Dale Carnegie's *How to Win Friends and Influence People*, published in 1936, was a result of courses in which he taught business and professional people 'to think on their feet and express their ideas with more clarity, more effectiveness and more poise'; it had sold nearly 5 million copies by his death in 1955. L. Ron Hubbard's Dianetics, first launched on the world in 1950, promised 'a condition of ability and rationality for Man well in advance of the current norm' and 'a complete insight into the full potentialities of the mind'. Norman Vincent Peale's *The Power of Positive Thinking* was first published in 1952; its chapters include 'Expect the Best and Get It' and 'I Don't Believe in Defeat'. The *Reader's Digest* has been promoting 'How to increase your word power' for decades.

More recent books include Bernard Haldane's *How to Make a Habit of Success* (1960), with chapter titles such as 'Open Your Life to Success' and 'Building Success into Your Thinking'; Robert J. Lumsden's *Twenty-three Steps to Success and Achievement* (1972), with chapters 'Make Maturity Your Goal', 'Increased Happiness for You' and 'Wider Mental Horizons'; and, on a more spiritual level, Will Schutz's *Profound Simplicity* (1979), was 'one of the first books to apply the learnings of the human potential movement to "real life" problems'.

Such books are still being written, but the last couple of decades have seen an explosion in the number of techniques, courses and seminars available, all offering ways to help you improve yourself. A cynic might suggest that a paperback book costing £6.99 will make only about 50p per copy for its author, while a weekend seminar can charge £300 apiece for only a fraction of the contents, and might encourage the attendee to come back for much more of the same – more advanced courses, for more advanced fees. A man can make millions by telling other people how they might make millions.

◆

Success-oriented America in particular has always been a fertile field for the planting of such self-improvement concepts. It is probably no coincidence that the country which brings up its children to believe that they can and will succeed, achieve whatever they aim for and be fulfilled has more adults going to one form or another of therapy than any other. If you don't succeed, if you don't reach the top, if you don't feel fulfilled, then you feel a failure; the opportunities are all there, in the land of opportunity, so it must be you who have failed. In America, a therapist will never be unemployed. It is probably also no coincidence that most of the human potential movements developed there.

Self-improvement seminars often seek to improve a person's awareness of and confidence in himself or herself by awakening and experiencing, in one phrase or another, 'the heartfelt energies' – which is a similar goal to that of many religions, without necessarily involving an external God. Could it be that such organizations have taken on a role analogous to religions in the past, and if so, is there still a need for religion? Certainly the fervour of many adherents to Personal Development movements is comparable to the fervour of a religious convert. Perhaps the benefits they gain are also comparable.

Some of the Personal Development movements – just like some of the alternative religions – have been criticized for their reluctance to let go of people once they have become involved. In the flush of enthusiasm as you successfully complete a course, with all the 'gains' you have made, you can easily be persuaded to sign on for the next one, perhaps at a 'special discount' if you put down a significant (and non-returnable) deposit immediately. Although there are noticeable benefits right from the start, there is also the promise of even greater benefits further up the ladder – or further up the bridge, as Scientology would say.

The best known of all these psychology-based self-improvement movements will be covered at some length. At different times and for different reasons Scientology has claimed the mantle of educative system, health improvement, therapy, philosophy and religion. Other organizations, at least publicly, eschew any spiritual connection.

Several of the organizations contacted for this book refused to have anything to do with it, on the grounds that they were not a religion; others simply didn't reply. Rather than researching solely from secondary sources – which effectively means repeating what other books have said – we have reluctantly decided to leave them out. This is regrettable, because several of these organizations, such as *est*, have, rightly or wrongly, received a bad press over the years. They could have used this book as an opportunity to refute any incorrect criticisms made of them or, where criticisms have been valid, to show that they have now cleaned up their act. Readers will have to draw their own conclusions from their arguments of silence.

NEURO-LINGUISTIC PROGRAMMING

Neuro-Linguistic Programming (NLP) is an approach rather than an organization; it is used by several different human potential movements. The information here was provided by John Seymour Associates, who offer NLP consulting and training mainly in London and Bristol.

'NLP is the art and science of personal excellence,' say Joseph O'Connor and John Seymour in their introductory book. It is 'a way of studying how people excel in any field and teaching these patterns to others'.[1]

NLP was developed in the mid-1970s by John Grinder, an Associate Professor of Linguistics at the University of California, Santa Cruz, and Richard Bandler, a psychology student at the university, with input from various others. The somewhat off-putting name encompasses the theory and practice of NLP. 'Neuro' reflects the fact that our experience and behaviour stem from the neurological processes of our senses and thoughts. 'Linguistic' refers to the fact that we use language to think logically and to communicate with others. 'Programming' refers to the way that we order and organize our ideas and actions to produce results.

Put them all together and NLP is a new way of looking at how people think, communicate and behave. It examines how people learn, and teaches more efficient ways of learning, and how to improve the memory. It shows how many of our reactions to events reinforce negativity, and how instead they can be made positive. It teaches how to communicate effectively and how to understand and interpret the signals from other people. It teaches people to question what they do and what they believe:

1 Why do you do what you do?
2 What does that mean to you?
3 What would happen if you didn't do that?
4 What is that like? What do you compare it to?
5 What is empowering to you about this?[2]

It may use different terminology and perhaps different methodology, but it is in the great tradition of Dale Carnegie and Norman Vincent Peale in that, in a phrase, it teaches people to be more successful.

The reason for NLP's inclusion here is twofold. First, several movements which do have a spiritual element, such as Insight (see p. 239) openly use NLP techniques and have NLP Masters among their leaders. Second, although it should be stressed once again that NLP itself is a process, a set of techniques, a methodology, and not a religious movement, or even a religious belief system, its function is similar to that of a religion, particularly many of the 'alternative' religions covered in this book.

'NLP offers specific and practical ways of making desired changes in our own and others' behaviour. It is about what works.'[3] Similar sentiments can be found in many of the Esoteric religious movements, both those within the Western Mystery Tradition and those which follow a more Eastern path, such as the School of Economic Science and the Gurdjieff/Ouspensky offshoots.

The 'philosophy' of NLP also sounds familiar:

It is about creativity, learning and change, and how you construct your reality. Put simply, the world we each live in is not the real world. It is a model of the world. A model that we each create unconsciously and live in as though it were the real world. Most human problems derive from the models in our heads rather than from the world as it really is. As you develop your practical understanding of how these inner models work, so you can learn to change unhelpful habits, thoughts, feelings and beliefs for more useful ones.

A Neo-Platonist or a Christian Scientist might say much the same thing, in surprisingly similar language – though possibly for different reasons. What ultimately distinguishes NLP from any of these religions or religious philosophies is that NLP teaches you to know yourself and better yourself. Esoteric religions teach you to know yourself, and through knowing yourself, the God within, to know better the God without.

◆

The *est* system (Erhard Seminars Training), now known as the Forum, which is run by the Centres Network, was founded by Werner Erhard (formerly Paul Rosenberg), a used-car and encyclopedia salesman. It was seized on by sales reps who wanted to improve their sales and thus their commissions. Exegesis was a British equivalent, with similar methods. When Exegesis folded as a human potential training movement in 1984, largely through the efforts of London Tory MP David Mellor, its staff set up a highly successful tele-sales company, putting their theory into practice.

Rather than going for sales reps, NLP courses tend to aim for executives, people climbing their way up the corporate ladder who want to know how to improve their chances. Many major companies, including top banks and building societies, privatized utilities, health authorities, county councils, police authorities and even government departments, have sent middle and senior management on NLP courses to improve their efficiency and increase their management potential. The self-employed and non-professionals are less likely to be able to afford the courses: the two-day introductory seminar costs £152.75 (1995 prices throughout).

Like many alternative religions, again particularly the Esoteric movements, there is a 'career ladder' within NLP. 'Many people find that experiencing the Introduction Seminar creates an enthusiasm and thirst for more. Practitioner level training is the place to go next.'

The 20-day practitioner course in London costs £1,833; the same course in 'the beautiful city of Bath' costs the same amount, plus residential fees.

Another set of courses, Trainer Training, is for teachers, lecturers, workshop leaders or anyone else wanting to improve their presentation skills. It should not be confused with Assisting and Coaching, and Apprentice Trainer, which teach Practitioners to become NLP Trainers themselves. There are certificates and diplomas for NLP Trainers. Above that there are certified Advanced Practitioners, Master Practitioners and Master Trainers.

Interestingly, the brief biographies of NLP Trainers always give the names of the people they themselves trained under. This could be seen as similar to new Eastern-origin religions tracing themselves back through a progression of gurus, and Esoteric movements claiming the authority of authenticity through their descent from previous movements.

In addition to a variety of NLP books, cassettes and videos, there is Personal Development software for £95, and a 'Biofeedback Meter GSR1 . . . to put you in touch with your body so that you can learn to master your emotional state. Digital or analogue displays. As sold to hypnotherapists and other relaxation teachers.' This is also £95 – considerably cheaper and perhaps more effective than a Scientology E-Meter.

INSIGHT

'Insight is very practical, offering a number of powerful yet simple techniques which you can take away and apply to your life daily, to allow you to do more of what you've always wanted to do.'[4]

Insight is often confused with *est* (Erhard Seminar Training), now known as the Forum. Although there is some surface similarity in their approach, techniques and aims, the two movements come from entirely different roots and have no connection.

BELIEFS AND PRACTICES

Insight draws on a number of different approaches, including Gestalt, Core System Psychology and Neuro-Linguistic Programming. Although it might not like the comparison, there is also some overlap with the theory behind Dianetics, in that unpleasant early experiences can have major effects on later life.

As life goes on, we have experiences that cause us to limit our expression in the world and to close down on our natural loving, spontaneity and creativity. These experiences can begin at birth and usually take place in childhood, where the patterns are laid down for later behaviour. An example of the kind of experience would be a small child being scolded for being noisy when it was simply expressing joy . . . So, rather than just being our natural unique selves, we develop fears and anxieties about life.[5]

The UK Insight organization conducts seminars roughly every two months, in a central London hotel. These take place on Wednesday, Thursday and Friday evenings, all day (and evening) on Saturday and Sunday, with a final session on the Monday evening – a total of around 48 hours. It's a cumulative process and people are discouraged from missing any of the seminar at all.

The seminar includes 'games and group processes involving the whole group; exercises done with a partner; periods when the facilitator will present information and new concepts; discussion and sharing of feelings; closed eye processes (sometimes called guided meditation or creative visualization). It is very varied, as people learn best when they are stimulated and interested.'

Aware of the adverse publicity attached to some similar courses in the past – particularly the early *est* movement – Insight are keen to stress that attendees at a seminar are not locked in the room, are free to leave when they want and are allowed 'regular water and loo breaks'. The sessions all end by midnight, so the usual criticism of sleep deprivation is also ruled out.

We are all a mixture of the person we really are, the person we fear we are and the person we pretend to be, say Insight. Like most of its teachings, this is not original; it is taught, sometimes with variations, by most human potential movements, including *est*.

The aim of the seminars is to help people to 'see who they really are underneath . . . They also become aware of the fears and limiting beliefs they have, and may also start to drop some of the pretence and outer behaviours'. These 'outer behaviours' are the face we present to the world, which is often not how we really are; an insecure person might project brash self-confidence, for example. 'On the seminar, people become more aware of how they are living their lives and more aware of how they may be holding themselves back. Often these things are unconscious. At the root of Insight's approach is the belief that each person starts life perfect and unlimited.' By revealing and dealing with their fears and anxieties, and those early negative experiences which are now limiting them, they can emerge with 'increased self-esteem and a clearer sense of their own unique qualities and strengths'. The Sunday session concludes with a candle-lighting 'graduation ceremony', which friends and family may attend.

The spiritual aspect of all this is implied in the introductory literature, but only in a broad sense. 'Where Insight differs from other personal development programmes is that at the centre of our philosophy is the heart, rather than the mind, and that the power of loving can heal everything.' Insight is portrayed as being '"spiritual" with a small "s" in that it deals with the human spirit', but it denies being religious. However, their philosophy or 'mission statement' – 'Our vision is for as many people as possible to have a positive and profound experience of themselves and their own power and light' – contains concepts reminiscent of 'awareness' and of the Light and Sound of ECKANKAR.

HISTORY

There is no mention in Insight's introductory literature of its origins, beyond 'Insight began in California in 1978, and came to the UK in 1979. It was founded by Russell Bishop, an educational psychologist, and John-Roger, a teacher.' In fact its history goes back some way before 1978, and gives a clue to the religious background to Insight's psychological and educational teachings.

Insight is just one aspect of a larger organization called the Church of the Movement of Spiritual Inner Awareness, or MSIA (pronounced Messiah). MSIA was founded in 1971 by John-Roger Hinkins (b. 1934), who started off in ECKANKAR (see p. 136), founded by John Paul Twitchell in 1965, which in turn has roots in Kirpal Singh's esoteric Hindu/Sikh Sant Mat teachings. Much of the spiritual teaching of MSIA is broadly the same as that of ECKANKAR, though some of the terminology has been changed (compare Christian offshoots, which usually keep the same terminology but change its meaning).

In 1963 John-Roger met Baba Sawan Singh on the spiritual plane, though apparently he was confused for some years about who it was he had met. Sawan Singh endowed him with Mystical Traveller Consciousness, which appears to be similar to being ECKANKAR'S Living ECK Master. As the Mystical Traveller, John-Roger has total awareness on all levels of consciousness. MSIA aims to teach this same awareness to others through its various component parts, which include the International Integrity Foundation, a holistic health centre, two colleges which train clergy and offer further degrees in theology and in Applied Human Relationships – and Insight, which is the most public face of MSIA.

Insight trainers or 'facilitators' are people who have been through several levels of training, including Insight IV, a five-week course in the USA; who have done at least two years on-the-job training in the seminar room; and who 'live the training to the best of their ability, and [are] a demonstration of what we teach'. Some of them have therapeutic qualifications, and many are Masters in Neuro-Linguistic Programming (see p. 237).

It would probably be unfair to see Insight as either a front or a recruiting ground for MSIA. The majority of people who attend the basic Insight seminar don't go on any further than that, and there are many reports of attendees gaining a vast amount from the seminar. Despite the order of their founding, it might be fairer to regard MSIA as providing, for those who want to go deeper, a spiritual development of the more psychological lessons learned through Insight.

THE EMIN

The Emin are one of the very few religious or semi-religious movements to have originated in Britain – though, like several of the other movements in this book, they say that they are not a religion as such; they are, rather, a group of people pursuing 'a natural philosophy and way of life'.[6] Like many other movements, they were stung by an article in the *Observer Magazine* (14 May 1995), 'A to Z of Cults', which described them as 'a highly secretive British cult' which held 'clandestine meetings'. In response, they point out that they have been holding public meetings for over 20 years; they have also recently published an introductory booklet.

HISTORY

The usual press story about the origins of the Emin has its founder Leo, then Raymond Armin, sitting under a tree on Hampstead Heath in London receiving enlightenment. The Emin say that as a boy, like many others, he had a favourite place to go and think about life, but that this story is 'really a simplistic misinterpretation of what, for any human, is a complex process'. In any case, this had nothing to do with the start of the movement *per se*. The Emin began some 30 years later, in 1972, when 'a group of people searching for the meaning and purpose of life, most of whom were widely travelled, academically qualified, and had spent years investigating numerous philosophies and religions' without finding satisfactory answers, happened to meet Armin 'through a chance encounter'.

The chance encounter was when Armin's son John, then an ambulance driver, picked up a young woman who was carrying a book of Sufi tales. John mentioned that his father read similar books, the two met, a few of the woman's friends joined them and the Emin began. *Emin* is apparently an Arabic word meaning 'Faithful One'.

Raymond Armin, born Raymond Schertenlieb in 1924, was the son of a Swiss immigrant to Britain. The family surname was changed to Armin; it was quite common to change Germanic surnames between the wars.

His early years, as told by the Emin, have much in common with other founders of religious movements, from Madame Blavatsky to L. Ron Hubbard. 'His quest to discover the truth about living began as a young boy . . . During his young adult life he extensively researched and studied world history, science, world religions, philosophy and a whole range of other subjects. National Service took him to the Far East, where he explored Indian and other Eastern religions and traditions. These explorations were not just academic . . . The paramount quest in his life was to be true and aligned to whatever causes each human to be.'

Leo never looked for followers, and the Emin do not see him as their founder or leader as such, 'but certainly the prime inspiration of those who formed the Emin endeavour'. When the early members of the Emin met him, 'They were staggered to find the great tangible results of his own researches and studies into many of the fundamental questions in living, which they found to be of uttermost use, not only in their own quest, but also in their everyday lives.' They persuaded him to provide them with writings and tapes of his researches, and began to pay him consultancy fees to enable him 'to pursue his research full-time for the benefit of the growing number of Emin companions'.

Within two years there were about 70 members: now there are between 400 and 500 in Britain, and a further 1,500 around the world. These numbers have been stable for the last eight years. Around 200 of the British members have been in the Emin for over ten years; Nick Woodeson and David Pearce, quoted throughout this entry, between them have '39 years of experience in the Emin Endeavour'. Leo himself has been living in semi-retirement in Florida for some years, though he still provides the Emin with new teachings.

Around 1986, seven Emin families established a new Israeli settlement, known as the Village of Maalé Tzvia, in northern Israel. 'It is important to bear in mind that the village is, firstly, a domestic Israeli settlement supported by the Jewish Settlement Agency and the government and, secondly, an Emin village, in the sense that the adults are Emin members who have sought to build a way of life for themselves which recognizes both local custom and Emin principles, tenets and understandings.' The Emin village has now grown to around 100 families, and is still expanding. Because of its success, 'It is now often used as a showcase example by the Israeli authorities.'

◆

The movement has had a number of names over the years and this has led to some confusion. These include the Faculty of Colour and the Emin University of Life. The first ten years they now see as experimental, trying out various paths and researching different areas. In 1977 they began 'a more advanced exploration', called the Eminent Way, which 'marked the transition of the Emin from external researches to internal processes, from learning to living'. Although the name is no longer widely used, some individual members still pursue this area of work, which involves meditation.

Like several other movements in this book, the Emin accept that they have made mistakes in the past: 'The whole evolution of the Emin endeavour has been trial and error because it is a real human endeavour.' Even Leo, who seems to be regarded simply as a wise man, rather than anything at all divine, has made mistakes in the way he has guided the movement. In 1978, for instance, he established a Church in America, and wrote a book called *The Poem of the Church of Emin Coils*. 'This was an attempt to establish a foundation upon which a religion could develop. This attempt was abandoned, and the book has long since been withdrawn.'

In 1978 the satirical magazine *Private Eye* alleged that Leo was a fraud. The Emin began the process of suing for libel, but dropped the case because of the expense. There was further controversy in 1983 and 1984 when Tory MP David Mellor tried to prevent the Emin from continuing to use a hall in Putney, London, which they had been using since 1976; a public inquiry ruled that they should be allowed to continue using it. Around the same time there were several articles and interviews with Leo and members of the Emin in local papers, none of which did the movement's credibility much good, though the Emin deny that Leo actually uttered the more sensational quotations attributed to him.

The movement is still developing. Leo's teachings, and the discoveries and researches of members, now form a vast archive. In 1993 'an effort was made to place all of the research that had taken place up to that time into a cohesive framework. Out from this came the "Emin Loom of Research Starters", which today forms the basis for the first few years of a person's engagement with the Emin.' Those undertaking this work are known as the Emin Stream. More advanced members follow two different streams, the Gemrod and the Acropolis.

BELIEFS AND PRACTICES

'The dictionary definition and the popular use of the word "belief" implies the acceptance *without proof* of things or statements. No one in the Emin is required to believe anything. People are encouraged to undertake their own research upon which they may prove, or disprove, the content of Emin teaching.'

Emin teachings are open to constant revision and development, as members explore subjects more deeply. All their publications bear the statement, 'This publication is sold on the condition that the reader understands that the content herein is entirely philosophical until such time as it may be proven as fact.' As well as allowing for continuous revelation, this presumably covers them against any possible errors of fact, and also against the possibility of disgruntled ex-members claiming they have been required to believe any particular principles.

The Philosophical Tenets of the Emin are:

1 That the creation is ordered by natural law and that it grows towards completion and that human life is a high point of this growth.
2 That the human also grows and is pressing toward its own evolution and completion.
3 That the human is spiritual and has a duty to the universe, to itself and to the rest of humanity.
4 That the endeavour of human life is to learn and develop and upgrade the ways and contents of the mental faculty and the whole human potential according to natural law.
5 That the human race is meant to be in unison and agreement concerning the conduct of life on earth.

6 That there is life after death and that this must be planned for and worked for individually.

7 That to be constructive and opportunity engendering is the true way to be properly participant in life.

From these Tenets come material responses, such as:

1 To uphold the rightful elected law of the land . . .

2 To seek to develop one's own potential to the uttermost and to use one's natural gifts to the full.

3 To be resistant to the lowering of standards . . .

4 To be constructive in the keeping of good order and stability . . .

5 To strive to be useful by one's own work . . . and to be supportive of natural freedoms . . .

6 To be pathfinder in various ways that unlock situations in learning which otherwise prevent further progress, and to try to expand boundaries of understanding as a duty to the future.

7 To seek to be constantly well informed and increasing so as not to offer hypocrisy or deception to others or to self from the standpoint of ignorance.

Generally there is a slightly old-fashioned courtesy about the Emin. For example, like the School of Economic Science (see p. 154) they tend to refer to women as 'ladies'.

♦

The emphasis in the Emin is on individual and group study and discovery. Leo's writings in the Emin Archives are seen more as guidelines than as gospel. The Emin Stream – the first few years of Emin work – is 'a live discovery into an array of subjects from theatre, the arts, barding, oratory, dance, to science, architecture, world history, the natural laws and the whole realm of personal development, behavioural sciences and becoming true to one's natural self'.

The 'Emin Loom of Research Starters' is a complex seven by seven chart. Down the left are two Connection Domains – 'Mentality Imagery' and 'Brain Perception'; two Alignment Domains – 'Emotions (Higher and Lower)/Feelings' and 'Process Reasonings/Instinct, Thinking, Moving Centres'; and three Reference Domains – 'Functions, Soul Related/White-Red-Blue, White-Pale Yellow-Pale Blue', 'Groundwork, Headwork, Heartwork, Practice, Meditation', and finally, 'Learning, Understanding, Mixing, Matching'. Along the top are 1. Governing Views – 'Genius'; 2. Governing Reason – 'Genetic'; 3. Governing Intentions – 'Generation'; and four further unlabelled columns.

The contents of the grid are an excellent example of the specialist use of language within a religious movement (Scientology is another good example). Language is used in such a way as to make sense to a member of the movement, who has been introduced to the concepts and terminology gradually and systematically, while being utterly baffling to the outsider. This accounts in part for the accusations of secrecy often made against alternative religious movements.

(Incidentally, this is not necessarily a criticism of such movements. Someone with no familiarity with standard Christian terminology would be equally baffled by such 'technical terms' as salvation, atonement and Trinity, let alone Paraclete, predestination or transubstantiation. When the New Testament was put into Basic

English, which has a vocabulary of only 850 words, it was found necessary to use 150 additional words because of the specialist nature of the text.[7]

Quoting just two examples taken at random from the 49 boxes of the 'Emin Loom' will illustrate the point:

2–5. That the human complex, carnal and electromagnetic, is plasmagenic theatre allowing, in which the cosmic relation and government is ⅓ expendable, ⅓ maintenance, ⅓ custodial.

3–6. That human in planetary domicile is evolutary, individually and/or collectively, in the presence of transference, which is the persuasions of human semi-conscious and superior conscious alignment by design and attribute and acumen.[8]

Senior members of the Emin move on from study based on the 'Emin Loom of Research Starters' to two further streams, Gemrod and the Acropolis. 'The Gemrod reflects the movement in a person's journey from learning to a more serious practical application and development . . . It has an emphasis on behavioural science and the improvement and refinement of attitude and values.' The Acropolis is 'the pinnacle of Emin research . . ., an "Emin think tank" attempt to pioneer into the unknown and to explore the potential of human evolution'.

Leo's books also use language in unusual ways. One of the primary Emin texts, Leo's first book, *Dear Dragon*, begins:

Hello, another person, whatever is your way and style. My name, self-chosen – for this, in truth, must it be – is POEM. Welcome to my purpose, that is not a story. Within this, you will learn and flavour much, that somehow, in some mysterious way, will move you, touch often something deep and powerful in your person.

Description of normal kind will not suffice; for the Blue Roses of Forgetfulness and that very fast something, seen from the corner of the eye, instantly gone, seen, but not understood, are only the path that leads to the first gate of passing through to the Way of the Dear Dragon . . .

Pemero sends you this gift . . . And although, you not remembering it in its entirety, I tell you, there are parts of you that will retain its essence eagerly.[9]

Dear Dragon is a mystical, poetical book, and its style of writing reflects this, but the language is strange, at times unwieldy, and often syntactically convoluted. A critic might ask – particularly as members of the Emin (like those of many other alternative religious movements) tend to be intelligent, cultured, middle-class people – why they do not at least tidy up Leo's grammar.

◆

Like several other movements covered in this book, the Emin are clearly, as they say, involved in developing human potential, using different terminology and techniques but perhaps reaching towards similar ends to, for example, Insight (see p. 239). Much of their terminology also reveals an Esoteric element analogous to, for example, the Builders of the Adytum (see p. 184) – for example, 'Birth on earth is the beginning of a universal organic immortality' and, 'Human life is designed to be "living spirit of God" in unquickened universal expansions.'[10]

In addition, among the many areas of study for the Emin are astrology and Tarot. Their own Gemrod Tarot pack (Major Arcana only) is substantially different from traditional designs; some of the titles have been changed, including the Lover to Life, the Hermit to the Searcher, Temperance to 'The Communication (the Searcher reaches Land's End)', the Devil to the Green Man and the World to the Nymph of Ability; the unnumbered Fool card has been dropped altogether. A later Major Arcana, marketed as the Frown Strong pack, also shows many differences from traditional packs, though this one does have a Fool equivalent, called 'The Card of Negation'.

'It is widely recognized that the Tarot has been significantly misrepresented and misused throughout the course of history. Early Emin research included the construction of a pictorial mosaic of understanding, based on the study of the laws and the influences that affect human development. This was an attempt to rediscover the original nature of the Tarot, which constituted a comprehensive encyclopedia of human development . . . definitely not a fortune-telling tool.'

The laws which are often mentioned both by the Emin and in accounts of them include several based on numbers. The law of two includes 'opposites/adjacencies, the male/female principles, energy and matter, etc. The law of four concerns cyclic phenomena, i.e the seasons, the phases of the moon, biorhythms, the four elements. The law of seven concerns the major planets, the spectrum colours, and the law of five concerns the five centres of the human, which are thinking, moving, instinctive, emotional and sexual.'

Although a previous book on new religious movements asserts dismissively that 'Leo's laws seem to be a bizarre mix of psycho-babble and New Age interests,'[11] it is clear that the Emin, like many other alternative religious movements, take an eclectic approach to their study and their teachings. If they find something useful, they use it. For example, both in their teachings of laws of number and in their emphasis on dance and music as means of approaching inner truths and exploring human potential, there are echoes of Gurdjieffian philosophy.

One of the most visible expressions of their work, for outsiders, is their use of music, dance, theatre and art as means to unlock human potential; the Emin are often first encountered in their theatre or dance work. Different groups of Emin musicians have produced a number of music CDs and cassettes which seek 'to capture and clothe in sound, rhythm and harmony the fine essence qualities and values that can balance, refresh and realign a person to cause much well-being'.[12] The use of colour is also important to the Emin: 'green promotes vigour, yellow promotes value, blue promotes regulation'[13] and so on.

One area which might be called 'New Age' is Aura Cleaning. The Emin teach that 'the electro-magnetic radiation of the human constitutes a field known as the aura. As the physical body needs regular cleansing, so does the aura. Headaches and irritability are often caused by imbalances in the aura. There are specific yet simple movements that we have developed to clear the pathways and balance the energy levels in the aura.' Former members mention groups of people flexing their fingers and flapping their arms rhythmically; the Emin say that what they call Electrobics works.

New members, after a few months, often take new names, a common practice in many religious movements both new (ISKCON) and old (Simon becoming Peter, Saul becoming Paul). The names are often colours or precious stones (Emerald, Opal), or qualities which the member wants to concentrate on (Patience, Hope). They can change their names at any point, to reflect their development.

They are also expected to contribute, depending on their financial circumstances, anything from a small amount up to £25 a week. This pays for 'the hire of halls, the purchase of equipment, and also includes salaries for administrators, consultancy fees for lecturers and commissioned researchers, including Leo'. Apparently they no longer wear a tabard-like cotton tunic and satin sash over their normal clothes at meetings; now, 'people wear what they want.'

Perhaps because the teachings of the Emin are constantly developing, there has been confusion over some matters. For example, in the (now withdrawn) *Poem of the Emin Coils*, Leo inveighed against homosexuality, as one 'unnatural condition or freak practice' among several others. Now, according to Woodeson and Pearce, 'the Emin does not refuse entry to homosexuals'. It does, like many of the Esoteric Schools, refuse to take on drug addicts or people with mental illness.

Some writers have made much of the different activities of men and women in the Emin. The movement stresses that it doesn't follow traditional stereotypes. 'Each gender obviously has its own nature, character, qualities and strengths which we recognize and seek to uphold . . . both genders are encouraged to be self reliant and independent . . . We study extensively the meaning and significance of gender both in its human characterization and its appearance through all planetary life.'

The Emin do not consider that they are the only ones with the truth. 'The Emin is not a religion. Personal spiritual development has always been possible for any human life . . . Emin companions hold their own religious beliefs. Many are Christians, Jews, Muslims, etc. We uphold the right of all individuals to pursue their own faith.' On morality, they say, 'We uphold anything that is constructive and progressive in the world, and stand against anything that is perverse or corrupt . . . We believe that common decency and good standards of moral behaviour are essential. We deplore the rapid erosion of these values.' At least in principle, anyone committing a criminal offence would be asked to leave – as would anyone seeking to use the Emin as a political forum.

The terminology might at times be unusual, but the aims of the Emin, and the various paths of study which they follow, appear to be an eclectic mixture of ideas common to many Esoteric, New Age and Personal Development movements. The main difference from most other semi-religious movements is that the Emin started from scratch rather than being based on a previously existing tradition.

TRANSCENDENTAL MEDITATION

Transcendental Meditation is not a religion, they say firmly; it is a scientific technique. Even purely as the latter it has a place in this section, because it aims to help develop the full potential of the individual. From the outside observer's point of view, however, it quite clearly has both specific religious origins and spiritual aims, though the movement emphasizes that it is practised by people of all religions and enhances the experience of their own religion.

The abbreviation TM is used here to mean both the type of meditation and the organization which teaches and promotes it.

HISTORY

The Maharishi Mahesh Yogi was born Mahesh Prasad Varma (or possibly J. N. Srivastava) in 1911 or 1918 (it is traditional for Indian gurus to put their early life behind them as no longer important, which accounts for the common difficulty in pinning down such factual details). He trained as a physicist at Allahabad University, gaining his degree in 1940, then went to study for 13 years under Guru Dev, then the Shankaracharya of the North (see p. 149), at Jyotir Monastery, Badarinath. Guru Dev died in 1953, and according to some sources there was a power struggle between two or three of his disciples, including Mahesh, before Sri Shantanand Saraswati became the new Shankaracharya of the North. The movement refutes this on the grounds that Mahesh was not a Brahmin by birth, so could not have become Shankaracharya. They also say that he has continued to honour the Shankaracharyas after Guru Dev.

Mahesh went into seclusion for two years before emerging in 1956, then set out on his mission to bring to the world the ancient mystical Hindu techniques of Transcendental Meditation taught to him by Guru Dev. Taking the title Maharishi (Sanskrit for 'Great Seer'), he established the Spiritual Regeneration Movement in Madras on 1 January 1958, in Los Angeles in 1959 and in Britain in 1960.

At the beginning of 1960 he gave some lectures at Caxton Hall in London. Several members of the Study Society (a Gurdjieff/Ouspensky group), including its leader Dr Francis Roles, and Leon MacLaren of the School of Economic Science, went to hear him and were introduced to TM. Both the Society and the School realized its value, and began to teach a version of it. In 1961 MacLaren organized a meeting for the Maharishi in the Albert Hall, and later that year the Society and the School jointly set up the School of Meditation, specifically to study and teach the principles and practical applications of meditation.

It has been suggested that the Maharishi fell out with the School of Meditation soon afterwards, either because students' fees were going to the School rather than to him, or more likely because its teaching of TM was 'polluted' by association with Gurdjieff/Ouspensky teachings. According to the TM movement, Roles never completed the teacher training course of TM. They say that 'the techniques involved in the School of Meditation are not the same as Transcendental Meditation, despite some superficial similarities. For example, a vital and distinctive feature about TM is that no attempt is made to control the mind.'[14]

Determined to spread his teachings around the world, the Maharishi started training people to teach the techniques of TM and set up a number of organizations, including the International Meditation Society in 1961, the Students International Meditation Society in 1965 and the Academy of Meditation in Rishikesh, India, in 1966.

In early 1968, through George Harrison's encouragement, the Beatles went to India to sit at the Maharishi's feet, which brought him a vast amount of publicity. Reports that the Beatles also gave the movement a great deal of money have been denied, although the publicity of their brief discipleship certainly brought large numbers of recruits to TM, along with their fees.

The Maharishi International University was established in Iowa in 1971, followed by what is now the International Association for the Advancement of the Science of Creative Intelligence. In 1972 the Maharishi announced his World Plan, to create one teaching centre per million people in the world, with the eventual target of one TM teacher per thousand people in the world. In 1976 he began teaching the TM-Sidhi Programme, which included Yogic Flying, and the idea of simultaneous meditation by many people beneficially affecting the world.

For some years TM was taught in schools and colleges in the USA, until this was challenged by Evangelical Christians, who saw in it the insidious encroachment of Hinduism. Court cases in 1977 and 1979 ruled that TM was in fact a religious activity, which meant that under the American Constitution it could not be taught in state schools. Although the TM organization disagreed with the ruling, they gave up the legal battle for the time being.

Even with these problems, nearly a million people had taken the basic TM course by 1980 – one of the most impressive results of any new religious movement. The figure today, say TM, is four million.

In 1982 TM set up the Maharishi University of Natural Law at Mentmore Towers in Buckinghamshire, which it had bought in 1978 for its UK headquarters. In 1985 the movement started promoting Ayur-Veda, an ancient Indian method of natural medicine. Then came the Maharishi's World Plan for Perfect Health in 1985, and Maharishi's Programme to Create World Peace in 1986. In 1980 TM established an Ideal Village in Skelmersdale, Lancashire, with a Golden Dome, completed in 1988, in which members meditate morning and evening.

The 1990s saw a move into British politics with the Natural Law Party, which puts up candidates in local, parliamentary and European elections. The party's headquarters is at Mentmore Towers, where the title of the TM organization, formerly the World Government of the Age of Enlightenment, was changed in 1994 to the Maharishi Foundation. Although the World Government 'never aspired to political government,' according to Kahn – 'its sovereignty is in the domain of consciousness, which is the unseen governor of life everywhere' – the Natural Law Party is a different matter; its political manifestos clearly speak of its becoming the government of Britain and implementing a wide range of political policies. It already has in place government ministers in charge of the Ministry for the Development of Consciousness, the Ministry of Cultural Integrity, the Ministry of Celebrations and Fulfilment, the Ministry of All Possibilities, and six others.

A plan to purchase the 400-hectare (1,000-acre) former US air base at Bentwaters in Suffolk for a full-scale University of Natural Law, offering accredited degree courses to 4,000 students, fell through in September 1995.

BELIEFS AND PRACTICES

Transcendental Meditation is described as 'a technology of consciousness' and 'the Science of Creative Intelligence', with the aim of developing the full potential of the individual. It is both a psychological and a spiritual process. It fulfils some of the same self-improvement functions as certain religious or semi-religious movements, and its techniques, or something like them, are used in several other movements – though Kahn disagrees.

'This is quite wrong. Nowhere do we find the technique of Transcendental Meditation taught, other than by instructors trained by Maharishi. If anything extraneous is introduced, then it is no longer Transcendental Meditation and the good benefits of Transcendental Meditation are no longer found.'

After basic training, which in 1995 cost £490, people are given a mantra, which is claimed to be specially chosen for each individual. Ex-members say, however, that the mantra is selected on the basis of sex and age from a list of only around 16 mantras altogether. Those who wish can go on to study more advanced techniques, including Yogic Flying. Other programmes include different areas of Vedic Science such as 'Maharishi Sthapatya-Veda, the science of Vedic architecture and town and home planning in accord with Natural Law; Maharishi Gandharva-Veda, the science of creating balance in individual and collective consciousness through music; Maharishi Jyotish, the Vedic Science of astrological prediction; and Yagya, the programmes for removal of obstacles resulting from cosmic influences.'

Every morning and evening users of TM meditate for 20 minutes. There are three major differences from most forms of meditation with mantras. First, the TM mantra has no meaning (in ECKANKAR, for example, the mantra 'HU' is supposed to be a sacred name of God); it is the sound itself which is sacred. Second, it isn't chanted, either aloud or mentally; instead, the meditator 'thinks' the sound. Third, says Kahn, 'The technique of TM is completely natural and effortless, involving no concentration or effort, and also not involving "thinking about" something, as is found in contemplation techniques.'

The movement makes tremendous claims for the benefits of TM. It brings you in touch with your own inner self; regular use increases your creative intelligence; you will be healthier in mind and body, and will live longer. The organization quotes figures which indicate that TM practitioners spend less time in hospital, have a much lower incidence of heart disease, are more resistant to infections and are less likely to suffer mental illness.

Critics argue, first, that any form of meditation, yoga or conscious relaxation has similar beneficial effects; and second, that TM's figures are not statistically sound for various reasons, including the way that the non-TM control groups are selected. The movement strongly disagrees with this, citing 'over 500 scientific research studies conducted on Transcendental Meditation, of which nearly 200 have been published in independent, peer-reviewed scientific or professional journals . . . The benefits of TM, backed by that huge weight of scientific research, are not merely matters of opinion. They are established scientific facts . . . All the authors of studies on Transcendental Meditation took pains to ensure that their research did not suffer from bias.'

◆

The other major claim of TM is rather more startling. If a large group of people are practising TM at the same time, it will have a peaceful effect on the immediate area. So, for example, they claim that as a result of the practice of TM and Yogic Flying in the Golden Dome in Skelmersdale, reported crime in nearby Merseyside reduced by 60 per cent between 1987 and 1992 – *relative to national crime trends*, a phrase it is easy to miss; on questioning they say that crime went down by 15 per cent in Merseyside, while increasing by 45 per cent nationwide. The reduction occurred, they say, because in March 1988 'participation in the Transcendental Meditation and TM-Sidhi programme passed the critical threshold of the square root of 1 per cent of the population'.[15]

So for a population of 1 million, 100 people practising TM and Yogic Flying together will have a noticeable effect; for 10 million it's 316, while for the 56 million in the UK you would need 748 meditators. Less than ten times that, 7,000 people meditating together are enough to cause significant changes for the entire population of the world. TM claims that this was done in 1983 and 1984, and that crime, accidents and illnesses worldwide were reduced for a three-week period. On several occasions TM claims to have reduced international tension.

'I would like again to emphasize that our "claim" that this was done in 1983 and 1984 is backed by scientific research. For this reason we do not consider it a claim,' says Kahn.

Figures made available by Merseyside Police, however, do not seem to support TM claims. Figures were not made available to the author for 1987 and 1988, but total recorded crime in the whole Mersyside area in fact rose year by year between 1989 and 1992. Recorded crimes did reduce in 1993 and again in 1994, perhaps due to 'many policing initiatives which have all helped to either prevent or detect crime'. Unfortunately this does not seem to be a continuing trend. 'Regrettably there has been a recent increase in crime on Merseyside; the reasons for this are complex and numerous.'[16]

Guy Hatchard, author of the TM study on crime reduction, however, insists that the statistics 'substantiate a sustained fall in Merseyside crime when compared to national crime trends between 1988 and 1993'.[17]

Even if there was a reduction in crime, can TM claim the credit? 'My study carefully examined nine other possible causes of reduced crime and found no evidence that they had had any significant impact on crime. These included economic factors, population movements and police practice,' says Hatchard. His study used 'Time Series Analysis – the most sophisticated statistical technique available to analyse complex social data. Using this technique our conclusion that reduced crime was due to Transcendental Meditation participation was found to be accurate to 9,996 parts in 10,000.'

It is not known how localized the effects are, or how much they are dissipated by distance, though Hatchard adds, 'My study also examined crime trends in Skelmersdale and found a consistent trend of falling crime relative to other police districts in Lancashire very comparable to that reported in Merseyside.'

♦

Also controversial is another aspect of the TM-Sidhi Programme, started in 1976: Yogic Flying. Early photographs showing smiling young people sitting cross-legged in mid-air didn't show the mattress 30 cm (12 in) beneath their knees, but in recent years there have been Yogic Flying competitions open to the press. In physical terms, Yogic Flying is usually accomplished by sitting cross-legged, and first rocking, and then bouncing, until one is able to bounce 30 cm or more into the air. To the outsider it might appear ludicrous, and a far way from true levitation, but TM say it is the moment of maximum spiritual awareness.

'Yogic Flying is accomplished by first bringing the mind to a state of restful alertness through the practice of Transcendental Meditation,' says Kahn. 'Yogic Flying is a phenomenon created by a specific thought projected from Transcendental Consciousness, the Unified Field of Natural Law, the field of all possibilities. Yogic Flying demonstrates perfect mind–body coordination and is correlated with maximum coherence, indicating maximum orderliness and integration of brain functioning, as has been measured by EEG research. Even in the first stage of Yogic Flying, where the body lifts up in a series of short hops, this practice gives the experience of bubbling bliss for the individual, and it generates coherence, positivity, and harmony for the environment.'

♦

The TM organization says that TM isn't a religion. However there are many aspects of its beliefs and practices which are spiritual. At the *puja* ceremony, for example, when a new member is instructed and given his or her mantra, the Maharishi's spiritual lineage back through Guru Dev is recited, there is a typical Hindu offering of fruit and flowers, and a song of gratitude to Guru Dev is sung. The TM movement, however, stresses that this is not a religious ceremony.

TM, the World Plan and the Natural Law Party are inextricably linked. The basis and the ideals of the Natural Law Party are clearly spiritual: 'Natural Law is the intelligence and infinite organizing power that silently maintains and guides the evolution of everything in the universe'; and 'a new principle . . . by which human life can be raised to the same level of perfection with which Natural Law eternally governs the entire universe'.[18]

TM itself might not be a religion, but such spiritually cosmological principles behind a political party very clearly underlie the basis of all religion – though Kahn sees it differently. The Natural Law Party, he says, 'was founded to bring the light of science into politics. It offers conflict-free politics and problem-free government. It is the only party offering programmes that are scientifically proven (other parties offer something that they *think* and *hope* will work), and it is the only party to put man and his happiness at the centre of politics.'

There is some concern among non-members about the political aspirations of the TM movement. History suggests, they point out, that however laudable their aims, and however godly their religion, we should beware of theocratic governments. Any religious movement hopes to improve society in one way or another, but the Natural Law Party, in addition to 'Stimulating the economy and eliminating unemployment . . . Lower taxation for all . . . Creating a healthy nation . . . Energy and environment creating a pollution-free nation' and other unarguably attractive manifesto headings, also promises, 'We will educate the population in Natural Law' and 'The first action of the Natural Law Party will be to implement programmes to eliminate negativity in collective consciousness.'[19]

SCIENTOLOGY

Scientology[20] is probably the most well known, widespread and wealthy of all the Personal Development organizations – and the most attacked. Arguments have raged for years over whether it is a religion or not. Some Scientologists have said that it isn't a religion at all, but simply a very efficient way of helping people deal with their lives. Critics have suggested that L. Ron Hubbard turned Dianetics, his original psychotherapy system, into the Church of Scientology because of the tax advantages of being a religion. Supporters say that whatever attacks are made on them, they believe in Dianetics and Scientology because they work. Critics say that whether Dianetics and Scientology are a religion, science, education system or therapy, the behaviour of senior Scientologists over the last couple of decades has been both illegal and immoral. The Church says that it has dealt with these problems.

Although the Church of Scientology provided several books and booklets, it did not in the end respond to repeated requests for answers to criticisms, despite agreeing to do so.

BELIEFS AND PRACTICES

The aims of Scientology are: 'A civilization without insanity, without criminals and without war, where the able can prosper and honest beings can have rights, and where man is free to rise to greater heights.'[21]

Before Scientology came Dianetics, based on L. Ron Hubbard's new theory of how the mind works. Our unconscious or 'reactive' mind stores the trauma of every unpleasant thing that has ever happened to us, in an almost pictorial form known as an 'engram'. Though we may forget the original incident, the engram is still active and may be triggered by association. For example, on a fine, sunny day you step out of a bakery in a seaside town and begin to cross the road; a blue car pulls out to overtake a red bus; it catches your leg, causing no serious injury, but it is at least momentarily painful, and quite a shock, and for a moment you're stunned. Although your conscious mind may eventually forget the incident, your reactive mind stores every detail. For the rest of your life the sight of a blue car or a red bus, or the smell of a bakery, or the cry of a seagull, or even the fact that it is a fine, sunny day, might trigger a 'remembered' pain in your leg, or cause you to start shaking with shock.

According to Hubbard, some of the most powerful engrams are received while you are still in the womb. The original *Dianetics* book, published in 1950, contains graphic accounts of a husband yelling at his pregnant wife and striking her in the belly. The foetus hears its father's words, and the reactive mind stores them. Though it cannot understand them at the time, those same words, heard in other contexts by the adult decades later, could trigger the engram, perhaps causing deep feelings of being unwanted or under attack.

(Hubbard appears to have had rather a negative image of marital relationships. In *Dianetics*, husbands are always beating up or raping their pregnant wives, and wives are forever trying to abort unwanted children. Such incidents lie behind many of the foetal engrams he describes.)

Through auditing, such engrams can be deleted. The auditor asks the subject questions, leading him or her back to the original incident which caused the engram. Once it is identified, its power is dissipated. The subject, known as a pre-clear (PC), holds two tin cans which are connected to an E-Meter in front of the auditor. In a similar way to a lie-detector, this measures electro-magnetic skin conductivity and resistance. After all engrams have been identified and disposed of, the PC goes Clear.

Many former Scientologists, who have left the Church for a variety of reasons, still believe in the efficacy of Dianetics. Like all forms of psychotherapy, counselling and confession, it clearly works to some extent and has some obvious benefits. At the very least, by unburdening themselves of their guilts and hang-ups, PCs feel better. Auditing sessions also seem to induce something akin to a light hypnotic trance, which leaves the PC feeling a 'buzz' of well-being – during which they are encouraged to write a euphoric report of the benefits of the session and sign up (and pay a deposit) for the next one.

◆

If this were all there was to Dianetics and Scientology few people, except perhaps the psychiatric professions, would find too much to worry about. But disposing of all the engrams acquired during your life, and even since conception, is not enough to enable you to go Clear. You also have to deal with any engrams from previous lives which are still troubling you. Scientology, like many other religions, believes in a form of reincarnation. Through auditing, you can recall aspects of your previous lives and dispose of the engrams. Eventually all engrams have gone and you have achieved Clear.

The precise meaning of 'Clear' seems to have changed over the years, but one definition is: 'A person who can be at cause knowingly and at will over mental matter, energy, space and time as regards the first dynamic (survival for self). A Clear is a being who has attained this state by completing the Saint Hill Clearing Course and has been declared Clear by the Saint Hill Qualifications Division.'[22]

At one time, to go Clear was the ultimate goal. The book *Dianetics* claims that someone who has reached Clear will have better health, better eyesight and hearing, will be able to deal with any psychosomatic illness and will have greatly increased intelligence. He (or she) will have become the optimum man (or woman). 'A clear, for instance, has complete recall of everything which has ever happened to him or anything he has ever studied. He does mental computations, such as those of chess, for example, which a normal [sic] would do in half an hour, in ten or fifteen seconds . . .'[23]

To reach Clear normally takes several hundred hours of auditing, which can cost several thousand pounds.

Hubbard distinguishes between the lesser state of 'release' and Clear: 'But a clear is a clear and when you see it you will know it with no further mistake.' It is necessary for an auditor to check over the next few months that there are no new engrams in the reactive mind, but if there are not, then 'the clear is definitely and without question, cleared. And he will stay that way.'[24]

The book speaks of many 'cases' having been cleared. In the early 1950s there were several well-publicized Clears – and some disastrous attempted public demonstrations of their powers. But all of these early Clears seem to have been forgotten by the mid-1960s. In a magazine published in 1967, we read:

> Saint Hill, February 14, 1967. A year ago to this day exactly, John McMaster completed his auditing on the Saint Hill Clearing Course to become the first Clear. On March 8, 1966 it was made official when John flew back from a Worldwide assignment in the United States and was checked out Clear by the Qualifications Secretary at Saint Hill. Shortly thereafter the news went out to the world in *Auditor* 14 that the last barrier to total spiritual freedom for Man had been vanquished by the incredible technology of L. Ron Hubbard.[25]

The Church says, 'Did L. Ron Hubbard go Clear? Yes. In order to map the route for others he had to make it himself,'[26] but in fact at that point Hubbard himself hadn't achieved Clear. He became Clear number 54, and his wife Mary Sue was Clear number 208. By the anniversary of John McMaster becoming the first Clear, there were 234 Clears; just over a year later there were 1,000 and by 1995 over 45,000 people had reached Clear.

The word 'technology', usually shortened to 'tech', is important. Hubbard had developed a process which, if followed exactly by auditors and pre-clears, would lead to Clear. No deviation from the tech was allowed: auditors could not add refinements, or even ad lib encouraging noises; PCs could not short-cut the process.

This is why, says the Church, they are so opposed to anyone else using the methodology Hubbard designed. Unless it is done *exactly* as he laid down, it can do more harm than good; not only does it not work, but it can actually damage people, making any Scientology-lookalike organizations not only charlatans but actively dangerous. The only organization which uses the correct methodology is the Church of Scientology; the tech is kept pure by the Religious Technology Centre: 'a non-profit organization formed in 1982 to preserve, maintain and protect the Scientology religion. Religious Technology Centre holds the ultimate ecclesiastical authority regarding the standard and pure application of L. Ron Hubbard's religious technologies'[27] (see also p. 265–6).

♦

More, perhaps, than in any other religious or semi-religious organization, there is a spiritual career path in Scientology. The road to Clear (Hubbard, in nautical terms, called it the Bridge) is 'reached by small certain steps, not by huge leaps'.[28] Not everything is revealed at once. As PCs progress up the ladder to Clear and beyond, they learn more and more of the philosophy which makes this a religion rather than just another form of psychoanalysis.

The cynical outsider might observe that if the new recruit had any idea what he was going to be expected to have to believe in a few years' time, he would never join any new religious movement. The believing insider would observe that in all areas of life there are things you can't understand or appreciate until you've had a progressive grounding in the subject. There's no point in handling theoretical physics to someone who hasn't grasped basic algebra; you don't expect someone struggling with their first French irregular verbs to appreciate fully the great French novelists and poets. So, as knowledge increases, understanding increases, and as understanding increases, more knowledge can be revealed. A fundamental precept of Scientology is: 'Be very, very certain you never go past a word you do not fully understand.'[29]

Again, as in many other alternative religions (and in semi-Esoteric organizations such as the Freemasons), there are clearly defined levels of attainment on the way up the career path, marked by levels of initiation, courses or grades. The completion of each level is the starting point for the next level up. There is always both an immediate goal to be aimed for, the next level, and an ultimate goal, the end of the path or the top of the ladder – the mountain peak. You start as one of countless millions, knowing nothing. Very quickly you become one of a few thousand, knowing something. As you progress through the levels you become more and more one of the select few.

Once a religion has been around for a while, the select few at the top of the ladder become a not-quite-so-select many. The solution to that is simple: when you eventually reach the ultimate goal, you discover that it is in fact just another staging post, the bottom level on a new, higher, more esoteric path, the first rung of another ladder.

The outsider might say that this is a clever way of keeping people within the religion; otherwise, once they've reached the top, where else is there for them to go except out? The insider might say, quite reasonably, that there is always more to be learned.

The new Scientologist learns early on that his inner self – what other religions might call his individual soul – is called a Thetan: 'the person himself . . . the identity that IS the individual'.[30] Beyond Clear is a further ladder: levels of Operating Thetan (OT) I–VIII were available before Hubbard's death, and there are currently 15 levels, though OT IX to OT XV are marked 'Not yet released' on the *Bridge to Total Freedom*, the Scientology Classification Gradation and

Awareness Chart of Levels and Certificates. Most of the first eight have apparently been redefined: OT I and OT IV–XV are described as 'New' on the chart.

It is vital, of course, that the knowledge gained at these very high levels is kept secret. If the most junior member were able to find it out, says the cynical outsider, it would remove the entire spiritual career structure. The junior member is not ready for such powerful higher knowledge, says the believing insider.

(As an analogy, trainee Anglican priests might be taught at theological college the academic principles of 'demythologizing' Christianity, but it doesn't do to let *hoi polloi* know that one is allowed to doubt the virgin birth, as the former Bishop of Durham found to his cost.)

Operating Thetan III ('The Wall of Fire') is the big revelation. The knowledge revealed at that level is so explosive, it must be kept secret. Anyone coming across it without the years of careful (and very expensive) training through all the preceding levels would be seriously damaged, and might even die from the knowledge – it is apparently 'rigged to kill' them. Even Hubbard himself nearly died learning of it. Scientologists at OT III level are allowed access to Hubbard's handwritten notes of his own experience.

Here, in brief, is a paraphrase of the OT III revelation.* Seventy-six million years ago a dictator named Xenu, worried about the overpopulation of the galaxy, persuaded the billions of people of the 75 inhabited planets in the Galactic Federation he ruled to go to earth (or Teegeeack). There he chained them up in volcanoes in Hawaii and dropped H-bombs on them. This was sufficiently traumatic to separate their inner selves (Thetans) from their bodies, and the bodiless Thetans were taken to Hawaii and Las Palmas, where they were frozen in alcohol and put in packages which were scattered around the solar system. They also had engrams implanted in them, including religion and sexual perversity. These Thetans, wanting to have bodies again, hitch a ride on the humans on earth. We are each covered in millions of 'Body Thetans' – which accounts for all the troubles of the human race over the millennia.

Once a Scientologist has reached OT III, he is enabled to deal with these Body Thetans, very carefully and precisely, in the same sort of way as dealing with engrams. Instead of being led by an auditor back to, say, a car bumping him on the leg, or a pre-birth memory of his father shouting at his mother, he is led back down the time-track to 76 million years ago, and helped to deal with the original trauma. The Body Thetans can then be woken up and encouraged to leave (or 'blow') from the Scientologist's body. This has to be done with great care, though; Body Thetans can cause illness and insanity if they become upset.

All religions have their central myths and this is the hidden myth at the heart of Scientology. There are further revelations beyond this – the new OT V is called 'The Second Wall of Fire', and the new OT VIII is called 'Truth revealed' – but their contents are not known.

◆

There was another whole set of mythology in Hubbard's 1952 book *The History of Man*, which was apparently produced by Hubbard while lying on a couch in company with an auditor and a tape recorder. As Christopher Evans points out,[31] the free-association images poured out when one is in a semi-trance-like condition,

---

*A note to the trepidatious: thousands of non-Scientologists have now read this without coming to any apparent harm.

just like the hypnagogic images which can flash randomly across someone's mind when they are falling asleep, are not normally taken at face value by psycho-analysts. Hubbard put them in a book.

The History of Man, according to the introduction a 'factual account of your last sixty trillion years', details the evolution of mankind through clams, molluscs known as Weepers or Boohoos, sloths, apes and the by-then-not-yet-disproved Piltdown Man. An Australian official inquiry into Scientology commented: 'For compressed nonsense and fantasy it must surpass anything theretofore written.'[32] Scientologists take the book as straight fact.

HISTORY

Scientology was founded by Lafayette Ron Hubbard (1911–86), a prolific and very much a hack science fiction author of the 1940s. (It is instructive to compare the opinions of Scientologists, most of whom, unlike in the early days of Dianetics, aren't SF fans, and SF fans, most of whom aren't Scientologists, on the quality of Hubbard's novels.)

SF experts have pointed out similarities between Hubbard's Dianetics and the fictional 'Science of Nexialism', a beneficial form of intense psychological conditioning, in some of the earliest stories of SF writer A. E. van Vogt, a close friend of Hubbard in the 1940s.

There is a widely quoted story, which may or may not be apocryphal, that Hubbard and a fellow SF writer were talking one night about that perennial preoccupation of writers, money. 'The easiest way to make a lot of money,' Hubbard is reported to have said – paraphrasing Eric Blair (George Orwell) by design or accident – 'is to found a new religion.' Another version of the tale is that Hubbard said this at a meeting. This is denied by the Church, which calls it 'an unfounded rumour'.[33]

Whatever the truth of it, Hubbard founded a new religion and made a lot of money.

Hubbard's life pre-Dianetics, including his military career and his time as an 'explorer', is a source of some controversy. There are persistent reports that he was involved in some way with 'the Great Beast' Aleister Crowley, British leader of the Ordo Templi Orientis. He deserted his first wife, Margaret (Polly), and his two children, and apparently took his best friend's girlfriend Sara, bigamously marrying her before divorcing his first wife.

Just a few of the conflicting claims about Hubbard's life will be mentioned here:

- Hubbard claimed to have travelled the world as a young man, and to have been an explorer. His opponents say that although he travelled, his claims of exploration are fictitious, or at least highly exaggerated.
- Hubbard claimed to have studied nuclear physics in 'the first [course] of its kind ever'. His opponents claim that he signed on for the course for one term, while studying other subjects, and that he failed the course with a D grade.
- Hubbard claimed to have at least two doctorates. Opponents claim he bought them for $20 or so from a mail-order 'college'.
- Hubbard claimed to have been a naval commander and a war hero. His opponents claim that he was only ever in command of an escort vessel on

one occasion, that he ordered it to open fire on an uninhabited island and that he was court-martialled for it.

- Hubbard claimed to have been invalided out of the US Navy with severe injuries. His opponents claim that the only medical treatment he had was psychiatric, and also for a duodenal ulcer.
- Hubbard claimed to have won 21 medals and decorations during the war; according to his US naval record the total was only four.

Hubbard was, by profession, a storyteller. According to fellow SF writers, he could produce detailed plots of SF stories off the top of his head. At American Fiction Guild lunches, everyone told tall stories about their exploits; the difference was that Hubbard seemed to expect people to believe his.[34]

The authorized version of Hubbard's life and endeavours is well documented by the Church.[35] It includes his achievements as an explorer, scholar and scientist.

At one point Scientologists claimed that Hubbard's true role in the Second World War was highly classified because of his intelligence work, and so could never be proved by official documentation. The Freedom of Information Act put paid to that. At another point they claimed that official Government and Naval records had been tampered with by enemies of Scientology. Then the Church decided that there should be an official, Scientology-approved biography of Hubbard. The person researching it, Gerry Armstrong, the stepson of Heber Jentzsch, President of the Church, was so disturbed by the disjunction between the 'approved' story and the facts that he left Scientology, taking sufficient information with him to prove the vast differences between the fiction and the truth. The Church tried everything it could in the courts to force Armstrong to hand back the material. In May 1984 Los Angeles Judge Paul G. Breckenridge commented: 'The organization clearly is schizophrenic and paranoid, and this bizarre combination seems to be a reflection of its founder. The evidence portrays a man who has been virtually a pathological liar when it comes to his history, background and achievements.'[36]

The Church sees Hubbard differently: 'Every few hundred or a thousand years, some genius rises and man takes a new step toward a better life, a better culture. Such a man is L. Ron Hubbard, the Founder of Scientology.'[37]

♦

Although a short piece about it was published in the Winter/Spring issue of the *Explorers Club Journal*, details of the new science of Dianetics were first revealed to the world in April 1950 in a 40-page article in the magazine *Astounding Science Fiction*,[38] to which Hubbard was a regular fiction contributor. Its influential editor, John W. Campbell, like many other SF writers and readers at the time, was initially an enthusiastic supporter of Dianetics, and had been plugging it in advance for months. (SF writer Isaac Asimov was an exception. He thought that Dianetics – 'out of which Hubbard would make his fortune and gain his godhead' – was 'gibberish'. According to Asimov, Campbell 'had broken with Hubbard and was out of the dianetics movement' by May 1951.[39]) Writer A. E. van Vogt initially ran the Los Angeles Dianetic Research Foundation, but split away early on to run his own version, firmly based on Dianetic principles, but without Hubbard's later religious ideas and, perhaps more importantly, without Hubbard.

The British SF writer and editor George Hay was secretary of the British Dianetics Association in the early 1950s and was probably the first to invite Hubbard to Britain. Hay has not been involved with Scientology for many years, but recalls the first meeting with Hubbard: 'This was in the early 50s, when Dianetics was being transmogrified into Scientology and the whole subject was liable to change overnight. Any scepticism this might have created was cancelled out by the combination of Hubbard's extraordinary powers (I can vouch for it that he could read minds as a matter of routine) and the gains that members of the group were getting.'[40]

The process of Dianetics worked for a lot of people; it was the organization which seemed to cause the trouble.

♦

In May 1950 Hubbard published *Dianetics, The Modern Science of Mental Health*, which laid down the basics of Dianetics, including the removal of engrams by auditing. The book was an immediate bestseller in therapy-conscious America, and small Dianetics groups sprang up all over the country.

Right from the very start there were problems. The Hubbard Dianetic Research Foundation was founded in 1950, and in 1951, when money was short, cash was put in by Don Purcell, who became President of the Foundation. In 1952 the Foundation went bankrupt and Hubbard sold all his interests to Purcell, including the copyright of the *Dianetics* book. Hubbard next founded the Hubbard Association of Scientologists International, and began suing Purcell for using his ideas. In 1954 Purcell, now associated with an early Dianetics splinter group, Synergetics, handed back the Dianetics copyrights to Hubbard.

In 1955 the Church of Scientology was incorporated as a non-profit making society. Within three years the US Internal Revenue Service (IRS) was attempting to withdraw its tax exemption.

In 1959 the E-Meter was developed, not by Hubbard, but by Volney G. Mathison. Although this very quickly enabled Dianetics auditors to run their sessions on a more scientific basis, it also got Hubbard into further trouble. In 1963 the powerful Food and Drugs Administration (FDA) raided the Scientology church in Washington, removing E-Meters on the grounds that it is illegal in the USA to practise any form of medical diagnosis or therapy unless qualified. A 1969 ruling allowed the use of E-Meters only on the assumption that they were totally ineffective in treating illness.

♦

According to the Church, the attacks on Dianetics and Scientology all originated from one source. After discussing the 'groundswell of public enthusiasm' which greeted the publication of the original *Dianetics* book in 1950, the Church continues: 'There were, however, a scant few among society's ranks who were not quite so enthusiastic, i.e. certain key members of the American medical/psychiatric establishment . . . They were well entrenched and well connected; and when they decided that Dianetics must be stopped to preserve their kingdom, they were fully prepared to make use of every one of those connections.'[41] These 'connections' apparently included the US intelligence services, the FBI, the IRS and the FDA. Thus began a bitter fight between the Church and the authorities.

L. Ron Hubbard was implacably opposed to the psychiatric profession, and the Church continues his campaign today. Most of the chapter 'Those Who Oppose Scientology' in *What Is Scientology?* is a virulent attack on the psychiatric profession; so is the first third of the 90-page brochure *A Description of the Scientology Religion.*

It began, perhaps, when two leading medical and psychiatric journals turned down Hubbard's initial paper on Dianetics. It was perhaps understandable that psychiatrists would not welcome a book on their subject written by a layman who told them that they were completely wrong. But it is more than simple pique on both sides. The psychiatric profession and Scientology appear to view each other as equally dangerous. The Church campaigns strongly against psychiatric malpractice around the world, including psycho-surgery, electro-convulsion therapy and personality-altering drugs. Through its Citizens Commission on Human Rights 'the Church has relentlessly exposed psychiatric criminality and oppression'.[42]

The psychiatric profession, according to the Church, is still attacking them, and is still behind other attacks on them: 'The previous pages might lead one to believe that the forty-year assault against Scientology has assumed large proportions, but the source must be remembered – that small but influential circle of psychiatrists. Nor have the means changed over the years: false allegations selectively planted in the media, then seeded into federal files as background "fact".'[43]

The battles continued. The Church of Scientology has clashed with governments around the world, and is rarely out of the courts. It has been embroiled in legal fights in many countries in its attempts to be classed as a tax-exempt religion.

An Australian Board of Inquiry reported in 1965 that: 'Scientology is evil, its techniques evil, its practice a serious threat to the community, medically, morally and socially; and its adherents sadly deluded and often mentally ill.' Some of its criticisms were couched in slightly less vehement terms, but were no less condemnatory: 'Scientology is a delusional belief system, based on fiction and fallacies and propagated by falsehood and deception . . . the world's largest organization of unqualified persons engaged in the practice of dangerous techniques which masquerade as mental therapy.'[44]

That same year Scientology and the use of E-Meters were banned in Australia. The ban was not reversed until 1983, and in 1984 Scientology was ruled to be a tax-exempt religion.

In 1968 the UK government banned any foreign Scientologists from coming to Britain either as students or to work. This effectively cut Hubbard off from his headquarters at Saint Hill, East Grinstead. The ban was not revoked until 1980.

In 1978, Hubbard was convicted of fraud by a court in Paris, and sentenced *in absentia* to four years in prison.

In a 1984 court case in Britain, Judge Latey said: 'Scientology is both immoral and socially obnoxious . . . In my judgement it is corrupt, sinister and dangerous . . . it is based on lies and deceit and has as its real objective money and power for Mr Hubbard, his wife and those close to him at the top.'

In 1985, in both France and Denmark, tax exemption was revoked, on the grounds that Scientology was a profit-making venture. In 1988, Scientology was charged with the theft of government documents in Canada. Also in 1988, there were court proceedings against Heber Jentzsch, President of the Church of Scientology, in Spain.

It is hardly surprising that Scientology has felt for years that it is under attack. To quote a French saying about human nature, *'Cet animal est très méchant; quand on l'attaque il se défend.'* Scientology sought to defend itself by going on the attack, and proved itself in the process to be somewhat more than merely *méchant*.

A Suppressive Person (SP) was defined as any Scientologist who violated Ethics, which could mean something as slight as questioning an order. SPs were 'bounced' down the career structure and were effectively sent to Coventry: their friends and even their family were ordered to 'disconnect' from them and forbidden to communicate with them in any way (cf. the Exclusive Brethren, see p. 70).

In one period of troubles between 1965 and 1968, many Scientologists were expelled from the organization, a large number of these being declared SPs. In 1966 Hubbard ordered that any critics of Scientology should be investigated, and anything that blackened their character should be revealed with 'wide lurid publicity'. They were told bluntly, 'We will look up – and will find and expose – your crimes.' In a later reversal of these orders, Hubbard said, 'We have no interest in the secrets and crimes of people and no use for them.'

In October 1968 Scientology defined the principle of Fair Game against SPs, or any other perceived threat to Scientology: '[They] may be deprived of property or injured by any means by any Scientologist without any discipline of the Scientologists. May be tricked, sued or lied to or destroyed.'

In response to criticism, Fair Game was officially abolished only a month later, though opponents say that the principle remained, and still remains. Indeed, one ex-Scientologist, Stacy Brooks Young, who worked in the mid-1980s in 'the PR Division of the Guardian's Office, which by that time had been renamed the Office of Special Affairs', has said in court:

> As a result of this work I became very familiar with the policies and practices of Scientology with regard to individuals and groups that criticize the organization. I have personal knowledge that the practices which were formerly called 'Fair Game' continue to be employed, although the term 'Fair Game' is no longer used. These tactics are laid out in many of the key policies that are studied and applied by staff of OSA.[45]

(According to Anton Selfe, public relations officer in the Office of Special Affairs UK of the Church of Scientology, the statements made by Stacy Brooks Young were 'lies'.[46])

Publicity about Scientology's strict internal discipline caused rapidly decreasing recruitment to the movement. In 1969, worried by this, Hubbard issued a Policy Letter overturning the policy: 'We will never need a harsh spartan discipline for ourselves.'

John McMaster, the very first Clear in 1966, left the Church of Scientology in 1969, disenchanted with Hubbard himself.

◆

Hubbard resigned as Executive Director of the Church of Scientology in 1966, and took to the sea, setting up the Sea Org (organization). This was an intensive training centre mainly for young Scientologists, many of whom had been brought up in the Church and were unswerving in their loyalty to Hubbard. 'The Commodore' spent the next ten years sailing around the world, mainly in the

Mediterranean and the eastern Atlantic coast. The Sea Org ships were banned from several ports because of their lack of seamanship.

Shipboard life, it is said, was harsh for everyone except Hubbard, whose Messengers, mainly young teenage girls, did everything from cooking his meals and washing his clothes (with 17 rinses to remove the smell of soap) to lighting his cigarettes for him. For anyone who stepped out of line in even the smallest way, or anyone who irritated Hubbard for whatever reason, punishments were severe. These allegedly included being locked in the bilge tanks or the chain lockers, sometimes for days at a time, or being 'overboarded' – thrown over the side, sometimes with their hands tied together. According to former members, even young children were put in the chain lockers.

(In 1986, after Hubbard's death, Flag Order No. 3905 was issued, forbidding Sea Org members to have children. Anyone who ignored this directive and became pregnant was 'busted' to a position on the staff of a Class IV Org, a poorly achieving local Scientology centre, whose staff are paid out of the receipts from their sales of Scientology books and courses. Alternatively: 'Some of these women went through extensive pressure methods to convince them to have an abortion. The severity of the Ethics handling was directly proportional to the prospective mother's desire and insistence to keep the child . . . it was considered Out Ethics to get pregnant. [Out Ethics in Scientology simply means your reasoning facilities are no longer thinking in a direction designed to promote Scientology and must be corrected.]'[47] This is despite Hubbard having made it clear that he regarded abortion as murder.[48] According to Selfe, the entire story about abortions is 'off the wall, insulting and gross'.[49])

Members of the Sea Org sign a billion-year contract to Scientology. For years the Commodore's Messenger Organization were the most highly respected members of the whole organization. They were the closest of anyone to Hubbard.

Although he was technically no longer in charge, Hubbard's word was still law. Thousands of HCOBs (Hubbard Communications Office Bulletins) were sent out over the years, giving instructions, regulations, restrictions and admonitions to members of the Church.

♦

One of the criticisms most often levelled against Scientology is that it takes over its members' lives, ordering them to behave in ways they might prefer not to – for example, forbidding Sea Org members to have children. There is no doubt that it is authoritarian, with exact rules and regulations laid down for every possible contingency. The Church says that the rigid structure of auditing sessions is because the system has been proved to work, and that auditors should be discouraged from adding 'improvements' or 'refinements' of their own; it is the exact process of auditing which has results, not the personality of the auditor.

The Ethics procedure has also come in for much criticism. This is a definition of Ethics from a Scientologist who was in the Church from 1967 to 1992:

> Ethics is the method of keeping everyone's mind controlled into thinking and seeing one way only to the point of ignoring major faults in the Scientology leaders, the organizations and the Hubbard technology itself . . .
>
> Once you have bit the bait and have completely joined Scientology, you are channelled in that vein of thinking from there on out with the use of Ethics procedures.[50]

In answer to a question about brainwashing, the Church says, 'The exact opposite is true. Scientology makes people spiritually free and enables them to think for themselves.'[51]

Another former member is even more condemnatory of Ethics: 'As it is a mixture of Barry Goldwater's Republicanism, Nazism, the less esoteric elements of communism, the sickly sweetness of television Christianity and the philosophy of Soldier Termites, it does indeed have an uniquely embracing quality but, regrettably, it makes no allowance for people to 'do their own thing'.[52]

Even a minor infringement can lead to a Condition of Liability: 'The being has ceased to be simply non-existent as a team member and has taken on the colour of an enemy.'[53] The immediate penalty is to tie a dirty grey rag around your left arm. For a major infringement you have to appear before a Committee of Evidence (Comm Ev). Comm Evs rule on four classes of offence: Errors, Misdemeanours, Crimes and High Crimes.

High Crimes include, among many others:

Testifying as a hostile witness against Scientology in public.
Announcing departure from Scientology (but not by reason of leaving an organization, a location or situation or death).
Seeking to resign or leave courses or sessions and refusing to return despite normal efforts.
Continued adherence to a person or group pronounced a Suppressive Person or Group by the Hubbard Communications Office.[54]

This last includes having any contact whatsoever with your husband or wife if they have been declared an SP.

◆

The late Dr Christopher Evans, in his 1973 book *Cults of Unreason*, devotes over 100 pages to Scientology. After detailing some of the above, and much else besides, he concludes:

Scientology's future, at the time of writing, is very uncertain, but it seems that it has probably passed the low-water mark of public unpopularity . . . the time has probably arrived when one should concentrate on what Scientology is all about now, and not be too diverted by its tumultuous past . . . The closer I have looked at Scientology the more I feel that it is changing for the better, and the more eager I believe its leader and its adherents are to forget its past.[55]

Evans was a little premature in his optimism.

In 1966 the Guardian's Office (GO) was set up as a sort of intelligence unit. According to a former member who worked in it, this was 'a highly confidential section of Scientology management which was known as the Guardian Office until 1982 and is today called the Office of Special Affairs. This section of Scientology is responsible for dealing with all external public relations, all matters relating to civil litigation or criminal matters, all governmental relations such as the IRS, and all critics of Scientology.'[56]

Unfortunately, like many government intelligence agencies, GO took on the role of dirty-tricks department, apparently digging up dirt on its opponents, including lawyers, politicians, psychiatrists and troublemaking ex-members, with the aim of silencing them or blackening their names. Although the Church now says that this *never* happens,[57] ex-members claim that information was sometimes drawn from PC files, information given in strictest confidence by pre-clears in their auditing sessions – including their guilts, their fears, their hang-ups and their misdemeanours.

GO agents were infiltrated into the American IRS and other government departments in 1976, both to track down the 'black propaganda' which the Church claimed the US government was using against Scientology, and to keep an eye on what the government departments were up to, to 'borrow' intelligence files on politicians and celebrities, and to plant information themselves.

In 1979, Hubbard's third wife, Mary Sue Hubbard, and eight other senior Scientologists, were found guilty of a wide range of criminal activities. They were fined £10,000 and imprisoned for between four and five years. The head and deputy head of the Guardians, who had fled to Britain in 1977, received similar sentences when they were returned to the USA in 1980. After many appeals, Mary Sue Hubbard eventually went to gaol in 1983, serving only one year.

The Church of Scientology now says that the Guardian's Office,

> initially created in 1966 as a unit to deal with the Church's legal and external affairs . . . had been infiltrated and set up to fail in its mission to protect the Church. It was influenced to abandon its original mandate and established itself as an independent autonomous unit, answerable to nobody. It was isolated . . . even from the Founder of the religion.

By the late 1970s,

> the Guardian's Ofice had abandoned any pretence of following the principles described in Mr Hubbard's writings . . . a handful of GO staff members had been influenced to adopt an 'anything goes' approach in dealing with government discrimination against the Church. These dupes infiltrated and burglarized several US government offices to obtain copies of files maintained and circulated about the Church. Obviously such activity was illegal and directly violated Mr Hubbard's policies . . . GO managed to keep its operations secret from Church management, staff and membership.[58]

The Church doesn't say who GO was 'infiltrated' by, or who 'influenced' its staff.

What is Scientology? mentions 'IRS illegalities', 'IRS attacks' and 'IRS dirty tricks' against the Church, and the planned 'infiltration of the Church with a network of undercover agents and the manufacture of evidence. Forged documents were to be seeded into Church files . . .'[59] It doesn't mention the Guardians Office, or its activities against the IRS.

◆

In 1980, in declining heath, Hubbard became a recluse. Only a handul of senior Scientologists ever saw him again. He began work on his ten-volume 'Mission Earth' science fiction series (most of which was published posthumously, leading to claims that at least some of it was 'ghost-written').

With the bad publicity of the revelations of illegalities at the highest levels, and with Hubbard's hand no longer on the tiller, the Church began to fragment. The numbers of people signing on to Scientology courses dropped dramatically, with a consequent serious loss of income for the Church. At the same time, because of the rigid systems laid down by Hubbard in his literally thousands of HCOBs, it was easy for Scientologists to inform on each other, and for whatever reasons many senior people were 'busted' to much lower positions.

Into the chaos, in 1981, stepped 23-year-old David Miscavige, who had been one of Hubbard's most trusted aides as a teenager in the Commodore's Messenger Organization (CMO) within the Sea Org. He was already on the Watchdog Committee, set up in May 1979 and consisting entirely of Messengers; by September 1979 the Watchdog Committee had taken control of the senior management of the whole of Scientology. Now Miscavige set up the All Clear Unit (ACU), ostensibly to fill in for Hubbard and prepare for when he came back to open prominence. Miscavige hired and fired and replaced various members of the CMO and the GO, for many years the two most powerful bodies in Scientology. Some of those who were deposed had been in Scientology since Miscavige was an infant, if not before he was born, and were highly respected very senior figures.

Within months the ACU had authority over the CMO.

Critics see Miscavige's actions as a coup: the Young Turk clearing out the Old Guard, all those who might challenge his new authority. The Church today sees it differently: 'When the GO's criminal activities were discovered by those who today form the core of the Church's leadership, the GO was disbanded, no small feat since it was the GO officials who held corporate control' – which seems to conflict with the previous statement that 'GO managed to keep its operations secret from Church management'. The statement continues:

> Sadly, there were also some people in the Church, but outside of the GO itself, who sympathized with the GO . . . In some cases, it was the Scriptures themselves they wanted to pervert for their own ends. Given these people had proved themselves to be avowed enemies of L. Ron Hubbard and the religion, they were excommunicated . . . This cleanup of the GO was led by Mr David Miscavige, who removed all corporate control from the hands of the GO, and dismissed all personnel who had been involved in illegalities or attempts to alter Mr Hubbard's technologies. Mr Miscavige and a team of Church executives then set up an entirely new corporate and administrative structure for the Scientology religion which has since served to keep the religion pure and in accordance with the teachings laid out by its Founder.[60]

Miscavige set up two further organizations, this time as legally independent, external companies: the Religious Technology Center (RTC) and Author Services Incorporated.

The handover to the RTC, which was to have complete control over the doctrine of the Church of Scientology, was supposed to be with Hubbard's full assent, though handwriting experts have pronounced Hubbard's signature on the relevant documents to be a forgery.[61] The notary public who legally witnessed the handover document was David Miscavige.

Author Services Incorporated (ASI), was set up to control the massive publishing empire based on Hubbard's books, both non-fiction and fiction. These include the Mission Earth 'dekalogy', which Scientologists see as innovative, thought-provoking and inspiring, but which is generally regarded by the science fiction world as embarrassingly bad hack work. Non-Scientologists have suggested three possible – and quite legitimate – reasons for the Church's intensive publicity for these books: they bring in much-needed revenue; the reverence which Scientologists give to *anything* that Hubbard wrote; and the more subtle idea of the value of spreading Hubbard's name and ideas as far and wide as possible – in essence, religious PR.

> Although ASI was established as a for-profit, non-religious corporation, in reality while DM [David Miscavige] was COB [Chairman of the Board of] ASI the staff of ASI ran the entire Scientology network. ASI had complete control over the management of all Scientology orgs and missions, all Office of Special Affairs activities, all transfers of funds between church accounts and LRH accounts, every aspect of the life of anyone who was a Scientologist, whether staff or public.[62]

By early 1982 the entirety of Scientology was under the absolute control of Miscavige and a few hand-picked allies – almost none of whom, including Miscavige himself, held any official position within the Church. One of the few who did, David Mayo, had been Hubbard's right-hand man and his declared heir-apparent to the running of the Church. By the beginning of 1983, along with many others of the old guard, Mayo had been declared a Suppressive Person. He left the Church of Scientology and set up one of the many lookalike splinter organizations, the Advanced Ability Centre.

Unsurprisingly, Miscavige's 'cleanup' of the entire organization made many enemies for both him and the reorganized Church. 'Today, some of these same people, no longer part of the Church, are loudly and bitterly critical of the Church's current management. It is these few apostates who are most often the ones who spread vitriol in the media about Scientology and Church leaders.'[63]

The fact that the RTC and ASI are external companies protects Miscavige – who is still chairman of the board of RTC – from the fate which befell so many senior Scientologists at the time: being busted for Ethics offences and being deposed.

According to an ex-member who was the Organizing Officer for ASI in 1982, and who 'worked directly for David Miscavige . . . to carry out his orders concerning the staff of ASI', this was very carefully planned.

> I have firsthand knowledge of the establishment of the corporate structure of Scientology as it now exists, having worked with the staff who were responsible for creating it. The purpose of this activity was to create an impenetrable, legally defensible network of corporations such that neither the IRS nor any other legitimate agency of government could 'pierce the corporate veil' of Scientology organizations, thereby freeing Scientology management to transfer funds between organizations without concern for the law.[64]

Miscavige has thus been protected from any legal moves against the Church, because technically he is not involved in the Church itself. However, at the time of writing there are moves to bring Miscavige himself to court.

Meanwhile, yet another new body was set up within Scientology: the International Finance Police. Its job was to squeeze much-needed money out of the many small Scientology Missions, and apparently it did so with a vengeance. Many more senior members, unhappy with the aggressive purges of the new regime, left the Church, joining Advanced Ability Centres or other splinter groups.

Most of those who left or were driven out of the Church by Miscavige still believed deeply in Dianetics and Scientology. Unlike those who had left in earlier years because they were unhappy with Hubbard's authoritarianism, many who left at this time still supported Hubbard, believing that he had lost control of his own Church.

♦

Though some had believed as early as 1983 that L. Ron Hubbard was dead, his death was announced by the Church of Scientology on 27 January 1986.

Miscavige 'moved the seat of power from ASI to the Religious Technology Center (RTC) in 1987, because it was more defensible to run Scientology from a non-profit corporation than from a for-profit corporation. At that point he appointed himself Chairman of the Board of RTC ("COB RTC"), which is his current title.'[65]

The Church of Scientology was finally recognized by the US Internal Revenue Service as a tax-exempt religion in 1993.

According to the Church it has around 8 million members, 100,000 of these in Britain. As these figures include people who have only had one or two introductory auditing sessions, it is not known whether they are current or cumulative.

CODA

Scientology has attracted vociferous criticism for many years. Numerous books have been written about it by opponents, including ex-members; other ex-members, some of them very senior, have split away to found rival organizations. The Church has terms for such opponents. Those who attempt to alter Scientology in any way are known as 'squirrels', presumably because they must, by definition, be nuts. Those who attack the Church are simply 'Enemies'. Another often-used term is 'wogs', meaning everyone who isn't a Scientologist. Many critics see this as offensive or uncaring, especially considering that Scientology's declared aim is to benefit the world.

In *What Is Scientology?*, the Church gives its answer to the question 'Why do some people oppose Scientology?'

There are certain characteristics and mental attitudes that cause a percentage of the population to oppose violently any betterment activity or group. This small percentage of society (roughly 2½ percent) cannot stand the fact that Scientology is successful at improving conditions around the world. This same 2½ percent is opposed to any self-betterment activity. The reason they so rapidly oppose Scientology is because it is doing more to help society than any other group.[66]

The very name Scientology has over the years acquired a bad reputation, which makes many people instantly suspicious. Possibly in part to avoid this, the Church of Scientology has set up a large number of different organizations under a wide variety of titles – many of them, to be fair, involved in very worthwhile areas of humanitarian work. These include the drug rehabilitation programme Narconon, the Citizens Commission on Human Rights, Committee on Public Health and Safety, American Citizens for Honesty in Government, Committee for a Safe Environment, National Commission on Law Enforcement and Social Justice, Religious Research Foundation, Concerned Businessmen's Association of America and The Way to Happiness Foundation – this last to improve society by improving individual morals and manners.

At the time of writing, the Church of Scientology is embroiled in a new controversy, over whether members, ex-members and opponents of Scientology should be allowed to discuss (and thus quote) the beliefs of the Church on the Internet. The Church is taking legal action against writers and operators of the Usenet discussion group alt.religions.scientology, this despite a clause in its Creed which reads: 'That all men have inalienable rights to think freely, to talk freely, to write freely their own opinions and to counter or utter or write upon the opinions of others.'[67]

It should not be forgotten that L. Ron Hubbard was a prolific pulp writer of science fiction and fantasy. The Church of Scientology points out that he also wrote in the western, adventure, romance, mystery and other genres, and says, 'Clearly the intention of those who attempt to classify Mr Hubbard as only a science fiction writer is to cast the shadow of "science fiction" over Dianetics and Scientology.'[68] It cannot be denied, though, that many of the teachings of Scientology – particularly the OT III revelation about Xenu, but also the 'superman' concept of the Clear and of the Operating Thetan – have science fictional overtones.

The veteran British SF editor George Hay mentions one of Hubbard's early novels, *The End Is Not Yet*, originally serialized in John W. Campbell's *Astounding Science Fiction* magazine in 1947. According to Hay, in this novel 'Hubbard outlined the reasons for the success *and for the eventual failure* of Scientology, long before he had brought it into existence.' Hay points out that while the Church, through ASI and its publishing offshoots, 'has done a great deal to get his fiction back into print, this particular work, at the time of writing, has been studiously ignored. Hubbard used to warn of the times ahead when alleged "followers" of his would carefully suppress some of his key work.'[69]

CONCLUSION

CONCLUSION

In 1910 the philosopher William James published a book of lectures on the psychology of the religious impulse entitled *The Varieties of Religious Experience*. This current book certainly demonstrates that variety. People reach out to God, each in his or her own way. People *want* to reach out to God. People want a relationship with God. And they want a religious experience. A variety of people require a variety of religious experiences. Who is to say that only one is right, and that all the others are wrong?

There are many reasons why people start a new religious movement – though very often they never actually intended to. But one of the reasons why people join what in this book we have called an 'alternative' religious movement is that the established religions and denominations have left them cold, have not answered their needs. There is obviously a place for middle-of-the-road 'Churchianity' in all religions; some people want that. There is also a clear need for a social gospel, and it was a pleasant surprise to discover how many of the movements in this book place a high emphasis on social and cultural work – but not at the expense of their spiritual work, which has perhaps been one of the mistakes of mainstream religion in recent years.

In almost every case the religious movements in this book – which are only a small sample of the many alternative religions – have a fire in their hearts, a real, genuine zeal to experience God and to serve God, by whatever name, in whatever way. When the mainstream Churches wake up and shake the dust off themselves from time to time – as with the Jesus Movement of the 1960s and early 1970s – it is because they have rediscovered that fire; they have put a personal relationship with God, and a genuine spiritual experience, first.

It could be suggested that those 'new religions' which have been in existence for a century or more and which now have falling memberships have perhaps lost that initial burning zeal; they have become organizations, rather than movements. They have, to a greater or lesser degree, become part of the very establishment they once set themselves against.

Perhaps in every generation there is a need for new alternatives to the mainstream. Perhaps, rather than fearing this and fighting against it, we should welcome it. Perhaps we should even rejoice in the fact that people are finding spiritual fulfilment – that people are finding God – in new ways every day. And perhaps we should accept that their way need not be our way.

PERSONAL COMMENT

It's a little sad that several of the religious movements seem prepared at times to fudge the truth about their history. If the founder had an unpredictable temper, or if some of the initial claims can be shown to be untrue, or if the movement made some mistakes in its first few years, surely it must be better to say so, to be honest about the fact that humans, including themselves and their leaders, are fallible. It would present a warmer, more truthful face to the outside world, and such frankness might, in the end, actually attract more members. Those movements such as ISKCON which accept that they made some serious errors a few years ago, or like the Worldwide Church of God, which now accepts that many of its founder's teachings were wrong, deserve our admiration for their courage in admitting their mistakes.

Similarly, secrecy breeds suspicion. Several movements, including the School of Economic Science and the Emin, now seem to be making a determined effort to be more open about their beliefs and practices, more open to scrutiny, more publicly visible. This cannot have been easy after years of keeping themselves out of public view and their new openness can only be applauded.

◆

I am not a member of, or a believer in, any of the religious movements discussed in this book. I have attempted to treat them all fairly, but it is inevitable that some personal bias may have shown from time to time. I feel more drawn to some than to others; I have a sneaking admiration for some; I find others intellectually fascinating; a fair number leave me cold; and one or two I find positively chilling.

Some of the religions that don't attract me in the slightest have thousands, or even millions, of followers. In some cases I personally find this difficult to understand – not necessarily that the adherents believe in them (the entirety of man's existence offers ample proof that people will believe anything, and who's to say that they're wrong?), but that they are prepared to accept conditions of membership which I myself would find intolerable. But then, once you believe, you will be prepared to live the life demanded of you; this is one of the characteristics of those religions which some critics perceive as dangerous.

◆

Practically every book on 'sects and cults' includes (to use their popular names) the Moonies, the Children of God, the Hare Krishna movement and the Scientologists – 'the usual suspects', as someone called them when discussing this book. The ones which really hit the headlines, however, are quite different. They are the ones which cause mass death, either to themselves or to others: the People's Temple, the Branch Davidians, the Order of the Solar Temple and possibly Aum Shinrikyo.

(According to one detailed press report,[1] there was actually little or no evidence to link Aum Shinrikyo or its leader, Shoko Asahara, at the time of his arrest, with the deaths of 12 people by a poison gas attack in the Tokyo underground system in March 1995. At the time of writing the case against them has not been proved either way, and they are not included in the following discussion.)

The more sensible experts on religious movements point out that each of these was probably fine to start off with, but then, for whatever reasons, ran out of control. Jim Jones of the People's Temple began as a sound, fairly mainstream Christian minister; David Koresh is still praised as a brilliant and caring Christian leader by those who survived the massacre at Waco; the Solar Temple was an Esoteric movement, originally probably little different from many others.

Things went wrong with each of them, the leaders and their movements. The leader became a personality figure, a guru, a messiah, sustained and enlarged by the devotion of his followers. The teachings, particularly on the imminent end of the world, became more and more divorced from the mainstream. The difference between the holy elect (themselves) and the wickedness of the rest of the world became more pronounced. The leaders and the members became increasingly paranoid, suspecting persecution and, by their behaviour, inviting it. Everything came to a head, with the disastrous consequences which have filled our TV screens.

Religious movements going this far out of control are very much the exception, but many of those described in this book – especially 'the usual suspects' – are tarred with the same brush by the tabloid papers and by some of the cult-watching organizations. It is largely to counter this popular misperception – to be blunt, this injustice – that this book has been written.

The more outspoken cult-watchers continually warn of another Waco about to happen. For some, it is a very real fear. The danger is that by spreading this fear, they may actually cause the very thing they're predicting. Several of the movements in this book feel persecuted by the cult-watchers and by the press. Persecution breeds paranoia. Paranoia can turn an unorthodox but essentially harmless religious movement into a dangerous and potentially explosive cult.

♦

There is absolutely no doubt that, as the various cult-watchers claim, some people over the years have been severely damaged physically, mentally, emotionally, spiritually, socially – and, of course, financially – by their membership of some of the movements in this book. Against that, many millions have found fulfilment, whether spiritually or in some other way, and their lives have become better and happier as a direct result of their beliefs.

To condemn every alternative religion because of a few, even to condemn those few because – to be brutally realistic – over the years a few hundred people have been hurt, out of the millions of members overall, seems a little unfair. It's also denying people freedom of religion.

It was sometimes difficult for me, when researching this book, to persuade religious movements that I wasn't going to treat them in the usual antagonistic way – especially when I said that I would point out criticisms of them. When I examined them, I found that most of the movements which have received the most criticism now accept that they have made mistakes in the past and have altered their practices as a result.

It seems not just unfair but possibly dishonest for the more outspoken cult-watchers to continue to attack movements for what they were like ten, 15 or 20 years ago, instead of looking at what they are actually like today. If we were all to be judged solely on the behaviour of our early years, few of us would score high marks for maturity. Movements, like individuals, do grow up.

Of the four movements which have received the most publicity as 'dangerous cults' over the last 20 years or so – the 'usual suspects' mentioned above – one is still embroiled in controversy and litigation, but the other three seem to have put their troubled past behind them and to have matured into more 'socially acceptable' organizations.

♦

There is an alternative viewpoint, of course. I have not joined any of these movements. I have deliberately not filled this book with graphic case-histories of the horrific experiences of ex-members. Perhaps I have had the wool pulled over my eyes by a number of the movements I have examined. Perhaps they really are as corrupt – even evil – as some of the cult-watchers would have us believe. Perhaps these movements deliberately and blatantly lied to me, persistently and consistently, in their literature, in their letters and in personal discussions. One must accept the possibility that this could be so; even the most cynical sceptic can be hoodwinked by an expert.

But I have, in general, been impressed by the openness and honesty of those I have corresponded with and met. They may have been practising 'Heavenly Deception', telling lies to protect the greater Truth, but I honestly don't believe so, in the great majority of cases. It is my belief that most of them are completely sincere in their beliefs and practices, and that they are just as honest and truthful as representatives of any mainstream Church.

Sometimes one has to accept what people say, on trust. If this seems naïve, and some of the cult-watchers would certainly say so, I am heartened by the fact that my conclusions seem to be shared by the academic experts on alternative religions, who have conducted many exhaustive studies, and who have no axe to grind beyond the search for truth.

◆

In this Conclusion the word 'cult' is used from time to time. Generally it is used more to represent the feelings and attitudes of outsiders, non-members of the movements covered in this book – concerned family and friends of a member, the cult-watching organizations, the media – than to imply that the alternative religions actually merit all the pejorative baggage associated with the word 'cult'.

WHY DO PEOPLE JOIN ALTERNATIVE RELIGIONS?

One of the cult-watching organizations once gave the remarkable statistic that a quarter of recruits to the more recent alternative religions are Jewish by birth. This may or may not be accurate, but it does become understandable when the profile of new members of alternative religions is examined. They tend to be intelligent, well-educated young people who have often had a religious upbringing (the members of the Jesus Army are very much an exception). They have been brought up to accept the importance of religious belief, and they have been taken to church or synagogue since childhood, but they often become disillusioned with the religion of their parents. They see their parents as having an unquestioned set of beliefs; when (as normal teenagers) they begin to question what they have been taught, this is discouraged, often with horror at what the parents see as the youngster's rejection of God's truth.

When teenagers leave home to go to college or university, they are officially encouraged to think for themselves, to question, to challenge. They meet, perhaps for the first time, people from different backgrounds, with radically different belief systems; they are no longer sheltered from, or actively discouraged from befriending, Sikhs or Muslims or others from different cultures who believe in their own religion just as absolutely as they themselves had been brought up to believe in the Jesus of the Church of England or the Yahweh of the synagogue.

Prime recruiting time is when someone is at university, or later, when they have their first job and are living for the first time in their own flat, alone, in a new town.

Let's take as a fictional example a young man called Hugh. He was brought up in a religious family, in this case Christian, though it could just as easily be Jewish, Muslim or anything else. He's 22, he's just left university and started his first job, and he's living on his own in a town where he knows hardly anyone.

Hugh began with the best of intentions, to go to church every Sunday, and he found a good church with the same sort of flavour as the one he was brought up in. But there's no one to encourage him to go there every single week. One Sunday morning it's raining – or he wakes up with a hangover, or with a new lover, or he just can't be bothered – and he doesn't go. It can be very easy to break the habits of a lifetime when you're in a different environment. Once he's skipped church one Sunday, and then again the next week, by the third week he's established a new habit, of not going.

The new habit is easier, and the freedom of the new lifestyle is more fun, but Hugh feels guilty about it. He knows his parents would disapprove if they knew, so he doesn't mention it; and if they mention it he hedges, or even lies.

Hugh rationalizes things to himself. He's learned a lot in recent years; he's learned something about other religions, so he no longer accepts that his own is unique, even though he may still believe that it's right. But he's learned of some of the weaknesses or uncertainties or fallacies of the religion he was brought up in, and he's actually a little angry that these were hidden from him as a child. He begins to intellectualize his turning away from practising the faith of his fathers.

But Hugh hasn't actually stopped believing in God. With a child-like belief, he knows that God is missing him in his church; and strangely, Hugh is missing God as well. There's an old cliché about everyone having a God-shaped hole inside themselves. If you've been brought up in a religion and you've now turned your back on it, you become very aware of that hole. It might be something missing deep inside yourself, if you had a real faith before; or it might be something missing in your life, if your church-going was more of a habit than a deep commitment.

What Hugh misses most of all is the companionship, the fellowship, of being with other people whom he's known for years, singing hymns together, praying togther, going to Bible study together. He misses all of this, though he doesn't really admit it, even to himself. He's turned away, and it's now very difficult to turn back. It's like saying sorry after a serious argument; he would have to admit that he was wrong. But there's still that hole. It's empty, and it's yearning to be filled.

And then Hugh meets someone who seems so much more alive than him – the guy is bubbling with it; there's a visible joy in him; it's shining in his eyes. The two of them get talking. Hugh becomes more aware of the *something* that he's missing and he realizes that this other person has it.

The guy's going to a meeting that night; why doesn't Hugh come along? Or, 'Why don't you come back to my place for an hour or so? I've a couple of friends I'd like you to meet. I'm sure you'll get on with them.'

Hugh realizes very quickly that they're religious, and that it's not a religion he's familiar with; in fact, it's one of those peculiar cults. He's deeply suspicious of the whole thing. But there again, they're decent people (not at all like he'd have expected them to be), and he's not stupid – he's not going to fall for a religious con; he's sensible enough not to get sucked in.

Within a couple of months he's inviting other people along. It's the most important thing in his life. It *is* his life. People can see it shining in his eyes.

♦

That's one scenario. It's not the only one, of course, but it is a fairly common one. It's the picture as we often hear it described by many of the cult-watching organizations, which are opposed to most of the new religious movements and talk in terms of them sucking people in.

BRAINWASHING, INDOCTRINATION AND CONDITIONING

A lot of rubbish is talked about brainwashing: the classic headline of 'Evil cult brainwashed my daughter'. The cult-watchers are split on this subject. Some see evidence of brainwashing everywhere; others point out that true brainwashing is extremely difficult and very rare.

There has been evidence, in some of the alternative religions (the ones usually called cults) – and far more so in the past than today – that new recruits are put on a low-protein diet and are kept awake night after night while being force-fed the teachings of the religion. Physically and emotionally weakened, they begin to accept everything that they are told. They are made to obey the leader of the group which recruited them, in every tiny detail; his word is absolute law. How much more, then, must they revere the founder of the religion if he is still alive, or his successors, the present leaders of the religion, if the founder has passed on to greater things.

As they progress through the ranks, members are careful not to voice any doubts they might have about doctrine or practices. They see the example that is made of those who do open their mouths. They are encouraged to watch each other for signs of weakness, and report them. Never knowing who might be watching them, they follow the prescribed line with open enthusiasm and zeal.

It's very reminiscent of Germany in the Third Reich, or of the former Eastern Europe communist bloc.

This sort of indoctrination or conditioning has almost certainly occurred in several alternative religions in the past, and perhaps still does in a few. But this is very much the exception, not the rule. The parents of youngsters who join most alternative religions do not need to fear this sort of indoctrination.

There is, however, another form of conditioning, which is less aggressive, more subtle and probably longer-lasting. Let's return to Hugh, our new recruit. That great gaping hole in Hugh's life has been filled. What's more, he's with a bunch of really wonderful people who share this belief, and this life, with him. He's grown to love them and he knows they love him. And if he finds himself, in some dark moment, doubting what he's become involved in, he's got others to support him, to strengthen his faith. They are his friends. They pray together, and read the Bible or the founder's teachings together, and worship together, and encourage each other.

Anyway, if he left, he'd feel so guilty. Why? Because he'd turned away from God, and God reached out and found him and brought him back to himself. And this time, God has shown him the right way. No longer is it the tired old religion of his parents, with all its hundreds of years of meaningless rituals, and all its faults, so obvious to him now. Now it's the true way to God, as revealed by his prophet, the blessed one, the founder of the movement.

Hugh had actually been conditioned by his parents to accept the church they took him to. They weren't doing it cynically or maliciously; they were doing it out of love for him. Technically it's called socialization. It's perfectly normal parental behaviour, but it's conditioning all the same. But now Hugh has replaced that initial set of conditioning with a new set.

Anyone from Britain who has spent a few weeks driving on the Continent, or in America, knows the problem of switching from driving on the left to driving on the right. For the first couple of days they're extremely careful, until driving on the right becomes a habit, and then there's little problem – until they return home. Then they have to remember to drive on the left again. Initially, they can't just throw away the conditioning of the last couple of weeks and go back to normal; they have to superimpose yet another new set of conditioning on top: 'I must remember to drive on the left. I must remember . . .'

Hugh's new conditioning has to be strong, to overcome the previous 20-odd years of parental and other societal conditioning. Once it is in place, it's very difficult to shake. He not only has the new set of beliefs, which he has learned in such a way that they are internally consistent and completely logical; he has also become bonded to a new set of friends, had a genuine and powerful religious experience, learned to revere and love the prophet or founder of the religion and his (or more rarely her) teachings and forged a strong new commitment to God.

All of this is very real. To expect him simply to be able to throw it away and return to the church of his youth, without a titanic inner struggle, is unrealistic.

The cult-watching organizations, some of which offer extremely good 'exit counselling' to people who are leaving a new religion, report that this is one of the main difficulties they encounter, even with people who are happy to leave. Getting rid of new conditioning is not easy. There are professional 'deprogrammers' who are skilled at stripping away the recently acquired conditioning – though many people have doubts about the morality of the 'reverse brainwashing' which some of these deprogrammers appear to use.

◆

It is noticeable that many people with a strong religious belief will say, 'I know this is true' rather than, 'I believe.' This applies to many Christians in mainstream Churches, especially born-again Evangelicals, just as much as to those in many of the alternative religions. It is a deep conviction of belief, a certainty. This is what makes it so difficult to argue someone out of their belief when trying to persuade them to leave their movement. Quite simply, they know that they are right. Whatever logical arguments you, the outsider, put up are irrelevant.

Paradoxically, this explains why a number of former members of alternative religions are converted to Evangelical Christianity. They have met someone, perhaps an exit counsellor, whose conviction is even stronger than their own; they fight, with a great clashing of belief systems and a mighty battle of wills, and they are outclassed. Effectively, they have exchanged one set of certainties for another – and for one without the social stigma of belonging to a 'cult'.

What about the others, those who don't convert to another faith? An outsider, perhaps a concerned parent or friend, or a 'professional carer', is asking them to give up the absolute certainty they have, the safe, solid knowledge that they are right, and replace it with what? The doubts and uncertainties that most people who aren't committed believers have. It's hardly surprising that many people choose to stay with their movement, even if there are other things about it which might be less than ideal.

◆

In addition, a member of any religious movement feels a tremendous bond with other members. They share a common set of beliefs and they have shared experiences. They have worshipped, prayed and studied together; they have stood in the rain together, witnessing to passers-by, or selling flowers or candles. They are united, they are one body, far more so than a crowd of fans at a football match or a rock festival. Even in the secular world, people often find that if they join an organization – a charity, or a political or environmental group, for example – most of the people they then spend their time with are members of the same group. For someone in a religious movement, this is even more so: all their friends, all the people they trust, are also members. And not only do they not have any friends outside the movement; they have learned to mistrust anyone outside the movement. In addition, like the early Christians, they have faced persecution together – another strong bond. All of this is even stronger if they live in a community, however large or small.

If they leave, they are not only giving up their beliefs, which is difficult enough; they are giving up their friends – their *family*. They are turning their back on everyone they know and love and trust. Both socially and spiritually, fellowship is an important part of belonging to a movement. To leave it behind is not easy.

In addition, if you have been a member of a movement, and again especially if you have lived in a community, you have grown used to doing certain things at certain times. You get up and go to bed, you study and worship, you meditate and recite mantras, you eat, you do manual work, all at set times. In a very real sense, you can become institutionalized. When you leave the movement, you are suddenly thrust into a world of chaos, where *you* have to take decisions, seemingly every moment of the day, where *you* are responsible for filling every moment of the day with *your* choice of activity. Ex-prisoners find this a problem. It's now accepted that even recently retired people, or people who have been made redundant, find this difficult to cope with. It can be a major problem for many people who leave a religious movement after much more than a few months. They are confused by their new freedom.

There is a further reason why some people may be reluctant to leave a religious movement. Over the years they have been a member, they have invested a vast amount of their time and energy – a vast amount of their life – into it; not to mention, in many cases, a vast amount of their money. They have been through all the early training exercises, the discipline, the lower levels necessary to prepare them spiritually, emotionally and intellectually for the higher levels of the inner group of members. They have very nearly reached the highest rungs of the ladder. They have put in a tremendous amount of study and effort and sweat and tears (and money) to get there. How can they possibly give it all up now, when they are so close to the final peak, the ultimate secrets which have yet to be revealed to them?

If they do – if they say, 'Stuff it' and walk out – there is a further psychological problem they may have to cope with. Once they are outside, looking back at what they have done, what they have believed, how they have lived for the last several years, from the totally new viewpoint of an ex-member, they might be hit by the amount of time and effort and everything else – the amount of their *life* – that they have wasted, thrown away, given over to something which (with the blessed view of somewhat bitter hindsight) was so full of contradictions and idiocies and awfulness. How could they have been so *stupid?*

The anticipation of such a realization can be part of what makes it so difficult for someone to leave, even if they are desperate to do so.

◆

In 1994 the BBC screened a powerful drama series, *Signs and Wonders*, written by Michael Eaton, which was very clearly based on the popular perception of the Moonies. A young woman, Claire, played by Jodhi May, is 'rescued against her will' from a cult headed by a Far Eastern 'Father', by a professional deprogrammer (James Earl Jones). What was particularly well portrayed was Claire's confusion at being torn away from the religion which had become her entire life, her terror at the damnation which must surely now be awaiting her and her blazing anger at her concerned mother (sympathetically played by Prunella Scales).

It was also interesting – and quite definitely true to life – that Claire was intelligent and artistic, and came from not just a 'good, middle-class home', but a home where she had had a traditional religious upbringing. David Warner played her father, a rather unhappy middle-aged Church of England vicar no longer sure if he really believed in God.

Signs and Wonders was (like the fictional story of Hugh) just one example, one version of the story. It was powerful, but it was clichéd. It showed a little of the love and joy and wonder and responsibility that Claire felt while she was a member of the religion, but that wasn't the story the series was telling. It concentrated on the drama of the kidnapping and the horrors that Claire went through before she was 'of sound mind' enough to be able to cry in her mother's arms. It didn't say, 'Forget Claire's parents for a moment. Look at Claire. Is she happy where she is? Is she fulfilled? Is she at peace? Should we leave her be?'

The joy and peace which Claire experienced, and the austerity and discipline of her life in the movement, probably differed very little from those of a young nun in a convent. Yet Roman Catholic parents, though they may feel sad at losing their daughter, would feel pride that she had given herself to the Lord. It's all a matter of perception.

CULT-WATCHING ORGANIZATIONS

In some cases there clearly have been incidences of indoctrination, sleep-deprivation, frugal meals, authoritarianism, deception and other abuses. There is no doubt that they have occurred in the past, and are probably occurring right now, somewhere. From the outsider's point of view this is offensive, wrong, even evil. The cult-watchers have brought it to public attention, and rightly so.

But perhaps they sometimes condemn when there is no real need to condemn. There is another form of often unconscious conditioning: for an outsider to hear the name 'Moonies' or 'Scientologists' or 'Children of God', and to flip into attack mode. It's all too easy to commit the logical fallacy of generalizing from the particular, saying that because one individual youngster has been damaged by one individual cult, then everyone in that movement is in danger, and that it, and all other 'peculiar' religious movements, must be destroyed.

There are a few cult-watchers who seem to believe this, who appear to view every cult, every alternative religious movement, as a threat to society. Some of the anti-cult organizations were founded by ex-cult members; there is no one more vehement than a convert from one cause to another, whether it is an ex-smoker or an ex-Moonie. Some critics have found such organizations just as disturbing as the cults they are attacking, especially (though this activity seems to have diminished) those which encourage the practice of kidnapping young people back out of a religion and forcibly deprogramming them.

The activities of the more outspoken cult-watchers have been described as religious McCarthyism: they look for evil everywhere – and because they are looking for it, they are always able to find it.

Indeed, some of the cult-watchers have been accused of being over-selective in the information they present about cults – or, to use a recent cliché, of being economical with the truth. Some, for example, provide harrowing case-histories which may well be completely true, but which are 15 or 20 years old – without mentioning that the religious movement in question has moved on from its practices of that time. Such massaging of the facts could perhaps be 'justified' in the cause of the greater truth that the public must be made aware of the dangerous nature of cults – but this is rather reminiscent of Heavenly Deception, this time used against the religions, rather than by them.

◆

Whenever there is a major 'cult' story, such as the Branch Davidians' inferno at Waco, or the deaths of members of the Solar Temple, representatives of cult-watching organizations appear on the radio and television to give informed comment. The two to appear most regularly in the UK media are Eileen Barker, Professor of Sociology at the London School of Economics and founder of INFORM, and Ian Haworth of the Cult Information Centre (CIC).

There are 'cult-watching' organizations in most countries; the addresses of some are given on page 306. Four of the most prominent in Britain are INFORM, Deo Gloria Outreach, FAIR and CIC.

INFORM (Information Network Focus On Religious Movements) was set up, originally with government funding, to do precisely that: to inform the outside world about the beliefs and practices of new religious movements (NRMs), an accurate and neutral term coined by sociologists including Eileen Barker to avoid the pejorative overtones of the words 'cult' and 'sect'. It collects, analyses and provides information 'about the diverse beliefs, practices, membership, organization and whereabouts of new religious movements, and about the consequences of their existence'. The information which it provides is 'as objective, balanced and up to date as possible'. It also acts as the hub of an international network of useful contacts for those with an interest or concern about NRMs. It organizes seminars and provides speakers; it doesn't provide counselling itself, but can put inquirers, including concerned parents, in touch with trained counsellors.

Deo Gloria Outreach 'aims to provide information and help to those encountering problems as a result of the activities of groups known as new religious movements, and to arrange counselling. Such help is offered to anyone in need, irrespective of their own religious convictions. It is part of the Deo Gloria Trust, a non-denominational Christian charity affiliated to the Evangelical Alliance.'

FAIR (Family Action Information and Resource [formerly Rescue]) 'offers advice and support to families as well as individuals who have been adversely affected by cult involvement'. It appears to be concerned mainly about the separation of cult members from their families. In addition to supplying speakers and publishing fact sheets, it 'issues warning leaflets to put young people on their guard'. The word 'rescue' in their former name didn't mean kidnapping and deprogramming. 'FAIR provides advice for cult members, but an individual's decision to leave a cult must remain his/her own. FAIR does not seek to convert cult members to any other belief. It merely aims to restore them to that state of mind in which rational judgements can be made.'

Cult Information Centre 'is concerned about the use of deceptive and manipulative methods used by cults to recruit and indoctrinate unsuspecting members of society. CIC believes that these cult methods present a threat to the well-being of the individual and the family. Consequently CIC sees the need for gathering and disseminating accurate information on cultism and aims to meet that need.' It provides information to the general public and the media, gives 'preventative educational talks' to schools and colleges, and 'offers information and support to ex-cult members'.[2]

The different use of language by the four organizations is quite telling.

Several of the movements in this book mentioned cult-watchers. There was a wide range of comment, which reflected the different approaches of the different organizations. The two extremes of comment were on CIC and INFORM.

Several movements were very critical of CIC. One said that they 'give very biased information and they are unwilling to visit to find out for themselves. They are quite dangerous in this approach as they whip up hysteria and fear rather than informing the general public objectively. This kind of approach can lead to NRMs withdrawing from mainstream society. Also when ex-members contact an organization like CIC they are more prone to become bitter rather than being helped through what can be sometimes a difficult period of adjustment.'

The same movement said of INFORM, 'They approach the subject of new religious movements from a more scientific and empirical approach, and they are open to being liaisons between individuals in and out of groups, give out factual information, and are there more as mediators and to help. Ex-members are more likely to be helped through the adjustment period and get on with their lives without having to bitterly attack the group of which they were members.'

In fact, the movements which mentioned it praised INFORM for its fairness and objectivity, even when it says things they disagree with. One said, 'Prof Eileen Barker of the LSE is admirable. The rest behave like propagandists, which I believe most fair-minded, thinking people wouldn't take seriously.'

These quotations are representative of the comments of several of the religious movements on these organizations.

On the subject of professional deprogrammers, one movement was particularly damning: 'They tend to understand very little about people's faith or beliefs and are generally more interested in money making than in individual freedom or right to religious expression or spiritual needs which all men have.'

Throughout this book we have asked movements for their response to criticisms. We also asked the four cult-watching organizations mentioned here for their comments.

Eileen Barker, speaking for herself as a sociologist of religion, says, 'I try to provide information as accurate and balanced as possible about the general scene in which the new religions operate, including society's response to them. I set up INFORM because some of the information provided by both the movements themselves and some of the other cult-watching groups was inaccurate, and most of them provided only selective or biased information.' Information from the movements themselves tended to be biased in their favour, she says, and information from the cult-watchers was biased against them. She believes that 'the results of scholarly research should be made more accessible to the general public'.

Deo Gloria Outreach are sceptical about movements claiming to have moved on from their past practices. 'Religious movements may say they have moved on in their practices, and may even appear to have done so, but it is not generally found that this moving on is anything other than a shallow approach. Most people respond to criticism by changing their front image, do they not?'

Audrey Chater, chairman of FAIR, is vehement in her response not to the quotations above, but to the opening paragraph of the next section, which she states 'is wrong. Most people are recruited into cults, sects or groups, and my organization would never agree that they "join". This is done by deceitful practices and promises which put pressure upon the victim to make a quick decision and once that has been achieved it is very difficult for them to leave. In making the statements which you have made you overlook the fact that lives are ruined by cult recruitment and families suffer terribly. The problem of cult influence is not a religious one – it is a human rights issue.'

CIC did not respond to our requests for a comment.[3]

SINCERITY AND HUMAN NATURE

Most members of the new religions are sincere believers. There are obviously exceptions, but most people who join new religions do so willingly and gladly, without overt coercion.

To talk of deliberate brainwashing of recruits is to presuppose a high degree of cynical manipulation on the part of all those who are already members of an alternative religious movement. It implies that they know that their religion is actually a con and that its sole purpose is to suck in new recruits and their money.

It is possible that there is a small element of truth in this assertion, in a very few cases, though almost certainly not at grass-roots level. This section and the next will look at two Churches as an example.

There have been several examples of alternative religions being taken to court for tax evasion or corrupt financial dealings, and the plush lifestyle of some of the leaders of these religions is well known. Herbert W. Armstrong, founder of the Worldwide Church of God, had a private jet, always stayed in the best hotels and had homes (and college campuses) whose opulence could hardly be believed. His response to criticism of his lifestyle was straightforward: only the best is good enough for God, and by living in this way he could show the world how God richly blesses his servants. The many thousands of his 'co-workers' who supported the Church with their tithes were assured that they were furthering God's work by paying for his expensive suits and gold watches and tie-pins.

To take another often-quoted example, L. Ron Hubbard, founder of Scientology, is reputed to have said that the best way to make a lot of money is to found a new religion. When he died, Hubbard is believed to have been worth several millions: the proceeds of the expensive courses and books on Dianetics.

This does not, of course, 'disprove' their religions. The vast majority of members of the Worldwide Church of God and the Church of Scientology are completely sincere in their beliefs, and are (from their point of view quite rightly) offended by accusations of financial motivations in their founders.

Neither does it necessarily prove insincerity on the part of these leaders. Without firm evidence, it would be completely wrong to accuse Armstrong and Hubbard of being motivated by money. Indeed, careful reading of their books shows quite the opposite: they very clearly did believe their own teachings and were sincere in their beliefs.

But they were human. The last few years have shown several more mainstream Christian preachers to be all too human: Jimmy Swaggart and others have fallen from grace very publicly.

There are probably several explanations, but there is one very simple one which would be recognized by many ordinary middle-of-the-road Roman Catholic and Anglican clergymen who start off their vocation fired by zeal, and by middle-age are plodding through the motions, like Claire's father in *Signs and Wonders*. On a wet November Sunday evening they would far rather curl up with a glass of wine in front of a warm fire and the TV than go out to take a service. It's almost worse if the church youth see the Sunday evening service as their fellowship meeting, and the fading priest has to inspire them with a message, than if he is taking Evensong for three old ladies and the verger; in the latter case, despite the discouragement, he can at least feel like a martyr.

THE FOUNDER AND THE ORGANIZATION

Consider what it is like for the founder of a new religious movement. He starts off with a message and a store-front church. Ten years later he has a string of a dozen churches, a magazine and a regular radio programme. Another ten years and he has a vast organization, with hundreds of churches in dozens of countries, a headquarters and branch offices, two or three teaching centres and a couple of thousand employees. These include not just the leaders of all the churches, and the secretaries to deal with the mail, but an administrator and his team, a financial manager and his team, a publications manager and his team, a director of studies for the teaching centres and his teams, scriptwriters, editors, producers and technical staff for the radio and TV programmes, cooks, cleaners and gardeners and heaven knows who else. If he's going to preach, he can't just get up and do it. He needs the whole organization of a major theatre, with house manager, stage manager, director, ushers, an MC, a choir, supporting cast, lighting and sound crews, and the rest.

It's no longer a man with a message; it's an organization with a figurehead. And he has to preach, whether he has a headache, or has had a row with his wife, or even if he's having doubts about the subject he's been given to preach on.

When he started, he worked out his own message, his own doctrine, and that was fine. Now there are doctrinal differences among his preachers and leaders, and the organization has a spiritual director who chairs a doctrinal council to rule on what is right and what is wrong. The founder might actually disagree with a doctrinal ruling, and agree with the thoughts of the young church leader who has just been reprimanded, but he no longer has a say in such things. He's no longer in control.

The organization runs the organization for the good of the organization. Does it actually matter if the financial director has been brought in from outside and isn't a believer? He's good at his job; he keeps the money under control, the money that pays for everybody else in the organization to do their jobs.

The founder isn't in control. Sometimes he feel that he's a liability to the organization; that all the various managers would be happier if he wasn't there, with the constant risk that he might throw a spanner in the works of the organization by saying something out of turn.

Whether this is why L. Ron Hubbard gave up direct involvement with his organization and went off to sea is an interesting question. Certainly, once he was permanently out of the way through death, there was a power struggle in the Church of Scientology, with a new leader throwing out the entire old guard and taking control in what was by many accounts a highly unpleasant *putsch*.

And certainly, within a few years of Herbert W. Armstrong's death, the beliefs of the Church, and the style, content and emphasis of its *Plain Truth* magazine, changed completely. The Millennialist British-Israelite prophecy which was the core of Armstrong's teaching was dropped altogether; the articles attacking evolution, one of Armstrong's great obsessions, vanished. *Plain Truth*, the public face of the Worldwide Church of God, became mellow, even bland, in comparison with what it used to be and is now a pale shadow of its former self, barely distinguishable from any other Christian-based magazine. Yet the magazine and the Church soldier on, month after month. The founder is dead, the message has been altered beyond recognition, but the organization must keep going.

In Armstrong's case, as in Hubbard's, the founder kept a tight grip on his organization. He would not stand for differences from his beliefs, whether in editorial style or in doctrine. He sacked many of his top leaders, including his own son, for daring to disagree with him. It's tempting to suspect a small sigh of relief among the remaining leaders when Herbert W. finally relinquished control by dying, and they were able to run the organization on somewhat less frenetic lines. Life in the Worldwide Church of God was probably less exciting than in the heady days of the 1960s and 1970s, but for a while it was probably a lot calmer and more stable – until the recent changes.[4]

(On a personal note, I feel tremendous sympathy for those on both sides of the current divide in the various Churches of God, and admire their honesty and courage. For those remaining loyal to the Worldwide Church of God, it cannot have been easy to see its doctrines rewritten from scratch, and nearly all of the teachings and writings of its founder rejected as 'inaccurate' or 'unbiblical'. For those who have remained loyal to the old doctrines, it cannot have been easy to turn their backs on the Church they worked in all their lives – and to reject the authority of the leadership of a very hierarchical Church. In both cases the personal upheaval must have been heart-rending, both on a spiritual level and in seeing formerly close colleagues, friends and even members of the same family going in different directions.)

FUNDAMENTALISM

It was mentioned above that many people with a strong religious belief will say, 'I know this is true' rather than 'I believe.' If you are born-again, you have assurance of salvation, and you know this. There's no doubt about it, no argument; there's nothing to discuss.

It's often this deep conviction of belief, this hard factual knowledge, which creates religious disagreements: two people or groups of people, with mutually incompatible beliefs, each knowing that they are right. Taken to an extreme, with Fundamentalists (of any religion, Christian, Muslim or whatever), it can lead to such a hardness of heart towards those who don't share the same beliefs that the Fundamentalist may try to censor the other person's right to express their beliefs.

The majority of Fundamentalists have two other things in common: morally they are puritanical and politically they are right wing. The teachings of Christian Fundamentalists on sex are indistinguishable from most of the early Church Fathers: homosexuality is evil, sex before marriage is sinful, sex within marriage is permissible for procreation, so long as you don't get too much enjoyment out of it. Sex on television is a clear sign of the evil days in which we live and must be fought against.

In California, Fundamentalists have taken the state to court to insist that children be taught creationism (as in Genesis) alongside evolution.

The rise of the politically active Christian Right in America concerns many people who are not Fundamentalists. The USA was founded on a Constitution which guarantees religious freedom and free speech; opponents of the Christian Right claim that Fundamentalists are using their right to the former to restrict other people's right to the latter. Recent US elections have seen Fundamentalists supporting candidates with increasingly extreme right-wing platforms.

History shows that when Church and state are working hand in hand, nonconformists of any kind tend to suffer. Behaviour slightly divergent from the norm is initially frowned upon, then officially criticized, then punished. And it is a small step from proscribing divergent behaviour to proscribing divergent beliefs. In any society with an official belief system, any variant belief becomes a heresy, and heretics begin to be persecuted.

When Fundamentalists of any religion gain political power, religious freedom disappears; blasphemy, a crime which has all but vanished from the courts of Western nations, is reinvoked.

There has been a rise in state Fundamentalism in recent years, and not just within Christianity. Author Salman Rushdie was sentenced to death by an Iranian religious leader for writing a novel which some Muslims found blasphemous (whether they had actually read it or not). The Bengali writer Tasuma Nasrin had to flee to Sweden for a similar reason; she criticized Islam (and thus by implication the Koran, say the Fundamentalists) for its treatment of women. Poets, novelists, journalists and intellectuals – 'free-thinkers' – are currently fleeing from Algeria, where hundreds have been killed by 'Islamists'. In Pakistan one Christian boy was murdered and his illiterate brother was very nearly executed (against the wishes of President Benizir Bhuto) for allegedly chalking up Christian slogans which offended Muslims. Also in Pakistan, members of the Ahmadi sect of Sufism can be arrested for doing anything 'to injure the feelings of a Muslim'; when three friends visited an Ahmadi in prison, one was stoned almost to death, while another was beaten to death and his eyes were gouged out.[5]

In both America and Britain, author Nikos Kazantzakis was vilified when his book *The Last Temptation of Christ* was turned into a film. People going to see the film were harangued and spat on by Fundamentalist Christians. In Britain, Fundamentalist Christians have firebombed Esoteric bookshops. In several Western countries, including Britain, women who are exercising their legal right to have an abortion have been harassed as they enter the clinic; in America several doctors who performed abortions have been shot dead by anti-abortionists who have the open support of Fundamentalist leaders.

The vast majority of both Muslims and Christians, including many Fundamentalists, would condemn such actions outright. But those who commit them do so in the righteous name of God – and it takes only one finger to pull a trigger.

For those who are worried about the rise of religious Fundamentalism, it can seem as if it is the spiritual equivalent of the National Front: bully boys with Bibles. Fundamentalism of such extremity, in any religion, is religious fascism. It denies other people their basic human right (enshrined in the articles of the United Nations, and in the Constitution of the United States of America and elsewhere) to believe and practise whatever religion they choose, and it denies freedom of speech. Take away these rights and we return to the days of the Inquisition and 'the burning times'.

This is what is so refreshing about the Quakers (the Society of Friends), the Unitarians and other 'free' Christian Churches who say that what a man believes is between that man and his god. It's what is so unusual about the Bahá'í Faith. While first Christianity was antagonistic to Judaism, and then Islam was antagonistic to Judaism and Christianity, Bahá'ís, who are the next in the sequence, are happy to accept all three as the right religion for their time and culture, as (they believe) the Bahá'í Faith is for today. And it's almost a hallmark of the Neo-Pagan movements, who accept each other's differences as valid paths for other people. All of these are intolerant of nothing except intolerance itself.

Many of the religious movements in this book which come over as the warmest, or the least threatening, are those which say, 'There are many paths to God; this is the one which we choose to follow.' The ones which leave a chill are those whose mission in life is to convert the whole world to their specific way of thinking, while condemning every other variety of religious belief.

SEX: SACRED OR SINFUL?

It has been said that the two most powerful drives in a human, besides the practical needs of food and shelter, are sex and religion. The sexual urge is strong in nearly everyone, as advertisers of everything from chocolate to cars recognize; and the urge to reach out and worship the divine (by whatever name) is also strongly present in most of us.

In early religions, and in much present-day Neo-Paganism, sex was celebrated as a joyous affirmation of life. 'Sex was felt from the first to be part, and a foundational part, of the great order of the world and of human nature; and therefore to separate it from Religion was unthinkable and a kind of contradiction in terms.'[6]

Many Old Testament kings, portrayed as godly men, had both wives and concubines. Even in the New Testament we are told that a bishop or a deacon must be 'the husband of one wife' (I Timothy 3:2, 12), suggesting that it was not unknown at the time for a man to have more than one wife – and also, incidentally, that priestly celibacy has no biblical basis.

Yet by the time of the Church Fathers the personal views of Paul were held up as the ideal: 'I would that all men were even as I myself . . . I say therefore to the unmarried and widows, It is good for them if they abide even as I. But if they cannot contain, let them marry: for it is better to marry than to burn' (I Corinthians 7:7–9).

To many of the Church Fathers celibacy was an inseparable part of their calling (even though marriage was both permissible and perfectly normal for Catholic priests and bishops at the time, and for many more centuries). They ruled that sex must occur only for procreation, and certainly mustn't be enjoyed. It was through sex that Original Sin was passed from one generation to the next. Some of the early Christian sects insisted on complete celibacy for all believers. Some present-day Christian Fundamentalist Churches also inveigh against just about all sexual behaviour that isn't essential. Many keep a strict eye on their younger members. Some, like the Jesus Army, advocate celibacy as the highest calling for believers.

The reasons for the Christian Church's antipathy to sex are many and complex. One which is particularly apposite to both the Church Fathers and present-day Christian offshoots is the importance of authority. One of the hallmarks of present-day Western society, whatever the party political labels, is liberal democracy. We shudder when we look at authoritarian dictatorship. We are able to believe and behave much as we wish, within democratically agreed social constraints. To a great extent the mainstream Christian Churches have (albeit at times reluctantly) accommodated themselves to this.

But for the Church Fathers, fighting against heresy, and for both the sects they were opposing and today's counterparts, authority was important. There must be no doubt in believers' minds as to whom they should obey, what they should believe and how they should behave.

Sexual activity is intensely personal and private. It involves, usually, two people concentrating on bringing intense pleasure to each other and to themselves. Sex at its best is loving, caring, and fun – and supremely joyous. Orgasm, for both men and women, can be an ecstatic, even a transcendent experience; it can lift them for a few moments into realms of joy otherwise unattainable in everyday life; it can be a glimpse of heaven on earth. It is no accident that the Anglican marriage ceremony includes the words, 'With my body I thee worship.'

Anything that is so powerful that it is possible to describe it in terminology which is usually the province of mystical religion, and yet which is completely out of the control of the Church, cannot possibly be encouraged.

The fact that most Neo-Pagan groups happily acknowledge the spiritual joy of sex does not endear them to Fundamentalists, amd provides ammunition for the sensationalist stories of 'witchcraft orgies' which from time to time appear in the tabloid press. Movements like the Church of All Worlds openly affirm sexual freedom between adults, and worship the god and goddess in each other.

The Family, formerly the Children of God, would not have raised anywhere near as much horror within established Christianity if they had held to conventional Christian views of sex. Instead, with a theological argument which can obviously be questioned but which must be accepted as part of their doctrine, they say that all adult members of a family (a community house) may make love with each other. They also point out that God created sex, and from the way it works, he obviously intended it to be thoroughly enjoyed.

Much the same applies to the Rajneesh movement, now known as Osho, and to the Raelian movement, both of which see sexual intimacy and sensuality as important parts of some forms of meditation. The Raelians also make it clear that they regard the guilt and repression that centuries of traditional religious teaching have implanted in people as harmful.

COUNTING THE DAYS

The new millennium is almost on us. For Christian-based Millennialist religions, the term refers to Christ's literal 1,000-year reign on earth, rather than to the year 2000 (or, to be accurate, 1 January 2001). The Millennium was supposed to start in 1844, 1864, 1874, 1914, 1975, 1985 or other quite specific years, but the magic of the year 2000 has a wider appeal, and several of the alternative religions are quietly (if they're sensible) or not so quietly (if they follow past form) hoping for The Big Event in that year.

If God has a sense of humour (and He or She really must have, to put up with the diversity of religions in His or Her name, and many of them the sole possessors of the Truth), one can imagine The Big Event being staged in 1998 or 2003, along with a celestial chuckle at the folly of mankind.

THE POWER OF MYTH

The Millennialist religions especially speak of 'the signs of the times'. It's not always realized that their strength is often drawn from their times. Especially over the last 30 years there has been a huge trend towards linking the Logical West with the Mystical East. Followers of the Maharishi Mahesh Yogi now explain Transcendental Meditation in socio-psychological terminology; recently they have moved into the political arena as well, founding their own Natural Law Party. Religion seems to have taken a back seat, at least in the public image they portray. Or perhaps religion, from the back seat, drives everything they do.

Other movements also seem to have dropped the mystical hippie-speak of their earlier years, to have cloaked themselves in sharp suits and Thatcherite ideology, and to have set up as training schools in personal development or trans-personal relationships.

Meanwhile, the Neo-Pagans of assorted hue are basically all shades of green. It's been said that they are the spiritual wing of the Green Party – or the converse.

Taking the word 'social' in its broadest sense, new religions follow social developments; if they want to survive they borrow from the buzz-speak of their day. This explains the complete transformation of, for example, movements such as the Divine Light Mission into Elan Vital. Those somewhat older new religions such as Christian Science and the Exclusive Brethren, which still appear rooted in the nineteenth century, just don't seem to have that essential spark to give them contemporary relevance. Unless they do something about it soon, in another generation, when those alive in the grey years of the 1940s and 1950s have all died, their membership will dwindle still more. It can take a century for a Church to fade away altogether. The Catholic Apostolic Church, founded in London in 1831 by Edward Irving, flourished for a while, but even in the 1860s it was beginning to lose impetus, though a small rump soldiered on. By 1975 its estimated membership, according to the *UK Christian Handbook 1994/95*, was only 50; five-yearly projections take it down to 40 in 1980, then 30, 25, 15, ten and five by the year 2005.

The Jehovah's Witnesses might last somewhat longer. Like several other new religions, they quickly learned that power lies in publishing. The same might have been said of the Worldwide Church of God until recently, except that they give away all their magazines and books rather than selling them. But they still have one of their formerly three university campuses, and the momentum of a huge business operation will surely carry them on for a while longer, even though they have currently fallen on hard times.

Dr Christopher Evans, in his *Cults of Unreason*, hinted at the reasons for the technological background to several of the new religions. Scientology has its E-Meters and its 76-million-year-old interplanetary betrayal; the Aetherius Society and the Raelians have their messengers in UFOs. Signs of the times indeed. Evans's selection of alternative religions is deliberately limited to support his point, but the point is still valid: 'We have seen that the focal areas for cultish interest are largely concerned with significant modern concepts or technology – science fiction, psychoanalysis, space travel, electronics and mysterious gadgetry of one kind and another.'[7] Alongside these, he says, are persistent beliefs in Atlantis, the Great White Brotherhood of Tibet and other Esoteric ideas. Evans speaks of 'the power of the myth'; this is a huge area we have barely touched on in this book. Of all the alternative religions we have covered, the Neo-Pagans are the most open in acknowledging and drawing on the power of myth, reawakening belief in the old gods of their lands.

One reason for the decline of the traditional mainstream religions has been their reluctance to move with the times, in more ways than one. The myths on which they are based (using the word 'myth' in its correct technical sense) have become outmoded; people in today's society have outgrown both the myths and the religions. The new religions have new myths, such as Joseph Smith digging up gold plates in America, or the Elohim appearing to Raël in France. Myths have power, whether they are new myths like these or the old myths of Odin, Freya and co. revitalized in the new Norse religious movements. Christian Churches which concentrate on a 2,000-year-old story miss the point of living myth; the reason for the Jesus Army's success is its emphasis on the living Jesus.

A SUGGESTION FOR SCEPTICS

Most non-Mormons find Joseph Smith's golden plates pretty hard to credit. Most people who aren't Neo-Pagans or members of Esoteric groups scoff at the idea of real magic. As for those who believe in extraterrestrials bringing religious and moral messages to mankind, a lot of people would quietly tap the side of their head.

But people – intelligent, sensible, rational, well-educated people – do believe in all these things. For them, these 'unbelievable beliefs' are absolutely real, demonstrably true. But how, cries the sceptic, how on earth can they be true?

An intriguing suggestion has recently been put forward which might provide a possible answer, while raising a hundred other questions. Few people in the West today would openly admit to believing in fairies, elves or dwarfs – the Little People – but it's not so long since perfectly ordinary people accepted their existence without any difficulty. (Belief in the Fair Folk was not limited to uneducated country-dwellers either. Robert Kirk, a Scottish Episcopalian minister – and a scholar and linguist – wrote *The Secret Commonwealth of Elves, Fauns and Fairies* in 1690.[8]) Some farmers' wives today still put down a saucer of milk in the barn every night. If challenged they might say it was for the farm cats, or for hedgehogs, but really it's to keep the hobgoblin or hearth-sprite in a good temper so it doesn't turn the cows' milk sour.

Patrick Harpur's *Daimonic Reality: A Field Guide to the Otherworld* (Viking, 1994) suggests that between hard physical fact and the fantasy creations of the imagination there is a middle zone, a sort of subjective reality which is objectively real to those who experience or observe it. The Fair Folk are part of it; so are visions of the Blessed Virgin Mary, sightings of ghosts and alien abductions in UFOs. Whether or not they physically exist is a non-question; for those who experience them, they are inarguably real.

This 'daimonic reality' could account for visions and voices seen and heard by religious mystics through the ages, and by everyone from mediums to 'channellers' today. It could account for the miracles of the saints and the magic of the Neo-Pagans. It could account for the absolutely, demonstrably real and genuine religious experiences of many thousands, perhaps millions of people. It could account for the *latihan* of Subud and the Toronto Blessing of Evangelical Christians. It could account for the fact that healing works, whether it is the Holy Spirit or the Goddess who has been invoked. It could account for Joseph Smith's golden plates; yes, they were real, for those who saw them 'with the eye of faith'. It could account for the meetings with the Masters experienced by ECKists and others in their dream travels. It could account for George King's Aetherius and Raël's Elohim.

It also makes sense of the paradox that the religious movements covered in this book (and many hundreds more) are all real and true to their followers, despite the fact that many of them are mutually exclusive. Anyone who has had a religious experience knows that it is true. Anyone who has witnessed the divine or the supernatural causing a miracle or magic knows that it is true. Anyone who has heard 'the still small voice of God' (or of the Goddess) deep in their soul knows that it is true.

For members of any one religion to claim a monopoly on truth is simply arrogance. To say, 'My religious experience is real, and of God; so yours must be false, and of the Devil' is demonstrating a blindness to other people's reality.

◆

Whether 'daimonic reality' is the solution or just another label for something which is by definition undefinable doesn't really matter. What does matter is that millions of people have found inner peace, a link to ultimate Truth and a relationship with God in many, many different ways.

And what is important is that they should be allowed to continue to do so.

NOTES

INTRODUCTION

1 *Webster's New Reference Library*, Thomas Nelson, Nashville, 1988 edition, p. 580.

1 A BRIEF HISTORY OF WORLD RELIGIONS

1 Personal correspondence.
2 Undated leaflet, 'Bahá'u'lláh: The Promised One', pp. 2–3.
3 *The Bahá'ís: A Profile of the Bahá'í Faith and Its Worldwide Community*, p. 35.
4 Ibid., p. 42.
5 Undated leaflet, 'The New Age', p. 2.
6 Ibid., p. 4.
7 Personal correspondence.
8 Personal correspondence.

2 VARIETIES OF CHRISTIANITY

1 Quoted in Ysenda Maxtone Graham, *The Church Hesitant: A Portrait of the Church of England Today*, Hodder & Stoughton, 1993, p. 224.
2 For more detail on the far-reaching effects of both Gnosticism and the Cathars, see David V. Barrett, *Secret Societies*, Blandford, 1997.

3 CHRISTIAN MOVEMENTS

1 J. Oswald Sanders, *Heresies and Cults*, Marshall, Morgan and Scott, 1962 edition, p. 66.
2 Unless otherwise stated, all quotations are from personal correspondence with Matthew F. Smith.
3 Betty Smith, quoted in undated booklet, *Unitarian Views of Jesus*.
4 *The Journal of John Wesley*, Moody Press, condensed version, n.d., p. 309.
5 These quotations are taken from the undated leaflet, *'What is the New Church?'*.
6 *The Pearl of Great Price*, 'History of Joseph Smith', 2: 64.
7 *Mormon* 9: 34.
8 Letter to F. D. Howe, 17 February 1834, quoted in Walter R. Martin, *The Kingdom of the Cults*, Marshall, Morgan and Scott, 1967 edition, p. 160.
9 *Encyclopedia of Mormonism*, Macmillan, 1992, p. 602.
10 Joseph Smith, *History of the Church*, 4:461.
11 *Enyclopedia of Mormonism*, p. 1403.
12 Unless otherwise stated, all quotations are from personal correspondence with Bryan J. Grant.
13 *Encyclopedia of Mormonism*, p. 560.
14 Ibid., p. 557.

15   *History, Beliefs, Lifestyle*, 1994, p. 16.
16   *Temples of the Church of Jesus Christ of Latter-day Saints*, 1988, p. 6.
17   *Encyclopedia of Mormonism*, p. 534.
18   *Doctrine and Covenants*, Section 89.
19   Quotations are from personal correspondence with the secretary of the Bible and Gospel Trust.
20   *Adventists: A Caring, Sharing Church World-Wide*, 1995, p. 4.
21   *Seventh-day Adventists Believe . . .: A Biblical Exposition of 27 Fundamental Doctrines*, Ministerial Association, General Conference of Seventh-day Adventists, 1988, p. iv.
22   *Questions on Doctrine*, 1957, p. 197.
23   Ibid., p. 193.
24   *Seventh-day Adventists Believe*, pp. 46–7.
25   *Adventists*, p. 14.
26   Personal correspondence.
27   Where quotations are from personal correspondence with Michael Ashton, his name is mentioned. All other quotations are taken from booklets from Christadelphian Publications, Birmingham, UK.
28   Fred Pearce, *Who are the Christadelphians?*, p. 8.
29   Fred Pearce, *Jesus: God the Son or Son of God?*, p. 2.
30   Ibid., p. 12.
31   Pearce, *Who are the Christadelphians?*, p. 8.
32   Pearce, *Jesus: God the Son or Son of God?*, p. 13.
33   Harry Tennant, *The Holy Spirit*, p. 3.
34   Pearce, *Who are the Christadelphians?*, p. 9.
35   Harry Tennant, *Back to the Bible*, n.d., p. 49.
36   Ibid., p. 42.
37   *Ambassador of the Coming Age*, 1866, p.2.
38   Mary Baker Eddy, *Miscellaneous Writings*, 1897, p. 24.
39   Mary Baker Eddy, *Science and Health, With Key to the Scriptures*, 1875, p. 107.
40   Ibid., p. 110.
41   *Christian Science Journal*, January 1901.
42   Ibid., March 1897.
43   *Media Guide to Christian Science*, 1993, pp. 8 and 2. All booklets are published by the Christian Science Committee on Publication.
44   *Christian Science Watchman*, Vol. 4, No. 5.
45   Eddy, *Science and Health*, p. 497.
46   Mary Baker Eddy, *Church Manual*, 1895, p. 17.
47   Eddy, *Science and Health*, p. 340.
48   Ibid., pp. 470, 472.
49   *Media Guide to Christian Science*, p. 19.
50   Ibid., p. 16.
51   *Facts about Christian Science*, 1959, p. 6.
52   *A Century of Christian Science Healing*, The Christian Science Publishing Society, 1966, p. viii.
53   *Facts about Christian Science*, p. 19.
54   Ibid., p. 20.
55   Eddy, *Science and Health*, p. 473.
56   *How Prayer Can Help You*, 1956, p. 7.
57   *Jehovah's Witnesses in the Twentieth Century*, 1989, p. 15.
58   Ibid., p. 3.
59   For detailed discussion of the name of God, see Doug Harris, *Awake! to the Watch Tower*, 1988, pp. 54–72, 246–7; and G. T. Manley, 'God, Names of', in J. D. Douglas (ed.), *The New Bible Dictionary*, Inter-Varsity Fellowship, 1962, pp. 477–80.
60   *Jehovah's Witnesses in the Twentieth Century*, p. 13.
61   Ibid., p. 16.
62   J. F. Rutherford, *Deliverance*, p. 222.
63   *The Watch Tower*, 15 September 1910.
64   Quoted in Harris, *Awake! to the Watch Tower*, pp. 143–4.

65 *Jehovah's Witnesses in the Twentieth Century*, p. 7.
66 *Awake!*, 22 June 1995, p. 8.
67 Ibid., p. 9.
68 Ibid., pp. 11–12.
69 Summarized from Herman L. Hoeh, *A True History of the True Church*, Radio Church of God, 1959, pp. 18–23.
70 Quoted ibid., p. 24.
71 *This is the Worldwide Church of God*, 1972, p. 15.
72 *The Autobiography of Herbert W. Armstrong*, Vol. 1, 1973 edition, pp. 366, 373–4.
73 John Bowden, *Herbert W. Armstrong and his Worldwide Church of God: An Exposure and an Indictment*, The Rationalist Association of New South Wales, 1973, pp. 14–17.
74 Garner Ted Armstrong, *The Origin and History of the Church of God, International*, Church of God, International, 1992, p. 40.
75 Ibid.
76 Herbert W. Armstrong, 'Why my son no longer stands "back to back" with me', *The Good News*, April 1979, p. 25.
77 Ibid.
78 Dated 25 April 1979, quoted in G. T. Armstrong, *The Origin and History of the Church of God, International*, p. 72.
79 Ibid., p. 52.
80 All quotations by Roderick C. Meredith are from an interview by Edwin H. Barnett and Sue Ann Pomicter, 24 October 1995 (Source: Internet), supplied by the United Church of God.
81 *The Autobiography of Herbert W. Armstrong*, Vol. 1, Ambassador College, 1967 edition, pp. 376–7: 1973 edition, p. 344; Worldwide Church of God, 1986 edition, pp. 398–9.
82 Ibid., 1967 edition, p. 450; 1973 edition, p. 408; 1986 edition, p. 476.
83 Dated 25 April 1979, quoted in G. T. Armstrong, *The Origin and History of the Church of God, International*, p. 82.
84 'About Our Founder', *Welcome to Our Fellowship*, 1995, p. 25.
85 *Statement of Beliefs of the Worldwide Church of God*, 1995, p. 8.
86 'Personal: Festivals of Praise', in *Plain Truth*, US edition, September/October 1995, p. 1.
87 Summarized from *The British Commonwealth and the United States in Prophecy*, Ambassador College, 1954, pp. 17–19: *The United States and British Commonwealth in Prophecy*, Ambassador College, 1967, pp. 115–18; *The United States and Britain in Prophecy*, Worldwide Church of God, 1980, pp. 93–9.
88 Ibid., pp. 19–22, 118–28, 99–104.
89 Undated leaflet, 'Church's statement regarding the identity of ancient Israel'.
90 This spokesman has since left the Worldwide Church of God.
91 Herbert W. Armstrong, *1975 in Prophecy*, 1956, p. 10.
92 Ibid., pp. 18, 19.
93 *The Autobiography of Herbert W. Armstrong*, Vol. 1, 1967 edition, p. 408; understandably, this passage is dropped from later editions.
94 'Where we have been, where we are going,' *Welcome to Our Fellowship*, 1995, p. 18.
95 *We're Often Asked . . .*, 1994, p. 6.
96 Herbert W. Armstrong, *Mystery of the Ages*, Worldwide Church of God, 1985, p. 42.
97 *We're Often Asked . . .*, p. 4.
98 *Statement of Beliefs*, 1995, p. 2.
99 'What *kind of* FAITH is required for *Salvation?*', 1952, p. 10.
100 *We're Often Asked*, p. 10.
101 Letter to co-workers dated 12 September 1985, quoted in *Autobiography of Herbert W. Armstrong*, Vol. 2, pp. 637, 640.
102 G. T. Armstrong, *The Origin and History of the Church of God, International*, pp. 32–3.
103 *We're Often Asked . . .*, p. 12.
104 Letter to Church co-workers dated 20 February 1995.
105 G. T. Armstrong, *The Origin and History of the Church of God, International*, p. 86.
106 Ibid.
107 Letter to Church co-workers dated 20 March 1995.
108 Letter to Church co-workers dated 20 February 1995.

109   In conversation with the author, 10 November 1995.
110   H. W. Armstrong, *Mystery of the Ages*, p. 224; see also pp. 206–7, 230–32.
111   *The Divine Principle Home Study Course 1: The Principles of Creation*, HSA-UWC, 1979, p. vii.
112   *Divine Principle*, HSA–UWC, 1973, p. 16.
113   *Toward the Ideal: An Introduction to the Unification Movement*, HSA-UWC, 1990, p. 8.
114   Ibid., p. 9.
115   *The Divine Principle Home Study Course 3: Mission of the Messiah*, HSA-UWC, 1980, p. 37.
116   Ibid., p. 39.
117   Morris Cerullo, *The New Anointing is Here: Handbook for the Harvest*, 1972, p. 4.
118   Ibid., p. 20.
119   Unless otherwise stated, all quotations are from Rachel Scott.
120   *Our Family's Origins*, World Services, Zurich, 1992, p. 1.
121   Ibid., pp. 1–2.
122   Ibid., p. 2.
123   Ibid., p. 3.
124   *Our Statement of Belief*, The Family, 1992, p. 5.
125   Personal correspondence.
126   Interview on *PM*, BBC Radio 4, 25 September 1995.

4   EASTERN MOVEMENTS

1   Unless otherwise stated, all quotations are by Bhagavat Dharma.
2   'Cleaning house and cleaning hearts: Reform and renewal in ISKCON, Part 1', in *ISKCON Communications Journal*, No. 3, January–June 1994, p. 47.
3   Ibid., Part 2, in *ISKCON Communications Journal*, No. 4, July–December 1994, p. 25.
4   Ibid., Part 1, p. 44.
5   All quotations are from Glen Whittaker.
6   ECKANKAR, ECK, Soul Travel and Mahanta are trademarks of ECKANKAR.
7   Paul Twitchell, *The Spiritual Notebook*, Illuminated Way Press, 1971, p. 198.
8   Ibid., p. 194.
9   Harold Klemp, *The Secret Teachings: Mahanta Transcripts Book 3*, ECKANKAR 1989, p. 139.
10   Todd Cramer and Doug Munson, *ECKANKAR: Ancient Wisdom for Today*, ECKANKAR, 1993, p. 5.
11   Quotations from Eve Illing are from personal correspondence.
12   Harold Klemp, *Cloak of Consciousness: Mahanta Transcripts Book 5*, 1991, pp. 1, 15.
13   Klemp, *The Secret Teachings: Mahanta Transcripts Book 3*, p. 139.
14   Twitchell, *The Spiritual Notebook*, pp. 57–8.
15   Ibid., p. 192.
16   Ibid., p. 104.
17   Ibid., p. 43.
18   Cramer and Munson, *ECKANKAR: Ancient Wisdom for Today*, p. 110.
19   Twitchell, *The Spiritual Notebook*, p. 152.
20   Ibid., p. 80.
21   Ibid., p. 131.
22   Ibid., p. 193–4.
23   Ibid., p. 152.
24   Cramer and Munson, *ECKANKAR: Ancient Wisdom for Today*, p. 60.
25   Twitchell, *The Spiritual Notebook*, p. 153.
26   Cramer and Munson, *ECKANKAR: Ancient Wisdom for Today*, p. 10.
27   Ibid., p. 30, 35.
28   Ibid., p. 70–71.
29   Twitchell, *The Spiritual Notebook*, p. 118.
30   Ibid., p. 112.
31   Ibid., p. 195–6.
32   Ibid., p. 42–3.
33   Cramer and Munson, *ECKANKAR: Ancient Wisdom for Today*, p. 7.

34 Unless otherwise stated, all quotations are taken from an undated Osho International leaflet: 'Can you give me a message to take to the world so that people there might understand you and your followers?'.
35 Cf. the similar words of Justin Martyr (see p. 42).
36 *The World of Meditation*, Osho International.
37 *Osho Commune International: An Invitation/Osho Multiversity.*
38 Ibid.
39 Ibid.
40 All quotations are from David Boddy, unless otherwise stated.
41 Peter Hounam and Andrew Hogg, *Secret Cult*, Lion, 1984, p. 83.
42 *The Art of Living: An Introduction to the Buddhism of Nichiren Daishonin*, SGI-UK, 1993, pp. 30–31.
43 Ibid., p. 19.
44 Ibid., p. 20.
45 Ibid., p. 22.
46 *Introducing SGI-UK*, p. 2.
47 Ibid., p. 3.
48 *The Art of Living*, p. 23.
49 Ibid., p. 32.

5   BACKGROUND

1 For example, J. D. Douglas (ed.), *The New Bible Dictionary*, IVF, 1962; Alan Richardson (ed.), *A Theological Word Book of the Bible*, SCM Press, 1957; William Smith, *Smith's Bible Dictionary*, Pyramid edition, 1967.
2 Smith, *Smith's Bible Dictionary*, p. 607.
3 Douglas (ed.), *The New Bible Dictionary*, p. 755.
4 J. Gordon Melton, *Encyclopedic Handbook of Cults in America*, Garland, 1992 edition, p. 109.
5 Anton LaVey, *The Satanic Bible*, 1969; Star Books edition, 1977, p. 21.

6   ESOTERIC MOVEMENTS

1 Rudolf Steiner, *Theosophy: An Introduction to the Supersensible Knowledge of the World and the Destination of Man*, 1922; Rudolf Steines Press, 3rd edition 1965, p. 5.
2 *The Reappearance of the Christ and the Masters of Wisdom*, 1994, p. 2.
3 Ibid.
4 *The Emergence Newsletter*, 1994, No. 3, p. 3.
5 Unless otherwise stated all quotations are taken from an untitled, undated Subud information leaflet.
6 Subuh, quoted in Robert Lyle, *Subud*, Humanus Ltd, 1983, pp. 91–2.
7 Quotations are from personal correspondence with H. C. Steinhart, General Secretary of Lectorium Rosicrucianum.
8 For more detail on the Rosicrucians, Freemasonry, the Order of the Golden Dawn and other Esoteric societies, and their influence, see David V. Barrett, *Secret Societies*, Blandford, 1997.
9 François Rabelais, *The Histories of Gargantua and Pantagruel, The First Book*, Chapter 57, first published in 1532. For the monks and nuns of the Abbey of Thélème:

in all their rule, and strictest tie of their order, there was but this one clause to be observed,
DO WHAT THOU WILT.
Because men that are free, well born, well bred, and conversant in honest companies, have naturally an instinct and spur that prompteth them unto virtuous actions, and withdraws them from vice, which is called honour.

10   Unless otherwise stated, all quotations are from the Builders of the Adytum's 1989 introductory booklet, *The Open Door*.

11   Rachel Pollack, *The New Tarot*, Aquarian Press, 1989, p. 137.

12   Personal correspondence.

13   Unless otherwise stated, all quotations are from the undated introductory booklet *The Society of the Inner Light: Work and Aims*.

14   All quotations are taken from the undated introductory booklet *Servants of the Light School of Occult Science*, 1987.

15   All quotations are taken from the undated introductory booklet *The London Group: Its Aims and Objectives*.

16   *Keepers of the Flame: A Fraternity*, 1986, p. 24.

17   Personal conversation.

18   Mark L. Prophet and Elizabeth Clare Prophet, *Saint Germain on Alchemy: Formulas for Self-Transformation*, Summit University Press, pp. 255–6.

19   *Profile: Elizabeth Clare Prophet/Teachings of the Ascended Masters*, Summit University Press, 1992, p. 7.

20   'The Life of Saint Issa' 4:12–13, in Elizabeth Clare Prophet, *The Lost Years of Jesus*, Summit University Press, 1987, p. 218.

21   This is Steinman's paraphrase; the actual verse reads, 'Jesus said, "He who will drink from my mouth will become like me; I myself shall become he, and the things that are hidden will be revealed to him."' James M. Robinson (ed.), *The Nag Hammadi Library*, Harper & Row, 1977, p. 307, 'The Gospel of Thomas', verse 108.

22   Prophet and Prophet, *Saint Germain on Alchemy*, pp. 446–7.

23   *Profile*, p. 8.

24   Video, *Climb the Highest Mountain: A Profile of the Church Universal and Triumphant*, 1994.

25   *Profile*, pp. 9–10.

26   *Church Universal and Triumphant: Tenets*, 1975, pp. 3, 4, 5, 7.

27   *Profile*, p. 16.

28   Ibid., p. 10.

29   *Telegraph Magazine*, 1 January 1994, p. 39.

30   *Royal Teton Ranch News*, Vol. 7, No. 2, February/March 1995, p. 8.

31   James R. Lewis and J. Gordon Melton (eds.), *Church Universal and Triumphant in Scholarly Perspective*, Center for Academic Publication, 1994, pp. 62, xii and *passim*.

32   *The Emissaries*, 1992.

33   Kate Hall, feature in the Findhorn magazine, *One Earth*.

34   *Mickleton House: Guidelines for Residents*, June 1995.

35   Undated leaflet, 'Lloyd Arthur Meeker: William Martin Alleyne Cecil'.

36   *Mickleton House: Guidelines for Residents*.

37   Ibid.

38   Unless otherwise stated, all quotations are from Kate Hall.

39   Lloyd Arthur Meeker, *The Divine Design*, Vol. 1, 1952.

40   Personal conversation.

41   Undated Aetherius Society information booklet.

42   Unless otherwise stated, all quotations are taken from the undated leaflet 'The Aetherius Society: Some basic principles included in its teachings'.

43   Aetherius Society information booklet.

44   Unless otherwise stated, all quotations are from the undated leaflet 'The Raelian Movement: Information'.

45   Personal correspondence.

46   *An Embassy for Extra-Terrestrials*, p. 7.

7   NEO-PAGAN MOVEMENTS

1   Personal correspondence.

2   Personal correspondence.

3   *Malleus Maleficarum*, Arrow, 1971 edition, p. 116.
4   Ibid., pp. 267–8.
5   Undated House of the Goddess leaflet (copyright HoG).
6   Margaret Murray, *The Witch-Cult in Western Europe*, 1921, Oxford University Press, p. 12.
7   Richard Cavendish, *A History of Magic*, Weidenfeld & Nicolson, 1987, p. 159.
8   Stewart Farrar, *What Witches Do*, 1971, 3rd edition 1991, Hale, p. 20.
9   House of the Goddess leaflet.
10 All quotations in this entry are from undated House of the Goddess leaflets.
11 *CAW Membership Handbook*, p. 4.
12 Unless otherwise stated, all quotations are from correspondence with Oberon Zell.
13 *CAW Membership Handbook*, p. 11.
14 Ibid., p. 21.
15 All quotations are from Rhuddlwm Gawr and Merridin Gawr, *The Word: The Greater Mysteries of Welsh Witchcraft*, Chapters 2 and 11.
16 Unless otherwise stated, quotations by Philip Shallcrass are from personal correspondence.
17 Stuart Piggott, *The Druids*, Thames and Hudson, 1968, Penguin edition, p. 143.
18 Letter to *Odinism Today*, No. 18, May 1995, p. 22.
19 Undated Henge of Keltria introductory leaflet.
20 Undated Order of Bards, Ovates and Druids introductory leaflet.
21 Summarized from Philip Carr-Gomm, *The Elements of the Druid Tradition*, Element, 1991, pp. 43–64.
22 Undated British Druid Order introductory leaflet.
23 *Odalstone*, No. 10, the news-sheet of Odinshof.
24 'Asatru – Ancient to Modern', undated press release.
25 Ibid.
26 Undated Odinic Rite leaflet: 'Odinists Say Yes to Life'.
27 Ibid.
28 The Ring of Troth membership application leaflet.
29 Personal correspondence.
30 *Odinshof Members' Handbook*.
31 Leaflet 'Welcome to the Odinic Rite'.
32 'Odinists Say Yes to Life'.
33 Ibid.
34 *Odinshof Members' Handbook*.
35 Undated Pagan Federation introductory leaflet.
36 Janet and Stewart Farrar and Gavin Bone, *The Pagan Path*, Phoenix, 1995, p. 167.
37 PaganLink Network leaflet: *A Guide to Paganlinking*.
38 Universal Federation of Pagans information booklet, 1992, p. 3.
39 Quoted in Farrar, Farrar and Bone, *The Pagan Path*, p.161.
40 Ibid., p. 161.
41 The University of Avalon Prospectus, September to December 1994.
42 The Isle of Avalon Foundation: Courses and Workshops, April 1995.
43 Leo Rutherford, in Eagle's Wing Centre for Contemporary Shamanism, course leaflet 'Elements of Shamanism'.
44 *The Findhorn Garden*, Findhorn Press, 2nd edition, 1988, p. 129.
45 Quotations are from the Fellowship of Isis Manifesto unless otherwise stated.
46 *The Handbook of the Fellowship of Isis*, p. 8.
47 Quotations are from personal correspondence with David Brock.

8   PERSONAL DEVELOPMENT MOVEMENTS

1   Joseph O'Connor and John Seymour, *Introducing NLP*, Aquarian Press, 1993, p.1.
2   Ibid., p. 183.
3   Unless otherwise stated, all quotations are from John Seymour Associates 1995 brochure, *Introducing NLP*.
4   Insight course flier.

5   Unless otherwise stated, all quotations are taken from the undated leaflet 'Everything you always wanted to know about Insight'.

6   Unless otherwise stated, all quotations are from personal correspondence with Nick Woodeson and David Pearce, two senior British members of the Emin. They stress, however, 'The Emin has no spokespeople; the people speak for themselves.'

7   *The New Testament in Basic English*, Cambridge, 1944, pp. v–vi.

8   'Emin Loom of Research Starters', 1995 edition.

9   Leo, *Dear Dragon*, 1976; 4th edition, Topaz Publishers, Israel, 1992, p. 15.

10 'Emin Loom of Research Starters', 2–1 and 3–7.

11 Jean Ritchie, *The Secret World of Cults*, Angus and Robertson, 1991, p. 216.

12 Essence Music Catalogue, 1993, p. 1.

13 Ibid., p. 3.

14 Unless otherwise stated, all quotations are from personal correspondence with Nigel Kahn of the UK press office of the Maharishi Foundation.

15 Natural Law Party European Election Communication, 1994, p. 6.

16 Personal correspondence from Merseyside Police Press Office, September 1995.

17 Quotations from Guy Hatchard taken from his letter to Nigel Kahn in response to a query by the author.

18 Natural Law Party European Election Communication, pp. 7, 4.

19 Ibid., pp. 4–5, 4, 6.

20 The terms Scientology, Dianetics, E-Meter, The Bridge, Saint Hill, Flag, OT, Hubbard and L. Ron Hubbard are trademarks owned by Religious Technology Centre; Narconon is a trademark owned by Able International.

21 *The Church of Scientology: 40th Anniversary*, 1994, p. 56.

22 *Scientology: The Field Staff Member Magazine*, Vol. 1, No. 1, p. 38.

23 L. Ron Hubbard, *Dianetics, The Modern Science of Mental Health*, New Era, 1950, p. 171.

24 Ibid., pp. 312, 313.

25 *The Auditor: The Journal of Scientology*, No. 21, February 1967, p. 2.

26 *What Is Scientology?*, Bridge Publications, 1993, p. 441.

27 *Reference Guide to the Scientology Religion*, Church of Scientology International, 1994, p. 18.

28 *Scientology: The Field Staff Member Magazine*, Vol. 1, No. 1, p. 23.

29 Hubbard, *Dianetics: The Modern Science of Mental Health*, p. vi.

30 *Scientology: The Field Staff Member Magazine*, Vol. 1, No. 1, p. 38.

31 Christopher Evans, *Cults of Unreason*, Harrap, 1973, pp. 42ff.

32 Kevin V. Anderson, *Report of the Board of Inquiry into Scientology*, Melbourne, 1965.

33 *Reference Guide to the Scientology Religion*, p. 42.

34 Russell Miller, *Bare-Faced Messiah*, Michael Joseph, 1987, p. 86.

35 See, for example, *What Is Scientology?*, pp. 25–53, *The Church of Scientology: 40th Anniversary*, pp. 49–55, *L. Ron Hubbard: A Profile*, 1995, pp. 1–124.

36 Quoted in Russell Miller, *Bare-Faced Messiah*, p. 485.

37 *What Is Scientology?*, p. 52.

38 This is not mentioned in the 593-page book, *What Is Scientology?*

39 Isaac Asimov, *In Memory Yet Green*, Avon, 1979, pp. 570, 587, 625.

40 Personal correspondence.

41 *What Is Scientology?*, p. 415.

42 Ibid., p. 290; see also pp. 290–300.

43 Ibid., p. 422.

44 Anderson, *Report of the Board of Inquiry into Scientology*.

45 Declaration by Stacy Brooks Young to the United States District Court, Central District of California, 1994 (Source: Internet).

46 Conversation with the author, 21 September 1995.

47 Declaration by Mary Tabayoyon to United States District Court, Central District of California, 4 April 1994 (Source: Internet).

48 Hubbard, *Dianetics: The Modern Science of Mental Health*, p. 132.

49 Conversation with the author, 21 September 1995.

50 Declaration by Mary Tabayoyon to United States District Court, Central District of California, 4 April 1994 (Source: Internet).
51 *Reference Guide to the Scientology Religion*, p. 33.
52 Cyril Vosper, *The Mind Benders*, Neville Spearman, 1971, p. 134.
53 Quoted in ibid., p. 138.
54 Quoted in ibid., pp. 147–8.
55 Evans, *Cults of Unreason*, pp. 131, 133, 134.
56 Declaration by Stacy Brooks Young to the United States District Court, Central District of California, 1994 (Source: Internet).
57 *Reference Guide to the Scientology Religion*, p. 35: 'This trust is never violated. The confidences given in trust during an auditing session are considered sacrosanct by the Church, and are never divulged.'
58 Ibid., p. 30.
59 *What Is Scientology?*, p. 421.
60 Ibid., p. 30–1.
61 Stewart Lamont, *Religion Inc.*, Harrap, 1986, pp. 95–6 and Appendix B.
62 Declaration by Stacy Brooks Young to the United States District Court, Central District of California, 1994 (Source: Internet).
63 *Reference Guide to the Scientology Religion*, p. 31.
64 Declaration by Stacy Brooks Young to the United States District Court, Central District of California, 1994 (Source: Internet).
65 Ibid.
66 *What Is Scientology?*, p. 466.
67 'The Creed of the Church of Scientology', para. 7, *The Church of Scientology: 40th Anniversary*, p. 1.
68 *Reference Guide to the Scientology Religion*, p. 42.
69 Personal correspondence; italics in original.

CONCLUSION

1 *Sunday Times Magazine*, 13 August 1995, pp. 19–24.
2 The details and quotations in these four paragraphs were taken from information leaflets published by the four organizations.
3 In April 1996, Ian Howarth of the Cult Information Centre was made bankrupt when the High Court ruled that he must pay £20,423 in libel damages to Landmark Education International Inc., an *est* offshoot.
4 There are now some 75 offshoots of the Worldwide Church of God. One of the earliest of these is currently fragmenting. Following his alleged 'misbehaviour', many of the ministers of the Church of God, International demanded that Garner Ted Armstrong step down from the leadership of his Church. When this didn't occur, over two-thirds of the membership, led by their ministers, left the Church in April 1996, forming a loose association of independent churches known as the Churches of God.
5 *Observer*, 14 May 1995.
6 Edward Carpenter, *Pagan and Christian Creeds: Their Origin and Meaning*, George Allen & Unwin, 1920, p. 184.
7 Christopher Evans, *Cults of Unreason*, Harrap, 1973, p. 252.
8 A new edition is available in R. J. Stewart's *Robert Kirk: Walker Between Worlds*, Element, 1990.

USEFUL ADDRESSES

For convenience, the addresses of the movements are arranged alphabetically within sections.

WORLD RELIGIONS

Bahá'í Faith
National Spiritual Assembly of the Bahá'ís of the United Kingdom
27 Rutland Gate
London SW7 1PD

Buddhism
The Buddhist Society
58 Eccleston Square
London SW1V 1PH

Friends of the Western Buddhist Order
Padmaloka
Lesingham House
Surlingham
Norwich NR14 7AL.

Church of England
Church House
Great Smith Street
London SW1P 3NZ

Hinduism, Sikhism
Bharatiya Vidya Bhavan (Institute of Indian Culture)
4A Castletown Road
London W14 9HQ

Islam
Islamic Cultural Centre and London Mosque
Regent's Lodge
146 Park Road
London NW8 7RG

Judaism
The United Synagogue
Woburn House
Tavistock Square
London WC1H 0EZ

Roman Catholicism
The Chase Centre
Catholic Enquiries
114 West Heath Road
London NW3 7TX

Sikhism
see Hinduism

Sufism
Sufi Order UK
London Sufi Centre
Beauchamp Lodge
2 Warwick Crescent
London W2 6NE

Zoroastrianism
88 Compayne Gardens
London NW6 3RU

CHRISTIAN ORIGINS

Christadelphians
The Christadelphian
404 Shaftmoor Lane
Hall Green
Birmingham B28 8SZ

Christian Scientists
The First Church of Christ, Scientist
2 Elysium Gate
126 New King's Road
London SW6 4LZ

The First Church of Christ, Scientist
175 Huntington Avenue
Boston
MA 02115–3187
USA

Church of God, International
PO Box 2530
Tyler
Texas 75710
USA

Evangelical Alliance
Whitefield House
186 Kennington Park Road
London SE11 4BT

Exclusive Brethren
Bible and Gospel Trust
99 Green Lane
Hounslow
Middlesex TW4 6BW

The Family
The Manor
Dunton Bassett
Leicester LE17 5JJ

BM Box 8440
London WC1N 3XX

Postfach 241
Zurich 8021
Switzerland

Global Church of God
16935 West Bernadino Drive
San-Diego
CA 92127–1634
USA

Jehovah's Witnesses
Watch Tower Bible and Tract Society
of Pennsylvania
IBSA House
The Ridgeway
London NW7 1RN

Watch Tower Bible and Tract Society
of Pennsylvania
Wallkill
New York
NY 12589
USA

Jesus Army
Jesus Fellowship Central Offices
Nether Heyford
Northampton NN7 3LB

Mormons
The Church of Jesus Christ of Latter-
day Saints
751 Warwick Road
Solihull
West Midlands B91 3DQ

The Church of Jesus Christ of Latter-
day Saints
50 East North Temple Street
Salt Lake City
Utah 84150
USA

Opus Dei
6 Orme Court
London W2 4RL

Quakers
Society of Friends
Friends House
Euston Road
London NW1 2BJ

Seventh-day Adventists
Stanborough Park
Watford
Herts WD2 6JP

Swedenborgians
The General Conference of the New
Church
Swedenborg House
20 Bloomsbury Way
London WC1A 2TH

Unification Church
42–44 Lancaster Gate
London W2 3NA

Unitarians
The General Assembly of Unitarian
and Free Christian Churches
Essex Hall
1–6 Essex Street
Strand
London WC2R 3HY

United Church of God
PO Box 5929
Thatcham
Berks RG19 6YX

Worldwide Church of God
PO Box 111
Borehamwood
Herts WD6 1LU

PO Box 92463
Pasadena
CA 91109–2463
USA

EASTERN ORIGINS

Elan Vital
PO Box 999
Hove
East Sussex BN3 1HX

ECKANKAR
PO Box 4496
London SW19 8XQ

PO Box 27300
Minneapolis
MN 55427
USA

ISKCON
Bhaktivedanta Manor
Letchmore Heath
Watford
Herts WD2 8EP

Nichiren Shoshu
Soka Gokkai International UK
Taplow Court
Taplow
Maidenhead
Berks SL6 0ER

Osho International
24 St James's Street
London SW1A 1HA

Osho Commune International
17 Koregaon Park
Poona 411 001
Maharashtra
India

School of Economic Science
90 Queen's Gate
London SW7 5AB

ESOTERIC MOVEMENTS

Aetherius Society
757 Fulham Road
London SW6 5UU

6202 Afton Place
Hollywood
CA 90028
USA

Anthroposophy
The Anthroposophical Society in
Great Britain
Rudolph Steiner House
35 Park Road
London NW1 6XT

Astara
800 W Arrow Highway
Box 5003
Upland
CA 91785
USA

Builders of the Adytum
5101–05 North Figueroa Street
Los Angeles
CA 90042
USA

Church Universal and Triumphant
Box 5000
Livingston
MA 59047
USA

Summit Lighthouse (UK)
65–66 Charlotte Road
London EC2A 3PE

Emissaries
Mickleton House
Mickleton
Chipping Campden
Glos GL55 6RY

I AM
St Germain Foundation
1120 Stonehedge Drive
Schaumberg
IL 60194
USA

Lectorium Rosicrucianum
BM LR7
London WC1N 3XX

Bakenessergracht 11–15
2011 JS Haarlem
The Netherlands

PO Box 9246
Bakersfield
CA 93309
USA

London Group
BM Vixack
London WC1N 3XX

Maitreya
Benjamin Creme
PO Box 3677
London NW5 1RU

Raelian Movement
BCM Minstrel
London WC1N 3XX

CP 225
1211 Geneva 8
Switzerland

CP 86
Station Youville
Montreal H2P 272
Canada

Servants of the Light
PO Box 215
St Helier
Jersey JE4 9SD
Channel Islands

Society of the Inner Light
38 Steele's Road
London NW3 4RG

Subud
Brecon Subud Centre
Watton Villa
Brecon
Powys LD3 7HH
Wales

Theosophy
The Theosophical Society in England
50 Gloucester Place
London W1H 4EA

NEO-PAGAN MOVEMENTS

Association of Cymmry Wicca
PO Box 674884
Marietta
GA 30067
USA

Church of All Worlds
PO Box 1542
Ukiah
CA 95482
USA

Covenant of the Goddess
Box 1226
Berkeley
CA 94704
USA

Eagle's Wing Centre for Contemporary Shamanism
58 Westbere Road
London NW2 3RU

Fellowship of Isis
Clonegal Castle
Enniscorthy
Eire

Findhorn Community
The Park
Findhorn Bay
Forres IV36 0TZ
Scotland

Hoblink
Box 22
4–7 Dorset Street
Brighton
East Sussex BL2 1WA

House of the Goddess
33 Oldridge Road
London SW12 8PN

Isle of Avalon Foundation
The Courtyard
2–4 High Street
Glastonbury
Somerset BA6 9DU

Pagan Federation
BM Box 7097
London WC1N 3XX

PaganLink
BM Web
London WC1N 3XX

**Sub-culture Alternatives Freedom
Foundation**
Sorcerer's Apprentice
6/8 Burley Lodge Road
Leeds LS6 1QP

Universal Federation of Pagans
PO Box 674884
Marietta
GA 30067
USA

Universal Life Church (Brythonic)
PO Box 15259
Portland
OR 97215
USA

DRUIDRY

British Druid Order
PO Box 29
St Leonards-on-Sea
East Sussex TN37 7YP

Druid Clan of Dana
Clonegal Castle
Enniscorthy
Eire

Henge of Keltria
PO Box 33284
Minneapolis
MN 55433
USA

Loyal Arthurian Warband
c/o 10 Sine Close
Farnborough
Hants GU14 8HG

Order of Bards, Ovates and Druids
PO Box 1333
Lewes
East Sussex BN7 3ZG

NORTHERN TRADITION

Odinic Rite
BM Edda
London WC1N 3XX

Odinshof
BCM Tercel
London WC1N 3XX

Ring of Troth and Rune Gild-UK
BM Aswynn
London WC1N 3XX

Ring of Troth
PO Box 212
Sheridan
IN 46069
USA

Rune Gild
PO Box 7622
Austin
Texas
USA

PERSONAL DEVELOPMENT MOVEMENTS

Emin
PO Box 48
Saffron Walden
Essex CB11 3PD

Insight
37 Spring Street
London W2 1JA

Neuro-Linguistic Programming
John Seymour Associates
17 Boyce Drive
Bristol BS2 9XQ

Scientology
Saint Hill Manor
East Grinstead
West Sussex RH19 4JY

6331 Hollywood Boulevard
Suite 1200
Los Angeles
CA 90028
USA

Transcendental Meditation
Mentmore Towers
Mentmore
Leighton Buzzard
Beds LU7 0QH

CULT-WATCHING ORGANIZATIONS

Catalyst
The Bridge Centre
Spa Common
Retford
Notts DN22 6LQ

Christian Research Institute
Box 500
San Juan Capistrano
CA 92693
USA

Cult Awareness Network
2421 West Pratt Blvd
Suite 1173
Chicago
IL 60645
USA

Cult Information Centre
BCM Cults
London WC1N 3XX

Deo Gloria Outreach
Selsdon House
212–220 Addington Road
South Croydon
Surrey CR2 8LD

DialogCentre UK
BM DialogCentre
London WC1N 3XX

FAIR
BCM Box 3535
London WC1N 3XX

INFORM
Houghton Street
London WC2A 2AE

Reachout Trust
24 Ormond Road
Richmond
Surrey TW10 6TH

BIBLIOGRAPHY

This Bibliography covers, in the main, books which are publicly available. It does not include the dozens of booklets and pamphlets produced by individual movements, which are referenced in the text.

It is divided into parts, as in the book, but with individual movements listed alphabetically for convenience.

Many of the more general reference works, of course, are relevant to several parts of the book. No distinction is made between books which are by movements and those which are about them, or between books which are unbiased and those which are biased, anti or pro; such a stance is often apparent from the title. A few particularly useful books are highlighted with an asterisk and a comment.

GENERAL

WORLD RELIGIONS

Brosse, Jacques, *Religious Leaders*, Chambers, 1991
Comte, Fernand, *Sacred Writings of World Religions*, Chambers, 1992
Crim, Keith, (ed.), *The Perennial Dictionary of World Religions*, Harper & Row, 1981
Hinnells, John R. (ed.), *A Handbook of Living Religions*, Pelican, 1984
—— *The Penguin Dictionary of Religions*, Penguin, 1984
Price, E. D., *The Story of Religions*, George Newnes, 1898
—— *Religious Systems of the World*, Swann Sonnenschwein, 1908
Smart, Ninian, *The World's Religions*, Cambridge University Press, 1989
Smith, Huston, *The Religions of Man*, Harper, 1958

ALTERNATIVE RELIGIONS, SECTS, CULTS AND HERESIES

Annett, Stephen (ed.), *The Many Ways of Being*, Abacus, 1976
Barker, Eileen, *New Religious Movements: A Practical Introduction*, HMSO, 1989
*Beit-Hallahmi, Benjamin, *The Illustrated Encyclopedia of Active New Religions, Sects and Cults*, Rosen, 1993
    Invaluable reference work spoiled by sloppy cross-referencing
*Christie-Murray, David, *A History of Heresy*, Oxford University Press, 1976
    Excellent historical account

Cozens, M. L., *A Handbook of Heresies*, Sheed & Ward, 1st edition 1928; 1974 edition

Davies, Horton, *Christian Deviations: The Challenge of the Sects*, SCM Press, 1954; 1961 edition

Evans, Christopher, *Cults of Unreason*, Harrap, 1973

Evans, John, *A Sketch of the Denominations of the Christian World*, Baldwin, Cradock & Joy, 15th edition 1827

*George, Leonard, *The Encyclopedia of Heresies and Heretics*, Robson Books, 1995

> Very wide and thorough coverage; published after the current work was completed

Harrison, Shirley, *Cults: The Battle for God*, Christopher Helm, 1990

Kellett, Arnold, *Isms and Ologies*, Epworth, 1965

Martin, Walter R., *The Kingdom of the Cults*, Marshall, Morgan & Scott, 1965

Melton, J. Gordon, *Biographical Dictionary of American Cult and Sect Leaders*, Garland, 1986

—— *Encyclopedic Handbook of Cults in America*, revised edition, Garland, 1992

—— *Encyclopedia of American Religions*, 4th edition, Gale Research, 1993

> Two extremely useful reference works

Petersen, William J., *Those Curious New Cults*, Keats Publishing, 1975

Ritchie, Jean, *The Secret World of Cults*, Angus & Robertson, 1991

Sanders, J. Oswald, *Heresies and Cults*, Marshall, Morgan & Scott, 1948; revised edition 1962

Sanders, J. Oswald and Wright, J. Stafford, *Some Modern Religions*, Inter-Varsity Fellowship, 1965; 4th edition 1963

*Shaw, William, *Spying in Guru Land: Inside Britain's Cults*, Fourth Estate, 1994

> Interesting anecdotal account of the author 'joining' several religions

Storm, Rachel, *In Search of Heaven on Earth*, Bloomsbury, 1991

Wallis, Roy (ed.), *Sectarianism: Analyses of Religions and Non-Religious Sects*, Peter Owen, 1975

CHRISTIAN ORIGINS

GENERAL

Chadwick, Henry, *The Early Church*, Pelican, 1967

Douglas, J. D. (ed.), *The New Bible Dictionary*, Inter-Varsity Fellowship, 1962

Lane, Tony, *The Lion Concise Book of Christian Thought*, Lion, 1984

Smart, Ninian, *The Phenomenon of Christianity*, Collins, 1979

INDIVIDUAL RELIGIONS

Branch Davidians

Linedecker, Clifford L., *Massacre at Waco*, True Crime/Virgin, 1993

Christadelphians
Tennant, Harry, *Back to the Bible*, Christadelphian Press, undated

Christian Science
A Century of Christian Science Healing, The Christian Science Publishing Society, 1966

Eddy, Mary Baker, *Science and Health, with Key to the Scriptures*, First Church of Christ, Scientist, 1906 edition

—— *Church Manual*, First Church of Christ, Scientist, 1908 edition

Church of God, International
Armstrong, Garner Ted, *The Origin and History of the Church of God, International*, Church of God, International, 1992

—— *Europe and America in Prophecy*, Church of God, International, 1994

Jehovah's Witnesses
Harris, Doug, *Awake! to the Watch Tower*, Reachout Trust, 1988

Tomsett, Valerie, *Released from the Watchtower*, Lakeland, 1971

You Can Live Forever in Paradise on Earth, Watch Tower Bible and Tract Society, 1982

Mormonism
The Book of Mormon, Church of Jesus Christ of Latter-day Saints, 1950 edition

Doctrine and Covenants & Pearl of Great Price, Church of Jesus Christ of Latter-day Saints, 1952 edition

Encyclopedia of Mormonism, Macmillan, 1992

Hansen, Klaus J., *Mormonism and the American Experience*, University of Chicago Press, 1981

Hoekema, A. A., *Mormonism*, Paternoster Press, 1973

Mullen, Robert, *The Mormons*, W. H. Allen, 1966

Opus Dei
Walsh, Michael, *The Secret World of Opus Dei*, Grafton, 1989

Quakers
Gorman, George H., *Introducing Quakers*, Quaker Home Service, 1969

Seventh-day Adventists
Seventh-day Adventists Believe . . .: A Biblical Exposition of 27 Fundamental Doctrines, Ministerial Association, General Conference of Seventh-day Adventists, 1988

White, Ellen G., *The Great Controversy*, 1888; Pyramid edition 1971

Unification Church
The Divine Principle Home Study Course: 1. The Principle of Creation: 2. The Fall of Man: 3. Mission of the Messiah, HSA-UWC, 1979, 1980, 1980

Moon, Sun Myung, *Divine Principle*, HSA-UWC, 1973

Worldwide Church of God
Armstrong, Herbert W., *The British Commonwealth and the United States in Prophecy*, Ambassador College, 1954

—— *1975 in Prophecy*, Radio Church of God, 1956

—— *The United States and British Commonwealth in Prophecy*, Ambassador College, 1967

—— *The United States and Britain in Prophecy*, Worldwide Church of God, 1980

—— *Mystery of the Ages*, Worldwide Church of God, 1985

—— *The Autobiography of Herbert W. Armstrong*, Vol. 1, Ambassador College, 1967 edition; 1973 edition; Worldwide Church of God, 1986 edition

—— *The Autobiography of Herbert W. Armstrong*, Vol. 2, Worldwide Church of God, 1987

Armstrong, Herbert W. and Armstrong, Garner Ted, *The Wonderful World Tomorrow: What It Will Be Like*, Ambassador College, 1966

Hoeh, Herman L., *A True History of the True Church*, Radio Church of God, 1959

—— *This Is the Worldwide Church of God*, Ambassador College, 1972

EASTERN ORIGINS

ECKANKAR
Cramer, Todd and Munson, Doug, *ECKANKAR: Ancient Wisdom for Today*, ECKANKAR, 1993

Twitchell, Paul, *The Spiritual Notebook*, IWP, 1971

ISKCON
Bhaktivedanta Swami Prabhupada, A. C., *The Science of Self-Realization*, Bhaktivedanta Book Trust, 1977

—— *Bhagavad-Gita As It Is*, Bhaktivedanta Book Trust, 1981 edition

Osho/Rajneesh
Sarito, Ma Deva (ed.), *Osho Zen Tarot*, Boxtree, 1994

School of Economic Science
Hounam, Peter and Hogg, Andrew, *Secret Cult*, Lion, 1984

ESOTERIC AND NEO-PAGAN MOVEMENTS

GENERAL

Bloom, William (ed.), *The New Age: An Anthology of Essential Writings*, Rider, 1991

Bray, Chris, *Newcomers' Guide to Essential Paganism, Witchcraft, Shamanism*, Sorcerer's Apprentice Press, 1994

Cavendish, Richard, *The Magical Arts: Western Occultism and Occultists*, Routledge, 1967; Arkana, 1984

—— *A History of Magic*, Weidenfeld & Nicolson, 1987; Arkana, 1990

*Cavendish, Richard (ed.), *Encyclopedia of the Unexplained*, Routledge & Kegan
    Paul, 1974; Arkana, 1989
        The most comprehensive and comprehensible work of its type; invaluable for
        any serious inquirer
Crow, W. B., *A History of Magic, Witchcraft and Occultism*, Aquarian Press,
    1968
Drury, Nevill, *Dictionary of Mysticism and the Occult*, Harper & Row, 1985
Farrar, Janet, Farrar, Stewart and Bone, Gavin, *The Pagan Path*, Phoenix, 1995
Gordon, Stuart, *The Paranormal: An Illustrated Encyclopedia*, Headline, 1992
*Guiley, Rosemary Ellen, *Encyclopedia of Mystical & Paranormal Experience*,
    HarperCollins, 1991
        Very wide-ranging and useful work
Haeffner, Mark, *The Dictionary of Alchemy*, Aquarian Press, 1991
King, Francis and Sutherland, Isabel, *The Rebirth of Magic*, Corgi, 1982
Knight, Gareth, *A History of White Magic*, Mowbrays, 1978
Kramer, Heinrich and Sprenger, Jakob, *Malleus Maleficarum*, 1486; Arrow
    edition, 1971
Lemesurier, Peter, *This New Age Business*, Findhorn Press, 1990
*Matthews, Caitlín and John, *The Western Way*, Vols 1 and 2, Arkana, 1985, 1986
        Essential reading on the Western Mystery Tradition
*Melton, J. Gordon, Clark, Jerome and Kelly, Aidan A., *New Age Almanac*,
    Visible Ink Press/Gale Research, 1991
        Very informative but appallingly organized, with no index and confusing
        order of contents
Nataf, André, *The Occult*, Chambers, 1991
—— *The Occult Census*, Sorcerer's Apprentice Press, 1989
*Parker, John, *At the Heart of Darkness*, Sidgwick & Jackson, 1993
        Useful account of 'Satanic ritual abuse', witchcraft and magical groups, but
        spoiled by sometimes sensationalist journalistic style
Shan, *The Pagan Index*, House of the Goddess, 1994
Spence, Lewis, *The Encyclopedia of the Occult*, Bracken Books edition, 1988
Underwood, Peter, *Dictionary of the Occult & Supernatural*, Fontana, 1979

INDIVIDUAL RELIGIONS

Church Universal and Triumphant

*Climb the Highest Mountain: A Profile of the Church Universal and
    Triumphant*, video, 1994
Lewis, James R. and Melton, J. Gordon (eds.), *Church Universal and Triumphant
    in Scholarly Perspective*, a special issue of *Syzygy: Journal of Alternative
    Religion and Culture*, Center for Academic Publication, 1994
Prophet, Elizabeth Clare, *The Lost Years of Jesus*, Summit University Press, 1987
Prophet, Mark L. and Elizabeth Clare, *Saint Germain on Alchemy*, Summit
    University Press, 1985
—— *The Lost Teachings of Jesus*, Vol. 1, Summit University Press, 1988

Druidry

Carr-Gomm, Philip, *The Elements of the Druid Tradition*, Element, 1991

Nichols, Ross, *The Book of Druidry*, Aquarian Press, 1990
Shallcrass, Philip (ed.), *A Druid Directory 1995*, British Druid Order

Findhorn
Findhorn Community, *The Findhorn Garden*, Findhorn Press, 2nd edition, 1988

Raelian Movement
Raël, *The Message Given to Me by Extraterrestrials: They Took Me to Their Planet*, AOM Corporation, Japan, 1986

Satanism
LaVey, Anton, *The Satanic Bible*, Star Books, 1977

Subud
Lyle, Robert, *Subud*, Humanus, 1983

Theosophy
Benjamin, Harry, *Everybody's Guide to Theosophy*, Health for All Publishing, undated
Steiner, Rudolf, *Theosophy*, Rudolf Steiner Press, 1922; 1970 edition

Wicca
Cabot, Laurie, *Power of the Witch*, Arkana, 1989
Farrar, Janet and Stewart, *Spells and How They Work*, Hale, 1990
Farrar, Stewart, *What Witches Do*, Hale, 3rd edition, 1991
Murray, Margaret A., *The Witch-Cult in Western Europe*, 1921; Oxford University Press edition, 1962
—— *The God of the Witches*, 1931, Oxford University Press edition, 1952
Shan, *Which Craft?*, House of the Goddess, 1986

PERSONAL DEVELOPMENT MOVEMENTS

Emin
Leo, *Dear Dragon*, 1976; Topaz Publishers, Israel, 1992 edition

Neuro-Linguistic Programming
O'Connor, Joseph and Seymour, John, *Introducing NLP*, Aquarian Press, 1993

Scientology
Hubbard, L. Ron, *Dianetics: The Modern Science of Mental Health*, New Era, 1950; 1981 edition
Lamont, Stewart, *Religion Inc.*, Harrap, 1986
L. Ron Hubbard: A Profile, Church of Scientology International, 1995
Miller, Russell, *Bare-Faced Messiah*, Michael Joseph, 1987
Vosper, Cyril, *The Mind Benders*, Neville Spearman, 1971
What Is Scientology?, Bridge Publications, 1993

CONCLUSION

Carpenter, Edward, *Pagan and Christian Creeds: Their Origin and Meaning*, George Allen & Unwin, 1920
Harpur, Patrick, *Daimonic Reality: A Field Guide to the Otherworld*, Viking, 1994
Stewart, R. J., *Robert Kirk: Walker Between Worlds – A New Edition of The Secret Commonwealth of Elves, Fauns & Fairies*, Element, 1990

INDEX